Internet Domain Names, Trademarks and Free Speech

ELGAR INTELLECTUAL PROPERTY AND GLOBAL DEVELOPMENT

Series Editor: Peter K. Yu, *Kern Family Chair in Intellectual Property Law and Director, Intellectual Property Law Center, Drake University, USA*

Rapid global economic integration and the increasing importance of technology and information goods have created the need for a broader, deeper and more critical understanding of intellectual property laws and policies. This uniquely-designed book series provides an interdisciplinary forum for advancing the debate on the global intellectual property system and related issues that intersect with transnational politics, international governance, and global economic, social, cultural and technological development. The series features the works of established experts and emerging voices in the academy as well as those practising on the frontlines. The series' high-quality, informed and accessible volumes include a wide range of materials such as historical narratives, theoretical explanations, substantive discussions, critical evaluations, empirical analyses, comparative studies, and formulations of practical solutions and best practices. The series will appeal to academics, policy makers, judges, practitioners, transnational lawyers and civil society groups as well as students of law, politics, culture, political economy, international relations and development studies.

Titles in the series include:

Intellectual Property and Sustainable Development
Development Agendas in a Changing World
Edited by Ricardo Meléndez-Ortiz and Pedro Roffe

Internet Domain Names, Trademarks and Free Speech
Jacqueline Lipton

Internet Domain Names, Trademarks and Free Speech

Jacqueline Lipton

Case Western Reserve University, USA

ELGAR INTELLECTUAL PROPERTY AND GLOBAL DEVELOPMENT

Edward Elgar

Cheltenham, UK • Northampton, MA, USA

Published by
Edward Elgar Publishing Limited
The Lypiatts
15 Lansdown Road
Cheltenham
Glos GL50 2JA
UK

Edward Elgar Publishing, Inc.
William Pratt House
9 Dewey Court
Northampton
Massachusetts 01060
USA

A catalogue record for this book
is available from the British Library

Library of Congress Control Number: 2010922130

ISBN 978 1 84844 414 0

Printed and bound by MPG Books Group, UK

Contents

Preface

I originally became interested in Internet domain names when I first learned of their existence in the mid-1990s. I had recently embarked on an academic career and was looking for a direction for my scholarly agenda. It seemed to me that domain names made for an extremely interesting subject of study. They were unlike any other form of intangible 'property' (for want of a more appropriate term). Like digital copyright works, domain names were valuable virtual assets. However, unlike copyrights, domain names were rivalrous. Only one person could own a given domain name at any given time. This led to a new set of questions about online property. While nonrivalrous digital copyright works raised issues of how to prevent uncontrolled online copying, domain names potentially raised the opposite problem – scarcity.

Even as the number of available generic Top Level Domains (gTLDs) and country code Top Level Domains (ccTLDs) has increased over the years (and will continue to increase)[1] only one person can hold any given iteration of a domain name at any one time. While Anna holds 'domain.com', Bill cannot own it, even though he might own 'domain.net' or 'domain.co.uk'. Domain names also differ from other digital assets in that they are simultaneously technological addresses and intuitive labels for the online presence of a person or organization. Courts have struggled to find an appropriate classification scheme for domain names. The names have been likened both to an intangible property right[2] and to a mere technological addressing system.[3] Domain names are also creatures of contractual license between a registrar and a registrant.[4]

The most immediate problem with domain names in the 1990s was the fact that domain names are very much like trademarks. They can indicate the source of products or services by incorporating a trademark: for

---

[1] ICANN, new gTLD Program, available at www.icann.org/en/topics/new-gtld-program.htm, last accessed October 19, 2009 (program to increase available generic Top Level Domains).

[2] *Kremen v Cohen*, 337 F.3d 1024 (9th Cir. 2003) (finding domain name to be property for the purposes of the Californian statutory tort of conversion).

[3] *Lockheed Martin v Network Solutions*, 194 F.3d 980 (9th Cir. 1999).

[4] *Network Solutions v Umbro International*, 529 S.E.2d 80 Va. (2000).

example, 'nike.com'. This opened the possibility for all kinds of trademark abuses, starting in the early days of the system with good, old-fashioned cybersquatting. Cybersquatting refers to the practice of registering domain names corresponding with other people's trademarks in an attempt to extort money from trademark holders for transfer of the names.[5] Because trademark holders were the most powerful lobby group impacted by these domain name practices, much of the discussion of domain name regulation from the 1990s onwards has focused on the protection of trademarks in the domain space.

This book is the first comprehensive discussion of issues that can arise in the domain space outside of traditional cybersquatting. It has now been ten years since the Internet Corporation for Assigned Names and Numbers (ICANN)[6] adopted the Uniform Domain Name Dispute Resolution Policy (UDRP)[7] to address global concerns about cybersquatting. This book raises questions about what we have learned in the ensuing years about domain name regulation. It addresses the limitations of existing regulatory regimes when confronted with competitions between multiple legitimate trademark holders; free speech issues; the desire to protect individual names and identities in the domain space; the need to facilitate democratic discourse; and the need to protect cultural and geographic indicators online.

This book has been a long time coming, and I have a number of people to thank for their help and support in its preparation. Much of the material in the following pages is developed from my earlier work on domain name regulation. I would like to acknowledge and thank the editors of the following publications for all their help, support and editorial expertise in preparing the articles that preceded this book: Lipton, *Bad Faith in Cyberspace: Grounding Domain Name Theory in Trademark, Property, and Restitution*, Harvard Journal of Law and Technology (forthcoming, 2010); Lipton, *From Domain Names to Video Games: The Rise of the Internet in Presidential Politics,* 86 Denver University Law Review 693 (2009); Lipton, *Celebrity in Cyberspace: A Personality Rights*

5 Jonathan Nilsen, *Mixing Oil with Water: Resolving the Differences Between Domain Names and Trademark Law*, 1 J. High Tech. L. 47, 51 (2002) ('Cybersquatting has been defined several ways. The most general definition of a cybersquatter is a person who registers a domain name that matches a well-known company for the purpose of ransoming it to that company.')

6 ICANN Is the body that administers the technical (and some of the policy) aspects of the domain name system. See www.icann.org for more information.

7 See www.icann.org/en/udrp/udrp-policy-24oct99.htm, last accessed October 19, 2009 (full text of the UDRP).

Paradigm for a New Personal Domain Name Dispute Resolution Policy, 65 Washington and Lee Law Review 1445 (2008); Lipton, *A Winning Solution for YouTube and Utube? Corresponding Trademarks and Domain Name Sharing*, 21 Harvard Journal of Law and Technology 509 (2008); Lipton, *Who Owns 'hillary.com'? Political Speech and the First Amendment in Cyberspace*, 49 Boston College Law Review 55 (2008); Lipton, *Commerce versus Commentary: Gripe Sites, Parody and the First Amendment in Cyberspace*, 84 Washington University Law Review 1327 (2006); and, Lipton, *Beyond Cybersquatting: Taking Domain Name Disputes Past Trademark Policy*, 40 Wake Forest Law Review 1361 (2005).

A number of colleagues have contributed to my thinking about domain names over the years, and it is probably dangerous to attempt a list as someone is sure to be accidentally omitted. Nevertheless, for what it's worth, I would very much like to thank: Olufunmilayo Arewa, Graeme Austin, Amitai Aviram, Taunya Lovell Banks, Margreth Barrett, Ann Bartow, Joseph Bauer, Patricia Bellia, Erik Bluemel, Bruce Boyden, M. Brent Byars, Anupam Chander, Kevin Collins, Frank Rudy Cooper, Robert Denicola, Joshua Fairfield, Brett Frischmann, Eric Goldman, Paul Heald, Deborah Hellman, B. Jessie Hill, Cynthia Ho, Mark Janis, Raymond Ku, Ilhyung Lee, Mark Lemley, Michael Madison, Andrea Matwyshyn, Mark McKenna, Andrew Morriss, Craig Nard, Elizabeth Rowe, Catherine Smith, Lawrence Solum, Robert Suggs, Michael Van Alstine and Diane Zimmerman. I would also like to acknowledge the law deans at Case Western Reserve University School of Law who supported this project in its various iterations over the years: Dean Gerald Korngold, Dean Gary Simson and Interim Dean Robert Rawson.

Particular thanks go to my friend, Peter Yu, for convincing me to develop my thoughts on domain name regulation into a book for this series, and to the staff at Edward Elgar, including Tara Gorvine who believed these thoughts were worth translating into a book. And most importantly, I must thank my family who coped stoically with the stress and anxiety of my attempts to balance the writing process with everything else going on in our lives. I could not have done this without the support and understanding of my husband, Patrick, and our two children, Sean and Brianne. Naturally, I take responsibility for any errors or omissions in the text, but the text would not be here without the unwavering support and advice from these people.

Jacqueline Lipton

Abbreviations

ACPA	Anti-Cybersquatting Consumer Protection Act (US)
ccTLD	country code Top Level Domain
CDA	Communications Decency Act (US)
ECJ	European Court of Justice
gTLD	generic Top Level Domain
ICANN	Internet Corporation for Assigned Names and Numbers
PCAA	Political Cyberfraud Abatement Act (California)
TDRA	Trademark Dilution Revision Act (US)
UDRP	Uniform Domain Name Dispute Resolution Policy
URL	uniform resource locator
WIPO	World Intellectual Property Organization

Introduction

From day one, the Internet domain name system has created puzzles for law and policy-makers. These challenges have included questions about whose responsibility it is to develop and enforce domain name policy, and on what basis policy decisions are to be made. The Internet Corporation for Assigned Names and Numbers (ICANN)[1] is formally tasked with the administration of the domain name system.[2] However, there has been some confusion over the years about the appropriate balance between ICANN's technical and policy functions.[3] It was originally assumed that ICANN was a purely technical body, and not a policy-making organization.[4] However, ICANN was fairly quickly forced to make policy in some areas related to its core technical functions.[5] An obvious example of ICANN's policy-making role is its implementation of an online dispute resolution procedure for Internet domain names, the Uniform Domain

[1] See www.icann.org, last accessed December 11, 2008. Details of ICANN's development and structure can be found in DAVID LINDSAY, INTERNATIONAL DOMAIN NAME LAW: ICANN AND THE UDRP, ch. 2 (2007); MILTON MUELLER, RULING THE ROOT: INTERNET GOVERNANCE AND THE TAMING OF CYBERSPACE, ch. 8 (2002).

[2] LINDSAY, *supra* note 1, at 66 (describing ICANN's mission as set out in article 1.1 of its Bylaws); see also Bylaws for Internet Corporation for Assigned Names and Numbers, available in full text at www.icann.org/en/general/bylaws.htm#I, last accessed December 11, 2008.

[3] *Id.* at 65 ('The scope of ICANN's responsibilities and functions has been one of the most controversial areas of DNS governance. In particular, the first years of ICANN's operations were characterised by debates over whether ICANN was a purely technical coordination body or whether it was primarily a policy-making body'.)

[4] *Id.* at 65 ('The scope of ICANN's mission received considerable attention during ICANN's structural reform process, with many claiming that ICANN had acted beyond its core technical functions.')

[5] *Id.* at 65 (noting that a 2002 report on reforming ICANN concluded that ICANN was necessarily involved in some policy-making activities, but that this role should be limited to activities reasonably related to its technical mission). See also Bylaws for Internet Corporation for Assigned Names and Numbers, art. I.1.3, available in full text at www.icann.org/en/general/bylaws.htm#I, last accessed December 11, 2008 ('[ICANN] coordinates policy development reasonably and appropriately related to [its] technical functions.').

Name Dispute Resolution Policy (UDRP).[6] Some policy-making has also been incorporated into ICANN's proposal for new generic Top Level Domains (gTLDs).[7]

Domestic legislatures and courts have also been involved in making domain name policy.[8] Some domestic legislatures have been more active than others in this area: for example, at both the federal and state levels, American legislatures have enacted laws that regulate certain conduct involving domain names.[9] The variations in approach between different legislatures naturally raise potential disharmonization concerns. Nevertheless, the different approaches create a variety of testing grounds that ultimately might assist in formulating the best approach to resolving domain name conflicts. When set against the backdrop of the more international UDRP, local experiments may prove useful in developing new approaches to specific disputes. At the same time, the UDRP might retain a baseline mechanism for expeditiously resolving some of the more pressing conflicts.

Some have argued that domain name regulation is no longer important because Internet users rely on search engines, rather than domain names, for navigating content on the World Wide Web.[10] So why write a book on domain name regulation?[11] In fact, there is little evidence that disputes over Internet domain names are becoming less prevalent in practice.

---

6 Full text available at www.icann.org/en/udrp/udrp-policy-24oct99.htm, last accessed December 11, 2008.

7 ICANN, New gTLD Program: Draft Applicant Guidebook (Draft RFP) (October 24, 2008), Module 3, full text available at www.icann.org/en/topics/new-gtlds/draft-rfp-24oct08-en.pdf, last accessed December 11, 2008.

8 Particularly with respect to application of trademark law to the domain space. See, for example, discussion in GRAEME DINWOODIE and MARK JANIS, TRADEMARKS AND UNFAIR COMPETITION: LAW AND POLICY 611–38 (2d edn 2007).

9 See, for example, 15 U.S.C. § 1125(d) (federal prohibition on cybersquatting involving a trademark); § 8131 (federal prohibition on cybersquatting involving a personal name); Cal. Elections Code, § 18320 (prohibiting activities described as 'political cyberfraud', some of which implicate Internet domain names); California's Business and Professions Code, § 17525–6 (regulating unauthorized registration and use of Internet domain names at the state level in California).

10 Eric Goldman, *Deregulating Relevancy in Internet Trademark Law*, 54 EMORY L.J. 507, 548 (2005) ('For some searchers, search engines have supplanted the DNS's core search function of delivering known websites. In turn, top search engine placements have eclipsed domain names as the premier Internet locations'.).

11 Interestingly, despite comments that domain names are decreasing in legal relevance, the literature on Internet domain names appears to be increasing. See, for example, LINDSAY, *supra* note 1; DAVID KESMODEL, THE DOMAIN GAME (2008); VADIM GOLIK and ALEXEY TOLKACHIOV, VIRTUAL REAL ESTATE (2006); TORSTEN

Recent statistics indicate that domain name disputes are actually on the rise.[12] The implementation of new gTLDs will also raise the specter of new classes of domain space disputes. The new system allows for people and organizations to apply for new gTLDs, such as '.hotel', '.camera', or '.fun'.[13] ICANN is anticipating disputes over such registrations on legal,[14] moral,[15] community[16] and string confusion[17] grounds.

In the early days of the domain name system, the policy focus was very much on the protection of trademarks in the domain space,[18] often to the detriment of other interests, such as free speech,[19] personal reputation or privacy.[20] The introduction of new gTLDs creates an opportunity to review, evaluate and make suggestions for future directions in domain name policy. This book contributes to the debate by identifying gaps in the current regulations and directions in which future policies might be developed.

BETTINGER, DOMAIN NAME LAW AND PRACTICE: AN INTERNATIONAL HANDBOOK (2005).

12 In fact, a survey of the biggest arbitrator of Internet domain name disputes under the 'UDRP' evidences that between 1999 and 2008, the number of disputes heard by the WIPO Domain Name Dispute Resolution Service rose from 199 complaints to 1,999: see www.wipo.int/amc/en/domains/decisionsx/index.html, last accessed January 14, 2009.

13 ICANN, New gTLD Program: Draft Applicant Guidebook (Draft RFP) (October 24, 2008), para. 3.1.2.2, available at www.icann.org/en/topics/new-gtlds/draft-rfp-24oct08-en.pdf, last accessed December 11, 2008.

14 *Id.* para. 3.1.2.2.

15 *Id.* para. 3.1.2.3.

16 *Id.* para. 3.1.2.4.

17 *Id.* para. 3.1.2.1.

18 See discussion in Jacqueline Lipton, *Beyond Cybersquatting: Taking Domain Name Disputes Past Trademark Policy*, 40 WAKE FOREST L. REV. 1361, 1363 (2005) ('[C]urrent dispute resolution mechanisms are focused on the protection of commercial trademark interests, often to the detriment of other socially important interests that may inhere in a given domain name. If the global information society continues down the current road of protecting these interests at all costs, other important social norms relating to Internet use will not have a chance to develop, and the Internet will become permanently skewed in favor of commercial trademark interests. Thus, society will miss out on the potential to develop the Internet in general, and the domain name system in particular, in new and useful ways.')

19 See Margreth Barrett, *Domain Names, Trademarks and the First Amendment: Searching for Meaningful Boundaries*, 39 CONN. L. REV. 973 (2007); Jacqueline Lipton, *Commerce versus Commentary: Gripe Sites, Parody and the First Amendment in Cyberspace*, 84 WASHINGTON UNIVERSITY L. REV. 1327 (2006).

20 Jacqueline Lipton, *Celebrity in Cyberspace: A Personality Rights Paradigm for a New Personal Domain Name Dispute Resolution Policy*, 65 WASHINGTON AND LEE L. REV. 1445 (2008).

Domain names comprise a unique form of online asset. They are the closest Internet analogy to real property.[21] This is because, unlike other forms of digital property, they are rivalrous. This means that one domain name can only be held by one person or entity at a time. However, unlike real property, domain names exist across domestic boundaries so domestic property law has limited application. Even nationally focused intellectual property laws are limited in the face of global online assets. The closest analogy to domain names in intellectual property law is probably found in trademark law. However, even trademark law effectively deals with non-rivalrous assets within fixed geographical boundaries. If two people develop the same trademark for different geographic or product markets, they can simultaneously hold trademark rights.[22] Unlike trademarks, any given domain name can only be held by one person. Of course, similar domain names can be simultaneously registered by different people: for example, one person could register 'alice.com' while another registers 'alicia.com', 'alice.net', or 'alice.co.uk'. However, only one person can hold any one of those names at any given time.[23]

Unlike real property, the most popular domain names – in the gTLDs like '.com' and '.net' – are effectively global in scope. They are not tied to any particular geographic region. Other online assets, including copyrights and trademarks, are not global in the same sense as domain names. Copyrights and trademarks derive from domestic legal systems as government-granted rights. These rights may be supported by international treaties.[24] However, they are domestic grants of rights rather than

---

[21] In fact, Paul Twomey, the Chief Executive of ICANN, has described recent moves to expand the number of gTLD extensions as: 'a massive increase in the geography of the real estate of the Internet'. See Danielle Nordine, *ICANN Proposes Major Domain Name Changes*, ITPRO, (June 23, 2008) available at www.itpro.co.uk/603930/icann-proposes-major-domain-name-changes, last accessed July 11, 2008.

[22] In the United States, this is often referred to as the 'concurrent use' doctrine: David Barrett, *The Future of the Concurrent Use of Trademarks Doctrine in the Information Age*, 23 HASTINGS COMM. AND ENT. L.J. 687, 689–92 (2001) (examining American legislative history of the 'concurrent use' doctrine in trademark law which allows different trademark-holders to use similar marks in different geographic areas).

[23] Of course, the same person can register multiple similar names so one person could, in fact, hold all four of these names simultaneously.

[24] See, for example, discussion of a variety of international intellectual property law treaties in MARSHALL LEAFFER, UNDERSTANDING COPYRIGHT LAW 551–68 (4th edn 2005). For a list of international intellectual property treaties administered by the World Intellectual Property Organization, see www.wipo.int/treaties/en/, last accessed January 19, 2009.

truly global assets. Of course, domestic laws might impact on individual rights in particular domain names.[25] Nevertheless, domain names exist outside domestic legal systems, while copyrights and trademarks are creatures of domestic law. Thus, domain names are arguably the first truly global Internet analog to real property.[26] They are an example of something that is like real property, but that exists in the borderless realm of cyberspace.

This raises interesting questions about domain names. In particular, issues arise about the need to balance competing interests in domain names, such as property and speech interests. While domain names are often traded as marketable commodities, they also have speech characteristics in that they are made of up strings of alphanumeric characters intended to mean something to Internet users. Domain name regulations need to accommodate, to the maximum extent possible, legal and cultural differences in different jurisdictions on questions relating to property and speech, as well as some other competing interests such as privacy. Regulations must also be enforced, which is problematic in the case of a truly global asset. Avenues for complaint about domain name registrations and uses need to be readily accessible to complainants, yet another tall order.

To date, the process of developing and enforcing balanced domain name policies seems to have stalled, except for some recent developments by ICANN in the area of the proposed new gTLDs. These developments largely reflect policy positions previously taken by ICANN with respect to existing gTLDs. These initial policy determinations were aimed largely at protecting trademark holders from the activities of cybersquatters. Cybersquatters registered domain names corresponding with trademarks and sought to profit from selling them to the corresponding trademark holder, or one of its competitors.[27] ICANN adopted the UDRP in 1999[28] to deal with this issue.[29] Much of the early drafting of the UDRP was

---

25 For example, trademark holders have often been successful in asserting trademark infringement and dilution claims against domain name registrants. See, for example, *Panavision v Toeppen*, 141 F.3d 1316 (9th Cir. 1998) (successful trademark dilution claim against a cybersquatter); *Planned Parenthood Federation of America Inc. v Bucci*, 42 U.S.P.Q.2d 1430 (S.D.N.Y. 1997) (successful trademark infringement and dilution claims against a domain name registrant).

26 See *supra* note 21.

27 See Nilsen, *supra* note 5.

28 Lindsay, *supra* note 1, at 105–6 (describing the final adoption of the UDRP by ICANN).

29 *Id.* at 99–106 (describing the priority given to the protection of trademarks online in the drafting of the UDRP).

conducted by the World Intellectual Property Organization (WIPO).[30] Perhaps understandably, WIPO tended to focus on protecting the interests of one of its main constituencies: trademark holders.[31]

Since the adoption of the trademark-focused UDRP, very little has been done in the way of global policy development to protect other interests in domain names. Such interests might include free speech,[32] privacy,[33] personality rights,[34] and rights in geographic and cultural indicators.[35] WIPO has maintained that some of these interests require further examination in the domain space,[36] but no specific action has been taken outside the new gTLD application process. Even competing commercial interests are not currently addressed particularly effectively under the UDRP. There are no specific rules for determining who has the best right to a given domain

---

[30] See www.wipo.int/portal/index.html.en, last accessed December 11, 2008. See also discussion in LINDSAY, *supra* note 1, at 99–120 (describing the drafting process between WIPO and ICANN).

[31] WIPO, *The Management of Internet Names and Addresses: Intellectual Property Issues*, Report of WIPO Internet Domain Name Process (April 30, 1999), para. 168, available at www.wipo.int/amc/en/processes/process1/report/finalreport.html, last accessed December 11, 2008 ('We are persuaded by the wisdom of proceeding firmly but cautiously and of tackling, at the first stage, problems which all agree require a solution. It was a striking fact that in all the 17 consultation meetings held throughout the world in the course of the WIPO Process, all participants agreed that 'cybersquatting' was wrong. It is in the interests of all, including the efficiency of economic relations, the avoidance of consumer confusion, the protection of consumers against fraud, the credibility of the domain name system and the protection of intellectual property rights, that the practice of deliberate abusive registrations of domain names be suppressed. There is evidence that this practice extends to the abuse of intellectual property rights other than trademarks and service marks, but we consider that it is premature to extend the notion of abusive registration beyond the violation of trademarks and service marks at this stage. After experience has been gained with the operation of the administrative procedure and time has allowed for an assessment of its efficacy and of the problems, if any, which remain outstanding, the question of extending the notion of abusive registration to other intellectual property rights can always be re-visited'.)

[32] See *supra* note 19.

[33] Lipton, *Beyond Cybersquatting, supra* note 18, at 1419 (suggesting the development of privacy rights in relation to domain name disputes involving personal names).

[34] See Lipton, *Celebrity in Cyberspace, supra* note 20.

[35] Thekla Hansen-Young, *Whose Name is it Anyway? Protecting Tribal Names from Cybersquatters*, 10 VIRGINIA J. LAW AND TECHNOLOGY 1 (2005).

[36] *Report of the Second WIPO Internet Domain Name Process* (September 3, 2001), available at www.wipo.int/amc/en/processes/process2/report/html/report.html, last accessed January 19, 2009. See, in particular, Chapters 4 and 5 on personal names and geographical indicators respectively.

name between, say, two competing legitimate trademark holders.[37] A presumption of 'first come, first served' currently prevails.[38]

This book identifies and categorizes different interests that may exist in domain names, as well as considering potential approaches to resolving disputes between competing interest holders. Some of these approaches could be implemented by ICANN, while others would require action by other bodies, such as domestic courts and legislatures. Emerging social norms and technological capabilities of the respective domain name registration systems might also play a role.[39] ICANN may need to formally adopt a broader policy-making role in the future. It may need to expressly protect a greater array of interests in domain names outside of the trademark arena. Perhaps the recent moves to protect trademarks alongside interests of public morality[40] and established communities[41] in the new gTLD registration procedure is a step in the right direction. However, a brief survey of ICANN's proposed dispute resolution procedures in the new gTLD system evidences that greater thought has been given to the protection of trademarks than other interests to date.[42] This step forward is also not reflected back with respect to disputes arising under existing gTLDs.

Importantly, we need to recognize that not all disputes involving

---

37 See, for example, discussion in Jacqueline Lipton, *A Winning Solution for YouTube and Utube? Corresponding Trademarks and Domain Name Sharing*, 21 Harvard J. Law and Technology 509, 510 (2008); Kesmodel, *supra* note 11, at 23 ('Domain names raised a host of new and perplexing questions in the field of intellectual-property law, especially when it came to trademarks. One problem was that only one company could register a domain, whereas under trademark law, multiple companies were entitled to use the same name, as long as they operated in different industries. That's why United Airlines, United Van Lines, and other companies using 'United' could peacefully coexist. But only one entity could register united.com. Trademark law also allowed for companies in different regions to share a name, but that was not practical on the borderless Internet'.)

38 Lipton, *A Winning Solution for YouTube and Utube?*, *supra* note 37, at 510.

39 Lawrence Lessig, *The Law of the Horse: What Cyberlaw Might Teach*, 113 Harvard L. Rev. 501 (1999) (famously identifying four regulatory modalities that will apply in cyberspace: legal rules, social norms, system architecture or 'code', and market forces).

40 ICANN, New gTLD Program: Draft Applicant Guidebook (Draft RFP), (October 24, 2008), Module 2, available at www.icann.org/en/topics/new-gtlds/draft-rfp-24oct08-en.pdf, last accessed December 11, 2008.

41 *Id.* at Module 3.

42 *Id.* at paras 3.5.2 (describing procedure for protection of trademarks in clear detail, as opposed to, say, paras 3.5.3 and 3.5.4, dealing in somewhat more vague terms with morality and public order confusion, and community objection, respectively).

domain names implicate trademarks. Increasingly, domain name speculators are turning to the registration of names of private individuals, acronyms and generic terms.[43] While some of these strings may coincide with trademarks, many will not. However, they may coincide with legitimate interests in personal identities, privacy, cultural interests, and the like.[44] This book commences with a description of the current regulatory framework for domain names in Chapter 1. It compares the structure and policy approach of the UDRP with domestic legislation at both the state and federal levels in the United States. Some of the domestic legislation focuses on protecting trademarks,[45] while other laws protect different interests, such as personality rights,[46] and interests in the integrity of the political process online.[47] This chapter illuminates the range of approaches available to regulating different aspects of domain name registration and use. It also identifies the various institutions that are involved in making and enforcing domain name policy at the present time.

Chapters 2 to 5 each focus on a specific set of interests that might arise in a given domain name. These chapters contemplate ways in which those often competing interests might be balanced against each other in practice. Chapter 2 focuses on competing commercial interests in a given domain name, such as the interests of multiple legitimate trademark holders with similar interests in the same domain name. Chapter 3 turns to the thorny question of the protection of free speech in the domain space. It considers ways in which decisions of UDRP arbitrators have started to shape the balance between free speech and trademark interests in domain names. Additionally, it considers whether any broader free speech protections are necessary. It focuses on the use of domain names for gripe sites, parody sites, fan sites, and general commentary or criticism. It examines alternatives for protecting and promoting free speech in the domain space outside of current policies and practices. Alternative approaches could include an attempt to zone online speech into different

---

43 See, for example, KESMODEL, *supra* note 11, at 181 (advising domain name speculators to focus on 'generic, commercially relevant words' for domain name registration purposes).

44 *Kremen v Cohen*, 337 F.3d 1024 (9th Cir. 2003) (involving conversion action with respect to the generic domain name 'sex.com'); see also discussion in KESMODEL, *supra* note 11, at 135–6.

45 See, for example, 15 U.S.C. § 1125(d).

46 See, for example, 15 U.S.C. § 8131(1) (protecting rights in personal names in the domain space against cybersquatting); California's Business and Professions Code, §§ 17525–17526.

47 See, for example, Cal. Elections Code, § 18320.

domain spaces, such as the '.xxx' gTLD that was proposed at one time for pornographic content.[48]

Chapter 4 focuses on the protection of personal names and identities in the domain space, noting that trademark law is often a poor fit for these interests. The interests an individual holds in her name or persona online may include privacy and autonomy interests, personality rights, political speech interests, and some business interests that may or may not overlap with a trademark. This chapter identifies the varying interests in a personal name that may be held by different classes of individuals such as celebrities, prominent athletes, politicians, public figures, private individuals and prominent business people. It considers different strategies for protecting the various rights an individual may seek to protect in her online name and persona.

Chapter 5 considers how best to protect politically, culturally and geographically significant terms in the domain space. There is little in the way of protection currently available for groups seeking to protect political, cultural and geographical interests in relevant names. While WIPO has addressed this issue in its domain name processes,[49] it has left resolution of the problem to a future date. One solution may be to create zones under new gTLDs where political,[50] cultural and geographic indicators could be protected. Alternatively, an expanded dispute resolution process could more specifically take account of non-trademark interests in domain names. The proposed dispute resolution procedure for new gTLDs does contemplate (albeit in vague terms) the protection of such names through a 'community objection' procedure.[51]

Chapter 6 considers conduct in the domain space that might more readily be labeled bad faith than conduct involving expressive, personal

---

[48] See discussion in Jennifer D. Phillips, *The Seamy Side of the Seamy Side: Potential Danger of Cyberpiracy in the Proposed '.xxx' Top Level Domain*, 7 North Carolina J. Law and Technology 233 (2005).

[49] See, for example, *Report of the Second WIPO Internet Domain Name Process* (September 3, 2001), paras 205–97, available at www.wipo.int/amc/en/processes/process2/report/html/report.html, last accessed January 19, 2009.

[50] For example, one commentator has suggested the creation of a '.pol' gTLD for political domain names: Matthew Sanderson, *Candidates, Squatters, and Gripers: A Primer on Political Cybersquatting and a Proposal for Reform*, 8 Election L.J. 3 (2008), available at www.liebertonline.com/doi/abs/10.1089/elj.2008.0013?cookieSet=1&journalCode=elj, last accessed March 16, 2010.

[51] ICANN, New gTLD Program: Draft Applicant Guidebook (Draft RFP) (October 24, 2008), para. 3.5.4, available at www.icann.org/en/topics/new-gtlds/draft-rfp-24oct08-en.pdf, last accessed December 11, 2008 (contemplating a community objection procedure to the registration of particular new gTLDs).

or cultural uses of domain names. It focuses on clickfarming and typosquatting. Clickfarming is a term generally used to describe situations where a person registers a domain name that corresponds with another person's trademark or name, and utilizes the associated website to make money out of advertising revenues from click-through advertisements.[52] Typosquatting has been defined as 'taking advantage of common misspellings made by Internet users who are looking for a particular site of a particular provider of goods or services, in order to obtain some benefit therefrom.'[53]

Clickfarming and typosquatting are not mutually exclusive. A person can register a domain name that is a common misspelling of another person's name or mark in order to set up a clickfarm. However, typosquatting can also arise more generally in situations that implicate any number of the interests identified above. A gripe site operator may, for example, employ a misspelling of a trademark to draw Internet users to her site in order to garner a bigger audience for her criticisms of the trademark holder. A fan of a celebrity may use a misspelling of the celebrity's name to draw Internet users to an unauthorized fan site. A political party or candidate could utilize a misspelling, or an unusual form,[54] of another candidate's name to draw the eyes of Internet users to information critical of, or otherwise harmful to, that other candidate.

Chapter 7 provides some preliminary insights as to the theoretical basis for any future domain name regulation, with particular reference to the possibility of moving away from trademark theory for cases that do not clearly implicate online trademarks. The discussion suggests a broader theoretical framework for future domain name regulation based respectively on trademark policy, property theory and restitution. The suggestion is that a tripartite policy basis for domain name regulation could better capture the different policies that need to be promoted in online commerce and discourse going forwards.

Chapter 8 concludes by briefly surveying some possible future direc-

---

[52] Jacqueline Lipton, *Clickfarming: The New Cybersquatting?*, 12 J. Internet Law 1 (2008). However, it should be noted that not all clickfarming involves taking advantage of another's name or trademark. See further discussion in Part 6.1, *infra*.

[53] *Expedia v Alvaro Collazo*, WIPO Arbitration and Mediation Center, Case No. D2003–0716 (October 30, 2003), available at www.wipo.int/amc/en/domains/decisions/html/2003/d2003-0716.html, last accessed December 11, 2008.

[54] For example, while Vice President Biden had registered 'www.joebiden.com' in the leadup to the 2008 presidential election, the republican party had registered the less often used form of his name, 'www.josephbiden.com' to establish a gripe site about then Senator Biden and his policy positions.

tions in domain name policy. This book does not, and is not intended to, provide comprehensive answers to all domain name regulation questions. It aims to identify, and to make suggestions for the resolution of, some of the current policy problems that exist for domain name governance. It is the author's hope that readers will take these suggestions for what they are worth. None of them is perfect, but the current system is also far from perfect, notwithstanding its relatively effective protections for trademark holders against cybersquatting. In modern domain name practice, this is a relatively rare case because the original cybersquatting phenomenon was largely a function of unfamiliarity by trademark holders with the commercial potential of the Internet in its early days. Today's domain name disputes tend to involve more difficult issues, such as competing interests in generic names, personal names and cultural identifiers, as well as competitions between multiple legitimate trademark holders. Hopefully, this book will serve to spark some additional debate about appropriate next steps in domain name governance at the domestic, and more importantly at the global, level.

1. Overview of domain name regulation

1.1 REGULATORY OPTIONS

A number of options currently exist for those seeking to assert rights in an Internet domain name against a prior registrant. The avenue chosen will largely depend upon the nature of the claim, and the jurisdiction in which the complainant resides. Despite the number of available avenues for dispute resolution, the current system suffers from significant gaps and limitations. Today's regulations focus on protecting trademarks, and occasionally personal names, against cybersquatters. Cybersquatting involves registering a domain name corresponding with someone else's name or mark with the intent to sell it for a profit.[1] Other conduct that may cause domain name conflicts is not specifically regulated. Examples of non-cybersquatting conflicts involve situations where multiple parties simultaneously hold legitimate trademark interests that correspond with the same domain name,[2] or where someone asserts expressive rights to comment on or criticize a trademark holder under a corresponding domain name.[3]

---

[1] Jonathan Nilsen, *Mixing Oil with Water: Resolving the Differences Between Domain Names and Trademark Law*, 1 J. HIGH TECH. L. 47, 51 (2002) ('Cybersquatting has been defined several ways. The most general definition of a cybersquatter is a person who registers a domain name that matches a well-known company for the purpose of ransoming it to that company'.)

[2] DAVID KESMODEL, THE DOMAIN GAME: HOW PEOPLE GET RICH FROM INTERNET DOMAIN NAMES 23 (2008) ('Domain names raised a host of new and perplexing questions in the field of intellectual-property law, especially when it came to trademarks. One problem was that only one company could register a domain, whereas under trademark law, multiple companies were entitled to use the same name, as long as they operated in different industries. That's why United Airlines, United Van Lines, and other companies using "United" could peacefully coexist. But only one entity could register united.com. Trademark law also allowed for companies in different regions to share a name, but that was not practical on the borderless Internet'.)

[3] See, for example, *Bridgestone-Firestone v Myers*, WIPO Arbitration and Mediation Center, Case No. D2000–0190 (July 6, 2000), available at www.wipoint/

This chapter outlines currently available domain name dispute resolution mechanisms, and highlights some of their limitations. Current mechanisms include (a) trademark infringement actions; (b) trademark dilution actions; (c) actions under the Anti-Cybersquatting Consumer Protection Act (ACPA) in the United States;[4] (d) arbitration under the UDRP; (e) actions under California's Business and Professions Code;[5] (f) actions under California's Political Cyberfraud Abatement Act;[6] (g) state actions relating to right of publicity tort in the United States;[7] (h) the possibility of other tort actions in various jurisdictions, including defamation and privacy torts.[8] These regulations are predominantly focused on protecting trademark interests and personal names in the domain space.

In the early days of the domain name system, the regulatory focus was on the protection of trademark interests against cybersquatters. Prior to 1999, the most common approach to this problem was through trademark infringement and dilution actions. Cybersquatters registered domain names corresponding with well-known trademarks at a time when the idea of electronic commerce was very new and many trademark holders had failed to appreciate the potential value in a domain name that matched its trademark. Cybersquatters sought to sell the domain names to the trademark holders – or sometimes to their competitors – for a profit.

A high profile example was Dennis Toeppen.[9] Toeppen registered multiple domain names corresponding with well-known trademarks in the early days of the Internet.[10] At the time, he did not believe there was

---

amc/en/domains/decisions/html/2000/d2000-0190.html, last accessed March 2, 2009 (registrant of a domain name successfully defended UDRP complaint on the basis of a right to free expression about his employer, despite the fact he utilized the employer's mark in his domain name).

4 15 U.S.C. § 1125(d) (anti-cybersquatting provisions involving trademarks). See also 15 U.S.C § 8131 (anti-cybersquatting provisions involving personal names).

5 Cal. Business and Professions Code, §§ 17525–17526.

6 Cal. Elections Code, § 18320(b), (c)(1).

7 ANNE GILSON LALONDE and JEROME GILSON, TRADEMARK PROTECTION AND PRACTICE para. 11.07[7] ('An individual's right of publicity is the right to control the commercial use of his or her identity – including name, likeness or other personal characteristics – by preventing others from appropriating that identity for commercial benefit'.)

8 See Restatement (Second) of Torts, § 652A-E (1977) (setting out the four established privacy torts in theUnited States).

9 Mr Toeppen maintains his own website at www.toeppen.com/, last accessed Feburary 28, 2009. The website includes details of his flirtations with cybersquatting in the 1990s.

10 *Id.*

any law against this conduct.[11] The Internet was widely regarded as a new frontier, much like the wild west.[12] Toeppen reasoned that he was merely staking a claim to valuable intangible property and was entitled to make a profit from it as the first claimant. This was not unlike making a land grab and then trying to sell the land to someone who valued it more highly. Toeppen was able to register the names at a minimal cost. Thus, even if he was not charging exorbitant fees for transfer of the names to the rightful trademark holders, he could make a very solid profit given that his time and costs in registering the names were minimal.

At the time, the only obvious option for complainants was trademark-based litigation. Generally, courts found in favor of trademark holders in these early cases on the basis of infringement or dilution.[13] Prevailing judicial attitudes at the time suggested some interesting things. First, judges seemed to be generally convinced that cybersquatting should be proscribed as a threat to the effective functioning of trademarks in online markets.[14] Secondly, early judicial attitudes to cybersquatting implicitly raise the question whether there was a pressing need for any new regulatory measures against cybersquatting at all. The courts' approach to early cybersquatting seemed to solidify an important presumption, being that protection of trademarks in the domain space should be an overriding goal of domain name regulation. Existing trademark law seemed equal to that challenge. It is questionable whether anything further was needed in the way of regulatory structure.

With the weight of judicial authority against cybersquatting, and in favor of a presumption that the protection of trademarks was a key goal of domain name regulation, the stage was set for the regulatory matrix to proceed with a very narrow focus. Indeed, the regulatory initiatives that followed most directly from these early cases solidified this attitude. Little thought was given to legitimate interests in domain names that might validly compete with trademark interests. Such competing interests might include free speech, or rights in personal names or cultural and geographic indicators. Likewise, little thought was given to protecting those with non-trademarked interests in a domain name against cybersquatters. Non-trademarked interests could

---

[11] *Id.*

[12] Jack Goldsmith and Tim Wu, Who Controls the Internet? Illusions of a Borderless World 17–18 (2008) (describing some early conceptions of the Internet as being a new electronic frontier akin to the Western frontier).

[13] See, for example, *Panavision v Toeppen*, 141 F.3d 1316 (9th Cir. 1998) (successful trademark dilution action against Dennis Toeppen with respect to the 'Panavision.com' domain name).

[14] *Id.*

include personal names or rights in a cultural or geographic indicator. The following sections consider ways in which various approaches to domain name dispute resolution have evolved to the present day.

1.2 TRADEMARK INFRINGEMENT

The trademark infringement action protects a trademark holder against an unauthorized use of a mark in commerce that is likely to confuse consumers as to the source of a particular product or service.[15] Infringement actions were successful in some early domain name cases on the basis that unauthorized registration and use of a domain name corresponding with someone else's mark would likely confuse consumers.[16] Trademark laws vary from jurisdiction to jurisdiction. American law in particular (codified in the Lanham Act) contains some notable points of departure from the laws of other jurisdictions. In particular, registration of a mark is less pivotal to its protection in the United States than in some other countries. This is because American trademark law is premised more on actual use of a mark in commerce than on registration.[17]

Additionally, the federal US Congress has been less prepared than legislatures in other countries to grant unequivocal proprietary status to trademarks.[18] Probably none of these distinctions is particularly relevant for trademark disputes involving the domain space, although it may

---

[15] Gilson, *supra* note 7, para. 5.01[1] (the general aim of trademark law is to prevent consumer confusion about the source of products or services).

[16] *Planned Parenthood Federation of America Inc. v Bucci*, 42 U.S.P.Q.2d 1430 (S.D.N.Y. 1997) (defendant's use of plannedparenthood.com domain name for messages critical of the Planned Parenthood organization was likely to confuse consumers as to the source of various services provided by the plaintiff); *Brookfield Communications Inc v West Coast Ent Corp*, 174 F.3d 1036 (9th Cir 1999) (use of 'moviebuff.com' domain name by one video library was likely to confuse customers of one of its competitors where each had some association with an iteration of the term 'Movie Buff' in its trademark).

[17] J.T. McCarthy, Trademarks and Unfair Competition para. 16.18 (2006) ('[I]t is not registration, but only actual use of a designation as a mark that creates rights and priority over others. The United States, unlike many civil law nations, has a rule of priority that is based on first-to-use, not first-to-register'.)

[18] For example, American trademark law, unlike equivalent laws in some other countries, prohibits assignments in gross; that is, assignments of trademarks without goodwill attached. See Gilson, *supra* note 7, para. 3.06[1] ('A trademark assignment, in order to validly transfer title in the mark, must carry the assignment of the good will which the trademark symbolizes. In other words, a trademark may not be validly assigned apart from its accompanying good will. An assignment

ultimately be that American trademark holders are in a weaker position than their counterparts in other countries if they cannot assert rights in trademarks in gross,[19] or rights in trademarks that have not yet been used in commerce.[20]

In the United States, trademark infringement actions are available for both registered[21] and unregistered marks,[22] as long as they are being used in commerce.[23] The main focus for both actions will be an assertion by the complainant that the domain name registrant confused consumers as to the source of trademarked goods or services.[24] Consumer confusion can be a sticking point in cybersquatting cases: for example, if the defendant is not actually selling any goods or services on her website, it may be difficult to ascertain how a consumer could be confused in the sense required by trademark law. One of the more well-known cases involving Dennis Toeppen provides a good example. With respect to the Panavision trademark, Toeppen had registered the 'panavision.com' domain name.[25] On the associated website, he sold no products or services. Instead, he displayed images of the town of Pana, Illinois.[26] This did not ultimately deter

without good will, known as an assignment ''in gross,'' does not transfer any legal rights to the assignee'.); 15 U.S.C. § 1060(a)(1) ('A registered mark or a mark for which an application to register has been filed shall be assignable with the good will of the business in which the mark is used, or with that part of the good will of the business connected with the use of and symbolized by the mark'.). This can be contrasted with, say, the Australian and British trademark laws in which assignments in gross are permissible. See, for example, Trade Marks Act 1995 (Austl), s. 106(3) ('The assignment or transmission may be with or without the goodwill of the business concerned in the relevant goods and/or services'.); Trade Marks Act, 1994 (UK), s. 24(1) ('A registered trade mark is transmissible by assignment, testamentary disposition or operation of law in the same way as other personal or moveable property. It is so transmissible either in connection with the goodwill of a business or independently'.).

19 *Id.*

20 See McCarthy, *supra* note 17, para. 16.18.

21 15 U.S.C. § 1114(1).

22 15 U.S.C. §1125(a)(1).

23 Gilson, *supra* note 7, para. 3.02[8][a]('In order to have ownership of a trademark, a party must use that trademark in commerce. Also, in order to establish federal jurisdiction for an infringement, dilution or unfair competition case, a plaintiff must plead and prove that the defendant's use or intended use of the infringing mark occurs "in commerce"'.)

24 *Id.* para. 5.01 ('The fundamental aim of trademark law is to avoid . . . consumer confusion about the source of products or services'.)

25 *Panavision v Toeppen*, 141 F.3d 1316 (9th Cir. 1998).

26 *Id.*; See also www.toeppen.com, last accessed February 28, 2009.

the court from finding trademark *dilution*.[27] However, such conduct does not necessarily satisfy the test for trademark *infringement* because there is no obvious consumer confusion. People typing 'Panavision.com' into their browsers and being confronted with a website containing images of the town of Pana are unlikely to be confused into thinking that the website belongs to the Panavision corporation.

Courts over the years have struggled with the concept of consumer confusion in the cybersquatting context. One court held that the fact that a website espoused online views that ran counter to the plaintiff trademark holder's views on family planning could satisfy the requirements of the Lanham Act on trademark infringement.[28] The court considered the fact that consumers might be deterred from finding the plaintiff's actual website after happening on to the defendant's website where the defendant had based its domain name on the plaintiff's mark: 'www.plannedparenthood.com'.[29] Over the years, courts have been increasingly prepared to find consumer confusion on the basis of 'initial interest confusion'.[30] Judges have held that the use of a plaintiff's trademark in a domain name or even potentially in a meta-tag[31] could amount to trademark infringement on the basis that consumers are initially diverted to the defendant's website when they were seeking the plaintiff's website.[32] Even if it would not be particularly onerous for the consumers to utilize the back button on their browser, or a search engine to find the site they were originally looking for, the fact that some consumers might be deterred from doing so has been sufficient to establish initial interest confusion for trademark infringement purposes.[33]

---

27 *Panavision v Toeppen*, 141 F.3d 1316 (9th Cir. 1998) (noting that trademark dilution has no consumer confusion requirement, See *infra*).

28 *Planned Parenthood Federation of America Inc. v Bucci*, 42 U.S.P.Q.2d 1430 (S.D.N.Y. 1997).

29 *Id.*

30 Greg Lastowka, *Google's Law*, 73 Brooklyn L. Rev. 1327, 1369–71 (2008) (providing a recent critique of the doctrine of initial interest confusion).

31 Gilson, *supra* note 7, at para. 11.07[6][a] ('Meta tags are codes that describe a website's properties and contents; they are not visible on the website itself, as displayed on the browser. When queried, many search engines look to a site's meta tags in determining whether a site is relevant and, if so, where to rank that site on its list of search results. The use of another party's trademark in one's meta tags can constitute meta tag misdirection and if this practice causes consumer confusion, it may be actionable'.)

32 *Brookfield Communications v West Coast Ent. Corp*, 174 F.3d 1036 (9th Cir. 1999).

33 *Id.* but See *Playboy v Netscape*, 354 F.3d 1020, 1034–6 (2004) (Judge Berzon criticizes *Brookfield* on initial interest confusion).

Another important requirement of trademark law generally, in both the infringement and dilution contexts, is that the conduct in question must be 'in commerce'.[34] This is particularly important in the United States, as the constitutional underpinning of the Lanham Act resides with the 'commerce clause' of the federal Constitution.[35] Courts have had little difficulty finding this requirement to be satisfied both in infringement and dilution proceedings.[36] For example, in the traditional cybersquatting context, the fact that a defendant has utilized a trademark in a domain name to extort money from the mark owner has been regarded as a sufficiently commercial activity to support a trademark dilution action.[37] In cases that are less like cybersquatting (because there is no actual attempt by the domain name registrant to sell the domain name) courts have nevertheless found the conduct to be in commerce. In the *Planned Parenthood* litigation, for example,[38] the court focused on the fact that the defendant was using his website to promote a book written by another person.[39] Additionally, the court noted that all Internet activity is conducted over a telecommunications system that users must subscribe to commercially, and that this fact should suffice to satisfy trademark law's 'in commerce' requirements.[40]

Of course, the trademark infringement action has some important limitations. The most obvious is that it only protects trademarks. It does not apply to cases that involve important, but non-trademarked, interests in domain names. Many people's names, for example, are not trademarked and may not be trademarkable.[41] Additionally, many cultural and geographic indicators are not trademarked or trademarkable.[42] Trademark

---

[34] 15 U.S.C. §§ 1114(1), 1125(a)(1).

[35] United States Constitution, article 1, section 8, clause 3 (provides that federal Congress has the power to regulate commerce with foreign nations, among the states, and with the Indian tribes).

[36] See, for example *Panavision v Toeppen*, 141 F.3d 1316 (9th Cir. 1998); *Planned Parenthood Federation of America Inc. v Bucci*, 42 U.S.P.Q.2d 1430 (S.D.N.Y. 1997).

[37] *Panavision v Toeppen*, 141 F.3d 1316 (9th Cir. 1998).

[38] *Planned Parenthood Federation of America Inc. v Bucci*, 42 U.S.P.Q.2d 1430 (S.D.N.Y. 1997).

[39] *Id.* at 13–14 (LEXIS page references).

[40] *Id.* at 11–12 (LEXIS page references).

[41] GILSON, *supra* note 7, at para. 2.03[4][d] ('Just as with descriptive terms, a trademark or trade name that consists of a personal name (first name, surname, or both) is entitled to legal protection only if it attains secondary meaning'.)

[42] *Id.* at para. 2.03[4][c] ('In general, geographic terms are legally protectible where they have attained secondary meaning, or where they lack geographic significance or meaning in association with the particular products or services. However, when such terms are used in their primary meaning to describe the place where a product is made or a service is performed, they are ordinarily unprotect-

infringement law also may not provide the perfect balance between commerce and speech in the domain space. While trademark law has traditionally struggled to find a balance between the rights of trademark holders and free speech,[43] the previous balance may not translate perfectly to cyberspace.[44] In particular, the global nature of cyberspace raises new challenges for trademark law. For example, it should not be presumed that whatever balance American courts have struck historically between trademarks and free speech necessarily reflects the cultural balances between speech and property in other countries.[45]

Trademark infringement also ultimately relies on the ability of the trademark holder to bring a successful court action. This can be a costly and protracted experience. It may be outside the means of many small players, including small businesses attempting to protect their trademarks online. Additionally, if defendants are in foreign jurisdictions, the prospects of actually being able to assert jurisdiction over them or to effectively enforce judgments against them can be insurmountable hurdles for some complainants.

1.3 TRADEMARK DILUTION

Trademark dilution differs from infringement in that it is not focused on consumer confusion. Dilution is instead concerned with protecting famous marks[46] from blurring[47] or tarnishment.[48] As enacted at the

---

able because they do not perform the trademark function of distinguishing the business source or origin of the product'.)

43 Gilson, *supra* note 7, at para. 11.08[4][l][i] (discussion of First Amendment defenses to trademark actions).

44 See, for example, discussion in Jacqueline Lipton, *Commerce versus Commentary: Gripe Sites, Parody and the First Amendment in Cyberspace*, 84 Washington University L. Rev. 1327 (2006); Margreth Barrett, *Domain Names, Trademarks and the First Amendment: Searching for Meaningful Boundaries*, 39 Conn. L. Rev. 973 (2007).

45 Goldsmith and Wu, *supra* note 12, at 158 (making a similar point in relation to defamation law).

46 15 U.S.C. § 1125(c)(2)(A) (statutory definition of 'famous mark' as inserted into the Lanham Act under the Trademark Dilution Revision Act, H.R. 683 of 2006) (TDRA).

47 15 U.S.C. § 1125(c)(2)(B) (defines 'blurring' as an 'association arising from the similarity between a mark or trade name and a famous mark that impairs the distinctiveness of the famous mark').

48 15 U.S.C. § 1125(c)(2)(C) (defines 'tarnishment' of a famous mark as an 'association arising from the similarity between a mark or trade name and a famous mark that harms the reputation of the famous mark'.)

federal level in the United States, the idea behind dilution is to prevent people from creating noise around a mark that might lessen the strength of the mark in terms of its capacity to identify the plaintiff's goods or services.[49] Thus, a dilution action could prevent the sale of Sony potato chips as potentially dilutive of the Sony corporation's marks for audio-visual and electronic equipment. In the United States, there is a non-commercial use exemption from trademark dilution liability.[50] Additionally, under revisions to the Lanham Act in 2006,[51] there is an expanded fair use defense to dilution that contemplates various forms of commentary on a trademark holder.[52]

Dilution actions have been used successfully against cybersquatters in the past.[53] This is because the use of someone else's trademark in a domain name for no particular purpose other than to sell the name to the trademark holder (or perhaps to a competitor of the trademark holder) could be said to be creating noise around the mark in a dilution sense.[54] Additionally, courts have had no trouble finding the 'in commerce' requirements of trademark law to be satisfied in dilution actions on the basis that the defendant was engaging in commerce by selling the domain names to corresponding trademark holders.[55]

As with trademark infringement, dilution actions are premised on the plaintiff holding a trademark. Moreover, in the case of dilution, the

---

49 Mark Lemley, *The Modern Lanham Act and the Death of Common Sense*, 108 YALE L.J. 1687, 1698–9 (1999) ('Dilution laws are directed against the possibility that the unique nature of a mark will be destroyed by companies who trade on the renown of the mark by selling unrelated goods, such as Kodak pianos or Buick aspirin'.); GILSON, *supra* note 7, at para.5A.01[1] ('Federal dilution law protects famous trademarks from unauthorized uses that are likely to impair their distinctiveness or harm their reputation. It enables owners of those marks to maintain their value as source indicators and as symbols of good will. While the law benefits only famous trademarks, it adds a potent weapon against the whittling away of the hard-to-measure distinctive quality of those marks'.)

50 15 U.S.C. § 1125(c)(3)(C).

51 Trademark Dilution Revision Act, H.R. 683 of 2006.

52 15 U.S.C. § 1125(c)(3)(A)(ii).

53 See, for example, *Panavision Int'l L.P. v Toeppen*, 141 F.3d 1316 (9th Cir.1998) (successful trademark dilution action against cybersquatter who was not using the name for any purpose other than attempting to sell it to the corresponding trademark holder).

54 *Id.* at 1327 (9th Cir. 1998) ('We reject [defendant's] premise that a domain name is nothing more than an address. A significant purpose of a domain name is to identify the entity that owns the website'.); ('[Defendant's] use of Panavision.com also puts Panavision's name and reputation at his mercy'.)

55 *Id.*

plaintiff must hold a *famous* mark.[56] Despite the fact that it has proved reasonably easy in the past for plaintiffs to establish that their marks are sufficiently famous to bring a dilution action,[57] the 2006 revisions to the federal dilution law in the United States may make it more difficult in the future. The new definition of famous mark contemplates a famous mark in very consumer-oriented terms with respect to the source of goods or services.[58] This may make it difficult for those who have in the past asserted trademarks in, say, some personal names or geographic and cultural indicators to establish sufficiently famous trademark interests for the purposes of a dilution action. Another impact of the 2006 revisions to the Lanham Act might arise because of the new commentary defense to trademark dilution.[59] This defense might more clearly excuse a purely expressive website from potential dilution liability.

---

56 15 U.S.C. § 1125(c)(1) ('Subject to the principles of equity, the owner of a famous mark that is distinctive, inherently or through acquired distinctiveness, shall be entitled to an injunction against another person who, at any time after the owner's mark has become famous, commences use of a mark or trade name in commerce that is likely to cause dilution by blurring or dilution by tarnishment of the famous mark, regardless of the presence or absence of actual or likely confusion, of competition, or of actual economic injury'.). 'Famous mark' is now defined for these purposes in 15 U.S.C. § 1125(c)(2)(A).

57 Lemley, *supra* note 49, at 1698–9. However, since the enactment of the TDRA in 2006, it may be more difficult to establish that a mark is famous than in the past due to the new definition of 'famous mark' now inserted into 15 U.S.C. § 1125(c)(2)(A). At least, courts may have to undertake an analysis of whether a mark is famous or not with regard to this provision.

58 15 U.S.C. § 1125(c)(2)(A) ('For purposes of paragraph [15 U.S.C. § 1125(c)(1)], a mark is famous if it is widely recognized by the general consuming public of the United States as a designation of source of the goods or services of the mark's owner. In determining whether a mark possesses the requisite degree of recognition, the court may consider all relevant factors, including the following: (i) The duration, extent, and geographic reach of advertising and publicity of the mark, whether advertised or publicized by the owner or third parties; (ii) the amount, volume, and geographic extent of sales of goods or services offered under the mark; (iii) the extent of actual recognition of the mark.')

59 15 U.S.C. § 1125(c)(3)(A)(ii) ('The following shall not be actionable as dilution by blurring or dilution by tarnishment under this subsection: (A) Any fair use, including a nominative or descriptive fair use, or facilitation of such fair use, of a famous mark by another person other than as a designation of source for the person's own goods or services, including use in connection with: . . . (ii) identifying and parodying, criticizing, or commenting upon the famous mark owner or the goods or services of the famous mark owner'.)

1.4 ANTI-CYBERSQUATTING CONSUMER PROTECTION ACT

1.4.1 Trademarks and the ACPA

In 1999, two things happened in response to trademark holders' concerns about cybersquatting. One was domestic legislation in the United States, the ACPA, and the other was a global arbitration procedure adopted by ICANN, the UDRP. This chapter addresses the domestic solution first, followed by a detailed consideration of the UDRP. Congress sought to achieve a variety of things with the ACPA. It wanted to create a more directed legislative prohibition against cybersquatting than had been available in the past. Additionally, it wanted to deal as best it could with some of the jurisdictional problems facing those involved in trademark disputes. Finally, it wanted to provide some protections against cybersquatting involving personal names.

The ACPA inserted new provisions into the Lanham Act to protect trademark holders against bad faith registrations of domain names corresponding with their registered or unregistered marks.[60] The ACPA originally created a civil action against a person who registers, traffics in, or uses a domain name corresponding with someone else's trademark with a bad faith intent to profit from the mark.[61] Bad faith is defined in terms that contemplate a knowing and unauthorized incursion into a complainant's trademark rights. The ACPA sets out a non-exclusive list of factors that courts may consider when ascertaining whether relevant conduct is in bad faith.[62] The factors include:

(a) the trademark or other intellectual property rights of the registrant in the domain name;[63]
(b) the extent to which the domain name consists of the legal name of the registrant or a name that is otherwise commonly used to identify that person;[64]
(c) the registrant's prior use of the domain name in connection with a bona fide offering of goods or services;[65]

---

60 15 U.S.C. § 1125(d).

61 15 U.S.C. § 1129(1). This provision has been removed from the Lanham Act and now appears at U.S.C. § 8131.

62 15 U.S.C. § 1125(d)(1)(B)(i) (making it clear that a court *may* consider the listed factors in making a determination of bad faith).

63 15 U.S.C. § 1125(d)(1)(B)(i)(I).

64 15 U.S.C. § 1125(d)(1)(B)(i)(II).

65 15 U.S.C. § 1125(d)(1)(B)(i)(III).

(d) the registrant's bona fide non-commercial or fair use of the mark in a site accessible under the domain name;[66]
(e) the registrant's intent to divert customers from the trademark owner's online location in a manner likely to cause consumer confusion or trademark dilution;[67]
(f) the registrant's offer to transfer the domain name to the trademark owner or a third party for financial gain without having used or intending to use the domain name for a bona fide offering of goods or services;[68]
(g) the registrant's provision of misleading false contact information when registering the domain name, the person's failure to maintain accurate contact information, or the person's prior conduct indicating a pattern of such conduct;[69]
(h) the person's registration or acquisition of multiple domain names which the person knows are identical or confusingly similar to marks of others, or dilutive of famous marks of others;[70] and,
(i) the extent to which the mark incorporated in the registrant's domain name is distinctive for the purposes of the dilution provisions of the trademark legislation.[71]

The ACPA further provides that a bad faith intent may not be found in a situation where the court determines that the registrant believed and had reasonable grounds to believe that the use of the domain name was a fair use or otherwise lawful.[72]

Although this legislation provides some clear rules against traditional Toeppen-style cybersquatting,[73] it raises some questions as well. The most

---

66 15 U.S.C. § 1125(d)(1)(B)(i)(IV).
67 15 U.S.C. § 1125(d)(1)(B)(i)(V).
68 15 U.S.C. § 1125(d)(1)(B)(i)(VI).
69 15 U.S.C. § 1125(d)(1)(B)(i)(VII).
70 15 U.S.C. § 1125(d)(1)(B)(i)(VIII).
71 15 U.S.C. § 1125(d)(1)(B)(i)(IX).
72 15 U.S.C. § 1125(d)(1)(B)(ii).
73 *Lucas Nursery v Grosse*, 359 F.3d 806, 810 (2004) (acknowledging that the paradigmatic harm that the ACPA was enacted to eradicate is the practice of cybersquatters registering several hundred domain names in an effort to sell them to the legitimate owners of a mark); *Northland Insurance Companies v Blaylock*, 115 F.Supp.2d 1108, 1123 (2000) ('Congress passed the [ACPA] to protect consumers and American businesses, to promote the growth of online commerce, and to provide clarity in the law for trademark owners by prohibiting the bad-faith and abusive registration of distinctive marks as Internet domain names with the intent to profit from the goodwill associated with such marks – a practice commonly referred to as "cybersquatting"'); *TMI Inc. v*

obvious is whether it was necessary at all. Courts were not apparently having trouble finding trademark infringement and dilution to be made out in the pre-ACPA cybersquatting cases.[74] Thus, the introduction of the ACPA without a clear legislative intent that it would *replace* infringement and dilution actions in the domain space now simply adds another string to a trademark holder's bow. Instead of streamlining litigation, plaintiff trademark holders can now plead the ACPA, trademark infringement, and dilution, in the alternative. Thus, litigation costs have arguably increased post-ACPA rather than decreased.[75]

Another concern with the ACPA is that it is very narrowly tailored to fit Toeppen-style cybersquatting cases. Its application to other domain name scenarios can be limited. For example, the idea of a *bad faith intent to profit* (which is central to an ACPA claim) has caused some consternation in cases involving gripe sites,[76] fan websites and parody sites. It is not clear whether random, innocuous comments that a defendant may be prepared to settle the case if a particular offer is made for a domain name may comprise the requisite bad faith intent to profit for the purposes of the ACPA.[77] If so, settling a dispute out of court becomes a difficult proposition. If any attempt by the defendant to name a price to settle is regarded as satisfying the bad faith intent to profit criteria, defendants will presumably be less inclined to agree to settlement negotiations for fear of attracting statutory liability.[78]

Maxwell, 368 F.3d 433, 439 (2004); *Lamparello v Falwell*, 420 F.3d 309 (2005) (the paradigmatic harm that the ACPA was intended to combat is the practice of cybersquatters registering several hundred domain names in an effort to sell them to legitimate owners of the marks – following *Lucas Nursery, supra*).

74 *Panavision Int'l v Toeppen*, 141 F.3d 1316 (9th Cir., 1998) (finding trademark dilution where the defendant had registered domain names corresponding with famous marks owned by the plaintiff and had put material unrelated to the plaintiff's marks or business on the relevant website); *Planned Parenthood Federation of America Inc. v Bucci*, 42 U.S.P.Q.2d 1430 (S.D.N.Y. 1997) (finding trademark infringement and dilution to be made out where defendant registered domain name corresponding with plaintiff's trademark for purposes of a website critical of plaintiff's point of view).

75 In fact, there is evidence that infringement, dilution and ACPA claims are pleaded in the alternative in practice. See, for example, *Bosley Medical Institute v Kremer*, 403 F.3d 672, 680 (2005).

76 A gripe site is a website set up to complain about an individual or entity, usually utilizing a domain name that in some way refers to the subject of the griping: for example, www.nikesucks.com for a website critical of the Nike corporation.

77 Lipton, *Commerce versus Commentary, supra* note 44, at 1349–50.

78 *Id.*

Particular bad faith factors in the ACPA can also be problematic in cases that do not fit the classic cybersquatting paradigm. For example, the factor that relates to multiple domain name registrations might be confusing in practice. It obviously contemplates a scenario where a cybersquatter like Toeppen has registered multiple domain names relating to different marks with the intent to extort money from a variety of trademark holders. It is not clear, however, how this factor might apply in a situation where a domain name registrant has registered multiple iterations of the same trademark (as opposed to a variety of different marks) in order to set up gripe sites and parody sites about the trademark holder. One example might be a cybergriper who wants to complain about Delta Airlines service, and registers the following domain names: 'deltasucks.com', 'deltaairlinessucks.com', 'ihatedelta.com', 'dellta.com' and 'deltareviews.com'.

This person is obviously not cybersquatting in the traditional sense as she probably does not wish to extort money for transfer of any of the names – although she might profit from the names in other ways, say, by selling advertising on relevant websites. Such a registrant might be presumed to be acting in bad faith for ACPA purposes, despite the fact that she is only guilty of bad will towards the trademark holder, and not a bad faith intent to profit from registration or use of the names. This problem might be mitigated if the ACPA's notion of multiple registrations were judicially confined (or legislatively revised) to relate to registering multiple domain names corresponding to *multiple* marks, rather than *one* mark. This would better match the situation where a domain name speculator is attempting to profit from selling names to various parties, rather than a situation where a griper is attempting to use multiple domain names to garner a larger audience for her complaints about one particular trademark holder.

Alternatively, this factor might be removed from the ACPA altogether. Clearly, the notion of multiple registrations was intended to combat Toeppen-style cybersquatting.[79] However, it may be unnecessary to include it in the legislation at all. Is it really relevant to a cybersquatting claim that the defendant has registered multiple domain names even if they correspond to multiple well-known trademarks? What does this factor tell the court in any given case about the registrant's specific intentions with respect to the plaintiff? Even in the case of a registrant who has registered multiple domain names corresponding with multiple marks, the registrant may be making legitimate uses of some of the names while cybersquatting

---

79 See discussion in *Panavision Int'l v Toeppen*, 141 F.3d 1316 (9th Cir. 1998).

on others. She may, for example, run gripe sites or parody sites (assuming these are legitimate uses) from some of the domain names, while using others to extort money from relevant trademark holders. The fact that she has registered multiple names corresponding with multiple marks does not necessarily give the court any specific guidance on her intentions with respect to the trademark holder's complaint in any given case. The court will still need to focus on whether or not the registrant is trying to profit from the sale of a domain name corresponding with the plaintiff's mark regardless of what she may be doing with any other domain names she may also have registered.

Some of the other bad faith factors in the ACPA might also be generally problematic: for example, what constitutes an 'offer to transfer the domain name to the mark owner or a third party for financial gain'?[80] Clearly the legislature had in mind schemes designed with the central aim of transferring names to rightful owners for profit. What about situations where a registrant is prepared to transfer the names, or might be prepared to transfer the names, but that was not the initial aim of registration? Again, could an offer to sell the name in the course of pre-litigation settlement negotiations amount to an offer to transfer the domain name to the rightful owner for financial gain? This might create a distinct disincentive to settle out of court.

While judicial decisions have not focused so much on this issue, there has been some confusion about the application of the related 'bad faith intent to profit' aspect of the ACPA. As Professor Snow has pointed out, the ACPA attaches liability for a bad-faith intent even after the registrant has registered the relevant domain name.[81] In other words, there is a temporal problem with the statute in that it does not require the bad faith intent to exist at the time of domain name registration.[82] This effectively means that any subsequent attempt to sell the name could be described as being in bad faith for the ACPA's purposes.[83]

Another problem with the 'bad faith intent to profit' requirement might arise when the defendant has set up a gripe site or parody site in such a

---

80 15 U.S.C. § 1125(d)(1)(B)(i)(VI).

81 Ned Snow, *The Constitutional Failing of the Anticybersquatting Act*, 41 Willamette L. Rev. 1, 41 (2005).

82 *Id.*

83 See, for example, *People for the Ethical Treatment of Animals v Doughney*, 113 F. Supp.2d 915, 920–1 (2000); *aff'd* 263 F.3d 359 (2001) (court held that defendant had requisite bad faith intent to profit from transfer of a domain name corresponding with plaintiff's mark even though his comment that the plaintiff could 'make him an offer' for the name occurred after the litigation commenced).

way that it is possible to argue some incidental financial benefit to the defendant or someone connected to the defendant. This could arise if the defendant uses the website to refer to, or to advertise, products or services that may or may not be relevant to the plaintiff's activities. If they are relevant to the plaintiff's activities, they may bolster the likelihood that the plaintiff will succeed on a trademark infringement claim.[84] If not, the possibility of an ACPA success still looms. As online advertising programs, such as GoogleAds, increase in popularity, it will be easier to establish a profit motive on the part of the domain name registrant, even if the profit has nothing to do with the registrant directly selling products or services in competition with the trademark holder.

There is also currently some judicial confusion as to whether an ACPA claim requires a showing of a commercial use of the mark by the defendant. Some courts have interpreted the ACPA's fourth bad faith factor[85] as imposing a burden on the defendant to satisfy the court that she has not used the relevant mark in commerce. At least one court has suggested that the fact that the website in question potentially deters customers from the plaintiff's online location might amount to a use in commerce.[86] However, not all courts have subscribed to this approach. In *Bosley v Kremer*, the Ninth Circuit Court of Appeals held that the ACPA does not contain a commercial use requirement.[87] The court was concerned that an approach that requires a commercial use – and all too readily finds it – could lead to a situation where otherwise constitutionally protected consumer commentary would be placed under the restrictions of the Lanham Act.[88]

Even courts that have recognized a commercial use requirement in the ACPA have split on the question whether the defendant's use of the website to link to other commercial websites would satisfy the requirement.

---

84 See, for example, *Planned Parenthood Federation of America Inc. v Bucci*, 42 U.S.P.Q.2d 1430, 1997 U.S. Dist. LEXIS 3338, 15 (S.D.N.Y. 1997) (suggesting that plaintiff and defendant were effectively competing in offering informational services on abortion and birth control).

85 Relating to 'the registrant's bona fide non-commercial or fair use of the mark in a site accessible under the domain name': 15 U.S.C. § 1125(d)(1)(B)(i)(IV).

86 See, for example, *People for the Ethical Treatment of Animals v Doughney*, 113 F.Supp.2d 915, 920 (2000); *aff'd* 263 F.3d 359 (2001) (this requirement appears to have been satisfied in the case by the fact that the defendant's website linked to the websites of organizations selling fur and animal products and potentially deterred the plaintiff's customers from finding the plaintiff's website – these factors also satisfied the plaintiff's traditional trademark infringement claim).

87 *Bosley Medical Institute v Kremer*, 403 F.3d 672, 680 (2005).

88 *Id.*

In *People for the Ethical Treatment of Animals v Doughney*,[89] for example, the court accepted as relevant to the commercial use issue the fact that the defendant's website linked to other sites where customers could purchase fur and animal products antithetical to the plaintiff's views and messages.[90] However, in similar circumstances, the Fourth Circuit Court of Appeals in *Lamparello v Falwell*[91] held that the defendant's linking of his commentary website to an Amazon.com webpage selling a particular book would not support an ACPA claim. This was because the inclusion of this link on his webpage 'does not diminish the communicative function of his website'.[92] The court in *Falwell* also suggested that the commercial use requirement is not satisfied here because the defendant 'did not even stand to gain financially from sales of the book at Amazon.com'.[93] This sounds reasonable, but also appears directly to contradict the reasoning in *Doughney* where the defendant likewise made no profits from the websites to which he linked.

The drafting and interpretation of the ACPA's provisions have serious implications for the protection of free speech in cyberspace. Several courts have already recognized the potential for speech to be chilled on the Internet as a result of over-zealous application of the ACPA. In *Northland Insurance v Blaylock*,[94] for example, Judge Doty in the District Court of Minnesota noted:

> While protecting the public interest clearly demands that the Internet be used responsibly and in conformance with intellectual property laws, the right of defendant to openly express his viewpoint should likewise not be curtailed absent clearer demonstration that the claims against him have merit . . . Public policy requires that preliminary injunctions, especially those that stand to potentially chill a person's right to free speech, no matter how disagreeable that speech may be, should only be granted in the most extraordinary of circumstances.[95]

However, courts have not given complete deference to the operators of gripe sites and parody sites whose Internet domain names correspond

---

89 *People for the Ethical Treatment of Animals v Doughney*, 113 F.Supp.2d 915 (2000); *aff'd* 263 F.3d 359 (2001).

90 *People for the Ethical Treatment of Animals v Doughney*, 113 F.Supp.2d 915, 919–20 (2000); *aff'd* 263 F.3d 359 (2001) (it is not clear to what extent this factor swayed the ACPA analysis as distinct from the trademark infringement analysis; however, it was clearly in the court's mind as relevant to the plaintiff's claims).

91 *Lamparello v Falwell*, 420 F.3d 309, 320 (2005).

92 *Id.*

93 *Id.*

94 115 F.Supp.2d 1108 (2000).

95 *Id.* at 1125.

with well-known marks. Moreover, the cases in which courts have been prepared to enjoin uses of particular domain names in the parody or commentary context are often difficult to distinguish from the cases in which courts have not been prepared to grant relief. The distinctions that courts make often rely heavily on justifications relating to multiple domain name registrations by a defendant and post-registration intentions to sell domain names to rightful owners. These are both problematic bad faith criteria for reasons set out above.

In *Lamparello v Falwell*,[96] for example, the Fourth Circuit Court of Appeals was not prepared to enjoin the defendant's use of a domain name comprising a misspelling of the plaintiff's name – 'fallwell.com' – for a website critical of the plaintiff's views on homosexuality. The court distinguished two similar cases[97] on the basis that the defendants in those cases had registered multiple domain names corresponding to marks held by various other people, and that, in one case, the defendant had made a comment in the course of the litigation that the plaintiff could make him an offer for transfer of the name.[98] As noted above, it is difficult to see how the multiple registrations of other domain names have any bearing on the use of a domain name corresponding to the plaintiff's mark where, in fact, the defendant is actually utilizing the name for an expressive purpose.[99]

1.4.2 Jurisdiction under the ACPA

Obviously, jurisdictional problems can arise in litigation involving domain names because the complainant and the registrant may be in different jurisdictions. The ACPA includes a provision to counteract some of these jurisdictional difficulties. It provides that the owner of a mark may file an *in rem* civil action against a domain name in the place where the domain name is registered or assigned[100] if the domain name violates any trademark rights,[101] and the plaintiff is unable to assert *in personam* jurisdiction

---

[96] 420 F.3d 309 (2005).

[97] *People for the Ethical Treatment of Animals v Doughney*, 113 F.Supp.2d 915 (2000); *aff'd* 263 F.3d 359 (2001), cited at 420 F.3d 309, 320–1 (2005); *Coca-Cola Co v Purdy*, 382 F.3d 774 (8th Cir. 2004), cited at 420 F.3d 309, 321 (2005).

[98] *People for the Ethical Treatment of Animals v*, 263 F.3d 359, 368 (2001).

[99] In *Panavision v Toeppen*, for example, Toeppen had registered two of Panavision's marks and used one for a website containing photographs of the town of 'Pana' in Illinois. The other *Doughney* merely contained the word 'hello': Jacqueline Lipton, *Beyond Cybersquatting: Taking Domain Name Disputes Past Trademark Policy*, 40 WAKE FOREST L. REV. 1361, 1388–9 (2005).

[100] 15 U.S.C. § 1125(d)(2)(A), (C).

[101] 15 U.S.C. § 1125(d)(2)(A)(i).

over the defendant,[102] or the plaintiff is unable to locate the defendant.[103] Orders made under these provisions are limited to cancellation, or transfer to the plaintiff of the domain name registration.[104]

This provision will be of limited use where the domain name in question is registered in a jurisdiction outside the United States. This was not such a problem in 1999 when the ACPA was enacted. At that time, all of the domain names with the most desirable '.com', '.net' and '.org' suffixes were registered with Network Solutions (now VeriSign Inc.)[105] in Reston, Virginia.[106] This meant that many American plaintiffs could bring their complaints in an American court. This has changed in recent years as the registration system has become decentralized under arrangements made with ICANN to introduce more registrars, and therefore more competition, into the domain name registration market.[107] One further limitation of the ACPA's *in rem* jurisdiction provisions is that they do not apply to disputes involving non-trademarked personal names or other interests in the domain space, such as rights in cultural or geographic indicators. The provisions only cover disputes that involve rights of a registered or unregistered trademark holder.[108]

1.4.3 Personal Name Cyberpiracy Protections

In 1999, Congress included specific personal name cyberpiracy provisions in the ACPA. These protections for personal names now appear in 15

---

102 15 U.S.C. § 1125(d)(2)(A)(ii)(I).

103 15 U.S.C. § 1125(d)(2)(A)(ii)(II).

104 15 U.S.C. § 1125(d)(2)(D)(i).

105 See www.verisign.com, last accessed March 2, 2009.

106 See discussion in MILTON MUELLER, RULING THE ROOT: INTERNET GOVERNANCE AND THE TAMING OF CYBERSPACE 2, 160–1 (2004); DAVID LINDSAY, INTERNATIONAL DOMAIN NAME LAW: ICANN AND THE UDRP para. 2.26 (2007).

107 See MUELLER, *supra* note 106, at 160–1; LINDSAY, *supra* note 106, para. 2.28.

108 15 U.S.C. § 1125(d)(2)(A)(i) (the provision is expressed to cover only situations where a domain name violates the rights of a registered trademark holder or the rights of an unregistered trademark holder against infringement or dilution of the mark). Interestingly, the provision does not appear expressly to cover the rights of an unregistered trademark holder against cybersquatting. As far as unregistered marks are concerned, § 1125(d)(2)(A)(i) only relates to contraventions of § 1125(a) and (c) which relate to infringement and dilution of an unregistered mark respectively. There is no express mention of the rights of an unregistered mark holder with respect to § 1125(d)(1) in the *in rem* jurisdiction provisions. Thus, arguably even though an unregistered mark is technically protected against cybersquatting under § 1125(d)(1), an unregistered trademark holder cannot avail herself of the *in rem* provisions of § 1125(d)(2) without first registering the mark.

U.S.C. § 8131. The basic prohibition on personal name cyberpiracy provides that:

> Any person who registers a domain name that consists of the name of another living person, or a name substantially and confusingly similar thereto, without that person's consent, with the specific intent to profit from such name by selling the domain name for financial gain to that person or any third party, shall be liable in a civil action by such person.[109]

The remedies for infringement of this provision include an order to transfer the domain name to the plaintiff or to cancel the domain name registration,[110] as well as orders for fees and costs to the prevailing party.[111] This provision broadens Lanham Act protections in the sense that it extends protection to rights in personal names that are neither trademarked nor trademarkable. There is no need for the plaintiff to establish a trademark in her name in order to bring a successful action. In other words, there is no requirement that the plaintiff establish secondary meaning in her name for trademark purposes.[112] This can be advantageous for many plaintiffs. However, the disadvantages of litigation in terms of jurisdiction, costs and time still dissuade most personal name claimants from proceeding under the personal name cyberpiracy provision. Most complainants still prefer to take action under the UDRP and take their chances in establishing at least common law trademarks in their personal names.[113]

The tendency to rely on the UDRP for personal name disputes puts pressure on UDRP arbitrators to accept the existence of trademarks in personal names in situations where such rights are questionable. Moreover, it has led to inconsistent and often arbitrary determinations under the UDRP about questions relating to the trademark status of particular personal names.[114] It may be preferable if the UDRP could be extended to cover personal names irrespective of trademark status. This would allow personal name claimants easier access to the cheaper, quicker

---

109 15 U.S.C. § 8131(1)(A).

110 15 U.S.C. § 8131(2).

111 15 U.S.C. § 8131(2).

112 Gilson, *supra* note 7, para. 2.03[4][d] ('Just as with descriptive terms, a trademark or trade name that consists of a personal name (first name, surname, or both) is entitled to legal protection only if it attains secondary meaning'.)

113 Jacqueline Lipton, *Celebrity in Cyberspace: A Personality Rights Paradigm for Personal Domain Name Disputes*, 65 Washington and Lee L. Rev. 1445, 1456–7 (2008).

114 *Id.* at 1449–50.

and more global[115] form of dispute resolution without having to resort to trademark rights.[116]

For the time being, the personal name cyberpiracy provisions may be useful in areas where trademark law has traditionally not been implicated. An obvious example is with respect to the names of prominent politicians and public figures. The personal name provisions allow such individuals to protect their identities in the domain space without having to establish secondary meaning. Of course, it may be that some politicians do have trademark rights in their names – and this may increasingly be the case with modern online politics, involving merchandising of campaign products.[117] Today's high profile politicians might avail themselves of the UDRP on the basis of trademark rights in their names.[118]

Of course, politicians and public figures may want to avoid the time, expense and negative publicity associated with any domain name disputes. It is also possible, if not likely, that politicians may avoid arbitration and litigation generally to avoid being regarded as humorless or thin-skinned, particularly if a website associated with their name contains critical or parodic information. Increasingly Internet-savvy politicians in the future will likely ensure that they avoid the pitfalls of domain name disputes in the first place by quietly securing domain names they might want for future campaigns or public projects before others have a chance to register them.[119]

One important distinction between the personal name cyberpiracy provisions in American Law and the UDRP is that, unlike the UDRP, the cyberpiracy provisions are not limited to particular gTLDs, such as '.com', '.net' and '.org'. While the UDRP is confined in its application to domain spaces for which it is expressly incorporated,[120] the personal name cyberpiracy provisions apply to all domain names, defined as 'any alphanumeric designation which is registered with or assigned by any domain name registrar, domain name registry, or other domain name

---

115 *Id.* at 1526–28.

116 See discussion at 1.5, *infra*.

117 See, for example, *Hillary Rodham Clinton v Michele Dinoia*, National Arbitration Forum, Claim No. FA0502000414641 (March 18, 2005), available at www.adrforum.com/domains/decisions/414641.htm, last accessed March 2, 2009 (holding that Hillary Clinton did have common law trademark rights in her name).

118 *Id.*

119 See discussion in Jacqueline Lipton, *From Domain Names to Video Games: The Rise of the Internet in Presidential Politics*, 86 DENVER UNIVERSITY L. REV. 693 (2009).

120 Although many domain name registries incorporate either the UDRP, or a set of rules modeled on the UDRP.

registration authority as part of an electronic address on the Internet'.[121] Thus, cyberpiracy action can be brought with respect to a domain name whatever its gTLD or ccTLD. This applies to both personal names and trademarks in the domain space as the ACPA definition of domain name applies to both 15 U.S.C. § 1125(d)(1) and § 8131(1)(A).[122] Thus, assuming that, say, Donald Trump can claim a trademark in his personal name, he might bring a complaint against a bad faith registrant of 'donaldtrump.com' under 15 U.S.C. § 1125(d)(1), § 8131(1)(A), or under the UDRP.[123] However, if his concern was with a bad faith registration of 'donaldtrump.name', or 'donaldtrump.us', he would be limited to proceedings under the first two options.[124]

It should be kept in mind that the personal name cyberpiracy protections are not supported by the *in rem* jurisdiction provisions found in 15 U.S.C. § 1125(d)(2). Those provisions require a trademark interest corresponding to a domain name.[125] Unless a plaintiff can assert a trademark in her personal name on the basis that it has acquired secondary meaning she will be forced to establish *in personam* jurisdiction against a defendant in order to proceed under § 8131(1)(A).[126]

One further limitation of the personal name cyberpiracy provisions is that the activities prohibited by § 8131(1)(A) are limited to bad faith attempts to sell a domain name for a profit. The provision would not apply to a situation where the registrant did not actually intend to sell the name. For example, someone running an unauthorized fan website about a celebrity would not run afoul of the provision unless she attempted to sell the name for a profit. Additionally, in a situation

---

121 15 U.S.C. § 1127.

122 15 U.S.C. § 8131(3). (In this section, the term 'domain name' has the meaning given that term in section 45 of the Trademark Act of 1946 (15 U.S.C. § 1127).)

123 As at the time of writing, this domain name was owned by the Trump Corporation and mapped directly onto Mr Trump's main website at www.trump.com, last accessed December 19, 2008.

124 In fact, as at the time of writing, both of these domain names appear to be 'parked' by GoDaddy (See www.godaddy.com) on behalf of cybersquatters.

125 15 U.S.C. § 1125(d)(2)(A)(i).

126 Lipton, *Celebrity in Cyberspace*, *supra* note 113, at 1474 (the actor Kevin Spacey, for example, failed to establish personal jurisdiction over a defendant in litigation for control of the domain name 'kevinspacey.com'. He then went on to successfully obtain control of the name in a UDRP proceeding); see also Kieren McCarthy, *Kevin Spacey Loses Pivotal Cybersquatting Court Case*, THE REGISTER, November 26, 2001, www.theregister.co.uk/2001/11/26/kevin_spacey_loses_pivotal_cybersquatting/ (discussing the issue of jurisdiction in the case involving the 'kevinspacey.com', domain name.

where someone has registered the name for purely personal reasons, or where the registrant is making a profit from using the name associated with a clickfarm with no intent to sell the name, the personal name protections will not apply.

1.5 UNIFORM DOMAIN NAME DISPUTE RESOLUTION POLICY

1.5.1 Basis of a UDRP Complaint

Because of its time, cost and jurisdictional advantages, most domain name disputes are brought under the UDRP. The UDRP is a privately-sponsored form of dispute resolution adopted by ICANN in 1999. UDRP disputes are heard by various accredited dispute resolution services, the largest of which is run by the World Intellectual Property Organization (WIPO).[127] Advantages of the UDRP over domestic litigation include the fact that the UDRP is international,[128] inexpensive,[129] fast[130] and predominantly online.[131] The UDRP does not oust the jurisdiction of national courts.[132] All domain name registrants are contractually bound to submit to a mandatory arbitration under the UDRP if a complaint is made about the registration of one or more of their domain names.[133] This is achieved by incorporating an agreement by the registrant to submit to the arbitration procedure in the initial domain name registration contract.[134]

There are currently four organizations authorized to hear UDRP disputes.[135] The organization that hears the most disputes has historically

---

[127] See www.wipo.int/amc/en/domains/, last accessed March 2, 2009.

[128] Because it is incorporated into domain name registration agreements and binds registrants regardless of the jurisdiction in which they reside: UDRP, para. 1; Lipton, *Celebrity in Cyberspace*, *supra* note 113, at 1448–9.

[129] Lipton, *Celebrity in Cyberspace*, *supra* note 113, at 1448–9.

[130] *Id.*

[131] See Rules for Uniform Domain Name Dispute Resolution Policy, adopted by ICANN on October 24, 1999, full text available at www.icann.org/en/udrp/udrp-rules-24oct99.htm, last accessed March 2, 2009.

[132] UDRP, para. 4(k).

[133] UDRP, para. 4(a).

[134] See www.icann.org/en/udrp/udrp-policy-24oct99.htm for list of domain names currently subject to UDRP, last accessed March 2, 2009.

[135] List of authorized dispute resolution service providers is available at www.icann.org/en/dndr/udrp/approved-providers.htm, last accessed March 2, 2009.

been the WIPO Arbitration and Mediation Center.[136] A UDRP dispute involves the submission of a complaint[137] to an ICANN approved dispute resolution service.[138] The dispute resolution service checks the complaint for compliance with ICANN's procedural requirements,[139] and then forwards it to the relevant domain name registrant.[140] The registrant has 20 days from the commencement of the proceeding to submit her response.[141] In certain circumstances, this time period may be extended by the dispute resolution service.[142] If the time is not extended and the registrant has not submitted a response to the complaint, the arbitration service is entitled to proceed to a decision on the complaint in the absence of a response.[143] If the registrant does submit a response, the arbitrator or panel appointed to the dispute provides a decision based on the complaint and the response.[144] There are generally no in-person hearings,[145] which is a significant advantage when disputants are located in different jurisdictions.[146]

As with *in rem* proceedings under the ACPA, the only orders that can be made by a UDRP arbitrator are an order to cancel the disputed domain name registration or an order to transfer it to the complainant.[147] The UDRP is limited to protecting trademark interests in the domain space.[148] This includes both registered and unregistered marks.[149] UDRP arbitrators have accepted the existence of secondary meaning in some

---

136 See www.wipo.int/amc/en/domains/resources/index.html, last accessed December 22, 2008.

137 Rules for the Uniform Domain Name Dispute Resolution Policy, para. 3(b); See also discussion in LINDSAY, *supra* note 106, para. 4.4.

138 Rules for the Uniform Domain Name Dispute Resolution Policy, para. 3(a); See also discussion in LINDSAY, *supra* note 106, para. 4.3.

139 Rules for the Uniform Domain Name Dispute Resolution Policy, para. 3(b); See also discussion in LINDSAY, *supra* note 106, para. 4.4.

140 See discussion in LINDSAY, *supra* note 106, para. 4.5.

141 Rules for the Uniform Domain Name Dispute Resolution Policy, para. 5(a); See also discussion in LINDSAY, *supra* note 106, para. 4.7.

142 Rules for the Uniform Domain Name Dispute Resolution Policy, para. 5(d); See also discussion in LINDSAY, *supra* note 106, para. 4.8.

143 Rules for the Uniform Domain Name Dispute Resolution Policy, para. 14(a); See also discussion in LINDSAY, *supra* note 106, para. 4.8.

144 Rules for Uniform Domain Name Dispute Resolution Policy, para. 15(a).

145 *Id.* para. 13.

146 For a more detailed discussion of the rules of procedure applying to UDRP arbitrations, See generally LINDSAY, *supra* note 106, ch. 4.

147 UDRP, para. 4(i).

148 *Id.* para. 4(a)(i).

149 Lipton, *Celebrity in Cyberspace*, *supra* note 113, at 1486 (UDRP often protects personal names as unregistered trademarks).

questionable cases, which has led some arbitrators to caution against the practice of too readily accepting trademarks in the names of famous people in particular.[150] Decisions involving personal names have been somewhat arbitrary and inconsistent, suggesting that perhaps UDRP arbitrators are struggling with the fact that complainants who are attempting to protect their names in the domain space have few viable options outside the UDRP.[151]

UDRP decisions are generally based on commercial considerations that resemble the key features of trademark infringement and dilution actions. Paragraph 4(a) of the UDRP requires that in order to bring a successful complaint, the complainant must establish that (i) the disputed domain name is identical or confusingly similar to a trademark or service mark in which she has rights;[152] (ii) the registrant has no rights or legitimate interests in the domain name;[153] and (iii) the domain name has been registered and is being used in bad faith.[154] These factors are cumulative. The complainant must establish all three to support a complaint.

The UDRP also contains some non-exclusive guidelines for a registrant to establish a legitimate interest in a disputed domain name in order to rebut the complainant's assertions. The legitimate interest guidelines in the UDRP include the following.

(1) Before any notice to the registrant of the dispute, the registrant had used or made demonstrable preparations to use the domain name or a name corresponding with the domain name in connection with a bona fide offering of goods or services.[155]
(2) The registrant (as an individual, business or other organization) had been commonly known by the domain name, even if she had acquired no trademark or service mark rights in the name.[156]
(3) The registrant is making legitimate noncommercial or fair use of the domain name without intent for commercial gain or to misleadingly

---

150 See, for example, *Bruce Springsteen v Jeff Burgar*, WIPO Arbitration and Mediation Center, Case No. D2000–1532, para. 6, available at www.wipo.int/amc/en/domains/decisions/html/2000/d2000-1532.html, last accessed March 2, 2009 (questioning whether UDRP arbitrators have too readily accepted claims of unregistered trademark interests in personal names).
151 See generally discussion in Lipton, *Celebrity in Cyberspace*, *supra* note 113.
152 UDRP, para. 4(a)(i).
153 *Id.* para. 4(a)(ii).
154 *Id.* para. 4(a)(iii), (b).
155 *Id.* para. 4(c)(i).
156 *Id.* para. 4(c)(ii).

divert customers, or to tarnish the trademark or service mark at issue.[157]

Clearly, this list has been drafted with trademark law in mind, although it is intended to be a nonexclusive list. Arbitrators are entitled to look at other evidence of legitimate interest. Some arbitrators have expressly identified free speech as a legitimate interest despite the lack of express mention of free speech in the UDRP.[158]

The UDRP is predominantly focused on protecting trademark rights. The complainant must establish a trademark interest that corresponds with the registrant's domain name, and the registrant has the option of establishing a legitimate use of the domain name in distinctly trademark-like terms. In other words, the registrant effectively has to prove to the satisfaction of the arbitrator that she has a valid trademark or service mark in the domain name,[159] or at least was known by that name as an individual or a business.[160] Alternatively, she could establish that she is making a non-commercial use of the name with no intent to confuse consumers or to dilute the complainant's mark.[161] In practice, this third limb of legitimate use may be increasingly difficult to establish in an age where many domain name registrants utilize some form of online advertising, such as GoogleAds, to defray the costs of maintaining their webpages.

The UDRP gives some guidance on the nature of a bad faith use of a domain name for the purposes of a complaint. As with the ACPA, these provisions are directed largely to concerns about bad faith cybersquatting. Unlike the ACPA, they are limited to conduct involving *registration and use* of a domain name in bad faith.[162] An ACPA action, on the other hand, contemplates a bad faith *registration, trafficking or use* of a domain name.[163] This seems like a minor technicality. However, arguably a domain name registrant could escape a finding of bad faith under the UDRP if she had used the name in bad faith, but had not initially registered it that way. In other words, someone who innocently registers a domain name that happens to correspond with someone else's trademark, but later seizes on

---

157 *Id.* para. 4(c)(iii).

158 *Bridgestone*, WIPO Case No. D2000–0190, para. 6, available at www.wipo.int/amc/en/domains/decisions/html/2000/d2000-0190.html (accepting free speech in the context of a gripe site as a 'legitimate interest' under the UDRP).

159 UDRP, para. 4(c)(i).

160 *Id.* para. 4(c)(ii).

161 *Id.* para. 4(c)(iii).

162 *Id.* para. 4(a)(iii).

163 15 U.S.C. § 1125(d)(1)(A)(ii).

an opportunity to use it for unfair commercial gain would technically not contravene the provisions of the UDRP. Of course, she might contravene provisions of domestic trademark law, including the ACPA in the United States.

The nonexclusive list of bad faith factors in the UDRP comprises the following:

(a) circumstances indicating that the registrant registered or acquired the domain name primarily for the purpose of selling, renting or otherwise transferring it to the complainant or to a competitor of the complainant for valuable consideration;[164]
(b) the registrant registered the domain name to prevent a trademark owner from reflecting the mark in a corresponding domain name, provided that the registrant has engaged in a pattern of such conduct;[165]
(c) the registrant registered the domain name primarily for the purpose of disrupting the business of a competitor;[166]
(d) by using the domain name, the registrant has intentionally attempted to attract, for commercial gain, Internet users to her website by creating a likelihood of confusion with the complainant's mark as to the source, sponsorship, affiliation or endorsement of the registrant's website or location or of a product or service available on that website or location.[167]

As with the ACPA, the concept of bad faith is drawn from trademark and unfair competition principles. Some of the UDRP's bad faith factors relate more closely to cybersquatting, while others reflect more traditional trademark concerns, such as the prevention of consumer confusion. Some aspects of the bad faith factors are open to debate: for example, the idea that the registrant registered a domain name to prevent a trademark holder from reflecting the mark in a corresponding domain name *provided that the registrant has engaged in a pattern of such conduct*.[168] It is not exactly clear why this proviso is necessary. Surely there will be circumstances in which a registrant might engage in conduct aimed to prevent a competitor from reflecting a mark in a corresponding domain name regardless of whether the competitor has engaged in a pattern of such conduct.

---

164 UDRP, para. 4(b)(i).
165 *Id.* para. 4(b)(ii).
166 *Id.* para. 4(b)(iii).
167 *Id.* para. 4(b)(iv).
168 *Id.* para. 4(b)(ii).

1.5.2 Advantages of the UDRP

The advantages of the UDRP relate to time and cost savings, avoidance of jurisdictional concerns, and ease of use. The procedure is much less expensive than litigation. Arbitration decisions can be made more quickly and cheaply than judicial decisions. Jurisdictional problems are minimized under the UDRP. Arbitrators automatically have jurisdiction over relevant disputes, and enforcement of arbitral orders is an easy administrative matter. There are also clear and simple procedural rules for UDRP disputes, relating to things like the appropriate language for the proceedings.[169]

One additional feature of the UDRP is that it does not implement a policy of *stare decisis*.[170] Arbitrators are not strictly bound to follow previous UDRP decisions.[171] They are not technically even bound to treat previous decisions as persuasive authority.[172] This could be good or bad, depending on the situation. The advantages of not following the doctrine of *stare decisis* include the fact that panelists can be flexible in applying the procedure to different kinds of situations involving different disputants in different jurisdictions. As national trademark laws and free speech laws vary, the lack of a rigid *stare decisis* doctrine allows UDRP arbitrators to more immediately meet the needs of the disputants in a given case. Additionally, it makes sense as a policy matter to encourage greater flexibility of outcome in what is intended as an arbitral mechanism, rather than a judicial procedure. Arbitration can be more amenable to the parties' individual needs without being too rigid in terms of outcomes.

However, the lack of a *stare decisis* doctrine can generate a lack of certainty. Additionally, one might argue that the inherent flexibility that comes with a lack of *stare decisis* is bad for the development of a body of principles about domain name disputes more generally if it leads to arbitrary and inconsistent decisions over time. This seems to be occurring in situations involving personal names. Rather than a clear set of principles emerging over time about the treatment of personal names in the domain space, the decisions are fragmented in their outcomes and difficult to reconcile.[173] The same may be said about disputes

---

169 Rules for Uniform Domain Name Dispute Resolution Policy, para. 11; See also discussion in LINDSAY, *supra* note 106, para. 4.11.

170 See discussion in LINDSAY, *supra* note 106, at 130.

171 *Id.*

172 *Id.*

173 See Lipton, *Celebrity in Cyberspace*, *supra* note 113, at 1449–50.

involving geographical indications, such as names of countries, cities or regions.[174]

With some of these considerations in mind, in March 2005, WIPO released an overview of UDRP panel views on selected UDRP questions.[175] This overview sets out some common questions addressed by UDRP arbitrators, cites examples of arbitral decisions dealing with those questions, and notes whether or not there is a consensus view on the issue in question and, if so, what that view is. If there is not a clear consensus view on a given question, the overview sets out common majority and minority views on the relevant issue. One important question addressed in the overview is how much precedential value should be given to previous UDRP decisions.[176] The consensus view is that: 'The UDRP does not operate on a strict doctrine of precedent. However panels consider it desirable that their decisions are consistent with prior panel decisions dealing with similar fact situations. This ensures that the UDRP system operates in a fair, effective and predictable manner for all parties'.[177] Thus, UDRP panelists will generally not dissent from a consensus view in the overview, even if they disagree with it.[178] UDRP panelists will generally follow a majority view from the overview unless they find a compelling reason to depart from it.[179]

1.5.3 Criticisms of the UDRP

The most obvious limitation of the UDRP is that it only protects trademarks in the domain space. Although arbitrators have been prepared fairly readily to accept unregistered trademarks in a variety of situations,[180] arbitral decisions still have to fit within the trademark model

---

174 LINDSAY, *supra* note 106, at 225–33.

175 WIPO, *WIPO Overview of WIPO Panel Views on Selected UDRP Questions* (March 23, 2005), available at www.wipo.int/amc/en/domains/search/overview/index.html, last accessed December 22, 2008; See also LINDSAY, *supra* note 106, para. 3.16.

176 See WIPO, *WIPO Overview of WIPO Panel Views on Selected UDRP Questions*, para. 4.1 (March 23, 2005), available at www.wipo.int/amc/en/domains/search/overview/index.html, last accessed December 22, 2008 ('What deference should be owed to past UDRP decisions dealing with similar factual matters and legal issues?').

177 See WIPO, *WIPO Overview of WIPO Panel Views on Selected UDRP Questions*, para. 4.1 (March 23, 2005), available at www.wipo.int/amc/en/domains/search/overview/index.html, last accessed December 22, 2008.

178 LINDSAY, *supra* note 106, at 128.

179 *Id.*

180 *Id.* at 229–31 (examples of UDRP arbitrators accepting unregistered trademark interests in geographic terms).

for a complaint to be successful. Differences in approach by arbitrators, compounded by thc lack of *stare decisis*, make for arbitrary results in practice. Complainants who cannot establish a trademark corresponding with a domain name will have no remedy, even though they may have rights such as personality rights,[181] privacy rights[182] or free speech rights.[183] Although some of these rights might be protected as legitimate interests under the UDRP in the hands of a domain name registrant if a third party complains about their registration, they are not rights that can be asserted by a complainant against a registrant in the absence of a corresponding trademark interest.

There are clear historical and political reasons why the UDRP focuses on trademarks.[184] In part, this was a result of the lobbying power of organizations involved in the governance of the domain name system.[185] In part, it arose from WIPO's role in crafting the UDRP, given that WIPO's key constituents are intellectual property rights holders.[186] Partly, it was simply the case that early in the development of the domain name system the most prevalent issues in domestic courts involved the protection of trademarks against bad faith cybersquatters.[187] At the time, the focus was on resolving these problems, rather than on predicting how to balance other interests in domain names.

Having focused on cybersquatting in the UDRP, ICANN then apparently scaled back its policy-making role. It did not move particularly fast on other concerns such as the protection of personal names and geographic indicators in the domain space. As a result, the protection of trademarks in the domain space has become, by default, the key concern of ICANN and the key focus of the UDRP. Some other technical processes were put

---

181 GILSON, *supra* note 7, para. 11.07[7] ('An individual's right of publicity is the right to control the commercial use of his or her identity – including name, likeness or other personal characteristics – by preventing others from appropriating that identity for commercial benefit.')

182 See, for example, Restatement (Second) of Torts, §§ 562A–E.

183 See, for example, United States Constitution, First Amendment ('Congress shall make no law respecting an establishment of religion, or prohibiting the free exercise thereof; or abridging the freedom of speech, or of the press; or the right of the people peaceably to assemble, and to petition the government for a redress of grievances'.)

184 See, for example, discussion in GOLDSMITH and WU, *supra* note 12, at 170.

185 *Id.*

186 MUELLER, *supra* note 106, at 190 ('[The White Paper] authorized WIPO, an entity entirely beholden to intellectual property owners, to create a set of policy recommendations for handling [domain name] disputes'.)

187 See, for example, *Panavision v Toeppen*, 141 F.3d 1316 (9th Cir. 1998).

in place when some new gTLDs were implemented, including '.name'. These new processes allowed for parties with relevant interests to defensively register a name they did not intend to use, or to ask to be notified if someone else attempted to register a name in which they had an interest.[188] However, many of these procedures still favored trademark holders rather than holders of other interests in domain names.[189] Additionally, these processes are not of much use to a complainant in the wake of a registration of a domain name in which they might have had an interest, but did not act prior to its registration.

Other criticisms of the UDRP include the fact that it favors trademark holder complainants to the detriment of original registrants. Statistics have established that a majority of UDRP arbitrations are decided in favor of the complainant who, by definition, must be a trademark holder.[190] These results may be unsurprising given that a complainant probably would not go to the trouble of bringing a UDRP proceeding unless she was concerned about misuse of a trademark. However, it is possible that, given competition between arbitration services, arbitrators might be more inclined to find in favor of complainants to make themselves more appealing to complainants.

One final point about the UDRP is that, despite its global reach, it is limited in practice to gTLDs and ccTLDs for which it has been specifically adopted.[191] These include '.com', '.net', '.org', as well as a variety of ccTLDs. However, as ICANN is not the body in charge of administrating the ccTLDs,[192] the UDRP will not automatically apply to relevant registration agreements unless the relevant administrative body affirmatively adopts it. As the UDRP procedure has proved popular in practice, it seems likely that it will be more widely adopted as more top level domains come into being.

---

188 Lipton, *Beyond Cybersquatting*, *supra* note 99, at 1420–1.

189 For example, when a new '.eu' domain was introduced, trademark holders were favored for registration in being granted a 'sunrise' period in which to register their trademarks in the '.eu' domain space before registration was opened to other applicants for domain name registration. See Policy Rules for .eu Domains, available at www.out-law.com/page-4516, last accessed March 8, 2009.

190 Michael Geist, *Fair.com? An Examination of the Allegations of Systemic Unfairness in the ICANN UDRP*, 27 Brooklyn J. Int'l L. 903, 905–6 (2002).

191 See Notes on UDRP, available at www.icann.org/en/udrp/udrp-policy-24oct99.htm, last accessed March 8, 2009 (list of gTLDs and ccTLDs for which the UDRP is incorporated by registration).

192 Mueller, *supra* note 106, at 207 (noting that ICANN's authority over country code level domains has always been ambiguous).

1.6 DOMAIN NAMES AND *SUI GENERIS* STATE LEGISLATION

1.6.1 California's Business and Professions Code

This section examines two pieces of Californian legislation that may impact on domain name disputes. One example is §§ 17525–17526 of California's Business and Professions Code. Section 17525(a) provides that:

> It is unlawful for a person, with a bad faith intent to register, traffic in, or use a domain name, that is identical or confusingly similar to the personal name of another living person or deceased personality, without regard to the goods or services of the parties.

Like § 1125(d) of the ACPA, but unlike 15 U.S.C. § 8131(1)(A), this provision covers activities of a defendant related to *registering, trafficking in or using* a domain name. Section 8131(1)(A) is limited to *registrations* of domain names corresponding with personal names with the intent to sell them for a profit. The UDRP requires a bad faith *registration and use* of a domain name, so is again narrower in scope than the Californian provision.

Given that California's Code provisions are focused on the protection of personal names, it is useful to compare them with 15 U.S.C. § 8131(1)(A). The Californian provisions are broader than the federal personal name cyberpiracy provisions in that they contemplate deceased as well as living persons and they include a list of bad faith factors that is broader than those in the federal provisions. For example, the Californian legislation includes as a bad faith factor an intention on the part of the registrant to mislead, deceive or defraud voters.[193] This may be relevant to situations where a politician complains about unauthorized use of her name in a domain name.[194] Where a registrant does not intend to sell the name for a profit, but is using it to, say, fraudulently raise money under a politician's name, the Californian legislation might apply where the federal personal name cyberpiracy protections would not.

As with the UDRP and the trademark-focused provisions of the ACPA,[195] the bad faith factors in the Californian Code are not intended

---

193 California Business and Professions Code, § 17526(j).

194 On this point, See also Cal. Elections Code, § 18320 which prohibits certain activities described as 'political cyberfraud'. This legislation, although not specifically targeted at personal name protection, may have the same results in practice as the Business and Professions Code with respect to some uses of politicians' names in the leadup to elections.

195 15 U.S.C. § 1125(d).

to be exhaustive.[196] However, unlike the UDRP and the ACPA, the Code contemplates a variety of remedies, including transfer of the domain name in question.[197] Along with the voter fraud provision, the other bad faith factors in § 17526 invite a court to consider:

(a) the trademark or other intellectual property rights of the domain name registrant;[198]
(b) the extent to which the domain name in question consists of the legal name or another name commonly used to identify the registrant;[199]
(c) the prior use of the domain name by the registrant with respect to a bona fide offering of goods or services;[200]
(d) the legitimate, noncommercial or fair use of the complainant's name in a website accessible under the domain name;[201]
(e) the intent of the registrant to divert consumers from the person's online location for purposes that could harm the goodwill in the name in question, either for commercial gain or with the intent to tarnish the person's name by creating a likelihood of consumer confusion;[202]
(f) an offer by the registrant to transfer the domain name to the rightful owner or a third party for substantial consideration without having used the name, or having the intent to use the name, with respect to a bona fide offering of goods or services;[203]
(g) the intentional provision of false or misleading contact information by the registrant when registering the domain name;[204]
(h) the registration or acquisition of multiple domain names that are identical or confusingly similar to the names of other living persons or deceased personalities; and[205]
(i) whether the registrant obtained consent from the rightful owner to register, traffic in or use the domain name.[206]

---

196 See California's Business and Professions Code, § 17526 ('in determining whether there is a bad faith intent pursuant to Section 17525, a court may consider factors, including, but not limited to, the following . . .').

197 *Id.* § 17528.5 ('in addition to any other remedies available under law, a court may order the transfer of a domain name as part of the relief awarded for a violation of this article'.).

198 *Id.* § 17526(a).

199 *Id.* § 17526(b).

200 *Id.* § 17526(c).

201 *Id.* § 17526(d).

202 *Id.* § 17526(e).

203 *Id.* § 17526(f).

204 *Id.* § 17526(g).

205 *Id.* § 17526(h).

206 *Id.* § 17526(i).

Some of these factors are reminiscent of the bad faith factors in the ACPA and the UDRP. The consideration of the intellectual property rights of the registrant,[207] as well as the question whether the domain name corresponds with the registrant's personal name,[208] are analogs to bad faith factors in the ACPA and UDRP. The same may be said of the factor relating to the registrant making a legitimate, noncommercial or fair use of the complainant's name in a domain name,[209] as well as the idea of the registrant having used the name with respect to a bona fide offering of goods or services.[210]

Some of the other factors raise different considerations than their counterparts in the ACPA and the UDRP. Factor (e), for example, talks about intent by the registrant to divert online traffic in a way that could harm the goodwill in the complainant's name *either* for commercial gain *or* with the intent to tarnish the person's name *by creating a likelihood of consumer confusion*. This factor is confusingly drafted. It appears that the key concern is with harm to goodwill in an individual's name, and there are two possible proscribed motives. The first is pure commercial gain and the second seems to mix the dilution and infringement policies from trademark law. In other words, the first proscribed motive is relatively straightforward and might include cybersquatting or clickfarming. However, the second proscribed motive seems to impute trademark-like attributes to a personal name and then conflates elements of the infringement and dilution actions in their application to the name.

This may confuse courts in practice. Trademark courts dealing with dilution by tarnishment are not used to considering consumer confusion in the same case, unless infringement has been pleaded in the alternative. Additionally, although this provision imputes a trademark-like status to a person's name, there is no suggestion that an action based on the blurring side of the trademark dilution spectrum is contemplated here. Thus, it seems that the main concern is with damage to a person's reputation by tarnishment.

Bad faith factor (f) may also be confusing, unless one understands that California is a state with strong right of publicity protections for both living and deceased personalities.[211] The right of publicity is a tort that prohibits commercial gain from unauthorized use of a person's name or

---

207 *Id.* § 17526(a).
208 *Id.* § 17526(b).
209 *Id.* § 17526(d).
210 *Id.* § 17526(c).
211 See Cal. Civil Code, § 3344.

likeness.[212] Bad faith factor (f) contemplates the existence of a rightful owner of an individual's name for domain name registration purposes. This is actually correct as a matter of law when you consider that in California a person's name or likeness may effectively be owned as a form of transferable property, even after the person has died. Thus, like a trademark, it may be transferred as property. This being the case, the factor is attempting to balance the interests of an owner of a personality right against any legitimate competing uses that a registrant may be making of the name. It may be read in conjunction with bad faith factor (i), contemplating situations where a domain name registrant has sought permission to register, traffic in or use a domain name that corresponds with another person's name.

Although these factors make sense under Californian law, they could be confusing in jurisdictions that do not have a right of publicity, or that have differently conceived rights of publicity. For example, in some states, the right of publicity terminates on a person's death. As the United States is alone in recognizing a right of publicity at all, and even then, the tort is a matter of disharmonized state law, provisions like this may be traps for the unwary when dealing with a domain name dispute if the complainant or her heirs or assigns are situated in California, or perhaps if the domain name is registered in California. In such cases, a domain name registrant could find herself unexpectedly haled into court in California on the basis of an action that does not exist in her own jurisdiction.

Like some of the other bad faith factors, factors (g) and (h) also mirror provisions of the ACPA in terms of conduct often associated with cybersquatting: the provision of false or misleading contact information, or the practice of registering multiple domain names corresponding with personal names. Similar comments may be made about the multiple registration factor in this context as might be made with respect to the ACPA.[213] However, it is worth noting the trademark language utilized in this provision. The Code's concern with domain names that are identical or confusingly similar to a living or deceased person's name again seems to connote trademark principles. These requirements conjure up the consumer confusion aspect of a trademark infringement action. Again, this may be less surprising in California than in some other jurisdictions

212 GILSON, *supra* note 7, para. 11.07[7] ('An individual's right of publicity is the right to control the commercial use of his or her identity – including name, likeness or other personal characteristics – by preventing others from appropriating that identity for commercial benefit'.)

213 15 U.S.C. § 1125(d)(I)(B)(i)(VIII); See discussion at 1.4.1, *supra*.

because California treats personal names and identities as trademark-like proprietary interests.

The Californian legislation is an interesting model of a comprehensive approach to the protection of personal names in the domain space. However, not all jurisdictions accept legal rights in personal names and personalities outside of trademark law to the same extent as California. Thus, the existence of these rights and associated laws in California could prove problematic in practice. Inconsistencies between national laws on the protection of personal names have also been recognized at the international level.

The WIPO Second Domain Name process commented on the disharmonized array of rights that might potentially protect personal names in the domain space.[214] This was used as an argument against creating any administrative procedures that would officially protect rights in personal names outside of trademark law.[215] The decision not to incorporate specific personal name protections in the UDRP has caused some problems in practice. Some arbitrators have taken the view that WIPO's suggestion that personal names are not specifically protected under the UDRP means that arbitrators should not protect personal names in the domain space as a general rule.[216] Others have been more flexible on that point,[217] or at least willing to allow unregistered trademarks in personal names.[218]

It may be that in years to come ICANN will need to formally extend the UDRP to personal names, even where those names are not trademarked, or to come up with some other means for protecting personal names and identities in the domain space.[219] If there is no separate procedure for protecting personal names, it is likely that UDRP arbitrators will increasingly be sympathetic to complainants and will all too readily find trademarks in personal names that may not have obvious secondary meaning. There is already some evidence of this, leading to inconsistent and arbitrary reasoning in practice.[220] In an era in which trademark law is coming

---

[214] See discussion in LINDSAY, *supra* note 106, at 211.

[215] *Id.*

[216] *Id.* at 218–19.

[217] *Id.* at 218–23.

[218] *Id.* at 221–3 (summarizing instances in which UDRP panelists have been prepared to find trademarks in personal names).

[219] See discussion in Lipton, *Celebrity in Cyberspace*, *supra* note 113 (suggesting a new mechanism for dispute resolution involving personal names in the domain space).

[220] See discussion in LINDSAY, *supra* note 106, at 221–3 (summarizing a large variety of situations in which UDRP arbitrators have been prepared to find trademarks in even unregistered personal names).

under increasing scrutiny on the Internet in terms of over-reaching its boundaries,[221] it might be a good idea for ICANN to cordon off the area of personal domain name disputes from the area of trademark disputes.

1.6.2 California's Political Cyberfraud Abatement Act

California's Political Cyberfraud Abatement Act (PCAA) prohibits engaging in acts of political cyberfraud. This term is defined to include an act concerning a political website 'that is committed with the intent to deny a person access to a political Web site, deny a person the opportunity to register a domain name for a political Web site, or cause a person reasonably to believe that a political Web site has been posted by a person other than the person who posted the Web site'.[222] 'Political website' is defined as 'a Web site that urges or appears to urge the support or opposition of a ballot measure'.[223] This is a narrow definition that was presumably intended to result in a limited practical application of the provision. The statute will only apply in the electoral context where a domain name is attached to a website that urges support or opposition to a ballot measure. This would include the election of a particular legislative or executive officer such as a Congressman, governor or even a president.

The PCAA gives further guidance on the nature of political cyberfraud in terms that contemplate:

(a) intentionally diverting or redirecting access to a political website to another person's website by the use of a similar domain name, meta-tags, or other electronic measures;[224]
(b) intentionally preventing or denying exit from a political website by the use of frames, hyperlinks, mousetrapping, popup screens, or other electronic measures;[225]
(c) registering a domain name that is similar to another domain name for a political website;[226] and,

---

221 See, for example, general discussion in Lastowka, *supra* note 30 (describing the variety of new trademark infringement actions arising in cyberspace, particularly with respect to popular search engines like Google); *Playboy v Netscape*, 354 F.3d 1020, 1034–6 (2004) (Judge Berzon crticizing *Brookfield* holding on initial interest confusion).

222 *See* Cal. Elections Code, § 18320(b), (c)(1).

223 *Id.* § 18320(b), (c)(3).

224 *Id.* § 18320(c)(1)(A).

225 *Id.* § 18320(c)(1)(B).

226 *Id.* § 18320(c)(1)(C).

(d) intentionally preventing the use of a domain name for a political website by registering and holding the domain name or by reselling it to another with the intent of preventing its use, or both.[227]

The legislation contemplates activities where rival politicians, political parties or political interest groups register or use domain names related to another person's (or party's) campaign in order to mislead or misdirect voters. It also appears to contemplate what has come to be called typosquatting.[228] This means registering an intentional misspelling of a particular word, phrase or name in the domain space to misdirect Internet users.[229] Factor (c) would likely include typosquatting because it contemplates registering a domain name similar to another domain name in the context of a political website. An example of typosquatting might be where someone registered, say, an intentional misspelling of California Governor Arnold Schwarzenegger's last name (for example, 'schwarzeneger.com' or 'shwarzenegger.com') in the context of a Californian gubernatorial election in order to mislead voters.

Although limited to the electoral context, this legislation is broader than the anti-cybersquatting laws in the sense that it would prohibit both registering a domain name with the intent to resell it *and* registering a domain name with the intent of preventing another from using it.[230] This second prohibition would cover situations where someone registers a political domain name for criticism or commentary purposes, or for pure commercial profit purposes such as running a clickfarm. A close look at the wording of the provision related to prohibited uses of domain names suggests that, unlike the ACPA and the UDRP, the PCAA is not especially concerned with intent to make a profit from selling a domain name. The PCAA specifically contemplates attempts to sell a registered domain name, but the stated purpose under the PCAA is not a commercial profit motive but rather an intention to prevent the use of the name,[231] presumably by a rightful holder of the name. This does not mean that the commercial sale of the name for a profit would not be covered by the PCAA. However, the court would likely look to the identity of the purchaser and her motives to ascertain whether the requisite intent existed: that is, an intent relating to infringing on a protected use of the name.

---

227 *Id.* § 18320(c)(1)(D).
228 LINDSAY, *supra* note 106, at 259–61.
229 *Id.*
230 Cal. Elections Code, § 18320(c)(1)(D).
231 *Id.* § 18320(c)(1)(D).

Under American law there may be some questions about the constitutionality of the PCAA in the sense that it arguably impinges on First Amendment freedoms of those who wish to engage in political discourse using specific domain names. There may be valid arguments, yet to be tested, that a law that prohibits certain registrations and uses of domain names in the political context is an unacceptable incursion on First Amendment freedoms. If such a challenge were mounted, the Californian government may need to prove that the legislation could survive either strict scrutiny as a content-based speech restriction on speech,[232] or intermediate scrutiny, if the legislation were found to be content neutral.[233]

It is arguably an open question whether a court would find the PCAA to be directed at speech per se, or only incidentally directed at speech, although there do seem to be good arguments that a law that impinges directly on what domain names can be used for expressive purposes might be regarded as content-based. In either case, the legislature would have to identify a compelling state interest that it was seeking to protect in enacting the legislation. The compelling state interest would obviously be the interest in fair and truthful elections. Even if the law impinges on speech, as it arguably does, this compelling state interest may override First Amendment concerns because elections stand at the heart of the democratic process. There are good reasons for promoting truthful speech in the electoral context.

In situations involving a political party's trademarked name or logo, where the conduct in question is cybersquatting, an aggrieved political party could resort to the UDRP, or relevant provisions of domestic trademark law, as well as potentially the PCAA for recourse. The PCAA would only be available if the complainant could establish some connection with the state of California: for example, the website was directed to Californian voters, or dealt with a Californian issue. In situations involving politicians' names in the domain space, complainants could resort to the UDRP or trademark protections under domestic law if the name could be regarded as an unregistered trademark. In the United States, the provisions of 15 U.S.C. § 8131(1)(A) would also be available, regardless of the trademark status of the name, if the registrant was seeking to sell the name for a profit.

---

232 R. Randall Kelso, *Standards of Review Under the Equal Protection Clause and Related Constitutional Doctrines Protecting Individual Rights: The 'Base Plus Six' Model and Modern Supreme Court Practice*, 4 U. Pa. J. Const. L. 225 (2002) (describing different standards of judicial review of legislative action in the United States).

233 *Id.*

Assuming a sufficient connection with California to bring a PCAA action, presumably an action under California's Business and Professions Code may also be available to protect a politician's name in the domain space. In particular, as noted in the preceding discussion, the Code expressly contemplates as a bad faith factor an intention on the part of the registrant to mislead, deceive or defraud voters.[234] The PCAA will have limited practical application to domain name disputes *except* in situations where there is a sufficient link with California and where a domain name is being misused in the context of an election. Where these requirements are satisfied, however, the PCAA at least provides the advantage to complainants that it contemplates situations where a domain name registrant does not intend to sell the name, but is using it for some other purpose.

If political cybersquatting and political cyberfraud become serious problems in the future, ICANN and domestic legislatures might need to consider action to better protect the political process.[235] For example, ICANN might require domain name registrants to agree to submit to an arbitration procedure like the UDRP if a politician or political party complained about registration even in the absence of a trademark right in the hands of the politician or political party. Such a procedure might include a new list of bad faith factors, perhaps drawing from the definition of political cyberfraud in the PCAA. Of course, if it turns out that most political organizations' names are regarded as trademarks, the UDRP would automatically apply to them in any event.

With respect to politicians' and public figures' personal names, the UDRP is limited in application. Politicians and public figures may have even less chance than, say, celebrities of convincing UDRP arbitrators that they hold trademark interests in their personal names. Even in situations where they can establish a trademark in their personal name, the UDRP will only protect them against cybersquatting, and not necessarily against uses of their names in the domain space that are aimed at preventing them from using intuitive domain names corresponding with their personal names. The UDRP is also limited in its operation to certain domain spaces, such as the '.com', '.net' and '.org' gTLDs. Domestic laws such as the Lanham Act, California's Business and Professions Code and the PCAA will have broader application outside these gTLDs.

---

[234] California Business and Professions Code, § 17526(j).

[235] LINDSAY, *supra* note 106, at 223 (noting that to date there have been few domain name disputes involving politicians' names); See also discussion in Jacqueline Lipton, *Who Owns 'Hillary.com'? Political Speech and the First Amendment in Cyberspace*, 49 BOSTON COLLEGE L. REV. 55 (2008).

1.7 TORT LAW: DEFAMATION, PRIVACY AND THE RIGHT OF PUBLICITY

Before leaving the discussion of current domain name regulations, it is worth briefly surveying some of the other legal doctrines that may apply to domain name disputes. The most obvious are the torts of defamation, privacy and right of publicity. All of these torts tend to be disharmonized laws both between countries and often within federal jurisdictions. Some jurisdictions do not have any sophisticated privacy laws. The United States is alone in its development of a right of publicity tort.

1.7.1 Defamation

Defamation law may impact on domain name disputes where the domain name in question involves a person's name. Defamation actions aim to protect an individual's reputation against harmful falsehoods.[236] The problem with attempting to apply defamation law in the domain space is that it will usually be the content of speech on an associated website that may be defamatory, rather than the domain name itself. Some courts may be prepared to consider the domain name and website as part of a unified whole, and therefore accept a defamation claim in relation to a domain name and its associated web content. For example, if I register your name as a domain name and defame you on the associated website, the court may be prepared to hold me liable on the basis of both the name and associated web contents. This may mean that a court is ultimately prepared to order cancellation or transfer of the domain name.

It is also possible that a domain name in and of itself could contain a defamatory character slur: for example, someone might register 'madonnaeatslivechickens.com'. In this context, the singer Madonna may be able to bring a defamation action in relation to the wording of the domain name itself. However, these situations are likely to be few and far between as domain names are most commonly used as intuitive mnemonics for finding websites, rather than for expressive purposes per se.[237]

---

236 Arlen Langvardt, *Section 43(a), Commercial Falsehood, and the First Amendment: A Proposed Framework*, 78 MINN. L. REV 309, 334 (1993) ('The common law defines defamation as the publication of a false and defamatory statement about the plaintiff. Defamatory statements, by definition, tend to harm the plaintiff's reputation'.).

237 A recent example involved a dispute over the domain name 'glennbeckrapedandmurderedayounggirlin1990.com'. See discussion in *Glenn Beck v Isaac*

1.7.2 Privacy Law

Privacy law will have limited application in the domain space. Again, its application will likely be limited to situations involving personal names in the domain space. An individual may seek to assert some kind of privacy interest in her persona in cyberspace. This may include attempts to prevent unauthorized uses of her name in the domain space, as well as in the content of relevant websites. It is arguable that some celebrity UDRP arbitrations seeking control of domain names are really about protecting privacy. There are several examples of celebrities bringing actions for transfer of domain names, which they then do not intend to use themselves.[238] This may be explained on the basis of privacy: that is, the celebrity wanting to control the use of her identity online to prevent unauthorized uses and disclosures of information.[239] Domain names in the '.com' space may be particularly implicated here as they are the most likely to be associated with a celebrity's authorized or official web presence. The '.com' form of a name is therefore the one that the celebrity herself may most likely seek to control either for her own profit purposes, or to protect her privacy.[240] The popularity of '.com' domains has continued, despite the introduction of the '.name' gTLD in 2000 for personal names.[241]

Different jurisdictions vary in the extent to which, and ways in which, they protect privacy interests. In the United States, privacy effectively branches into four distinct torts: (a) intrusion into seclusion;[242] (b) false light publicity;[243] (c) public disclosure of private facts;[244] and (d) misappropriation.[245] None of these torts is a likely candidate effectively to protect an individual's ability to control her name in the domain space. The misappropriation tort is closely aligned with the right of publicity tort and is discussed in more detail below.[246]

Eiland-Hall, WIPO Arbitration and Mediation Center, Case No. D2009–1182 (October 29, 2009), available at http://randazza.files.wordpress.com/2009/11/decision-d2009-1182.pdf, last accessed December 8, 2009.

238 Lipton, *Beyond Cybersquatting*, *supra* note 99, at 1414–15 (citing the example of 'juliaroberts.com' in this respect).

239 *Id.*

240 *Id.*

241 *Id.* at 1368.

242 Restatement (Second) of Torts, § 652B.

243 *Id.* § 652E.

244 *Id.* § 652D.

245 *Id.* § 652C.

246 See 1.7.3, *infra*.

The intrusion into seclusion tort is not applicable to the domain name context because it requires a physical invasion of the plaintiff's private space.[247] The torts related to false light publicity and public disclosure of private facts will suffer many of the same limitations as defamation in relation to domain names.[248] They both relate to disseminations of information about a person, rather than uses of labels in the domain space to identify a person. As with defamation, if the domain name is inextricably linked with web content that contravenes one of the privacy torts, an action may be successful on that basis. Also, presumably if a domain name registrant utilized a domain name such as the 'madonnaeatslivechickens.com' name, this may contravene the false light publicity tort (if the allegation that Madonna eats live chickens were false) or the public disclosure of private facts tort (if the allegation were true and this fact had been kept private). However, as noted above, most domain names are not expressive of factual matters other than the fact that they may resolve to a website that contains information about the person identified in the domain space.

The privacy torts are likely to be extremely limited in their application to cases involving registrations and uses of domain names relating to personal names. This may well be an appropriate result as a policy matter. The Internet is an important global communications medium. Torts aimed at protecting privacy and reputation should arguably not impinge too readily on what is basically an addressing system in a significant communications medium. On the other hand, some UDRP arbitrators have been sympathetic to those who wish to prevent unauthorized uses of their personal names in the domain space.[249] The balance between these privacy-like interests and the interests in free communication and easy addressing of websites online may require more detailed consideration at the international level. ICANN may need to develop more focused policies and procedures to balance speech, privacy and personal identity interests online.

The preceding discussion has focused on The United States privacy

---

[247] See, for example, California Civil Code, § 1708.8(a) ('A person is liable for physical invasion of privacy when the defendant knowingly enters onto the land of another person without permission or otherwise committed a trespass in order to physically invade the privacy of the plaintiff with the intent to capture any type of visual image, sound recording, or other physical impression of the plaintiff engaging in a personal or familial activity and the physical invasion occurs in a manner that is offensive to a reasonable person'.).

[248] See 1.7.1, *infra*.

[249] See, for example, *Julia Fiona Roberts v Russell Boyd*, WIPO Arbitration and Mediation Center, Case No. D2000–0210 (May 29, 2000), available at www.wipo.int/amc/en/domains/decisions/html/2000/d2000-0210.html, last accessed November 6, 2007.

torts. Other jurisdictions deal with privacy in different, albeit equally problematic, ways. In the European Union, for example, the Data Protection Directive[250] attempts to protect privacy rights as fundamental human rights in the context of the processing of personal data.[251] The concept of processing personal data is defined to mean 'any operation or set of operations which is performed upon personal data, whether or not by automatic means, such as collection, recording, organization, storage, adaptation or alteration, retrieval, consultation, use, disclosure by transmission, dissemination or otherwise making available, alignment or combination, blocking, erasure or destruction'.[252] Although this seems to contemplate processing of individual data records, such as in a digital database, the definition has been interpreted broadly by the European Court of Justice (ECJ) to include making information about an individual generally available on a website.[253] Although recent ECJ authority contemplates information made available in the text of the webpage associated with a domain name, there is no necessary reason why the reasoning could not also apply to information made publicly available in the domain space.

With respect to domain names, there may be some question as to whether particular iterations of a personal name in the domain space would satisfy the definition of personal data as contemplated in the Directive. 'Personal data' is defined as 'any information relating to an identified or identifiable natural person ('data subject'); an identifiable person is one who can be identified, directly or indirectly, in particular by reference to an identification number or to one or more factors specific to his physical, physiological, mental, economic, cultural or social identity'.[254] If a domain name in question only states an individual's name, it may not fall within this definition. The name of a person may not be 'information relating to an identified or identifiable natural person'. Rather, it may be the actual *identity* of the person with which personal data, such as the person's age, height, and weight, could be associated. If this is a correct interpretation of the definition of personal data, a domain name containing nothing more than

---

250 Directive 95/46/EC of the European Parliament and of the Council of October 24, 1995 on the protection of individuals with regard to the processing of personal data and on the free movement of such data.

251 *Id.* art. 1.

252 *Id.* art. 2(b).

253 *Re Bodil Lindqvist*, paras 46–8 (ECJ, Luxemborg, November 6, 2003, full text available at http://curia.europa.eu/jurisp/cgi-bin/gettext.pl?lang=en&num=79968893C19010101&doc=T&ouvert=T&seance=ARRET, last accessed December 16, 2008).

254 Directive 95/46/EC, *supra* note 250, art. 2(a).

a person's name may not fall within the scope of the Directive. However, a domain name and its associated website taken together may fall within the scope of the Directive assuming that the website contained personal data about the individual in question.

There is also a question whether some information in the domain space would potentially be excluded from the scope of the Directive because of the 'personal use' exception in the Directive.[255] The Directive exempts from its operation the processing of personal data 'by a natural person in the course of a purely personal or household activity'.[256] If a private individual registered a domain name corresponding with someone else's name, would this be covered by the exemption, assuming that the registration and use of a domain name otherwise amounted to the processing of personal data? The *Bodil Lindqvist* case suggests that the private use exemption would not apply here.[257] The ECJ held that making information generally available on a website would not satisfy the definition of a purely personal use for the purposes of the Directive. Thus, in some cases, particular uses of a personal domain name in concert with web content about the person in question might possibly contravene the Directive. However, as with defamation liability, generally these cases are more about web content than about domain names per se.

Overall, the Directive by itself is likely to be of limited, if any, assistance to those seeking to assert a privacy right in a personal name in the domain space. As with The United States privacy law, this result may be appropriate as a policy matter. It may be that interests of easy communication in the global information age should trump certain privacy assertions. However, no international determinations have yet been made about the appropriate balance of privacy interests and free speech in the domain space. Additional policy work may be required here to resolve these questions.

1.7.3 Right of Publicity

In the United States, the right of publicity, as well as the privacy tort relating to misappropriation,[258] may be relevant to some domain name disputes

---

255 *Id.* art. 3(2).

256 *Id.*

257 *Re Bodil Lindqvist*, paras 46–8 (ECJ, Luxemborg, November 6, 2003, full text available at http://curia.europa.eu/jurisp/cgi-bin/gettext.pl?lang=en&num=79968893C19010101&doc=T&ouvert=T&seance=ARRET, last accessed December 16, 2008).

258 See 1.7.2, *supra*.

involving personal names. There have already been some judicial actions involving the right of publicity in the domain space.[259] These cases are few and far between, presumably because plaintiffs are deterred by costs and jurisdictional problems associated with litigation. Additionally, where personal name complainants have opted for litigation over the UDRP, some have chosen trademark law instead of the right of publicity.[260] This may be because federally harmonized trademark law has advantages over the disharmonized state-based right of publicity.[261]

The right of publicity is the right of an individual to control the commercial use of his or her name, likeness, signature or other personal characteristics.[262] It has been likened to a trademark right in that it protects the goodwill inherent in a famous person's identity.[263] It reserves to the individual the exclusive right to the commercial exploitation of his or her name, likeness, signature or product endorsement. It is related to the misappropriation tort in the United States[264] by virtue of the fact that each relates to control of an individual's persona against unauthorized commercial appropriation.[265] The key difference between the two is that the right of publicity generally protects the commercial interests of a celebrity, while the misappropriation tort generally protects rights to human dignity of a private individual.[266]

The right of publicity has developed in different states within the United States variously as a matter of common law[267] or state legislation.[268] High profile examples of right of publicity actions include cases involving the unauthorized use of Elvis Presley's name and likeness after his death,[269]

---

259 See, for example, *Paul Wright v Domain Source Inc.*, 2002 U.S. Dist. LEXIS 16024 (2002); *Trudeau v Lanoue*, 2006 U.S. Dixt. LEXIS 7956 (2006); *Stephan Schmidheiny v Steven Weber*, 285 F.Supp. 2d 613 (2003).

260 See, for example, *Lamparello v Falwell*, 420 F.3d 309 (2005); *Stephan Schmidheiny v Steven Weber*, 285 F.Supp.2d 613 (2003).

261 Lipton, *Celebrity in Cyberspace*, *supra* note 113, at 1488–9.

262 GILSON, *supra* note 7, at para. 2B.01.

263 *Id.*

264 Restatement (Second) of Torts, § 652C.

265 JON MILLS, PRIVACY: THE LOST RIGHT 173–7 (2008) (explaining technical differences between the two torts).

266 *Id.*

267 Kentucky, for example, has a common law basis for the right of publicity: See discussion in G. DINWOODIE AND M. JANIS, TRADEMARKS AND UNFAIR COMPETITION: LAW AND POLICY 823–7 (2d edn, 2007).

268 See, for example, Indiana Code Title 32 (Property), art. 36 (Publicity), chap. 1 (Rights of Publicity).

269 *Estate of Elvis Presley v Russen*, 513 F.Supp.1339 (1981).

John Wayne's likeness on greeting cards,[270] Martin Luther King's likeness on unauthorized plastic busts,[271] Rosa Parks' name as a song title,[272] Arnold Schwarzenegger's likeness as a bobblehead doll,[273] and Rudolph Giuliani's likeness on an advertisement run on city buses in New York.[274] The publicity rights tort has also been extended to lookalikes and soundalikes of famous people. Relevant cases include the use of a Vanna White lookalike robot in a television commercial,[275] and the use of imitators of Bette Midler's[276] and Tom Waits'[277] distinctive singing voices in advertising campaigns.

In the domain name context, most cases will involve the right of publicity tort, rather than privacy law's misappropriation tort, because it is more likely that enterprising domain name registrants will seek to register famous individuals' names than private individuals' names. Whether the motive is profit or commentary, there is less reason for anyone to register a private person's name. Of course, when multiple people share a name, this might be the basis for a dispute between them over control of the name, particularly if one of them is a celebrity. However, these kinds of disputes are unlikely to attract either of the misappropriation-focused torts because such situations generally will not involve an unauthorized profit motive.

Unlike the UDRP, the right of publicity and misappropriation privacy torts do not require the plaintiff to establish a trademark corresponding

---

[270] See discussion in Michael Madow, *Private Ownership of Public Image: Popular Culture and Publicity Rights*, 81 CALIF. L. REV. 125, 141–3 (1993).

[271] *Martin Luther King Jr, Center for Social Change Inc. v American Heritage Products*, 694 F.2d 674 (11th Cir. 1993) (the estate of Martin Luther King, Jr sought an injunction to prevent the defendant from selling plastic busts of Dr King).

[272] *Rosa Parks v LaFace Records*, 329 F.3d 437 (2003) (involving publicity rights of Rosa Parks in the context of a song title using her name in relation to a hip hop recording that had nothing in particular to do with her or her work).

[273] Charles Harder and Henry L. Self III, *Schwarzenegger vs. Bobbleheads: The Case for Schwarzenegger*, 45 SANTA CLARA L. REV. 557 (2005); William Gallagher, *Strategic Intellectual Property Litigation, the Right of Publicity, and the Attenuation of Free Speech: Lessons from the Schwarzenegger Bobblehead Doll War (and Peace)*, 45 SANTA CLARA L. REV. 581 (2005); David Welkowitz and Tyler Ochoa, *The Terminator as Eraser: How Arnold Schwarzenegger Used the Right of Publicity to Terminate Non-Defamatory Political Speech*, 45 SANTA CLARA L. REV. 651 (2005).

[274] *New York Magazine v The Metropolitan Transit Authority of the City of New York*, 987 F.Supp. 254 (1997).

[275] *Vanna White v Samsung Electronics America Inc.*, 971 F.2d (9th Cir. 1992); *cert denied*, 508 U.S. 951 (1993).

[276] *Bette Midler v Ford Motor Company*, 849 F.2d 460 (1988).

[277] *Tom Waits v Frito-Lay Inc.*, 978 F.2d 1093 (1992).

with her personal name. These torts are uniquely aimed at the protection of an individual name or likenesses irrespective of trademark rights. Interestingly, the right of publicity tort has been recognized as comprising moral elements as well as purely commercial elements.[278] This may make it more useful in some respects for the protection of personal names in the domain space in cases where a commercial motive on the part of the registrant is hard to establish. The key moral harm that has been protected by the right of publicity is more like a privacy protection than a property protection. The obvious example is where unauthorized commercial use is made of an individual's name or likeness in circumstances where that individual wants to maintain privacy of her image, rather than control commercial profits derived from her image.

The Bette Midler[279] and Tom Waits[280] cases are good examples of this. They are situations where the celebrities bringing the actions did not themselves want to make money from commercial advertising campaigns. Tom Waits, in particular, had a well-known policy against commercial endorsements. Thus, the harm to him from the unauthorized use of a soundalike in a commercial was not economic, but was rather moral in terms of his ability to appear to remain true to his principles against advertising. A parallel may be made here with domain name cases like the one involving the actress Julia Roberts. Ms Roberts did not seek control of the domain name 'juliaroberts.com' to make a commercial profit herself. Rather, she did not want anyone to use the domain name, presumably seeking to avoid any official-looking commercial presence online as a matter of principle.

Of course, for a successful right of publicity action, the complainant must establish an unauthorized commercial profit motive on the part of the defendant. In situations where a domain name registrant has registered and is using a domain name corresponding with a famous person's name for pure commentary purposes, such as an unauthorized fan website, this prohibited profit purpose may be absent. Thus, a right of publicity action would be unavailable. If, on the other hand, the registrant is prepared to sell the domain name either to the rightful owner or to someone else, that may be a sufficient profit motive for a successful action. Additionally, using the website for a clickfarm to profit from advertising could also satisfy the commercial profit requirement. Even an unauthorized fan site might run afoul of the right of publicity if the owner of the site profits from online advertisements.

More difficult questions might arise in the political context where a

---

278 Roberta Rosenthal Kwall, *Fame*, 73 INDIANA L.J.1, 36–7 (1997).

279 *Bette Midler v Ford Motor Company*, 849 F.2d 460 (1988).

280 *Tom Waits v Frito-Lay Inc.*, 978 F.2d 1093 (1992).

politician's or public figure's name is used in the domain space for unauthorized critical commentary. Where there is no profit motive on the part of the registrant, the right of publicity action is presumably not available. Where, however, the registrant uses the site for mixed commentary and commercial purposes, the issue may be more difficult. If, for example, someone registers 'billclinton.com' for the purpose of criticizing the former president, but is also prepared to sell the name for a profit, or is using the website for online advertising alongside the Clinton commentary, it is not clear whether the former president could successfully bring a right of publicity action.

First, one needs to answer the question whether politicians and public figures, as opposed to celebrities, might avail themselves of the right of publicity at all. Although the cases are few and far between, there seems to be no express legal prohibition on a politician bringing a right of publicity action.[281] A number of suggestions have been made as to why politicians tend not to bring right of publicity actions more frequently. These suggestions include: (a) politicians are often not generally concerned with commercial use of their image because 'it is not their typical business';[282] (b) politicians do not wish to invest resources into such claims;[283] (c) politicians want to avoid negative publicity that may arise from such claims,[284] partly because they do not want to appear 'humorless or soft-skinned';[285] and (d) politicians are aware that the sale of

---

[281] LINDSAY, *supra* note 106, at 223 (summarizing cases involving politicians' names); see also *Martin Luther King, Jr, Ctr. for Soc. Change, Inc. v Am. Heritage Prod., Inc.*, 694 F.2d 674, 677–80 (11th Cir. 1983) (incorporating Supreme Court of Georgia certified question holding that the right of publicity extends to 'public figures who are [not] public officials' in the sense of holding public office); *N. Y. Magazine v Metro. Transit Auth.*, 987 F.Supp. 254, 260–9 (S.D.N.Y. 1997) (holding that defendant transit authority could not use refusal to violate right of publicity statute to defend against exclusion of advertisements that depicted Mayor Rudolph Giuliani in a less than complimentary light, and that an attempt to prevent display of the advertisements on public buses in New York City was an infringement of the magazine's First Amendment rights to political commentary 'of public interest', notwithstanding that it was commercial speech). See Tyler Ochoa, *The Schwarzenegger Bobblehead Case: Introduction and Statement of Facts*, 45 SANTA CLARA L. REV. 547, 547 (2005).

[282] Charles Harder and Henry Self III, *Schwarzenegger vs Bobbleheads: The Case for Schwarzenneger*, 45 SANTA CLARA L. REV. 547, 567–8 (2005).

[283] *Id.* at 568

[284] *Id.*

[285] William Gallagher, *Strategic Intellectual Property Litigation, the Right of Publicity, and the Attenuation of Free Speech: Lessons from the Schwarzenegger Bobblehead Doll War (and Peace)*, 45 Santa Clara L. Rev. 581, 583 (2005).

products bearing their name or likeness might be protected by the First Amendment.[286]

However, assuming that First Amendment concerns can be dealt with on a case by case basis, there appear to be no good reasons why the right of publicity tort should not be available to politicians and public figures as a matter of principle. Where the concern is with an unauthorized *commercial* use of a name or likeness, rather than an expressive or political use, there seems to be no reason to deny a politician access to the tort.

To the extent that a complainant's concern is about unauthorized commercial profits (such as in the case of cybersquatting and clickfarming) the right of publicity, and the associated privacy misappropriation tort may be possible avenues of recourse where a domain name corresponds with a personal name. Of course, as with all domestic laws, right of publicity actions will raise cost, time and jurisdictional concerns that are not as pronounced under avenues such as the UDRP. However, in circumstances where the UDRP is of uncertain application, say because the complainant does not have a trademark in her name, the right of publicity or misappropriation tort might be viable options.

1.8 CHAPTER SUMMARY

This chapter has surveyed the current regulatory matrix for Internet domain name disputes. It has illustrated the fact that despite a number of available avenues for complaints, the system is not globally, or even nationally, harmonized. Some interests, such as trademark rights, are protected in multiple ways, including under the UDRP and national trademark laws. Other interests, such as privacy and speech, are less clearly or coherently protected. ICANN has made a good start on domain name dispute resolution with its adoption of the UDRP to protect trademarks in the domain space. However, the domain name registration system and resultant disputes have continued to evolve while the dispute resolution machinery has not. It may now be time for additional thought to be given to policies underlying domain name registration and use.

This chapter has set out the operation of a variety of available domain name dispute resolution avenues, and has identified their advantages and disadvantages for complainants and domain name registrants alike. In particular, it has addressed the following.

(1) The evolution of trademark law in the domain space from early

---

286 *Id.*

trademark infringement and dilution actions in the 1990s to the enactment in the United States of the ACPA aimed specifically at protecting trademarks and personal names against cybersquatting.

(2) The implementation of the UDRP by ICANN and its limitation to the protection of trademark interests, albeit on a global scale. Its practical benefits relate to time, cost and the avoidance of jurisdictional problems. Its disadvantages are mainly its limited focus to trademark-related cybersquatting. While it protects trademarks effectively in the domain space, it might be useful to adopt a broader policy at this point that protects other interests, including personal names and geographical and culturally significant terms.

(3) *Sui generis* state legislation dealing with the protection of personal names in the domain space, and the prevention of conduct involving domain names to mislead the public in the electoral context. The two pieces of legislation examined were California's Business and Professions Code, and California's Political Cyberfraud Abatement Act. This legislation has limited application and raises time, cost and jurisdictional concerns.

(4) The application of general tort law to domain name disputes. In this context, the focus was on defamation law, privacy law and the right of publicity tort. As with *sui generis* state legislation, these torts tend to be disharmonized both internationally and often also within a federal jurisdiction such as the United States. They have limited reach and may only apply to particular kinds of domain name disputes. For example, the right of publicity will only apply to a situation where a defendant is seeking to make an unauthorized commercial profit from a domain name corresponding with an individual's name.

Subsequent chapters delve in more detail into options for striking a more nuanced balance between competing interests in domain names, including competing trademark interests, free speech rights and privacy interests.

2. Competing trademark interests

2.1 COMPETING TRADEMARKS IN THE DOMAIN SPACE

Since the inception of the domain name system there have been many examples in which several parties with legitimate trademark rights assert claims to the same domain name. One example is 'delta.com' in which a number of trademark holders have claimed interests, including Delta Airlines and Delta Faucets. The domain name system basically operates on a 'first-come, first-served' basis unless the first registrant is infringing on another's trademark rights in bad faith. Where multiple trademark holders have the same or similar marks in different product markets or different geographic regions, the registration of a corresponding domain name by one of them is unlikely to trigger the bad faith requirements of the various regulatory mechanisms.[1]

'First come, first served' as a registration policy has its limitations. In a contest between two or more parties, each of whom has an interest corresponding with the same domain name, the first to register generally will prevail, unless the parties privately agree to transfer the name. There is nothing necessarily wrong with this as a policy rule. However, it does highlight the fact that the rivalrous nature of domain names means that the system does not map well on to the trademark system. The trademark system allows multiple parties to hold the same mark, provided that they operate in different product or geographic markets, whereas the domain name system only allows one entity to register a domain name at any given time.

This chapter considers whether there are better ways for the domain name system to accommodate multiple trademark interests. Domain name sharing is one option. Nothing in the current domain name registration system prevents trademark holders from reaching private domain name sharing arrangements.[2] However, nothing in the system facilitates

---

[1] See Chapter 1 for a detailed discussion of current domain name regulations.

[2] There is no legal or technological reason why trademark holders cannot enter into such contracts, although there may be few economic incentives to do so. One good example of a private domain name sharing arrangement arose with respect to the domain name 'playtex.com': see Jacqueline Lipton, *A Winning Solution for Youtube and Utube: Corresponding Trademarks and Domain Name Sharing*, 21

such agreements. To date, this option has not been popular in practice, probably due to the time and costs associated with negotiating sharing arrangements, in contrast to simply negotiating for transfer of a desired name, or, in the alternative, registering a different name to the original registrant. For example, Delta Airlines might register 'delta.com' while Delta Faucets registers 'deltafaucet.com'.

This chapter considers the limitations of the domain name system in cases involving competing trademark holders. It also examines possibilities for facilitating domain name sharing in appropriate circumstances. It commences with a description of how existing regulations apply to disputes involving multiple trademark interests, and the limitations of those regulations in these contexts. The discussion then moves to alternate approaches to resolving problems caused by multiple competing legitimate trademark interests in the same domain name. It considers the impact of new gTLDs as a mechanism to potentially lessen the pressure on the trademark system by providing more domain name options for competing trademark holders.[3] It then examines market solutions and ICANN-facilitated solutions that might encourage sharing or transfer of names between multiple trademark holders in appropriate cases. The chapter concludes with a brief identification and discussion of emerging issues in the domain space that might implicate competing trademark interests. These emerging issues include the proposed introduction of new gTLDs by ICANN and the recent development of alphanumeric URLs on Facebook that may incorporate trademarks.

2.2 COMPETING TRADEMARKS: LIMITATIONS OF CURRENT REGULATIONS

In the physical world, multiple companies can hold the same or similar trademarks in different markets or different geographic areas.[4] The Internet

---

HARV. J. LAW AND TECH 509, 519–24 (2008) (on domain name sharing generally). *See also* Eric Goldman, *Deregulating Relevancy in Internet Trademark Law,* 54 EMORY L.J. 507, 546 (2005) ('[S]ome domain names resolve to a "gateway page" (also referred to as a "shared page" or "intermediate page") for the sole purpose of allowing multiple trademark owners or licensees to "share" the domain name through links on the page to their respective sites' (citation omitted)).

[3] See ICANN, new gTLD Program: Draft Applicant Guide book (Draft RFP) (October 24, 2008), available at www.icann.org/en/topics/new-gtld-program.htm, last accessed June 29, 2009.

[4] Stuart Weinstein, *The Cyberpiracy Prevention Act: Reconciling Real Space Sectoral and Geographic Distinctions in the Use of Internet Domain Names Under*

allows one company to have a global reach with its registered domain name, a reach which it may or may not need depending on its business practices and future plans. Thus, where a company has registered a domain name that corresponds with more than one trademark, disputes may arise as to which trademark holder should be entitled to the name. In many cases, the party with the deepest pockets will secure the name because it has the greatest wherewithal to fight or bargain for the name. Some may see this as an unobjectionable market solution, while others may see it as an unfortunate extension into cyberspace of the kinds of market pressures that occur in the physical world. If cyberspace is regarded as a forum where large and small businesses alike have an equal chance of success because of the low costs of setting up an online enterprise, we might like to think about whether there are other results that could be promoted in cases where different parties with the same mark compete for the same domain name.

Of course, different people can always register *similar* domain names. Delta Air Lines could use 'delta.com' while Delta Faucets used 'delta.biz' or 'delta.org'. However, this division of similar domain names across gTLDs tends not to occur in practice, partly because nothing stops one trademark holder from registering multiple iterations of a domain name. Delta Air Lines could use many domain names with 'delta' in them. Regardless of the different gTLDs available, domain name registrants will probably still prefer to hold the '.com' version of a relevant domain name because it is the most intuitive version of their mark in the domain space.

The current situation potentially wastes resources because multiple domain names are registered by the same company and used for the same website. This is contrary to ICANN's reasons for creating multiple new gTLDs.[5] Additionally, this allocation of domain space can make it difficult for Internet users to find particular websites. If a given trademark holder very aggressively registers multiple iterations of a domain name that also

---

the Lanham Act, 9 U. Miami Bus. L. Rev. 158 (2001) ('[A]n entity may use an identical mark as another, as long as he does not use that mark within the same sector or industry. As with geographical protection of a user's mark, the scope of protection is determined as an evidentiary matter, looking at the likelihood of consumer confusion'. (citations omitted)).

[5] Wallace Koehler, *ICANN and the New Magnificent Seven*, SEARCHER, February 2001, 56 (noting that new gTLDs were needed because all the 'good' domain names, particularly those corresponding to valuable trademarks, were already taken). In theory, the introduction of new gTLDs would have allowed new registrants to register variations of existing names. In practice, however, many of the new names were reserved for trademark holders. Goldman, *supra* note 2, at 545 ('[N]ew TLDs in the recent years have abandoned the "first to register" relevancy algorithm, giving priority to trademark owners.')

corresponds to someone else's trademark, Internet users may have trouble finding the website of the less aggressive trademark holder because all the obvious iterations of the domain name are held by the more aggressive trademark holder. Again, one might argue that this is a perfectly acceptable market solution. The most aggressive company, the one that puts more time and resources into acquiring appropriate domain names, should reap the rewards. However, if domain name regulation aims to provide more consumers with more opportunities to deal with more companies, the more powerful companies from the physical world should not necessarily be entitled to monopolize relevant domain names.

Search engine technology might alleviate some of these concerns. Even without a memorable or intuitive domain name, a good search engine can often find a relevant site, prioritizing it so it appears somewhere on its first page of search results.[6] However, even with sophisticated search engine technology, the trademark holder who has monopolized multiple iterations of a domain name has an advantage because it will be easier for Internet users to guess and remember its domain names. Users do not have to rely on search engines to find the website of the more aggressive trademark holder in the way they must to find the websites of less aggressive trademark holders. Also, provided that search engines continue to rely on domain names in their search algorithms, the power to hold more domain names corresponding with a particular mark may have advantages in the search context.[7]

Domain name sharing might be a preferable solution in some cases involving corresponding marks. The domain name system could be expanded to facilitate the sharing of a domain name between two or more trademark holders. One way to facilitate sharing would be to have the domain name map onto a shared, main webpage that contains hyperlinks to each trademark holder's separate page.[8] Sharing could reduce the amount of wasted resources. This solution may be more efficient for both trademark holders and their online customers.[9]

In the United States, a trademark holder has at least four avenues for complaining about someone else's registration of a domain name that corresponds with its trademark. The avenues include trademark infringement and dilution, as well as the possibility of an action under the Anti-

---

6 See Goldman, *supra* note 2, at 532–52 for a detailed explanation of the operation of modern search engines.

7 Lipton, *A Winning Solution*, *supra* note 2, at 543–4.

8 Goldman, *supra* note 2, at 546.

9 Methods for facilitating domain name sharing arrangements are discussed below: See 2.4, *infra*.

Cybersquatting Consumer Protection Act (ACPA) or an arbitration under the Uniform Domain Name Dispute Resolution Policy (UDRP).[10] These dispute resolution mechanisms all suffer from the same problem. They are all designed to determine who has the better trademark interest corresponding with a given domain name in cases where someone is acting in bad faith. The result will be an allocation of the domain name to a single trademark holder. These avenues are helpful to a trademark holder who complains of domain name registration by someone who does not have a legitimate interest corresponding to the domain name: for example, a cybersquatter. However, they are not designed to resolve disputes between competing trademark holders.

2.2.1 Trademark Infringement and Competing Trademarks

Prior to the enactment of the ACPA and the adoption of the UDRP, domain name disputes were generally brought under existing provisions of the Lanham Act in the United States: those relating to trademark infringement and trademark dilution. In a traditional trademark infringement action, the holder of a registered[11] or unregistered[12] trademark seeks relief where a defendant has created consumer confusion regarding the source of goods or services sold under the mark.[13] To establish trademark infringement, the plaintiff must establish ownership of a trademark right in the relevant domain name, as well as a likelihood of consumer confusion.[14] In early cases, it was not difficult for trademark holders to establish trademark interests corresponding to domain names.[15] However, proving consumer confusion was more problematic. It was not clear that mere registration and use

---

[10] See Chapter 1 for a detailed discussion of these regulatory options in the domain name context.

[11] 15 U.S.C. § 1114(1).

[12] 15 U.S.C. § 1125(a)(1).

[13] Anne Gilson Lalonde and Jerome Gilson, Trademark, Protection and Practice para. 5.01 ('The fundamental aim of trademark law is to avoid . . . consumer confusion about the source of products or services.').

[14] See *Hasbro, Inc. v Clue Computing, Inc.*, 66 F Supp.2d 117, 121(D. Mass. 1999) ('*To prevail on a trademark infringement claim, a plaintiff must show* (1) use and therefore ownership of the mark (2) use by the defendant of the same mark or a similar one, and (3) likelihood that the defendant's use will confuse the public, thereby harming the plaintiff.').

[15] See, for example, *Panavision Int'l, L.P. v Toeppen,* 141 F.3d 1316, 1326–7 (9th Cir. 1998) (explaining the importance of a company being able to use its trademarks that correspond to domain names). Although *Panavision* was a trademark dilution case, not an infringement proceeding, for both causes of action plaintiffs are still required to show ownership of a trademark that corresponds with the domain name.

of a domain name corresponding to the plaintiff's trademark would confuse consumers about the source of the given products or services when the website did not refer to any of the goods or services sold by the plaintiff.[16]

This is likely to be the case with many actions involving competing trademark holders, at least when the marks are used in different product markets. More complex problems will arise where marks are used for similar products in different geographic markets. Similar trademarks can exist for similar goods or services in different geographic markets.[17] American courts have held that different companies may use similar marks for similar products in different geographic locations.[18] This principle also commonly operates at the international level. Two different companies, for example, were entitled to use the 'Healthy Choice' mark for frozen dinners in two different countries, the United States and Australia.[19] Another example is the 'Scrabble' mark for the popular board game. This mark is registered to one company in North America and another outside of North America.[20]

While trademark infringement actions have established that two trademarks can coexist in different product and service markets, or in different geographic markets, the domain name system has complicated the issue, particularly with respect to geographic markets. In the physical world, the concurrent use doctrine provides that businesses operating in different geographic markets can continue using similar trademarks, even when they are selling similar goods or services. However, when the businesses

---

[16] See *Hasbro, supra* note14, 66 F.Supp.2d at 121.

[17] In the United States, this is often referred to as the 'concurrent use' doctrine. David Barrett, *The Future of the Concurrent Use of Trademarks Doctrine in the Information Age,* 23 HASTINGS COMM. AND ENT. L.J. 687, 689–91 (2001) (examining American legislative history of the 'concurrent use' doctrine in trademark law).

[18] *Id.* See, for example, *Nat'l Ass'n for Healthcare Commc'ns, Inc. v Cent. Ark. Area Agency on Aging, Inc.,* 257 F.3d 732, 737 (8th Cir. 2001) (granting an injunction against a federal trademark owner and allowing the mark's use by another user in an a six-county area where that user had already used the mark); *Dawn Donut Co. v. Hart's Food Stores, Inc.,* 267 F.2d 358, 360 (2d Cir. 1959) (holding no likelihood of confusion when plaintiff and defendant used similar marks in different product markets).

[19] *ConAgra Inc. v McCain Foods (Aust) Pty Ltd* (1992) 33 F.C.R. 302 (Austl.)

[20] Hasbro, Inc. holds the relevant trademarks in the United States and Canada while J.W. Spear & Sons Ltd of England, a subsidiary of Mattel, Inc., holds these trademarks in other countries. See Welcome to WorldWide Scrabble, www.scrabble.com, last accessed May 12, 2008. Scrabble.com is an example of a privately negotiated domain name sharing arrangement.

move into the world of online commerce and want to use domain names corresponding with their trademarks, the situation is unsettled. If two companies that operate in different geographic markets in the physical world each hold the same or a similar mark, it is not clear what should happen when one of them attempts to register the 'trademark.com' version of the mark as a domain name.

Presumably, the relevant website will be accessible from most places in the world, including the geographic locations of both trademark holders. Any notion that the concurrent use of the two marks in the physical world would not confuse consumers is lost in cyberspace. Even if a trademark holder uses a corresponding domain name to do business within a limited region, the availability of the trademark holder's webpage in other places may nevertheless create consumer confusion. In any event, businesses that establish webpages at particular domain names often ultimately plan to expand their geographic reach. Thus, there are some situations that the current domain name system cannot equitably resolve. The existing 'first come, first served' approach may not be the most efficient outcome depending on one's point of view.

Later in this chapter, we consider the possibility of other ways to deal with these kinds of conflicts. For example, domain name sharing may help here. If parties opt to, or can be encouraged to, share domain names in at least some cases, costly and often ultimately wasteful trademark litigation might be avoided. An example where sharing might have proved more useful than protracted trademark litigation can be found in the case of *Hasbro, Inc. v Clue Computing, Inc.*[21] The *Hasbro* case concerned registration of the domain name 'clue.com' by a small computer company called Clue Computing. *Hasbro* complained that its customers were being confused by the online presence of the smaller player accessible under the 'clue.com' name.[22] Clue Computing had chosen the domain name as a joke relating to people who were 'clueless' about computers.[23] Hasbro was concerned that the domain name registration was confusing because it corresponded to Hasbro's registered trademark for its popular Clue board game.[24]

Hasbro failed in its trademark infringement action against Clue Computing because it failed to establish sufficient consumer confusion to support its claim.[25] This result might appear unremarkable as a matter of

---

21 66 F.Supp.2d 117 (D. Mass. 1999).
22 *Id.* at 119.
23 *Id.*
24 *Id.*
25 *Id.* at 124.

trademark law. Hasbro had not managed to provide sufficient evidence of actual consumer confusion.[26] The court also expressed concern about protecting legitimate, competing uses of a domain name.[27] The court alluded to the 'first come, first served' basis of domain name registration, noting that '[i]f another Internet user has an innocent and legitimate reason for using the famous mark as a domain name and is the first to register it, that user should be able to use the domain name, provided that it has not otherwise infringed upon or diluted the trademark'.[28]

It may be unobjectionable in a situation where there is no demonstrable consumer confusion that the original domain name registrant should be entitled to maintain its registration of the name, even in a case of similar marks. However, might other solutions be possible, or even preferable, in these kinds of cases? While trademark infringement actions may be particularly useful against a party who has registered a domain name in bad faith, there are some cases in which two parties can each claim a legitimate trademark interest corresponding to the same domain name. Domain name sharing may be a more appropriate avenue for resolving some of these situations than trademark infringement litigation.[29]

2.2.2 Trademark Dilution and Competing Trademarks

Outside of an infringement action, a trademark holder might file a dilution claim against the registrant of a domain name corresponding to its trademark.[30] A dilution action protects the holder of a famous mark[31] against blurring or tarnishment of the mark.[32] When two trademark holders have trademark interests corresponding to the same domain name, how might

---

[26] *Id.* (concluding that Hasbro had produced only 'a few scraps of evidence' of actual consumer confusion).

[27] *Id.* at 133.

[28] *Id.*

[29] See discussion at 2.4, *infra*.

[30] 15 U.S.C. § 1125(c); *Panavision v Toeppen*, 141 F.3d 1316 (9th Cir. 1998).

[31] A new definition of famous mark was recently inserted into the Lanham Act by the Trademark Dilution Revision Act of 2006, Pub. L. No. 109–312, 120 Stat. 1730 (codified as amended at 15 U.S.C.A. § 1125(c)). A famous mark is a mark that is 'widely recognized by the general consuming public of the United States as a designation of source of the goods or services of the mark's owner.' 15 U.S.C.A. § 1125(c)(2)(A).

[32] 15 U.S.C. § 1125(c)(1); *see* GILSON, *supra* note 13, para. 5A.01[1] ('Federal dilution law protects famous trademarks from unauthorized uses that are likely to impair their distinctiveness or harm their reputation. It enables owners of those marks to maintain their value as source indicators and as symbols of good will.').

a dilution action help? The action certainly creates challenges for the complainant. For one thing, a mark must be famous to be the subject of a dilution action. Although traditional trademark jurisprudence allowed this requirement to be satisfied relatively easily,[33] the 2006 revisions to the dilution statute that clarify the meaning of 'famous mark' in this context may make this requirement more difficult to satisfy in practice.[34] For example, if a trademark holder is a small, local concern that operates predominantly in a small geographic area, the fame of the mark may be questionable.

In the past, trademark dilution actions have been unsuccessful in the domain name context in cases of competing trademark interests. In the *Hasbro* case,[35] for example, the plaintiff Hasbro was concerned about dilution as well as infringement. However, Hasbro did not succeed on its dilution claims. The court held that a trademark holder does not automatically have a right to monopolize a corresponding domain name through a dilution action.[36] To prevail in an action for dilution by tarnishment would have required Hasbro to show that Clue Computing had used Hasbro's mark in an unwholesome manner or for a low quality product; the court found that Hasbro could not sustain such a showing.[37]

Dilution by blurring, on the other hand, requires that 'the marks must be similar enough that a significant segment of the target group sees the two marks as essentially the same'.[38] This view of dilution by

---

33 Mark A. Lemley, *The Modern Lanham Act and the Death of Common Sense,* 108 YALE L.J. 1687, 1698–9 (1999) (noting that some courts have found trademark dilution even without engaging in a 'fame' analysis).

34 The 'famousness' factors provided by the new statute are: (i) the duration, extent and geographic reach of advertising and publicity of the mark, whether advertised or publicized by the owner or third parties; (ii) the amount, volume and geographic extent of sales of goods or services offered under the mark; (iii) the extent of actual recognition of the mark; and (iv) whether the mark was registered under the Act of March 3, 1881, or the Act of February 20, 1905, or on the principal register: 15 U.S.C.A. § 1125(c)(2)(A). Although federal courts have not consistently interpreted the statutory test for fame, one court has described a situation in which a mark may not be famous. See *Green v Fornario*, 486 F.3d 100, 105 (3d Cir. 2007) ('[I]t seems several steps short of probable that a [baseball player] with such a brief, and largely undistinguished, professional career limited to one team in one area would have a name that is "widely recognized by the general consuming public of the United States"').

35 *Hasbro v Clue Computing*, 66 F.Supp.2d 117, 133 (D. Mass. 1999); see 2.2.1, *supra*.

36 *Hasbro, id.*

37 *Id.*

38 *Id.* at 135 (quoting J. THOMAS MCCARTHY, 3 MCCARTHY ON TRADEMARKS AND UNFAIR COMPETITION PARA. 24:90.1 (4th edn 1996)).

blurring seems almost to import a consumer confusion requirement into the dilution action even though consumer confusion is technically not an element of the action. However, the fact that courts take this view of dilution illustrates the difficulties potentially faced by a trademark holder attempting to establish that a competing trademark holder has improperly registered a domain name that happens to correspond with both of their marks.

In any event, one might question whether the policy underlying trademark dilution is appropriate for cases involving multiple trademark holders with competing interests in the same domain name. The dilution action is intended to prevent trademarks that businesses have built up through the investment of significant time and effort from being blurred or tarnished in the minds of consumers.[39] When the dilution provisions were added to the Lanham Act, Congress did not have the domain name system in mind. Domain names may create challenges for trademark holders that are better resolved through channels other than traditional infringement and dilution actions. Allowing the trademark holder with the deepest pockets potentially to monopolize the domain name that corresponds to the trademark is not the purpose of trademark dilution. Alternative solutions, such as domain-name sharing, might provide better results for society and a greater potential for development of online commerce in general, and the domain name system in particular, in future years.

2.2.3 The Anti-Cybersquatting Consumer Protection Act and Competing Trademarks

The ACPA was designed to prevent bad faith cybersquatting: registration of a domain name corresponding with someone else's name or mark with the intent to sell it for a profit.[40] It requires the defendant to have had a bad faith intent to profit[41] from registering, trafficking in or using a

---

[39] GILSON, *supra* note 13, para. 5A.01 ('Federal dilution law protects famous trademarks from unauthorized uses that are likely to impair their distinctiveness or harm their reputation. It enables owners of those marks to maintain their value as source indicators and as symbols of good will.')

[40] Jonathan Nilsen, *Mixing Oil with Water: Resolving the Differences Between Domain Names and Trademark Law*, 1 J. HIGH TECH. L. 47, 51 (2002) ('Cybersquatting has been defined several ways. The most general definition of a cybersquatter is a person who registers a domain name that matches a well-known company for the purpose of ransoming it to that company.')

[41] 15 U.S.C. § 1125(d)(1)(A)(i).

domain name that corresponds[42] to a relevant trademark.[43] The legislation incorporates a number of factors that a court may consider in determining whether the defendant's conduct meets the bad faith requirement. These factors include: (1) the trademark or other intellectual property rights of the registrant in the domain name;[44] (2) the extent to which the domain name corresponds to the registrant's personal name;[45] (3) the registrant's prior use of the domain name in connection with a bona fide offering of goods or services;[46] (4) the registrant's bona fide noncommercial or fair use of the relevant trademark in a site accessible under the domain name;[47] (5) the registrant's intent to divert customers from a corresponding trademark holder's online location to its own location in a way that could harm the goodwill associated with the trademark;[48] (6) whether the registrant has offered to transfer the name to another for financial gain without having used or having intended to use the name for a bona fide purpose;[49] (7) the provision of false contact information by the registrant on the domain name registry;[50] and (8) the registrant's acquisition of multiple domain names that the registrant knows are identical or confusingly similar to other people's trademarks.[51]

Although the ACPA can be applied effectively against bad faith cybersquatters, its application in cases of multiple competing trademark interests is more problematic. If a trademark holder can prove that a second trademark holder in fact registered a domain name (or a trademark and then a corresponding domain name) with the intent to extort money from the complainant, the holder may have a cause of action under the ACPA. For example, suppose a business registers the trademark 'Fluffy Animal Organization' and then registers the corresponding domain name, 'fao.com'. The registrant meets the first ACPA factor,

---

42 15 U.S.C. § 1125(d)(1)(A)(ii) contemplates domain names that are identical or confusingly similar to a mark and domain names that are identical, confusingly similar to or dilutive of a famous mark.

43 15 U.S.C. § 1125(d)(1)(A)(ii).

44 15 U.S.C. § 1125(d)(1)(B)(i)(I).

45 15 U.S.C. § 1125(d)(1)(B)(i)(II).

46 15 U.S.C. § 1125(d)(1)(B)(i)(III).

47 15 U.S.C. § 1125(d)(1)(B)(i)(IV).

48 15 U.S.C. § 1125(d)(1)(B)(i)(V). The registrant can interfere with the goodwill represented by the mark 'either for commercial gain or with the intent to tarnish or disparage the mark, by creating a likelihood of confusion as to the source, sponsorship, affiliation, or endorsement of the site'. *Id.*

49 15 U.S.C. § 1125(d)(1)(B)(i)(VI).

50 15 U.S.C. § 1125(d)(1)(B)(i)(VII).

51 15 U.S.C. § 1125(d)(1)(B)(i)(VIII).

ownership of a trademark interest corresponding to the domain name. But if the well-known toy store FAO Schwarz has its own trademark interest corresponding to the domain name 'fao.com', the registrant may be liable to FAO Schwarz in an action under the ACPA if the remaining factors suggest a bad faith intent to profit from sale of the domain name to FAO Schwarz.

However, in a case where the domain name registrant registered the trademark for a legitimate purpose, the resolution of the conflict with FAO Schwarz may be more difficult. If the domain name registrant really is a legitimate organization called the Fluffy Animal Organization, and the registrant can establish that the organization is making a bona fide use of 'fao.com', an ACPA action by FAO Schwarz would likely not be successful. It may be, however, that the toy company could instead bring a trademark dilution action, arguing that its mark is famous and that the registrant's use of the domain name blurs or tarnishes its mark. FAO Schwarz might also be able to bring a trademark infringement action. If, for example, the registrant of 'fao.com' sells fluffy animal toys on its website, FAO Schwarz might be able to argue that the registrant's activities are causing consumer confusion as to the source of FAO Schwarz's products, since FAO Schwarz also sells fluffy animal toys.[52]

Nevertheless, there may be cases where none of these trademark actions are available. For example, at least three companies have, or have had, similar trademarks rights corresponding with the domain name 'delta.com' in different product markets over the years. They include Deltacom Business Solutions,[53] Delta Faucets[54] and Delta Air Lines.[55] Each of these companies has an established mark involving the term 'delta' in juxtaposition with another word or phrase, such as 'business solutions', 'faucets' or 'airlines'. At least two of these companies are commonly referred to by 'Delta' alone. The airline and faucet companies could likely claim this distinction. Thus, each of them has a colorable claim for control of the corresponding domain name 'delta.com'. If one of these companies were to register the domain name 'delta.com', it would be difficult for the others to establish bad faith intent to profit from its sale to another company, and lack of legitimate interest in the original registration for the purposes

---

52 See discussion of this hypothetical in Lipton, *A Winning Solution*, *supra* note 2, at 527–9.

53 See www.itcdeltacom.com/business_solutions.asp, last accessed June 29, 2009.

54 See www.deltafaucet.com/, last accessed on June 29, 2009.

55 See www.delta.com/index.jsp?Log=1&MkCpgn=SEzzzw1a&s_kwcid=TC|8489|delta%20airlines||S|e|1295365688, last accessed June 29, 2009.

of the ACPA. As of the time of writing, the domain name is registered to Delta Airlines, having previously passed through the hands of some of the other 'delta' trademarked companies.

A trademark infringement action would be equally unlikely to succeed. Consumer confusion is not likely in a case where the companies operate in different product markets. While a dilution action could succeed if the plaintiff were to claim a sufficiently famous mark, if the domain name is held by the most famous trademark holder, the other 'Delta' corporate concerns are unlikely to convince a court that their marks are being diluted by the airline's use of 'delta.com'. None of the trademark-based litigation strategies is particularly fruitful here. In cases where the most global, powerful or well-known of the multiple trademark holders has secured the most intuitive corresponding domain name, we might simply argue that the market has taken care of itself. We might also argue that the faucet and financial services companies are not particularly losers here as long as they can be located using a search engine.

However, there may be cases where there is no clear hierarchy amongst the trademark holders with respect to the name. There may likewise be cases where all the marks in question correspond *exactly* to the same domain name, unlike the above situations where 'delta' in each corporate name is paired with another word or phrase. For example, if there are three companies called 'Floral Art' all in different product markets[56] and equally well known, it is not clear who should have the better right to the domain name 'floralart.com' as a matter of policy, all else being equal. If all the names are equally well-known and all companies arguably deserve a shot at the most intuitive domain name, it is not clear that the 'first come, first served' approach is the most appropriate policy. Perhaps this is the kind of case where a domain name sharing strategy could be useful.

2.2.4 The Uniform Domain Name Dispute Resolution Policy and Competing Trademarks

The UDRP is a private dispute resolution mechanism developed by ICANN and incorporated into the domain name system via contract between each domain name registrant and the registrar.[57] As part of the

---

[56] Consider, for example, that one company is a florist, another is a photography business that specializes in nature scenes, and the third monograms flowers and other designs on T-shirts and other consumer clothing items.

[57] See discussion at 1.5, *supra*.

domain name registration agreement, the registrant agrees that if someone else complains about the registration, the registrant will submit to a UDRP arbitration to resolve the dispute.[58] As compared with trademark litigation, UDRP proceedings are simple, fast, inexpensive and predominantly online. The main limitation of the UDRP for disputes involving competing trademark holders is that, like the ACPA, the UDRP was designed to prevent bad faith cybersquatting. It does not focus on other kinds of conflicts that involve legitimate competing interests in a given domain name.

Paragraph 4(a) of the UDRP provides that the procedure is only available in disputes where (a) the domain name at issue is identical or confusingly similar to the complainant's registered trademark or service mark; (b) the registrant has no rights or legitimate interests corresponding with the domain name; and (c) the domain name was registered and is being used in bad faith. The UDRP and the ACPA define bad faith in similar terms. Under the UDRP, bad faith involves registration of a domain name with the intent to sell it to the rightful trademark holder or to prevent the rightful trademark holder from using it.[59] The UDRP includes additional bad faith factors largely drawn from trademark policy. One factor is the intent to disrupt the business of a competitor by using a domain name that corresponds to the competitor's trademark.[60] Another factor is the intent to attract the complainant's customers by using the domain name to confuse customers about the connection between the activities conducted through the registrant's website, and the goods or services identified by the complainant's trademark.[61]

The only remedies currently available to a complainant under the UDRP are cancellation of the domain name or transfer to the complainant.[62] Such remedies are available if a UDRP arbitrator or panel of arbitrators decides both that the complainant has established bad faith registration and use of the name[63] and that the registrant has not adequately established a legitimate interest corresponding to the name.[64] The

---

58 UDRP, para. 4(a).
59 *Id.* paras 4(b)(i), (ii).
60 *Id.* para. 4(b)(iii).
61 *Id.* para. 4(b)(iv).
62 *Id.* para. 4(i) ('The remedies available to a complainant pursuant to any proceeding before an Administrative Panel shall be limited to requiring the cancellation of your domain name or the transfer of your domain name registration to the complainant.')
63 *Id.* para. 4(b).
64 *Id.* para. 4(c).

UDRP provides a vague definition of 'legitimate interest', by setting out a nonexclusive list of potential legitimate interests that a registrant may seek to establish in a domain name.[65] The list includes trademark-like interests, such as using the domain name in connection with a bona fide offering of goods and services,[66] as well as making a legitimate noncommercial or fair use of the domain name.[67]

The first legitimate use factor would most likely cover the problematic situation where two or more competing trademark holders assert trademarks that are identical with or confusingly similar to a given domain name. Most UDRP arbitrations in these cases would not result in an order to cancel or to transfer the domain name. The complainant may therefore reason that it is not worth the time and effort of bringing a UDRP proceeding if the registrant can establish a legitimate trademark interest corresponding to the domain name. Provided that the original registrant is a legitimate trademark holder with a trademark corresponding to the disputed name, a UDRP proceeding by another corresponding trademark holder will likely prove fruitless.

2.3 ADDITION OF NEW GENERIC TOP LEVEL DOMAINS

One potential answer to the problem of multiple competing trademark interests in the domain space has historically been the introduction of new generic Top Level Domains (gTLDs). In 2000, ICANN introduced seven new gTLDs[68] in an effort to spread around the number of legitimate interests that could be reflected in a given word or phrase in the domain space.[69] One of these new domain names, '.biz', might well have competed with '.com' as an intuitive pointer to a commercial entity. Another, '.name', might have taken pressure off attempts by celebrities and their fans to register famous individuals' names in the '.com' domain space,

---

65 *Id.* para. 4(c).

66 *Id.* para. 4(c)(i).

67 *Id.* para. 4(c)(iii).

68 They were '.biz', '.info', '.pro', '.name', '.aero', '.coop' and '.museum'. See MILTON MUELLER, RULING THE ROOT: INTERNET GOVERNANCE AND THE TAMING OF CYBERSPACE 204 (2004).

69 Koehler, *supra* note 5, at 56 (noting that new gTLDs were needed because all the 'good' domain names, particularly those corresponding to valuable trade marks, were already taken). In theory, the introduction of new gTLDs would have allowed new registrants to register variations of existing names. In practice, however, many of the new names were reserved for trademark holders.

such as 'juliaroberts.com' and 'tomcruise.com'.[70] However, what ultimately transpired was that existing trademark holders took precedence in many of the new gTLD spaces over other legitimate interests that might otherwise have been reflected in those spaces.[71]

Nothing prevented one trademark holder from monopolizing many relevant domain spaces by registering multiple iterations of its mark in the domain space. The popular online retailer Amazon.com, for example, has registered both 'amazon.com' and 'amazon.biz', along with a variety of intuitive country code domains (ccTLDs) corresponding with its Amazon trademark.[72] Further, despite the new gTLDs, registrants still favor '.com' names for official online businesses. They assume that most customers (and most search engine algorithms) will gravitate to 'trademark.com' domains.[73] The initial addition of the seven new gTLDs in 2000 did little to alleviate problems faced when multiple trademark holders asserted competing interests in the same domain name.

In 2000, ICANN tightly controlled the new gTLDs.[74] The addition of the new names resulted from an application process that was adjudicated by ICANN's board.[75] During the process, certain potentially promising gTLDs were refused by ICANN. They included proposals for gTLDs related to the sex and pornography industries (such as '.sex' and '.xxx')[76] as well as those related to children in particular (such as '.kids').[77] ICANN also turned down an application to adopt a '.web' gTLD.[78] One of the reasons ICANN shied away from accepting some of these gTLDs sprang from fears that it would be venturing too close to content regulation if it adopted domain names like '.sex', '.xxx' and '.kids'. Milton Mueller has noted, for example, that 'ICANN did not want to take responsibil-

---

70 Issues relating to registration of personal names in the domain space are taken up in Chapter 4.

71 Goldman, *supra* note 2, at 545 ('[N]ew TLDs in the recent years have abandoned the "first to register" relevancy algorithm, giving priority to trademark owners.').

72 See, for example, www.amazon.fr/, last accessed June 29, 2009; www.amazon.ca/, last accessed June 29, 2009; www.amazon.co.uk/, last accessed June 29, 2009; and www.amazon.co.jp/, last accessed June 29, 2009.

73 For example, the 'amazon.biz' domain name simply links back to the 'amazon.com' webpage.

74 See discussion of the process in MUELLER, *supra* note 68, at 201–5.

75 *Id.* at 202–3.

76 Jennifer Phillips, *The Seamy Side of the Seamy Side: Potential Danger of Cyberpiracy in the Proposed '.xxx' Top Level Domain*, 7 NORTH CAROLINA J. LAW AND TECHNOLOGY 233 (2005).

77 MUELLER, *supra* note 68, at 203.

78 *Id.* at 204–5.

ity, by awarding a .kids top-level domain, for certifying that the content and operators of Web sites in that domain would post child-appropriate material'.[79]

In 2008, ICANN developed a more open stance to the development of new gTLDs. In an effort to enhance 'diversity, choice, and competition' in the domain space,[80] ICANN has established a program to allow individuals and organizations to apply for any new gTLD. Successful applicants would be allowed to serve as registrars for new gTLDs.[81] While the program is still in development, it is not clear that even this new system will alleviate problems relating to multiple competing trademark holders. Unless the new system adopts a limit as to the number of gTLDs that may be registered by any given trademark holder, nothing will stop one trademark holder from registering multiple iterations of its mark in the most intuitive gTLD spaces. Additionally, the new gTLD proposal assumes that '.com' names might ultimately lose their appeal as the real estate of choice in the domain space. Only time will tell if this turns out to be the case in practice. However, past practices suggest that the '.com' space is unlikely to lose its luster.

2.4 DOMAIN NAME TRANSFERS AND SHARING

2.4.1 Private Negotiations

An obvious solution to the problem of competing trademark interests in the same domain name is to let the market take care of itself. Market solutions may involve private negotiations for either domain name transfers or domain name sharing. Given that many online players will want to control the most intuitive '.com' spaces, negotiating for transfers from prior registrants may be the favored option. This approach carries obvious benefits in that it does not require any specific policy determinations to be made, and no particular regulatory oversight is necessary. Businesses that have invested sufficient time and money into developing their brands, and that are willing to bargain with those who may have previously registered desirable domain names, will be able to reflect their marks in relevant

---

79 *Id.* at 204.

80 See www.icann.org/en/topics/new-gtld-program.htm, last accessed June 29, 2009.

81 See www.icann.org/en/topics/new-gtlds/comments-e-en.htm#matrix, last accessed June 29, 2009 (most updated revisions to proposed new application procedures).

domain names. Of course, one downside of this approach is that powerful players with deep pockets may come to dominate the most intuitive domain spaces, often to the detriment of smaller players. Some may regard this as an unfortunate result given the potential of the Internet to allow more enterprises, whether large or small, an opportunity to connect with customers easily and globally online.

There might be less waste in the domain space, and in transactions involving domain names, if more cooperative approaches to domain name registration could be developed. One possibility would be to expand the UDRP to facilitate domain name sharing. This might not only supplement the sharing arrangements currently possible through private agreement,[82] but also communicate the policy message that sharing is, in some cases, preferable to negotiating for a transfer of a given domain name. The problem with relying on purely private arrangements with no outside assistance is that the current system provides little to no incentive for parties to negotiate sharing arrangements. Even when parties do have sufficient commercial incentives to negotiate sharing arrangements, the absence of established sharing norms may make the idea seem too risky to pursue without any external assistance. The establishment of a sharing system facilitated by a third party, such as UDRP arbitrators, might encourage competing trademark holders to negotiate domain name sharing arrangements.

Non-assisted private domain name sharing arrangements seem to work only in a small number of cases. One example of when such an arrangement might occur is the sale of a division of a business, where the seller retains trademark interests in the parts of the business that are not being sold, but transfers or licenses similar trademarks to the purchaser. This occurred with the sale of Playtex Company's apparel division to Hanes in 1991.[83] The Playtex trademarks used with respect to apparel were sold with the division, while the trademarks used for baby products remain with the original company. The 'playtex.com' domain name is now shared between the two entities.[84]

To share the domain name, Playtex and Hanes have established a shared webpage under the 'playtex.com' domain with links to each company's individual home page. The domain name is registered to the Playtex Marketing Corporation,[85] a corporation that apparently holds all of the

---

82 Lipton, *A Winning Solution*, *supra* note 2, at 534.
83 *Id.* at 532.
84 *Id.*
85 *Id.* at 532–3.

relevant trademarks.[86] The shared webpage proclaims: 'Although we may have a name in common . . . [w]e are two completely separate companies'.[87] The page is then divided into two sections that each hyperlink to a different company. The left-hand section links to the webpage for Playtex Products (which has the domain name 'playtexproducts.com'), and the right-hand section links to the webpage for Playtex Apparel (which has the domain name 'playtexbras.com').

In this example, consumers can find the company they are looking for by: (1) knowing or guessing the individual domain names for each company and typing them directly into a web browser; (2) searching for the relevant company or its product lines with an Internet search engine; or (3) intuitively guessing the 'playtex.com' name and typing it into a web browser, then following the appropriate link from the shared website. The sharing arrangement makes online navigation easier by giving Internet users an additional means to find their desired destination. Additionally, it avoids wasted resources because neither company monopolizes or seeks to monopolize multiple domain names corresponding to its trademark through litigation or arbitration.

Private sharing arrangements are likely to work when the sale of part of a company and its trademarks creates incentives for both parties to cooperate. Private sharing arrangements may also be negotiable in some other circumstances where the trademark holders competing for a domain name have other incentives to cooperate. For example, there might be sufficient financial incentives for similar-sized trademark holders with competing trademarks of similar value to share domain names rather than engaging in litigation or arbitration over establishing better rights in a name.

Private sharing agreements might also be attractive when different parties each own a similar trademark that they have concurrently used in different geographic areas. The 'scrabble.com' domain name is an example. The Scrabble trademark is registered to different companies in different regions. Hasbro owns the Scrabble trademark in the United States and Canada, while a British subsidiary of Mattel owns the mark in the rest of the world.[88] Each company has held and used these marks for a long period of time and each is equally well-established within its own territory. The website at 'scrabble.com' requires the user to select the user's location, which then routes the user to the appropriate company's home page.[89]

---

86 *Id.* at 533.
87 See www.playtex.com/, last accessed June 29, 2009.
88 Lipton, *A Winning Solution*, *supra* note 2, at 534–5.
89 *Id.*

Part of the reason why parties have generally opted to negotiate, litigate or arbitrate for transfer, rather than sharing, of domain names may be that this is how registrants understand the system to work. Since the early days of the domain name system, the emphasis has been on sole ownership of domain names. It is true that at any one time only one party can formally register a given domain name. This limitation is a technological constraint of the system. However, there is no reason why the registrant cannot be a holding company, like Playtex Marketing Corporation, which manages shared interests in similar trademarks that correspond to the same domain name. Most entities appear to have equated the idea that only one entity can *register* a domain name at a given time with the idea that only one entity can *use* the domain name at a given time.

Establishing mechanisms to facilitate domain name sharing might change this perspective. If there are a viable number of competing interests, and sufficient incentives to share, the domain name system could be adjusted to facilitate sharing in more cases. Currently, in many situations, the barriers to reaching an agreement may be too high for parties to successfully negotiate a private sharing arrangement. Thus, the facilitation of sharing by a third party mediator may be appropriate. If enough agreements can be facilitated by a third party (such as an arbitrator under a modified version of the UDRP) new norms might develop that encourage domain name sharing in appropriate cases without the need for third party intervention.

2.4.2 Incorporating Domain Sharing into the UDRP

As the system currently stands, UDRP arbitrators are likely the most readily able to facilitate sharing agreements. For arbitrators to act as facilitators, the UDRP could be modified to provide not only for transfer and cancellation orders,[90] which are currently available, but also for sharing agreements.[91] As with the current procedures under the UDRP, any sharing agreement facilitated by UDRP arbitrators should not necessarily preclude other avenues of redress for a party dissatisfied with the arbitral outcome.[92] Even if modified to provide for sharing agreements, the UDRP is a creature of contract and cannot oust courts of otherwise competent jurisdiction. A party could still choose to litigate its trademark interests in the wake of an unsatisfactory UDRP arbitration.[93]

---

90 UDRP, para. 4(i).
91 See generally discussion in Lipton, *A Winning Solution*, *supra* note 2.
92 UDRP, para. 4(k).
93 *Id.*

The UDRP has already facilitated the quick and easy resolution of cybersquatting cases. It has also reduced the pressure on judicial systems in this context. A similar result could be achieved in cases involving competing trademark holders if domain name sharing could be facilitated under the UDRP. The UDRP could simply be modified to ensure cost-effective sharing arrangements when viable and appropriate. This might be done by inserting a new provision into the UDRP for disputes in which a complainant is asserting that it has legitimate trademark interests in a domain name that is already validly registered to another trademark holder. Instead of, or in the alternative to, seeking a transfer or cancellation order, the complainant could request a sharing arrangement.[94]

This approach contradicts current thinking about the domain name system. We are used to the idea that if a registrant has a legitimate trademark interest corresponding to a given domain name and was the first to register the name, that registrant should be entitled to retain sole registration. This view persists because the system has paid little attention to other trademark holders who might simultaneously be in a position to assert legitimate interests corresponding to the same domain name. There is no necessary policy reason why multiple competing trademark interests could not be incorporated into the domain name system in ways that make less wasteful use of certain domain names.

If a new provision were to be added to the UDRP to facilitate domain name sharing in cases of multiple trademark interests, it would probably be appropriate to give the registrant an opportunity to oppose the request to share the name in certain situations. For example, a registrant might argue that the complainant's interest in the domain name is not sufficiently strong to support a sharing arrangement. Consider, for example, the hypothetical Furry Animal Organization discussed above.[95] If FAO Schwarz had registered 'fao.com' (as indeed it has) and the owner of the Furry Animal Organization trademark brought a complaint under a new UDRP domain name sharing process, FAO Schwarz might avoid a sharing order if it could establish to the satisfaction of an arbitrator that the Fluffy Animal Organization's mark is insufficiently close to 'FAO' to warrant a domain name sharing order. A registrant might also oppose an application for a sharing order with evidence that the complainant had only registered the relevant trademark for the purpose of forcing a sharing arrangement on the complainant, or using

---

94 Lipton, *A Winning Solution*, *supra* note 2.

95 See discussion at 2.2.3, *supra*.

the threat of an unwanted sharing arrangement to extort money from the registrant.[96]

In situations where a complainant does have a legitimate interest in a trademark that corresponds to the registrant's domain name, a revised UDRP could empower an arbitrator or panel to require the parties to share the domain name. The sharing itself could be implemented in a number of ways. The parties might, for example, nominate an entity to act as registrant of the domain name and to host a shared website that would link to each company's individual website, much like the Playtex scenario described above.[97] Alternatively, the domain name could be registered to one of the trademark holders or to a new corporate entity jointly operated by the trademark holders, or to a private individual nominated by the trademark holders. Thus, a domain name sharing order would in effect be an order to transfer the domain name to whichever entity was nominated to hold the domain name on behalf of the trademark owners.[98]

In order to streamline this aspect of the sharing arrangement, the disputing parties could be required to nominate a 'sharing agent' at the start of the UDRP proceedings to whom the name would be transferred in the event that a sharing order was made. This could be difficult in practice where the parties are not on good terms, but at least such a requirement might provide some incentives for the parties to start communicating with each other in a cooperative spirit. Another alternative would be for ICANN to provide domain name sharing companies incorporated as shelf companies for this purpose. Such companies might ultimately be transferred jointly to the disputing parties in the event that a domain sharing order was made by a UDRP arbitrator.[99]

The use of a third party holding company, either supplied by ICANN or established by the parties, would in many cases be preferable to maintaining the domain name registration in the hands of either of the trademark holders individually. This is because ICANN, its registrars and its arbitrators control the technical aspects of the system, but not web content. It is much easier to enforce an order governing the identity of the domain name registrant than to enforce an order governing what appears on the associated webpage. In other words, the best way for domain name administrators to enforce a sharing arrangement is to

---

96 Lipton, *A Winning Solution*, *supra* note 2, at 537.
97 See 2.4.1, *supra*.
98 Lipton, *A Winning Solution*, *supra* note 2, at 537.
99 *Id.* at 538.

ensure joint ownership of the shared domain name. If one of the parties retains sole ownership of the disputed domain name, it would be difficult for the other party to enforce an order to share if the registered party later refused to establish the necessary hyperlinks to the other party's website.

The parties subject to a domain name sharing order may need assistance with some of the technical aspects of the domain name sharing arrangement. In particular, they may need help hyperlinking the new, shared webpage to their individual webpages. The individual webpages may require new domain name registrations, or they could be subpages accessible under the shared domain. To facilitate sharing, it would be useful if ICANN could establish some form of domain name sharing assistance mechanism to help domain name sharers with these technical aspects of the process. ICANN's help would reduce some of the financial burdens related to sharing agreements, particularly between small businesses that might not have ready access to web development personnel.

Outside of ICANN, a private market might develop for such services. There are already independent web-design services available, and some of these companies might be interested in branching out into the domain name sharing business. The creation of such services by ICANN or private parties might encourage domain name sharing agreements, whether or not the UDRP is ever expanded to facilitate them. The availability of domain name sharing assistance services might encourage sharing in cases where the parties would be happy to share, but do not know how to go about it and are worried about the costs involved.

If sharing orders were to be incorporated into the UDRP, it might be wise to allow a complainant to argue sharing in the alternative to an order for transfer or cancellation. There may be cases where a complainant's preference is to obtain a transfer or cancellation order, but failing that, the complainant would be prepared to share the domain name. Such cases might be decided in the same proceeding by the same arbitrator or panel, in effect as a consolidation of the complainant's different claims.[100]

To achieve these ends, the UDRP would not require much alteration. New sharing order aspects of the UDRP would not affect its basic operation. It would remain a contractual arrangement that does not oust the jurisdiction of competent courts.[101] The procedural rules governing

---

100 *Id.* at 539.
101 UDRP, para. 4(k).

UDRP disputes would remain the same.[102] Even the provisions relating to transfers and cancellations of domain names during and subsequent to arbitrations[103] would not require revision. An order to share a domain name would simply be an order to transfer the name to an entity that would hold the name on behalf of the parties. The UDRP's representations that determine when a domain name registrar will effect such a transfer (for example, when it receives an order from an arbitral tribunal)[104] would therefore not require revision.

Importantly, under such a procedure, domain name arbitrators would not be asked to make determinations that are particularly more complex than the determinations they are currently asked to make. Under the UDRP as presently drafted, arbitrators routinely decide who has a legitimate interest in a domain name and who may be using a domain name in bad faith. In cases where an arbitrator was satisfied that both parties have a legitimate interest in the name, the arbitrators would simply have an additional option to mandate a domain name sharing solution, rather than to deny transfer or cancellation of the name – as would currently happen if the registrant established a legitimate interest in the domain name.

2.4.3 Evaluating UDRP-mandated Domain Sharing

One advantage of incorporating domain name sharing into the UDRP would be the potential for disputes adjudicated in this way to generate data about how many of these disputes are likely to arise in practice, and how many of them might effectively be resolved in this way. If a sharing option resulted in little to no sharing and parties continued to either fight for sole control of names or to negotiate private arrangements between themselves, little would have been lost. However, if sharing norms began to develop as a result of a UDRP domain name sharing process, this may lead to less waste in the domain space over time. If third-party facilitation of sharing under the UDRP could ultimately create new cyberspace sharing norms, private parties would then be in a position to base their negotiations on those norms rather than on the current combination of the 'first come, first served' and 'better rights' rules.

These kinds of developments would not likely resolve all disputes over domain names between legitimate trademark holders. Even if the UDRP

---

102 Rules for the Uniform Domain Name Dispute Resolution Policy, available at www.icann.org/en/udrp/udrp-rules-24oct99.htm, last accessed June 30, 2009.

103 UDRP, para. 3.

104 *Id.* at para. 3(c).

were revised to facilitate sharing, some situations would arise that could not be resolved in this way. One example might be in cases where too many parties assert competing trademark interests in the same domain name for sharing to be effective in practice. The more parties are involved in a dispute over the same name, the more likely at least one party will object to the terms of a sharing arrangement. Even in cases where all parties are prepared to share as a matter of principle, the sheer number of trademark holders may make a shared webpage difficult to navigate and ultimately perhaps hardly more helpful than a general list of search results. The potential advantages of sharing an intuitive domain name could be lost here.

Even in cases involving only two parties, there may be situations where sophisticated parties with well-known or valuable trademarks might prefer private negotiations in the hope of gaining exclusive rights to a given domain name. There is nothing particularly wrong with this. The idea of implementing a sharing process under the UDRP is not intended to be the only way in which competing trademark holders could resolve conflicts involving a domain name. Ultimately, a UDRP-facilitated sharing system might be most useful to businesses with lesser known trademarks, or trademarks that are well known only in a limited geographic area.

2.5 RELEVANCE OF SEARCH ENGINES

Many would argue that mechanisms to facilitate domain name sharing are unnecessary in cases of competing trademark interests because increasingly sophisticated search engines will ultimately surpass domain names as a method for helping Internet users find relevant information online. Indeed, some have argued that search engines have already surpassed domain names as search tools.[105] While this is a strong argument, and while search engine providers continue to fine tune their search algorithms to help Internet users find information, domain names will continue to be important in practice. Thus, the development of systems that facilitate optimum uses of domain names where competing parties assert legitimate interests in the same name will continue to be of concern to the global Internet community.

Despite the prevalence and popularity of sophisticated search engine

---

[105] Goldman, *supra* note 2, at 543–8 (describing how domain names underperform as search tools compared to Internet search engines).

technology, many people continue to use domain names for Internet searching. In fact, there is evidence that Internet users often type domain names into Internet search engines in the hopes of locating one or more relevant webpages.[106] Part of the reason why domain names may be prioritized by Internet searchers, even those using search engines, is that domain names continue to be a significant part of most search engines' algorithms.[107] The ability of a trademark holder to secure an intuitive domain name may assist the business in obtaining priority in search results. Additionally, many Internet search engine users no doubt gravitate towards items in search results that contain a domain name that intuitively corresponds with the search term they used.

Domain names also retain an important referential function in that they allow people to easily refer others to specific websites. I am more likely to direct a colleague to 'nike.com' than to describe the search steps I took to find Nike's official website. Finally, if domain names were not important in the age of sophisticated Internet search engines, parties would not continue to litigate, arbitrate and negotiate over them. However, domain names continue to be hot property, as evidenced by the increasing number of domain name disputes arbitrated under the UDRP,[108] as well as by ICANN's project to increase the number of available gTLDs within the system.

2.6 EMERGING ISSUES: NEW GTLDS AND DESCRIPTIVE FACEBOOK URLS

New developments in the domain space are likely to implicate competing trademark interests in new ways. The proposed introduction of new gTLDs by ICANN is one example. The potential for the adoption of many new gTLDs will likely raise conflicts in the domain space that have not arisen before. For example, who should have the better rights to control, and register names in, a new '.delta' gTLD? ICANN is adopting

---

106 *Id.* at 547–8.

107 *See* Topranker.in, Importance of Domain Names for Search Engine Optimization, www.topranker.in/important_seo_tips_for_domain_name.htm# seo_tips_for_domain_name, last accessed May 12, 2008 (explaining that search engines give top priority to keywords that also appear in the site's domain name).

108 See WIPO, *Record Number of Cybersquatting Cases in 2008, WIPO Proposes Paperless UDRP*, available at www.wipo.int/pressroom/en/articles/2009/ article_0005.html, last accessed June 30, 2009.

procedures that will protect trademark rights in the event of a conflict involving an application to register a new gTLD that incorporates a trademark.[109]

Another area of emerging interest is that of the relatively recent Facebook URLs.[110] These URLs allow Facebook members to utilize words and marks in their Facebook addresses.[111] Thus, Facebook users can now register pages with URLs like 'facebook.com/delta'. Companies and individuals may want to utilize this system to personalize their official Facebook pages. Businesses can utilize the service for advertising their products and communicating with their customers.[112] The system again raises issues of what should happen when two or more trademark holders assert similar interests in the same Facebook URL, such as facebook.com/delta. Facebook maintains a private grievance procedure to deal with disputes over these URLs, but again there is little guidance for trademark holders as to how Facebook would deal with situations of competing trademark holders' interests in the same URL.

Presumably, trademark infringement, dilution and ACPA infringement actions are available to trademark holders with respect to both the new gTLDs adopted by ICANN and Facebook URLs. However, for reasons addressed above, if the registrant is using the relevant descriptor for a bona fide offering of goods or services under its own trademark, the complainant may not have very much luck. The UDRP will not apply to disputes involving new gTLDs unless the registrars of the relevant gTLDs expressly adopt the Policy. The UDRP will also not apply to the Facebook situation because the domain name registrant of the 'facebook.com' name is Facebook itself. The subpages are created by Facebook's contracts with its members. Complainants about particular subpages therefore only have recourse to Facebook, and not to UDRP arbitrators.

It may be that a sharing policy along the lines described above could

---

109 ICANN, New gTLD Program: Draft Applicant Guidebook (Draft RFP) (October 24, 2008), para. 3.5.2, available at www.icann.org/en/topics/new-gtlds/draft-rfp-24oct08-en.pdf, last accessed December 11, 2008 (contemplating protections for existing trademarks in the gTLD space).

110 URL stands for Uniform Resource Locator which specifies where content is available on the Internet.

111 See, for example, discussion in Stoel Rives L.L.P., *Trademark Law Alert: New Personalized Facebook URLs May Infringe Your Trademarks and Brands* (June 11, 2009), available at www.stoel.com/showalert.aspx?Show=5515, last accessed July 6, 2009.

112 See, for example, www.facebook.com/coca-cola, last accessed on July 6, 2009.

be adopted and incorporated into registration agreements for existing and new gTLDs for cases involving multiple trademark holders. Additionally, Facebook may want to consider adopting a private sharing arrangement for competing trademark holders that want to make use of the same Facebook subpage. However, there may be little incentive for Facebook to do so unless Facebook pages develop a greater prominence in online commercial life. Currently, it is mainly regarded as a social networking site, even though some businesses maintain a commercial presence there.[113]

2.7 CHAPTER SUMMARY

Trademark-protecting regulations effectively protect trademarks in the domain space against bad faith incursions by those seeking to profit from opportunistic registration of domain names corresponding with marks. However, those regulations are less effective in cases where multiple trademark holders compete for registration and use of the same domain name. Because similar trademarks can be used in different markets, trademarks are, in a sense, nonrivalrous. The same mark can be held simultaneously by different businesses, provided they operate in different product or geographic markets.

Domain names, on the other hand, are effectively rivalrous, in the sense that only one person can register a domain name at any given time. This does not mean, however, that only one person can effectively *use* the same domain name simultaneously if a domain name sharing arrangement can be negotiated. There may be advantages to considering ways in which domain names could be shared by two or more corresponding trademark holders in cases where each such an arrangement would be to the businesses' mutual advantage.

This chapter has addressed the following.

(1) The limitations of existing regulations in effectively dealing with situations where multiple trademark holders compete for registration and use of the same domain name.

(2) Past practices and current proposals for creating more gTLDs in attempts to take pressure off the '.com' space and to allow more entities to reflect their trademarks and other legitimate interests in the domain space.

---

[113] At the time of writing, businesses like Pepsi, Coca-Cola and McDonalds had Facebook pages, although other well-known businesses like Nike, Burger King and the Disney Corporation did not have a Facebook presence.

(3) Limitations on the creation of new gTLDs in situations involving competitions between multiple competing trademark holders.

(4) Strategies for facilitating domain name transfers and sharing arrangements in situations where multiple trademark holders have legitimate interests in the same domain name. In particular, a proposal for amending the UDRP to incorporate domain name sharing strategies as an alternative to a transfer or cancellation order is suggested for situations involving multiple trademark holders competing for use of the same domain name.

(5) Emerging issues in the domain space, such as new gTLDs and personalized Facebook URLs, where competition between multiple trademark holders may arise.

Subsequent chapters consider balances between trademark interests and other legitimate interests in domain names, including free speech interests, in both the political and commercial contexts, and some privacy interests.

3. Domain names and free speech

3.1 SPEECH IN THE DOMAIN SPACE

> 'We limit linguistic monopolies because ultimately we value the freedom to communicate above the freedom to own: the language of liberty is seldom heard where liberty of language has been removed from the commons.'[1]

Current domain name regulations focus on protecting trademarks in the domain space against bad faith commercial incursions, largely in the form of cybersquatting.[2] A variety of options are available for trademark holders to protect their marks in the domain space, including actions for trademark infringement[3] and dilution,[4] as well as actions under the newer anti-cybersquatting provisions of the Lanham Act in the United States.[5] More globally, and inexpensively, the Uniform Domain Name Dispute Resolution Policy has proved a popular dispute resolution mechanism for cybersquatting disputes.[6] As trademark protections online have broadened in scope, the tension between trademarks and free speech has intensified.

When trademark rights were limited to the prevention of consumer confusion via the traditional trademark infringement action, free speech was less likely to be implicated. However, when trademarks are protected against unauthorized uses that relate to things other than consumer confusion and may, in fact, involve commentary, criticism, artistic expression, and the like, the First Amendment can and should come into play.[7]

---

[1] Kevin Gray, *Property in Thin Air*, 50 CAMBRIDGE L.J. 252, 286 (1991).

[2] Jonathan Nilsen, *Mixing Oil with Water: Resolving the Differences Between Domain Names and Trademark Law*, 1 J. HIGH TECH. L. 47, 51 (2002) ('Cybersquatting has been defined several ways. The most general definition of a cybersquatter is a person who registers a domain name that matches a well-known company for the purpose of ransoming it to that company.')

[3] 15 U.S.C. §§ 1114(1), 1125(a)(1).

[4] 15 U.S.C. § 1125(c).

[5] 15 U.S.C. §§ 1125(d).

[6] Full text available at www.icann.org/en/dndr/udrp/policy.htm, last accessed July 6, 2009.

[7] Robert C. Denicola, *Trademarks as Speech: Constitutional Implications of the Emerging Rationales for the Protection of Trade Symbols*, 1982 WIS. L. REV.

Trademark law and the First Amendment increasingly collided prior to the rise of the Internet. Obvious examples are the infamous *Enjoy Cocaine* poster[8] and the *Cocaine is the Real Thing* T-shirts,[9] parodying the well-known Coca Cola trademark; the use of L.L. Bean's registered trademark in a sexually explicit parody in High Society magazine;[10] and the use of the famous Olympic-rings mark in a poster protesting state plans to convert the Olympic Village in Lake Placid into a prison after the winter games.[11]

The domain name system adds new challenges to the already complex balancing act between trademark rights and free speech. This is because the Internet is both an important global communications medium and a commercial marketplace. Conflicts between speech and commerce are inevitable. Online, trademark holders can reach larger customer bases than ever before. Nevertheless, people should be free to utilize the Internet for expressive purposes. As the Internet is global in scale, international harmonization of relevant rules potentially becomes extremely difficult, particularly with respect to rules that impact on foundational cultural values such as free speech.

Moreover, the domain name system raises a scarcity problem online that impacts both free speech and trademark holders. Only one person can register a particular domain name at any given time. In other words, domain names are like real estate: they are effectively rivalrous. Only one person can be the registrant of a given name. Thus, we need to craft policies to help determine whether a 'trademark.com' domain name, for example, should be protected in the hands of someone who wants to comment on, or criticize, the trademark holder. Alternatively, should such a name be presumptively reserved to the trademark holder?

This chapter highlights the balance between speech and trademark rights in the domain space. It commences with a brief survey of globally

---

158, 166 (1982) ('The first amendment . . . does not operate to restrict the rights afforded trademark owners under traditional doctrine. Trademark law, however, has sometimes ventured beyond the confines of the [consumer] confusion model. Those seeking to extend the scope of trademark protection have championed models more closely allied with property than with tort. When consumer confusion ceases to be the touchstone, however, the accommodation between trademark law and the First Amendment becomes more problematic.').

8 *Coca-Cola Co. v Gemini Rising, Inc.*, 346 F.Supp.1183 (E.D.N.Y. 1972).

9 *Id.* at 1189 note. 5 (referring to a consumer complaint about the T-shirts that was not litigated in the case and did not involve the defendant in this case).

10 *L.L. Bean, Inc. v Drake Publishers, Inc.*, 811 F.2d 26 (1st Cir. 1987).

11 *Stop the Olympic Prison v U.S. Olympic Comm.*, 489 F.Supp.1112 (S.D.N.Y. 1980).

diverse perspectives on free speech. It then outlines ways in which courts have attempted to balance free speech against trademark interests in the pre-Internet world. It sets out the framework within which judges and arbitrators have to maneuver in the Internet context. The discussion then turns to ways in which judges and arbitrators have attempted to balance trademarks and free speech in the domain name context with particular reference to gripe sites and parody sites.

A number of regulatory options for balancing trademark interests and free speech in the domain space are identified, including (a) clarifying and streamlining the common-law tests for trademark infringement and Anti Cybersquatting Consumer Protection Act (ACPA) infringement in the online context; (b) creating special new domain name spaces for parody, commentary, and criticism, such as a new '.sucks', '.parody', '.fun' or '.crit' gTLD;[12] and (c) creating a specific judicial or legislative presumption that utilizing a pejorative word like 'sucks', 'parody' or 'critical' within a domain name (such as 'trademarksucks.com') will be prima facie evidence of a non-infringing use of the mark. These suggestions are not mutually exclusive and might all be developed simultaneously by relevant entities, including courts, legislatures and private bodies such as ICANN. The chapter concludes with a look to the future of free speech in the domain space. It includes consideration of emerging issues involving speech in the domain space, including problems that may be raised by the introduction of new gTLDs by ICANN.

3.2 FREE SPEECH RIGHTS

One obvious problem inherent in an attempt to identify or streamline approaches to the trademark/speech balance online is the fact that speech rights differ from country to country in terms of their constitutional basis and scope. While trademark law is relatively well harmonized between developed nations, free speech is divergent in its basis, scope and history. Trademarks are accepted as a form of intangible personal property,[13] or

---

[12] Of course, this will be possible under ICANN's plans to introduce new gTLDs: see ICANN, New gTLD Program: Draft Applicant Guidebook (Draft RFP) (October 24, 2008), available at www.icann.org/en/topics/new-gtld-program.htm, last accessed July 6, 2009.

[13] See, for example, Trade Marks Act 1995 (Austl.), s. 21(1) (defining a trade mark as a form of personal property); Trade Marks Act 1994 (Eng.), s. 2(1) ('A registered trade mark is a property right obtained by the registration of the trade mark under this Act').

quasi-property,[14] right in most countries under registered trademark legislation. Such rights are usually subordinate to constitutionally guaranteed rights like free speech in many countries, although the balance may be achieved in different ways depending on the jurisdiction.

An initial question in approaching the global problem of balancing speech against intangible property interests relates to the nature of the speech right itself. Most people are familiar with the powerful First Amendment speech guarantees in the United States.[15] The First Amendment protects citizens against government incursions on freedom of speech or of the press.[16] Although the First Amendment is aimed at government action, the notion of 'government' has been interpreted broadly in this context. It now applies to a variety of executive actions outside of pure federal legislation.[17]

First Amendment jurisprudence has a detailed and complex history. An understanding of the intricacies of the relevant literature is beyond the scope of this text.[18] However, the First Amendment guarantee of speech is a strong constitutional protection that should, as a matter of policy, override an intangible property right to the extent that the exercise of the property right creates an unacceptable burden on speech. Property rights should not generally abridge a citizen's right to participate in the free exchange of information and ideas in a democratic society.

Other countries have taken different approaches to free speech. Australia, for example, has a very limited implied constitutional guarantee

---

[14] On the American position, see Mark Lemley, *The Modern Lanham Act and the Death of Common Sense*, 108 YALE L.J. 1687, 1687–8 (1999) ('Commentators and even courts increasingly talk about trademarks as property rights; as things valuable in and of themselves, rather than for the product goodwill they embody'); Stacey L. Dogan and Mark A. Lemley, T*rademarks and Consumer Search Costs on the Internet*, 41 HOUS. L. REV. 777, 788 (2004) ('Trademarks are not property rights in gross, but limited entitlements to protect against uses that diminish the informative value of marks'). Trademarks are not described as 'personal property' in the Lanham Act.

[15] The First Amendment to the United States Constitution states that 'Congress shall make no law respecting an establishment of religion, or prohibiting the free exercise thereof; or abridging the freedom of speech, or of the press; or the right of the people peaceably to assemble, and to petition the Government for a redress of grievances'.

[16] *Id.*

[17] See, for example, *Mainstream Loudoun v Bd of Trustees of the Loudoun Co. Library*, 2 F.Supp.2d 783 (E.D. Va. 1998) (First Amendment scrutiny applied to Internet filtering policy adopted by public library).

[18] Interested readers might consult STEVEN HEYMAN, FREE SPEECH AND HUMAN DIGNITY (2008).

of free speech that tends to be restricted in practice to situations involving speech pertaining to federal politicians.[19] Thus, it is necessary to bear in mind that online battles between speech and property rights might play out differently in countries with weaker free speech guarantees than the United States.

Another interesting comparison is the United Kingdom, where a constitutional guarantee of free speech has relatively recently been enacted into domestic law under the Human Rights Act 1998.[20] This legislation adopts the principles set out in the European Convention on Human Rights,[21] including article 10 as pertains to free expression:

> 1. Everyone has the right to freedom of expression. This right shall include freedom to hold opinions and to receive and impart information and ideas without interference by public authority and regardless of frontiers. . .
>
> 2. The exercise of these freedoms, since it carries with it duties and responsibilities, may be subject to such formalities, conditions, restrictions or penalties as are prescribed by law, and are necessary in a democratic society, in the interests of national security, territorial integrity or public safety, for the protection of health or morals, for the protection of the reputation or rights of others, for preventing the disclosure of information received in confidence, or for maintaining the authority and impartiality of the judiciary.

Free speech is now recognized as a constitutional right in the United Kingdom, along with other signatory countries to the Convention. Now, British courts are expressly asked to balance speech against concurrent duties and responsibilities including 'conditions, restrictions or penalties as are prescribed by law, and as are necessary in a democratic society'. It remains to be seen whether trademark interests meet this definition or whether free speech might now more freely trump commercial trademarks in the United Kingdom. While this text focuses predominantly on American law, the global picture should be kept in mind, specifically with respect to cultural values such as free speech which vary significantly from country to country.

---

[19] See, for example, discussion in Ben Roxburgh, *Australian Perspective: Legitimizing Free Speech – Perils and Pitfalls*, 3 CAROLINA PAPERS: DEMOCRACY AND HUMAN RIGHTS 1 (Spring, 2002), available at http://cgi.unc.edu/research/pdf/Roxborough.pdf, last accessed July 9, 2009.

[20] Human Rights Act 1998 (Eng.); full text available at www.legislation.gov.uk/acts/acts1998/ukpga_19980042_en_1, last accessed July 9, 2009.

[21] European Convention on Human Rights (1950), full text available at www.hri.org/docs/ECHR50.html, last accessed July 9, 2009.

3.3 FREE SPEECH UNDER TRADITIONAL TRADEMARK LAW

3.3.1 Trademark-related Actions and Free Speech

In theory, there should be no conflict between trademark law and free speech. The purpose of trademark law is to prevent consumer confusion with respect to the source of products and services.[22] The unauthorized use of trademarks for expressive purposes should not technically amount to trademark infringement, either because such uses are not in commerce,[23] or because they should not cause consumer confusion.[24] There is also a debate as to whether, or the extent to which, a trademark 'use' is required as a prerequisite to an infringement action, at least in the United States. In other words, if the defendant is not using the mark *as a trademark* – or making a trademark use of it – there should be no infringement action available to the plaintiff.[25] If a use of a trademark is purely expressive, for example, to comment on a trademark holder's labor practices, this arguably would not be a trademark use to the extent that doctrine is accepted

---

22 Denicola, *supra* note 7, at 165 ('Reliance on the confusion rationale as the primary basis of [trademark infringement] liability has effectively insulated trademark doctrine from constitutional attack. The necessity of establishing that the challenged use generates a likelihood of confusion restricts judicial intervention to instances in which the mark is used to misrepresent the source or sponsorship of goods or services. The regulation of such deceptive or misleading commercial speech presents no constitutional difficulties'); Dogan and Lemley, *supra* note 14, at 786 ('Most people think of trademark law in terms of what it forbids: the use of another party's trademark, or something resembling it, in a way that will cause confusion among consumers in the marketplace. Courts commonly describe the goal of trademark law as avoiding consumer confusion, which has the corollary effect of preventing the appropriation of a producer's goodwill.').

23 15 U.S.C. §§1114(1)(a), 1125(a)(1) (in commerce requirements from American trademark law).

24 *Id.*; *Mushroom Makers, Inc. v R.G. Barry Corp.*, 441 F.Supp.1220, 1225 (S.D.N.Y. 1977) ('The touchstone of trademark infringement under the Lanham Act . . . is "likelihood of confusion": whether a substantial number of ordinarily prudent purchasers are likely to be misled or confused as to the source of the different products'.); ANNE GILSON LALONDE and JEROME GILSON, 2, TRADEMARK PROTECTION AND PRACTICE para. 5.01[1] ('The issue of whether the use of the same trademark or two similar marks by different parties is likely to cause confusion among the purchasing public is central to most trademark cases'.).

25 Graeme Dinwoodie and Mark Janis, *Confusion Over Use: Contextualism in Trademark Law*, 92 IOWA L. REV. 1597 (2007); Stacey Dogan and Mark Lemley, *Grounding Trademark Law Through Trademark Use*, 92 IOWA L. REV. 1669 (2007).

as part of American trademark law.[26] In this case, the person making the expressive use of the mark should technically be under no threat of a trademark infringement order being made against her. However, even the threat of a trademark infringement action may have a chilling effect on speech.

As trademark law has developed in recent decades, particularly online, the rights of trademark owners have become more expansive, arguably at the expense of free expression.[27] Courts and commentators are now obliged to pay more attention to the need to protect free speech in the face of increasingly powerful trademark interests. To fully appreciate the ways in which free speech has played into trademark law in recent decades, it is necessary briefly to review the basic trademark-related actions: that is, the actions for infringement and dilution. It is important to understand how courts have historically attempted to balance free speech with trademark interests in the context of these more longstanding trademark rights before considering how the balance should play out online, specifically under newer regulations like the ACPA and the Uniform Domain Name Dispute Resolution Policy (UDRP).

Trademark *infringement* has generally been premised on two interconnected aims. The first is to protect the public when purchasing a product or service to ensure that the purchasers get what they think they are paying for in terms of goods or services from a particular source.[28] The second aim of trademark law is to ensure that those who invest in developing goodwill in a particular mark are protected against unfair misappropriations of that goodwill.[29] In the United States, the Lanham Act contains two trademark infringement provisions, dealing with infringement of registered and unregistered trademark rights respectively.[30] Each provision is

---

[26] *Id.*

[27] Denicola, *supra* note 7, at 166; Lemley, *supra* note 14, at 1710–11 ('As trademarks are transformed from rights against unfair competition to rights to control language, our ability to discuss, portray, comment, criticize, and make fun of companies and their products is diminishing'); Greg Lastowka, *Google's Law*, 73 Brooklyn L. Rev. 1327, 1369–71 (2008) (providing a recent critique of the doctrine of initial interest confusion which extends the reach of trademark infringement online).

[28] Graeme B. Dinwoodie and Mark D. Janis, Trademarks and Unfair Competition 16–17 (2004) (citing S. Rep. No. 1333, 79th Cong., 2d Sess. 3 (1946)); Dogan and Lemley, *supra* note 14, at 786 (noting the benefits to both consumers and producers of consumers having access to 'truthful information about the source of products and services').

[29] *Id.*

[30] 15 U.S.C. §§ 1114(a) (infringement of registered trademarks), 1125(a)(1) (infringement of unregistered trademarks).

premised on the idea of an unauthorized use in commerce of a mark in a manner that is likely to cause consumer confusion.

Over time, American courts have developed varying iterations of a likelihood-of-confusion test as part of the inquiry into whether a trademark has been infringed. As Professors Dinwoodie and Janis have noted, even though the tests between the different circuit courts vary, they all fit the same general pattern.[31] They all include factors such as (a) the alleged infringer's intent; (b) actual confusion; and (c) a variety of factors that can be referred to as market factors, such as the relationship between the goods and services in question and the relationship between respective trade channels.[32]

The infringement action may be contrasted with the dilution action which does not require a likelihood of confusion analysis. Dilution has become an expansive notion because it recognizes damage to a trademark holder irrespective of the existence or likelihood of consumer confusion.[33] The dilution action has been criticized for potentially eroding the traditional foundations of trademark law, historically premised on preventing consumer confusion as to the source of goods or services. The American federal dilution statute specifically provides that a likelihood of consumer confusion is not necessary for a dilution action.[34]

The federal dilution provisions in the United States recognize two different kinds of dilution: dilution by blurring and dilution by tarnishment.[35] Blurring relates to an 'association arising from the similarity between a mark or trade name and a famous mark that impairs the distinctiveness of the famous mark'.[36] Tarnishment relates to an 'association arising from the similarity between a mark or trade name and a famous mark that harms the reputation of the famous mark'.[37] Dilution actions are

---

31 Dinwoodie and Janis, *supra* note 28, at 469.

32 *Id.*

33 *Id.* at 563–6.

34 15 U.S.C. § 1125(c)(1) ('Subject to the principles of equity, the owner of a famous mark that is distinctive, inherently or through acquired distinctiveness, shall be entitled to an injunction against another person who, at any time after the owner's mark has become famous, commences use of a mark or trade name in commerce that is likely to cause dilution by blurring or dilution by tarnishment of the famous mark, *regardless of the presence or absence of actual or likely confusion*, of competition, or of actual economic injury.') (emphasis added).

35 15 U.S.C. §§ 1125(c)(2)(B) (dilution by blurring), 1125(c)(2)(C) (dilution by tarnishment).

36 15 U.S.C. § 1125(c)(2)(B).

37 15 U.S.C. § 1125(c)(2)(C).

only available for famous marks.[38] Prior to 2006, it was relatively easy for a plaintiff to establish the requisite degree of fame of a mark under the common law.[39] However, revisions to the Lanham Act in 2006, under the Trademark Dilution Revision Act, incorporated a new statutory definition of famous mark for the purposes of a dilution action.[40] The statute now provides that a mark is famous if:

> it is widely recognized by the general consuming public of the United States as a designation of source of the goods or services of the mark's owner. In determining whether a mark possesses the requisite degree of recognition, the court may consider all relevant factors, including the following:
> (i) The duration, extent, and geographic reach of advertising and publicity of the mark, whether advertised or publicized by the owner or third parties.
> (ii) The amount, volume, and geographic extent of sales of goods or services offered under the mark.
> (iii) The extent of actual recognition of the mark. . .[41]

It remains to be seen how courts will interpret the degree of fame required in order to support a dilution action in the future. Prior to 2006, the Congressional intent behind dilution was to restrict the action to a 'relatively small class of nationally known trademarks whose fame is sufficiently great that the risk of blurring by multiple noncompeting uses is significant'.[42] Presumably the 2006 revisions are intended to return dilution policy to focus on cases involving marks of this stature in light of the fact that the common law test for fame was too readily extended beyond the original intention. Prior to 2006, courts had been prepared to extend protection to local marks even if somewhat obscure,[43] and to noncompeting, nonidentical marks.[44] Some courts were also prepared to find dilution without engaging in a fame inquiry at all.[45]

The easier it is for plaintiffs to establish dilution, the higher the threat for free speech. This is because, in the absence of a consumer confusion requirement, a broadly applied dilution law is likely to catch uses of a trademark that are expressive if they affect the selling power of the mark,

---

38 15 U.S.C. §§ 1125(c)(1), 1125(c)(2)(A).

39 Lemley, *supra* note 14, at 1698–9 (noting the ease with which courts have been prepared to find marks to be sufficiently famous for the purposes of the dilution statute).

40 15 U.S.C. § 1125(c)(2)(A).

41 *Id.*

42 Lemley, *supra* note 14, at 1698.

43 *Id.*

44 *Id.* at 1699.

45 *Id.* at 1698–9.

regardless of whether consumers are confused by the use. Like the infringement action, the dilution action contains an 'in commerce' requirement.[46] However, this has been relatively easy for plaintiffs to satisfy online. Some courts have gone as far as suggesting that any use of a trademark on the Internet could be commercial because the Internet itself is a commercial medium.[47]

One interesting new development in the 2006 revisions to the dilution statute was the expansion of available statutory defenses to dilution. The defenses expressly recognized in the Lanham Act now include:

> (A) Any fair use, including a nominative or descriptive fair use, or facilitation of such fair use, of a famous mark by another person other than as a designation of source for the person's own goods or services, including use in connection with:
> (i) advertising or promotion that permits consumers to compare goods or services; or
> (ii) identifying and parodying, criticizing, or commenting upon the famous mark owner or the goods or services of the famous mark owner.
>
> (B) All forms of news reporting and news commentary.
> (C) Any noncommercial use of a mark.[48]

This goes some way towards protecting free speech. It clearly aims to protect speech in the context of comparative advertising; parody, criticism and comment in relation to the mark or the trademark holder, news reporting and non-commercial use. This should theoretically codify the position at common law. As noted above, theoretically, trademark law should not impinge on the First Amendment at all, as it is only intended to protect the ability of marks to serve as effective source identifiers in relation to goods and services. However, as the reach of trademark law has been expanded by courts in practice, particularly in the dilution context, Congress has had to step in to confine trademark law to more appropriate boundaries, particularly in relation to balancing trademark holders' rights against the free speech rights of others.

3.3.2 Trademark Infringement and Free Speech

In the trademark infringement context, three approaches have developed that balance rights to free expression against the proprietary interests

---

[46] 15 U.S.C. § 1125(c)(1).

[47] See, for example, discussion in *Planned Parenthood Federation of America Inc. v Bucci*, 42 U.S.P.Q.2d 1430 (S.D.N.Y. 1997).

[48] 15 U.S.C. § 1125(c)(3).

of trademark holders. The application of these approaches has varied from case to case, and to some extent, from circuit to circuit. They have largely developed in cases involving parodies of a trademark. The three approaches may be described as (a) adding a parody factor to the traditional common-law multifactor likelihood-of-confusion test;[49] (b) requiring a stricter showing of all of the likelihood-of-confusion factors when the use of the mark is part of a political, social or artistic message;[50] and (c) applying the traditional test for trademark infringement and then conducting a separate balancing of free speech rights with the trademark holder's rights.[51]

It has also been suggested by some commentators that courts appear to have acknowledged a distinct parody defense to trademark infringement. However, this view is not universally accepted.[52] It is possible that what has been described as the 'parody defense' is in reality a judicial conclusion that there is no likelihood of confusion in the given case.[53] Free speech has also been accommodated to some extent by the fair use defense to trademark infringement.[54] This is particularly apparent in the nominative use subcategory of the fair use defense recognized by some courts.[55] The Lanham Act permits unauthorized use of another's mark as a fair use when the mark is used only in a descriptive sense and in good faith.[56] The nominative use test has typically been judicially applied as follows:

---

49 GILSON, *supra* note 24, para. 5.05[10][b].

50 *Id.*

51 *Id.*

52 *Id.* at para. 5.05[10][a] ('Is parody a sufficient excuse, or even an affirmative defense to a charge of trademark infringement? The better view is that parody is not an affirmative defense in a trademark case, but that the humorous intent and any free speech rights of the parodists must be factored into the court's analysis'.).

53 See DINWOODIE and JANIS, *supra* note 28, at 750.

54 15 U.S.C. § 1115(b)(4).

55 GILSON, *supra* note 24, para. 11.08[3][d] ('Some courts recognize a judge-made variation on the statutory fair use doctrine, calling it "nominative fair use" and allowing the use of another's trademark under certain limited circumstances. In these cases, a defendant uses a trademark that refers to another party's product, such as a television station using the mark BOSTON MARATHON in connection with its broadcast of the marathon'); *New Kids On The Block v News Am. Publ'g, Inc.*, 971 F.2d 302, 308 (9th Cir. 1992).

56 15 U.S.C. § 1115(b)(4) ('The use of the name, term, or device charged to be an infringement is a use, otherwise than as a mark, of the party's individual name in his own business, or of the individual name of anyone in privity with such party, or of a term or device which is descriptive of and used fairly and in good faith only to describe the goods or services of such party, or their geographic origin'.).

> First, the product or service in question must be one not readily identifiable without use of the trademark; second, only so much of the mark or marks may be used as is reasonably necessary to identify the product or service; and third, the user must do nothing that would, in conjunction with the mark, suggest sponsorship or endorsement by the trademark holder.[57]

The nominative use test protects uses of a mark when the potential defendant has no other realistic option for referring to the mark. This is often the case with trademarks associated with famous people,[58] popular music groups[59] and sports teams.[60] The district court explained in litigation between Playboy Enterprises and the 1981 Playmate of the Year, Terri Welles, over alleged trademark infringement of the 'Playmate of the Year 1981' mark on Ms Welles' website:

> [T]here is no other way that Ms Welles can identify or describe herself and her services without venturing into absurd descriptive phrases. To describe herself as the nude model selected by Mr Heffner's magazine as its number-one prototypical woman for the year 1981 would be impractical as well as ineffectual in identifying Terri Welles to the public.[61]

Obviously, nominative use protects certain informational uses of a mark, largely in connection with the sale of other goods or services in good faith. It therefore has limited relevance to questions about the protection of purely expressive uses of a mark in contexts such as criticism, commentary or parody, although some of the other approaches to balancing free speech with trademark interests, described above, may apply in these cases. Of course, even in nominative use cases, the trademark is being used in an expressive sense, albeit generally with an underlying commercial purpose on the part of the user.

---

[57] *New Kids On The Block v News Am. Publ'g, Inc.*, 971 F.2d 302, 308 (9th Cir. 1992).

[58] *Playboy v Terri Welles*, 279 F.3d 796 (2002).

[59] *New Kids On The Block v News Am. Publ'g, Inc.*, 971 F.2d 302, 308 (9th Cir. 1992).

[60] *Playboy v Terri Welles*, 279 F.3d 796, 802 (2002) ('In *New Kids*, we gave the example of the trademarked term, "Chicago Bulls". We explained that "one might refer to the 'two-time world champions' or 'the professional basketball team from Chicago' but it's far simpler (and more likely to be understood) to refer to the Chicago Bulls."').

[61] *Id.* at 802.

3.3.3 Trademark Dilution and Free Speech

Speech may be protected in the face of a dilution action in a number of contexts. These are now largely codified in the Lanham Act as a result of the 2006 revisions to the statute.[62] A mark has to be sufficiently famous to support a dilution action.[63] Although originally not a significant hurdle for plaintiffs,[64] the famousness requirement may be more difficult for plaintiffs to satisfy in the wake of the 2006 revisions to the federal dilution statute.[65] Purely noncommercial uses of a mark will not support a dilution action, both because of the 'in commerce' requirement of the action,[66] and because noncommercial use is an express defense to a dilution action.[67] Other defenses to a dilution action relevant to free speech are the news reporting defense[68] and the extended statutory fair use defense, which includes using a mark for purposes of 'identifying and parodying, criticizing, or commenting upon the famous mark owner or the goods or services of the famous mark owner'.[69] Prior to the 2006 revisions to the Lanham Act, it was not so clear that activities such as parody, criticism or comment would be regarded as non-dilutive of a mark, or would be excused under dilution law. The 2006 express fair use defense now makes these cases much easier. This is particularly important in the domain name context, as many domain name disputes have involved uses of trademarks in the domain space in the context of a gripe site or parody site about the trademark holder.[70]

---

62 See discussion at 3.3.1, *supra*.

63 15 U.S.C. § 1125(c)(1), (2)(A).

64 Lemley, *supra* note 14, at 1698–9 (noting the ease with which courts have been prepared to find marks to be sufficiently famous for the purposes of the dilution statute).

65 15 U.S.C. § 1125(c)(2)(A).

66 15 U.S.C. § 1125(c)(1).

67 15 U.S.C. § 1125(c)(3)(C).

68 15 U.S.C. § 1125(c)(3)(B).

69 15 U.S.C. § 1125(c)(3)(A)(ii).

70 For example, in *People for the Ethical Treatment of Animals v Doughney,* 113 F.Supp.2d 915, 920 (E.D. Va. 2000), *aff'd* 263 F.3d 359 (4th Cir. 2001), the District Court for the Eastern District of Virginia held that the defendant's parody site utilizing the plaintiff's PETA mark in its domain name (peta.org) satisfied the commercial use requirement of dilution law because the website included links to commercial enterprises engaged in conduct that was contrary to the plaintiff's animal protection efforts. In contrast, in *TMI, Inc. v Maxwell,* 368 F.3d 433, 436 (5th Cir. 2004), the Fifth Circuit Court of Appeals held that a gripe site utilizing the plaintiff's trademark in its domain name was not a commercial use of the mark and did not fall within the ambit of anti-dilution law; *Bosley v Kremer*, 403 F.3d 672 (2005).

3.3.4 Trademarks, Titles and Free Speech

One aspect of traditional trademark law that deserves particular attention involves the use of marks in book, song and movie titles. Cases involving titles may have particular relevance for a discussion of trademarks and free speech in the domain space. Domain names operate much like titles in that they serve as descriptive labels for an underlying work. In the case of the book, song and movie titles, the associated work is the book, song or movie. In the case of domain names, the associated work is the web page associated with the domain name.

Generally speaking, courts in the United States have been prepared to protect expressive uses of trademarks in the context of book, song and movie titles provided that consumers are not misled by the use of the mark, and that the title is relevant to the associated work.[71] Prime examples include the 'Barbie Girl' song where Mattel's 'Barbie' trademark was used expressively in a song title.[72] Another relatively well known example involves a movie entitled 'Ginger and Fred'.[73] Here, Ginger Rogers' trademarked name was used in the title of a film about a cabaret act that impersonated the famous dancers, Fred Astaire and Ginger Rogers.[74] Courts likely extend particular deference to book, song and movie titles in trademark cases because of consumers' expectations about the function of a title in identifying and describing an underlying work.

---

[71] *Mattel v MCA Records*, 296 F.3d 894, 902 (9th Cir. 2002) ('A title is designed to catch the eye and to promote the value of the underlying work. Consumers expect a title to communicate a message about the book or movie, but they do not expect it to identify the publisher or producer.'); *Rogers v Grimaldi,* 875 F.2d at 994, 1001 (2d Cir. 1989) (noting that at most some members of the public might draw an incorrect inference that Ginger Rogers was somehow involved with a film entitled Ginger and Fred, but that risk is so outweighed by interests in artistic expression as to preclude trademark infringement); *Mattel,* 296 F.3d at 901 ('We expect a title to describe the underlying work, not to identify the producer, and Barbie Girl [the song] does just that.'); *Rogers*, 875 F.2d at 1001 (noting that the film title Ginger and Fred is 'entirely truthful as to its content in referring to the film's fictional protagonists who are known to their Italian audience as "Ginger and Fred"').

[72] *Mattel, Inc. v MCA Records, Inc.,* 296 F.3d 894 (9th Cir. 2002). In this case, Mattel failed to obtain an injunction against the producers of a popular song entitled 'Barbie Girl' and relating to the 'Barbie Girl' image in society.

[73] *Rogers v Grimaldi,* 875 F.2d 994 (2d Cir. 1989). In this case, the movie star Ginger Rogers failed to obtain an injunction against the use of the Ginger and Fred movie title in the context of a film about two Italian cabaret performers who made a living imitating Ginger Rogers and Fred Astaire.

[74] *Id.*

This approach might guide the development of a framework for balancing free speech interests against trademark interests in domain names. The deference that courts have given to titles should not, of course, be overstated. There is no clear test for the protection of titles that could create certainty as to whether a particular title does or does not infringe a mark. As with other trademark cases, courts have developed a series of guidelines to help address the issue of trademark infringement in the title context: for example, some courts have been less likely to find infringement in the case of a mark utilized in a title where the use parodies the owner of the mark, rather than a different topic.[75] Thus, the 'Barbie Girl' song title is protected because the underlying song makes fun of ideas clearly related to the 'Barbie' image in society.[76] The song contains lyrics such as:

> I'm a Barbie girl in the Barbie world
> Life in plastic, it's fantastic
> You can brush my hair, undress me everywhere
> Imagination, life is your creation[77]

and

> I'm a blonde single girl in the fantasy world
> Dress me up, take your time, I'm your dollie
> You're my doll, rock and roll, feel the glamour and pain
> Kiss me here, touch me there, hanky-panky.[78]

The song's aim is not to infringe or dilute Mattel's trademark, but to comment on the cultural values that are embodied in the concept of a 'Barbie'-like existence. On the other hand, the use of marks relating to Dr Seuss books, including the title *The Cat in the Hat*, was found to be a trademark infringement where the use of the marks had no relevance to the associated product at all. The marks in this case were used in a completely unrelated commentary on the O.J. Simpson trial. The court concluded that the marks were used as a commercial draw for no apparent purpose other than attracting consumers who might not otherwise have noticed the defendant's work.[79] In this case, a distinction was drawn by the court between making fun of a trademark holder with an unauthor-

---

[75] GILSON, *supra* note 24, para. 5.05[10][b].

[76] *Mattel,* 296 F.3d at 901.

[77] Aqua, *Barbie Girl* (1997), full text available at www.anysonglyrics.com/lyrics/a/aqua/barbie-girl.htm, last accessed July 4, 2009.

[78] *Id.*

[79] *Dr Seuss Enter. v Penguin Books USA, Inc.*, 109 F.3d 1394 (9th Cir. 1997).

ized use of its mark, and making fun of something else trading unfairly on the trademark holder's property rights.[80] With respect to the trademark infringement action, the court tied its reasoning back to the idea of the likelihood of consumer confusion:

> The cry of 'parody!' does not magically fend off otherwise legitimate claims of trademark infringement or dilution. There are confusing parodies and non-confusing parodies. All they have in common is an attempt at humor through the use of someone else's trademark. A non-infringing parody is merely amusing, not confusing.[81]

This case again illustrates how important the notion of consumer confusion has been in the trademark infringement context in ensuring that expressive uses of a trademark are given some degree of leeway by courts. Of course, in the Dr Seuss case, the expressive use was not protected, but it was because the court effectively found the use to be a form of deceptive trade practice. Opinions may vary on whether this kind of expressive use should be protected in the balance between free speech and trademark law. However, the case does exemplify ways in which courts have used the consumer confusion doctrine as a test for free speech protection in the United States.

Perhaps the solution for protecting free speech in the trademark context, both online and offline, should substantially revolve around consumer confusion. Courts are familiar with this test in cases involving expressive uses of trademarks. Most expressive uses of a mark are likely not to be confusing consumers about the origins of goods and services. Thus, like the question as to whether there is a parody defense to trademark infringement, the question of infringing song, movie and book titles really boils down to the fundamental trademark inquiry as to whether consumers would likely be confused by a particular use of a mark. There may be a developing judicial presumption against consumer confusion in title cases, and this may usefully be translated to the domain name context. Relevant cases may include situations where the use of a particular domain name is unlikely to cause confusion because it serves mainly an identifying and descriptive function in relation to the underlying webpage and does not confuse consumers as to the source of particular goods or services. This would presumably cover most gripe site and parody site cases, even those using a trademark or a variation of a mark within the domain name.

Of course, the development of such an approach still leaves an open

---

80 *Id.* at 1405–6.

81 *Id.* at 1405.

question about trademark dilution, where consumer confusion is not the touchstone of the action. In the 'Barbie Girl' litigation, a claim for trademark dilution against the distributors of the 'Barbie Girl' song failed on the basis that the reference to the Barbie doll in the song and its title fell within the noncommercial use exception to a dilution action.[82] The court considered the legislative history of the dilution statute in identifying the relevant congressional intent. With respect to the pre-2006 dilution statute, the court found that the noncommercial use exception was included in the legislation to ensure the preservation of First Amendment interests with respect to noncommercial expression.[83] Although the defendant's speech in the 'Barbie Girl' song and song title was commercial in that it was part of a commercially released recording, the court held that it was not purely commercial and so could fall within the noncommercial use exemption to trademark dilution.[84]

In so holding, Judge Kozinski noted:

> although the boundary between commercial and noncommercial speech has yet to be clearly delineated, the 'core notion of commercial speech' is that it 'does no more than propose a commercial transaction' . . . If speech is not 'purely commercial' – that is, if it does more than propose a commercial transaction – then it is entitled to full First Amendment protection.[85]

The judge also suggested that the 'Barbie Girl' song was not purely commercial speech because it also 'lampoons the Barbie image and comments humorously on the cultural values Aqua [the pop band] claims she represents'.[86]

Whether or not this is precisely what Congress intended in its definition of noncommercial speech, it seems intuitively to be a good line to draw for the purposes of this discussion. If there is a judicial presumption, or at least a judicial leaning, against trademark dilution in cases where the unauthorized use of a mark is for purposes of identifying and describing

---

82 *Mattel,* 296 F.3d at 894. This was the non-commercial use exception in the pre-2006 statute, which is reproduced in the 2006 statute along with the extended fair use defense: 15 U.S.C. § 1125(c)(3).

83 *Id.* at 905–7. See also GILSON, *supra* note 24, at para. 5A.01[9][b] ('The most important exception to Dilution Act liability is for the "noncommercial use of a mark". This exception makes clear that the Act is intended to prevent the courts from enjoining speech that has been recognized to be constitutionally protected.').

84 *Mattel,* 296 F.3d at 906.

85 *Id.* (quoting *Hoffman v Capital Cities/ABC, Inc.,* 255 F.3d 1180 (9th Cir. 2001), quoting *Bolger v Youngs Drug Prods. Corp.,* 463 U.S. 60 (1983)).

86 *Id.* at 907.

an underlying work that does not compete commercially with the trademark holder's products or services, this may be very useful in the domain name context. Where a domain name is used to identify the contents of an associated website that is a parody or criticism of a trademark holder, the same reasoning should ring true. This is because domain names, like movie and song titles, clearly can, and often do, serve identifying and descriptive functions with respect to their associated websites.

The question is whether it is necessary to perform a detailed likelihood-of-confusion or dilution analysis in such cases, or whether we can begin to acknowledge an *ex ante* presumption that such uses are noncommercial (for dilution purposes) and will not confuse consumers (for infringement purposes). This may create a workable balance between trademark law and free speech interests, and the presumption may cut against a discernable judicial trend to extend trademark rights in a way that might chill expression on the Internet.[87] However, before adopting this approach it is necessary to identify ways in which courts have been approaching this problem in the domain name context so far. We also need to consider the impact of more recent domain name regulations on these problems, such as the provisions of the ACPA and the UDRP.

3.4 FREE SPEECH IN THE DOMAIN SPACE

3.4.1 Free Speech and the Anti-Cybersquatting Consumer Protection Act

Chapter 1 set out the options available for trademark holders concerned about unauthorized uses of domain names corresponding with their marks. These options include traditional trademark infringement and dilution actions. Trademark holders can also resort to the provisions of the ACPA and the UDRP. Both of these measures are focused predominantly on the prevention of cybersquatting: that is, the registration of domain names

---

[87] See, for example, concerns that the doctrine of initial interest confusion is unnecessarily expanding the reach of trademark infringement actions online: *Playboy v Netscape*, 354 F.3d 1020, 1035 (2004) ('I do not think it is reasonable to find initial interest confusion when a consumer is never confused as to source or affiliation, but instead knows, or should know, from the outset that a product or web link is not related to that of the trademark holder because the list produced by the search engine so informs him. There is a big difference between hijacking a customer to another website by making the customer think he or she is visiting the trademark holder's website (even if only briefly), which is what may be happening in this case when the banner advertisements are not labeled, and just distracting a potential customer with another *choice*, when it is clear that it is a choice.')

that match well-known trademarks with the intention of profiting from selling the names.[88] This practice became prevalent in the early days of the World Wide Web when many corporations with well-known marks had not yet realized the importance of registering domain names corresponding with their marks.[89] One of the most famous cybersquatters was Dennis Toeppen, who registered over a hundred domain names corresponding with well-known marks with the intention of profiting from selling them.[90] Traditional cybersquatters were generally regarded as acting in bad faith in a moral, and ultimately also a legal, sense, largely as there was arguably no socially useful justification for their activities.[91]

Aggrieved trademark holders either negotiated with cybersquatters for transfer of the domain names, or resorted to litigation under existing trademark law – infringement and dilution actions. Courts were generally sympathetic to trademark holders, finding infringement or dilution even in cases where there was no obvious consumer confusion or commercial use.[92] In *Panavision International v Toeppen*,[93] for example, the Ninth Circuit Court of Appeals found trademark law's in commerce requirement to be satisfied for dilution purposes on the basis that the defendant cybersquatter's business was registering domain names corresponding with well-known trademarks and selling them to rightful trademark owners.[94]

In *Planned Parenthood v Bucci*,[95] the court identified two ways in which the in commerce requirement for trademark infringement and dilution was

---

88 Nilsen, *supra* note 2, at 51.

89 Jacqueline Lipton, *Beyond Cybersquatting: Taking Domain Name Disputes Past Trademark Policy*, 40 Wake Forest L. Rev. 1361, 1370–1 (2005).

90 *Id.* at 1370.

91 *Id.* at 1387–92 (describing the development of the idea that cybersquatting was an immoral commercial practice and extending traditional trademark actions to combat this practice based on notions of bad faith).

92 *Panavision Int'l v Toeppen,* 141 F.3d 1316 (9th Cir. 1998) (finding trademark dilution where the defendant had registered domain names corresponding with famous marks owned by the plaintiff and had put material unrelated to the plaintiff's marks or business on the relevant website); *Planned Parenthood Federation of America Inc. v Bucci,* 42 U.S.P.Q.2d 1430 (S.D.N.Y. 1997) (finding trademark infringement and dilution to be made out where defendant registered domain name corresponding with plaintiff's trademark for purposes of a website critical of plaintiff's point of view).

93 141 F.3d 1316 (9th Cir. 1998).

94 *Id.* at 1325 ('Toeppen's "business" is to register trademarks as domain names and then sell them to the rightful trademark owners . . . This is a commercial use.').

95 42 U.S.P.Q.2d 1430 (S.D.N.Y. 1997).

satisfied. First, the cybersquatter's actions affected the plaintiff's ability to offer its services over the Internet.[96] Secondly, Internet users constitute a national, if not international, audience who must use interstate telephone lines to access the Internet, and the nature of the Internet itself satisfies the in commerce requirement.[97] The *Planned Parenthood* court further held that there was a likelihood of consumer confusion because the defendant was offering informational services about abortion and birth control.[98] Additionally, the court took the view that a disclaimer on the defendant's website distinguishing itself from the plaintiff's services would not sufficiently cure the confusion.[99]

Planned Parenthood was technically not a classic cybersquatting case because the defendant in question was utilizing the Planned Parenthood mark in its domain name for a website promulgating a point of view opposed to the Planned Parenthood Organization on abortion and birth control.[100] In many ways, that case is more akin to the situations under consideration later in this chapter – gripe sites and parody sites. The defendant in *Planned Parenthood* was not seeking to extort money from the plaintiff for transfer of the domain name. Rather, he sought to retain and use the domain name to promulgate his own views online, and to attract an audience that might otherwise be seeking Planned Parenthood's official website.

As noted in Chapter 1, Congress enacted the ACPA predominantly to combat concerns about traditional cybersquatting, such as the online conduct of Dennis Toeppen.[101] The ACPA creates a civil action against a person who traffics in or uses a domain name corresponding with a trademark with a bad faith intent to profit from the mark.[102] The statute sets out a nonexclusive list of factors that courts may consider when ascertaining whether relevant conduct is in bad faith. These factors include:

---

96 *Id.* at 1434.

97 *Id.*

98 *Id.* at 1437–8.

99 *Id.* at 1441 ('Due to the nature of Internet use, defendant's appropriation of plaintiff's mark as a domain name and home page address cannot adequately be remedied by a disclaimer. Defendant's domain name and home page address are external labels that, on their face, cause confusion among Internet users and may cause Internet users who seek plaintiff's website to expend time and energy accessing defendant's website . . . [A] disclaimer on the defendant's home page would not be sufficient to dispel the confusion induced by his home page address and domain name.').

100 Lipton, *Beyond Cybersquatting, supra* note 89, at 1393.

101 See 1.1, *supra*.

102 15 U.S.C. § 1125(d).

(a) the trademark or other intellectual property rights of the registrant in the domain name;[103]
(b) the extent to which the domain name consists of the legal name of the registrant or a name that is otherwise commonly used to identify that person;[104]
(c) the registrant's prior use of the domain name in connection with a bona fide offering of goods or services;[105]
(d) the registrant's bona fide noncommercial or fair use of the mark in a site accessible under the domain name;[106]
(e) the registrant's intent to divert customers from the trademark holder's online location in a manner likely to cause consumer confusion or trademark dilution;[107]
(f) the registrant's offer to transfer the domain name to the trademark holder or a third party for financial gain without having used or intending to use the domain name for a bona fide offering of goods or services;[108]
(g) the registrant's provision of misleading false contact information when registering the domain name, the person's failure to maintain accurate contact information, or the person's prior conduct indicating a pattern of such conduct;[109]
(h) the person's registration or acquisition of multiple domain names which the person knows are identical or confusingly similar to marks of others, or dilutive of famous marks of others;[110] and
(i) the extent to which the mark incorporated in the registrant's domain name is distinctive for the purposes of the dilution provisions of the trademark legislation.[111]

The statute also sets out a good faith defense to an ACPA action that may apply in situations where the domain name registrant believed and had reasonable grounds to believe that the use of the domain name was a fair use or otherwise lawful.[112] While this defense makes no specific mention of free speech, it might have been the legislative intent that free speech

103 15 U.S.C. § 1125(d)(1)(B)(i)(I).
104 15 U.S.C. § 1125(d)(1)(B)(i)(II).
105 15 U.S.C. § 1125(d)(1)(B)(i)(III).
106 15 U.S.C. § 1125(d)(1)(B)(i)(IV).
107 15 U.S.C. § 1125(d)(1)(B)(i)(V).
108 15 U.S.C. § 1125(d)(1)(B)(i)(VI).
109 15 U.S.C. § 1125(d)(1)(B)(i)(VII).
110 15 U.S.C. § 1125(d)(1)(B)(i)(VIII).
111 15 U.S.C. § 1125(d)(1)(B)(i)(IX).
112 15 U.S.C. § 1125(d)(1)(B)(ii).

would be encompassed in the notion of a domain name use being a fair use or otherwise lawful. However, it would have been useful if Congress had expressly acknowledged this point, much as it did in the context of the new defenses to a dilution action, where 'fair use' now expressly incorporates uses such as parody, commentary and criticism.[113]

Interpretation of the ACPA has raised some practical difficulties in the context of domain name disputes involving free speech. For example, the notion of a bad faith intent to profit, which is central to an ACPA claim, has caused some problems of interpretation in cases involving gripe sites and parody sites.[114] Further, the bad faith factors have not proved to be very helpful in cases that do not fit the traditional cybersquatting paradigm. Consider a situation in which a person has registered multiple iterations of a domain name containing a trademark for the purposes of criticizing or lampooning the trademark holder.[115] Is this the kind of multiple registration that the ACPA contemplates as one of the bad faith factors?[116] It would seem that the ACPA's notion of multiple registrations should relate to registering multiple domain names corresponding to multiple marks, rather than corresponding to just the one mark, if the legislation is aimed at Toeppen-style cybersquatting.[117]

One might also query whether this factor should have been included in the legislation at all. Clearly, it was included to combat conduct such as

---

[113] See discussion at 3.3.1 and 3.3.3, *supra*.

[114] Jacqueline Lipton, *Commerce versus Commentary: Gripe Sites, Parody, and the First Amendment in Cyberspace*, 84 WASHINGTON UNIVERSITY L. REV. 1327, 1349 (2006) ('the [ACPA] attaches liability for a bad-faith intent even after the registrant has registered the relevant domain name. In other words, there is a temporal problem with the statute in that it does not require the bad faith intent to exist at the time of the domain name registration. This . . . means that any subsequent attempt to sell the name for profit that could in some way be described as bad faith could run afoul of the ACPA. This might include an offer to sell the name to a complainant after a dispute has arisen, thus bolstering the complainant's grounds for an ACPA claim.'); *People for the Ethical Treatment of Animals v Doughney*, 113 F.Supp.2d 915, 920–21 (E.D. Va. 2000), *aff'd* 263 F.3d 359 (4th Cir. 2001) (finding defendant had requisite bad faith intent to profit from a transfer of a domain name corresponding with a plaintiff's mark in a parody website context on the basis of a comment by the defendant that the plaintiff could 'make him an offer' for the name after the action had been brought against him).

[115] See, for example, *Bosley v Kremer*, 403 F.3d 672 (9th Cir. 2005) (defendant registered two domain names corresponding with plaintiff's marks for the purposes of a gripe site about the plaintiff's business).

[116] 15 U.S.C. § 1125(d)(1)(B)(i)(VIII).

[117] Lipton, *Beyond Cybersquatting*, *supra* note 89, at 1370 (summary of Toeppen's conduct).

Toeppen's in the early days of the domain name system. In other words, the aim was to catch people who registered multiple domain names corresponding with multiple marks where the registrant's intent was to extort money from trademark holders for transfer of the names.[118] However, this factor may be needlessly confusing in current practice. Is it really relevant to a cybersquatting claim that the defendant has registered multiple domain names, even if they correspond to multiple well-known trademarks? Arguably, this factor does not tell the court very much about the defendant's conduct with respect to the plaintiff's mark in particular.

A traditional cybersquatter who registers names with the sole intent to profit from transferring them might have registered (a) multiple domain names corresponding with multiple marks; (b) multiple domain names corresponding with one mark; or (c) one domain name corresponding with a mark. In the case of registering multiple domain names corresponding with multiple marks, the registrant may make legitimate use of some of the domain names, while holding the others hostage for profit from the rightful owners. She may, for example, run gripe sites or parody sites from some of the domain names, while using others to extort money from relevant trademark holders. She may, in fact, run gripe sites or parody sites from all of the domain names and let it be known that they are available for sale if a trademark holder wants them. Alternatively, she may run gripe sites or parody sites from all of the domain names and say nothing about sale, hoping that people will simply make her an offer. The fact of multiple registrations in and of itself does not necessarily tell the court very much to aid in a determination about the defendant's purposes in registering any particular domain.

Looking at other bad faith factors in the ACPA, there may also be difficulties of interpretation in ascertaining the nature of an offer to transfer the domain name to the trademark owner or a third party for financial gain.[119] Clearly the legislature had in mind schemes designed with the central aim of transferring names for profit.[120] It is not clear how courts should deal with situations where a registrant is prepared to transfer a domain name to the trademark holder, even though that was not the initial aim of the registration. Oftentimes, parties to an ACPA action will attempt to negotiate a settlement, and an offer by the defendant to transfer the name to the plaintiff will ensue in the course of settlement negotiations.

---

[118] See discussion in *Panavision v Toeppen*, 141 F.3d 1316 (9th Cir. 1998).

[119] 15 U.S.C. § 1125(d)(1)(B)(i)(VI).

[120] This is evident when one considers that the whole thrust of the ACPA is to prevent attempts to make unlawful profits from transfer of domain names in bad faith: 15 U.S.C. §1125(d)(1)(A).

There is currently no clear guidance as to when or whether such offers could trigger the bad faith provisions of the ACPA in subsequent litigation if a settlement is not reached beforehand.

Although judicial decisions have not focused so much on the bad faith factor relating to an offer to transfer the name, courts have been confused about the application of the related bad faith intent to profit aspect of the ACPA.[121] The statute attaches liability for a bad faith intent to profit even after the registrant has registered the relevant domain name.[122] In other words, there is a temporal problem with the legislation. The statute does not require the bad faith intent to exist at the time of domain name registration. This means that any subsequent attempt to sell the name for profit that could be described as bad faith could run afoul of the ACPA. This might include an offer to sell the name to a complainant after a dispute has arisen. Such a result could bolster the complainant's grounds for an ACPA claim. It could also potentially chill attempts to settle a dispute prior to adjudication for fear that any offer to negotiate a sale will be used later as evidence of a bad faith intent to profit from the domain name.

Most attempts to sell a domain name corresponding with a trademark could, in some way, be regarded as bad faith, at least from the trademark holder's point of view. This does not mean that the argument will always be successful, but it does mean that the narrow tailoring of the ACPA to combat Toeppen-style cybersquatting creates significant potential for confusion in application to nontraditional cases, including cases involving expressive uses of domain names.

Another problem with the bad faith intent to profit requirement can arise when the defendant has set up a gripe site or parody site on which

---

[121] See, for example, *People for the Ethical Treatment of Animals v Doughney*, 113 F.Supp.2d 915, 920–1 (E.D. Va. 2000), *aff'd* 263 F.3d 359 (4th Cir. 2001) (finding defendant had requisite bad faith intent to profit from a transfer of a domain name corresponding with a plaintiff's mark in a parody website context on the basis of a comment by the defendant that the plaintiff could 'make him an offer' for the name after the action had been brought against him); *Northland Insurance Co. v Blaylock*, 115 F.Supp.2d 1008, 1124 (D. Minn. 2000) (plaintiff argued that an inference could be made that defendant's intent in registering a domain name corresponding with its trademark for a gripe site was to use the domain name to extract money from the plaintiff in order to compensate the defendant for perceived losses from dealing with the plaintiff; the court said the argument had some merit but rejected it in preliminary proceedings because the record did not sufficiently reflect a bad faith intent to profit on the part of the defendant with respect to the domain name registration).

[122] See discussion in Ned Snow, *The Constitutional Failing of the Anticybersquatting Act*, 41 WILLAMETTE L. REV. 1, 41 (2005).

the defendant, or someone connected to the defendant, receives a financial benefit from advertising products or services that may or may not be related to the plaintiff's activities. This might include situations where the defendant is financing the website using a clickfarm,[123] or situations where the defendant simply refers to products or services that may in some way be related to the plaintiff's business.[124] In fact, a reference on the defendant's website to products or services that are in some way related to the plaintiff's activities might bolster the likelihood that the plaintiff will succeed on a trademark infringement claim.[125] If not, the possibility of an ACPA success still looms large.

Some confusion has also arisen as to whether ACPA claims require a showing of commercial use of the mark by a defendant, in the same way that may be required for an infringement or dilution action.[126] It is possible, for example, that the bad faith factor relating to 'bona fide noncommercial or fair use'[127] of a domain name by a registrant implies that a commercial use requirement may be a prerequisite for a successful ACPA action. Alternatively, it may imply a strong presumption of a need for a commercial use by the defendant in order to support an ACPA claim. At least one court appears to have suggested that the ACPA does have a commercial use requirement and that the requirement may be satisfied if the defendant's website potentially deters customers from the plaintiff's online

---

[123] Jacqueline Lipton, *Clickfarming: The New Cybersquatting?*, 12 J. INTERNET L. 1 (2008) ('[Clickfarming] may be defined as the use of a domain name corresponding to another person's trademark or personal name to gain advertising revenues through click-on advertisements').

[124] *Planned Parenthood Federation of America Inc. v Bucci*, 4 U.S.P.Q.2d 1430, 1433 (S.D.N.Y. 1997) (suggesting that plaintiff and defendant were effectively both competing in offering informational services on abortion and birth control, even though the defendant's site was more or less a pure commentary site with some references to commercial products – books and radio shows – that were not actually provided by the defendant).

[125] *People for the Ethical Treatment of Animals v Doughney*, 113 F.Supp.2d 915, 920 (E.D. Va. 2000), *aff'd* 263 F.3d 359 (4th Cir. 2001) (finding that the commercial use requirement of trademark infringement law was satisfied by the fact that the defendant's website linked to the websites of organizations selling fur and animal products and potentially deterred the plaintiff's customers from finding the plaintiff's website, even though the defendant's website was clearly a parody of the plaintiff, and the links to websites selling fur and animal products were antithetical to what the plaintiff stood for).

[126] *Bosley Med. Inst., Inc. v Kremer*, 403 F.3d 672, 681 (2005) (noting confusion in lower court about commercial use requirement for ACPA proceedings, and holding that there is no commercial use requirement for an ACPA action).

[127] 15 U.S.C. § 1125(d)(1)(B)(i)(IV).

location.[128] Not all courts subscribe to this approach. In *Bosley v Kremer*, for example, the Ninth Circuit Court of Appeals held that the ACPA does not contain a commercial use requirement.[129]

Even courts that have recognized a commercial use requirement in the ACPA have split on the question whether the defendant's use of the website to link to other websites where goods and services are available would satisfy the requirement. In *People for the Ethical Treatment of Animals v Doughney*,[130] the court accepted as relevant to the commercial use requirement the fact that the defendant's website linked to other sites where customers could purchase fur and animal products antithetical to the plaintiff's views.[131] However, in similar circumstances, the Fourth Circuit Court of Appeals in *Lamparello v Falwell*[132] held that the defendant's linking of his commentary website to an Amazon.com webpage selling a particular book would not support an ACPA claim because the link on his webpage 'does not diminish the communicative function of his website'.[133] The court also suggested that the commercial use requirement was not satisfied because the defendant 'did not even stand to gain financially from sales of the book at Amazon.com'.[134] This analysis appears reasonable, but it also directly contradicts the holding in *Doughney*.

The drafting and interpretation of the above-mentioned provisions of the ACPA have implications for the protection of free speech in cyberspace. Some judicial or legislative clarification may now be desirable on the kinds of situations that will not run afoul of the legislation where speech is implicated. Several courts have recognized the potential for speech to be chilled on the Internet as a result of overzealous application of the ACPA. In *Northland Insurance v Blaylock*,[135] the court noted:

> While the public interest clearly demands that the Internet be used responsibly and in conformance with intellectual property laws, the right of defendant to openly express his viewpoint should likewise not be curtailed absent clearer demonstration that the claims against him have merit . . . Public

---

128 *People for the Ethical Treatment of Animals v Doughney*, 113 F.Supp.2d 915, 920 (E.D. Va. 2000), *aff'd* 263 F.3d 359 (4th Cir. 2001).

129 403 F.3d 672, 680 (9th Cir. 2005).

130 113 F.Supp.2d 915, 919–20.

131 *Id.*

132 420 F.3d 309, 320 (4th Cir. 2005). This case involved a personal name as a trademark. Chapter 4 considers the extent to which personal names should be accepted as trademarks in the domain space.

133 *Id.*

134 *Id.*

135 115 F Supp.2d 1108 (D. Minn. 2000).

> policy requires that preliminary injunctions, especially those that stand to potentially chill a person's right to free speech, no matter how disagreeable that speech may be, should only be granted in the most extraordinary of circumstances.[136]

Nevertheless, a number of courts have not deferred to the expressive interests of gripe site and parody site operators whose Internet domain names correspond with well-known marks. Moreover, the cases in which courts have been prepared to enjoin uses of particular domain names in the parody or commentary context are often difficult to distinguish from the cases in which courts have not been prepared to grant relief. This becomes obvious when one compares the *Doughney* and *Falwell* cases. The distinctions that courts make often rely heavily on justifications relating to multiple domain name registrations by a defendant and post-registration intentions to sell domain names to rightful owners. These can both be problematic bad faith criteria, for reasons already discussed.

In *Falwell*, for example, the court was not prepared to enjoin the defendant's use of a domain name comprising a misspelling of the plaintiff's name (www.fallwell.com) for a website critical of the plaintiff's views on homosexuality. The *Falwell* court distinguished two similar cases[137] on the basis that the defendants in those cases had registered multiple domain names corresponding to marks held by various other people. The *Falwell* court further noted, by way of distinction, that in one of those cases, the defendant had made a comment in the course of the litigation that the plaintiff could 'make him an offer' for transfer of the name.[138] It is difficult to see how the multiple registrations of other domain names have any bearing on the use of the domain name corresponding to the plaintiff's mark where, in fact, the defendant is actually utilizing the name for a purely expressive purpose. These situations may be distinguished from classic Toeppen-style cybersquatting cases where the defendant is not using the domain name to communicate anything in particular.[139] Clearly, the registration of multiple domain names is contemplated as only one of the bad faith factors in the ACPA, and

---

[136] *Id.* at 1125.

[137] *Coca-Cola v Purdy*, 382 F.3d 774 (8th Cir. 2004) and *People for the Ethical Treatment of Animals v Doughney*, 113 F.Supp.2d 915 (E.D. Va. 2000), *aff'd* 263 F.3d 359 (4th Cir. 2001).

[138] *Falwell*, 420 F.3d at 321.

[139] Lipton, *Beyond Cybersquatting, supra* note 89, at 1388–9 (noting that Toeppen himself was not making particularly expressive uses of the domain names he had registered that corresponded with other people's trademarks).

courts can be swayed by the other factors despite multiple registrations of domain names. However, it seems that utilizing the bad faith factors from the ACPA can lead to results that are counterintuitive when they are applied to situations that are not on all fours with classic Toeppen-style cybersquatting.

One additional problem with the ACPA is that it is a national law that does not have many, if any, analogs in other jurisdictions. There are some American state laws that impact on cybersquatting and that implicate free speech to a greater or lesser degree depending on the circumstances.[140] Thus, in the global context of the Internet, one might add to the above uncertainties in application of the ACPA some jurisdictional concerns about when and whether the provisions of the ACPA will apply in a given case. Where a defendant is not in the United States and the domain name in question is not registered in the United States, an ACPA action may well not be available to a plaintiff.[141] This jurisdictional limitation may serve to protect free expression in cases where an out-of-jurisdiction defendant uses an American mark in a domain name to criticize or otherwise comment on the trademark holder. However, in cross-border situations, it will be necessary also to consider the potential reach of the UDRP in these kinds of cases.

3.4.2 Free Speech and the Uniform Domain Name Dispute Resolution Policy

The UDRP is a private dispute resolution system that is implemented under the domain name registration contract for generic Top Level Domains (gTLDs) such as '.com', '.org' and '.net'. When a person registers such a domain name, she becomes contractually bound to submit to a private arbitration if someone complains about registration of the name.[142] Like the ACPA, the UDRP's focus is on protecting trademark interests and preventing bad faith registrations and uses for nonlegitimate purposes.[143] The main motivator for the adoption of the UDRP by ICANN was to combat the practice of cybersquatting that had become prevalent in the mid-to late 1990s. The main advantages of the UDRP are that it is fast, inexpensive, effectively global in scope, and disputes are

---

140 See, for example, 1.6, *supra.*

141 15 U.S.C. § 1125(d)(2)(D) (*in rem* proceedings for domain name disputes where personal jurisdiction cannot be established; situs of domain name is place of registration).

142 UDRP, para. 4.

143 *Id.* para. 4(a), (b).

adjudicated remotely thereby limiting the need for in person appearances in domestic courts.[144]

To succeed in a UDRP arbitration, a complainant must establish that (a) a domain name is confusingly similar to a trademark in which the complainant has rights;[145] (b) the registrant has no legitimate interests in the domain name;[146] and (c) the domain name has been registered and is being used in bad faith.[147] The UDRP includes a list of bad faith factors much like those in the ACPA. The UDRP's bad-faith factors include circumstances indicating that (a) the registrant intended to transfer the domain name to the complainant or to a third party for a profit;[148] (b) the registrant transferred the name to prevent the holder of a trademark from reflecting the mark in a corresponding domain name, provided that the registrant has engaged in a pattern of such conduct;[149] (c) the registrant registered the name primarily for the purpose of disrupting the business of a competitor;[150] or (d) the registrant has used the name to attempt to attract Internet users to its own online location by creating confusion as to the sponsorship or affiliation of the registrant with the complainant's mark.[151]

As with the ACPA, the registrant can avail herself of a legitimate interest defense in appropriate cases.[152] The UDRP sets out some factors that arbitrators may consider in deciding whether a use of a domain name by a registrant is legitimate for UDRP purposes. These factors include (a) before any notification of the dispute, the registrant used, or made demonstrable preparations to use, the relevant domain name in connection with a bona fide offering of goods or services;[153] (b) the registrant has been commonly known by the relevant name;[154] and (c) the registrant is making a legitimate noncommercial or fair use of the name without intent for commercial gain to mislead consumers or tarnish a trademark.[155]

---

144 Jacqueline Lipton, *Celebrity in Cyberspace: A Personality Rights Paradigm for Personal Domain Name Disputes*, 65 Washington and Lee L. Rev. 1445, 1497 (2008) (citing procedural advantages of the UDRP over domestic trademark law).

145 UDRP, para. 4(a)(i).

146 *Id.* para. 4(a)(ii)

147 *Id.* para 4(a)(iii).

148 *Id.* para. 4(b)(i).

149 *Id.* para. 4(b)(ii).

150 *Id.* para. 4(b)(iii).

151 *Id.* para. 4(b)(iv).

152 *Id.* para. 4(c).

153 *Id.* para. 4(c)(i).

154 *Id.* para. 4(c)(ii).

155 *Id.* para. 4(c)(iii).

The UDRP thus reflects the same policy aims as the ACPA, even though it achieves them slightly differently, and of course the UDRP is procedurally different to the ACPA in that it is a private arbitration mechanism as opposed to a statute. Theoretically, the First Amendment is not implicated by the UDRP in the same way as it is by the Lanham Act. This is because the UDRP is not a Congressional enactment, subject to First Amendment guarantees.[156] Some UDRP arbitrators have expressly recognized this in practice:

> It may well be that Respondent is making a 'fair use' of complainant's marks in their 'consumer complaint' websites and that the contents of those sites are constitutionally protected in the United States. It is, however, neither necessary nor appropriate to make such an evaluation here. The issue to be determined under paragraph 4(a)(ii) of the [UDRP] is more restricted and specific.[157]

A UDRP arbitration is not decisive of the parties' respective rights in the sense that the dispute can still be litigated before a domestic court under national trademark law.[158] However, just because the UDRP is not technically subject to the First Amendment, and is not necessarily the final word on any given dispute, does not mean that free speech is not implicated by the policy. In fact, because of the global reach of the policy, and the fact that domestic litigation may be too costly for some disputants, the UDRP could have a greater impact on free expression than domestic trademark law.

A brief consideration of the key provisions of the UDRP evidences that it suffers from some of the same limitations as the ACPA in that it focuses on the protection of trademarks, and its drafting gives less weight to specific competing interests such as free speech.[159] However, the drafting of the UDRP is somewhat different from the ACPA. As a result, it may strike a more appropriate balance between trademarks and speech than the ACPA. For example, while the ACPA does not create a temporal link between the development of a registrant's bad faith motives and the time of registration of a domain name, the UDRP does contemplate such a link. In other words, the UDRP contemplates that a domain name should be transferred to the complainant where the domain name in question '*has*

---

156 See the First Amendment to the United States Constitution, *supra* note 15.

157 *Estée Lauder v Hanna*, WIPO Arbitration and Mediation Center, Case No. D2000–0869 (September 25, 2000), para.6B, available at www.wipo.int/amc/en/domains/decisions/html/2000/d2000-0869.html, last accessed March 16, 2010.

158 UDRP, para. 4(k).

159 See discussion in Lipton, *Beyond Cybersquatting*, *supra* note 89, at 1374–7.

been registered and is being used in bad faith'.[160] The UDRP's list of bad faith factors is also generally drafted in terms of bad faith registration of a name as opposed to an intent that developed at a later time, for example, after the commencement of litigation, as was the case in the *Doughney* litigation.

The requirement that bad faith be shown at the time of registration avoids some of the problems that arise under the ACPA where there was not necessarily a bad faith profit motive at the time of registration, but later on (after a dispute arises), the registrant considers making a profit from selling the name. In these situations under the ACPA, the registrant is in a no-win situation because, even if she registered the domain name without a bad faith profit motive, any subsequent attempt to sell the name might trigger the bad faith requirement and thus bolster the complainant's case. Under the UDRP, at least, the complainant has to establish that the domain name in question was initially registered in bad faith, and has subsequently been used in bad faith.

This still leaves an open question as to whether the registration and use of a domain name for purposes of a gripe site or parody site would satisfy the UDRP criteria. In particular, the question arises as to whether free speech is, or should be, protected by the 'non-commercial or fair use' aspects of legitimate use in paragraph 4(c)(iii). This clause definitely leaves room for UDRP arbitrators to protect free speech in the form of criticism, commentary or parody, provided that there is no concurrent consumer confusion or tarnishment of a relevant mark.[161]

The problem for UDRP arbitrators is that there is no clear test as to when a commentary site is a fair or legitimate use. This is not necessarily a criticism of the UDRP. In many ways, it is useful that a policy intended to apply globally to situations that may involve significant cross-border cultural variations on human values such as free speech maintains some vagueness in wording to give arbitrators some flexibility in its application. However, there are trade-offs between flexibility and certainty. A comparison of two early UDRP decisions involving consumer commentary and gripe sites demonstrates the arbitrary results that can arise under the UDRP in this respect. These decisions illustrate that, despite the global nature of the UDRP, arbitrators are likely to be influenced, at least to some extent, by the domestic trademark laws with which they may be particularly familiar.[162]

---

160 UDRP, para. 4(a)(iii) (emphasis added).

161 *Id.* para. 4(c)(iii).

162 See, for example, *Bridgestone Firestone, Inc. v Myers,* WIPO Arbitration and Mediation Center, Case No. D2000–0190 para. 6 (July 6, 2000) available at www.wipo.int/amc/en/domains/decisions/html/2000/d2000-0190.html, last

In *Estée Lauder, Inc. v Hanna*, a UDRP arbitration panel ordered a domain name registrant who had registered deliberate misspellings of the complainant's mark as domain names (estelauder.com and estelauder.net) to transfer the names to the complainant.[163] The respondent's motive appeared to have been profit as he worked for a firm of personal injury lawyers who represented litigants against large corporations.[164] The websites in question contained comment forms for visitors to complain about Estée Lauder to the Better Business Bureau or to the site operator, although the site operator was not identified.[165] The registrant had apparently engaged in similar conduct with respect to other well-known trademarks.[166] The complainant alleged that the registrant was a cybersquatter and was creating confusion as to the affiliation or sponsorship of the relevant sites.[167] The registrant responded that its use was noncommercial and that it included clear disclaimers on its websites for the purpose of avoiding any such confusion.[168]

In deciding that the registrant was not making a legitimate use of the relevant domain names, the arbitrator drew a distinction between the domain names themselves and the website contents in terms of the registrant's rights to free speech:

> Respondent may well, and likely does, have extensive rights of free speech to provide a platform to criticize Complainant and a right to the fair use of the Complainant's marks in so doing. The contents of Respondent's websites may also be a perfectly legitimate use of those rights. But Respondent could well have chosen to use a domain name that was not confusingly similar to Complainants and/or in which Complainant has no rights; it intentionally chose not to do so . . . Respondent's free expression rights do not here give it a right or legitimate interest in the domain names at issue.[169]

This statement may be contrasted with the decision of a UDRP arbitration panel in *Bridgestone Firestone v Myers*.[170] As with *Estée Lauder*,

---

accessed March 2, 2009 ('The discussion and decision herein will . . . be governed by the terms of the [UDRP], although reference by analogy may be made to principles of U.S. law, as two of the Complainants are U.S. corporations, Respondent is a U.S. resident, and both parties have cited U.S. law in their submissions.').

163 WIPO Case No. D2000–0869, available at www.wipo.int/amc/en/domains/decisions/html/2000/d2000-0869.html.

164 *Id.*

165 *Id.*

166 *Id.*

167 *Id.* para. 5.

168 *Id. para.* 6B.

169 *Id.*

170 *Bridgestone*, WIPO Case No. D2000–0190, available at www.wipo.int/amc/en/domains/decisions/html/2000/d2000-0190.html

the panel in *Bridgestone* accepted a right to free expression as a legitimate interest under the UDRP.[171] However, unlike *Estée Lauder*, the arbitrator in *Bridgestone* felt that the use of a domain name corresponding with a well-known mark for the purposes of a gripe site with no obvious commercial motive would not justify a decision to transfer the name to the trademark holder.[172] The registrant, an ex-employee of the complainant, had registered www.bridgestone-firestone.net which corresponded with the complainant's marks. In terms of the argument that the registrant sought commercial profit because the website in question contained an offer to transfer the domain name to the complainants, the arbitrator felt that commercial sale was not the registrant's primary purpose in registering or using the name.[173] Thus, there was no bad faith registration or use.

The *Bridgestone* arbitrator was mindful of the delicate balance necessary to promote free speech on the Internet while at the same time protecting legitimate trademark interests online:

> Although free speech is not listed as one of the [UDRP's] examples of a right or legitimate interest in a domain name, the list is not exclusive, and the Panel concludes that the exercise of free speech for criticism and commentary . . . demonstrates a right or legitimate interest in the domain name under Paragraph 4(c)(iii). The Internet is above all a framework for global communication, and the right to free speech should be one of the foundations of Internet law.[174]

In this light, the arbitrator did not feel that registrants wanting to establish gripe sites should be restricted to particular iterations of trademarks in their domain names, such as www.trademarksucks.com, to designate a site for criticism or commentary.[175] However, the limits of the reasoning are somewhat murky in that it is not clear that the arbitrator would have been favorably disposed to a gripe site operator using a '.com' gTLD, as opposed to '.net' or '.org':

> In the cybersquatting cases, the domain names in question generally were trademark.com domain names, which prevented the trademark holder from utilizing the customary commercial domain name for its 'official' site . . . Here, however, the domain name registrant has not usurped the '.com' domain,

---

171 *Id.* para. 6.
172 *Id.*
173 *Id.*
174 *Id.*
175 *Id.*

but has utilized only the '.net' domain, has posted disclaimers on the website homepage, and has included criticism and commentary on the site so that a reasonably prudent Internet user can tell that the site is not the trademark holder's 'official' site.[176]

Here, there seems to be a presumption that the use of a '.com' gTLD corresponding to a trademark will be in bad faith, while the use of any other gTLD will not necessarily support such a presumption:

> Since there are now seven generic top level domains, with more in the process of being approved, as well as some 240 country top level domains, there are hundreds of domain name permutations available to complainants. Respondent's use of one of those permutations other than the principle '.com' domain name for purposes of critical commentary is a legitimate noncommercial and fair use.[177]

This may be a sensible approach. However, one obvious downside is that it relegates those wanting to comment on a particular trademark holder to a lesser domain space than the trademark holder itself. Assuming that Internet users will find at least some sites by guessing at domain names rather than using search engines, gripe site and parody site operators can potentially reach a larger audience if they can use '.com' versions of names than if they are relegated to other gTLDs. Additionally, as many search engines utilize algorithms that incorporate domain names, the registration of the most intuitive version of someone's mark in a domain name may well reach a larger prospective audience even of search engine users.[178]

Is it possible to reconcile decisions like *Estée Lauder* and *Bridgestone*? The *Estée Lauder* panel based the distinction on the fact that the registrant in *Bridgestone* had only registered a '.net' version of the relevant name whereas

---

[176] *Id.* The arbitrator further cited the Ninth Circuit Court of Appeals case of *Avery Dennison Corp. v Sumpton,* 189 F.3d 868, 880–1 (9th Cir. 1999), which held that '.net' generally applies to networks and '.com' generally applies to commercial entities, so a factfinder might infer that trademark dilution does not occur with a '.net' registration. This is another good example of a UDRP arbitrator looking to domestic trademark law for guidance on principles of good faith versus bad faith registration and use.

[177] *Bridgestone*, WIPO Case No. D2000–0190 para. 6, available at www.wipo.int/amc/en/domains/decisions/html/2000/d2000-0190.html.

[178] Lastowka, *supra* note 27, at 1336–7 (noting that search algorithms employed in sophisticated search engines like Google tend to generate search results based on combinations of meta-tags, domain names, full text searches, and popularity rankings of webpages.)

the registrant in *Estée Lauder* had entered the '.com' arena.[179] However, the *Bridgestone* decision in and of itself does not in practice create an effective protection for free speech because, as noted above, UDRP arbitrations are not the end of the story if the aggrieved party at the end of the dispute wants to continue in a domestic court. In particular, the *Bridgestone* panel expressly acknowledged that the UDRP does not allow for a formal hearing of a trademark dilution claim that was also alleged against the registrant by the complainant.[180] Thus, the victory at arbitration may have been a minor hurdle for the registrant facing a potential trademark dilution claim. Even a threatening post-arbitration letter from the complainant alleging trademark dilution could have chilled the registrant's speech.

An attempt to balance free speech with commercial trademark interests in the domain space must involve a policy that encompasses the application of all relevant parts of trademark law. It would be pointless to clarify the confusions underlying the ACPA and the UDRP in the hope of promoting a better balance between trademarks and free speech while allowing the balance to be offset by overzealous application of, say, trademark dilution law. This must be kept in mind while considering the various options for future development. The following discussion on future directions is not necessarily comprehensive, but it is an attempt to draw together threads of ideas that have been suggested in the past to better balance free speech with trademark rights online.

3.5 PROPOSALS FOR AN IMPROVED SPEECH–TRADEMARK BALANCE

3.5.1 Free Speech Zones in the Domain Space

One possibility for more appropriately balancing free speech interests against trademark interests in the domain space might be to zone the

---

179 *Estée Lauder, Inc. v Hanna*, WIPO Case No. D2000–0869, para. 6C, available at www.wipo.int/amc/en/domains/decisions/html/2000/d2000-0869.html ('One salient difference with the case at hand is that in *Bridgestone* the respondent had registered the "net" domain name only, and this was an important factor in the Panel conclusion that . . . respondent was not misleadingly diverting internet users to his site. Here, respondent had registered and linked both the "net" and "com" versions of a name confusingly similar to that of complainant's marks in order to enhance the possibilities of diversion.').

180 *Bridgestone*, WIPO Case No. D2000–0190, para. 6, available at www.wipo.int/amc/en/domains/decisions/html/2000/d2000-0190.html.

domain space along the lines suggested by the UDRP arbitrator in *Bridgestone*.[181] This would involve developing a rule that trademark holders are entitled to the 'trademark.com' versions of their marks in the domain space. Those wishing to comment on trademark holders would then be relegated to a different gTLD, such as '.net' or '.org'. Some courts and arbitrators have already begun to accept such a rule.[182] There might be other possible permutations of this approach, such as creating new gTLDs specifically for gripe sites and parodies, such as '.sucks', '.stinks', '.bites', '.fun' or '.humor'. If this were done, a rule could be instituted that trademark holders could claim all of the standard gTLDs, including '.net' and '.org', while commentators would be relegated to the new gTLDs.

Of course, such a rule would have to be built into the new gTLD program currently underway at ICANN. The program has rules for arbitrating between applicants for new gTLDs on the basis of trademark interests and some other legitimate concerns.[183] An attempt to formally zone the domain space would have to include special rules relating to new gTLDs intended to be reserved for the purposes of commentary or criticism. Particular registrars might have to administer those names and ensure their appropriate use in practice. Even though the intention would be to promote speech online, the relegation of expressive speech to certain online zones could be regarded as a form of censorship.

Another potential variation of this approach might be the one that was rejected by the UDRP arbitrator in *Bridgestone.* The idea would be to require those wanting to establish gripe sites or parody sites to use domain names such as 'www.trademarksucks.com'.[184] No new gTLDs would need to be created or specially administered in support of this approach. There would also be no need to keep commentators out of the '.com' domain space provided that they included pejorative terms like sucks, stinks, or perhaps parody, fun or humor as part of the domain name. Additionally,

---

[181] See discussion at 3.4.2, *supra*.

[182] See *Bridgestone*, WIPO Case No. D2000–0190, para. 6 available at www.wipo.int/amc/en/domains/decisions/html/2000/d2000-0190.html (citing the Ninth Circuit Court of Appeals case *Avery Dennison Corp. v Sumpton,* 189 F.3d 868 (9th Cir. 1999), *supra* note 176.

[183] See ICANN, New gTLD Program: Draft Applicant Guidebook, (Draft RFP) (October 24, 2008), Module 3, available at www.icann.org/en/topics/new-gtlds/draft-rfp-24oct08-en.pdf, last accessed July 6, 2009.

[184] See *Bridgestone*, WIPO Case No. D2000–0190, para. 6, available at www.wipo.int/amc/en/domains/decisions/html/2000/d2000-0190.html ('The Panel sees no reason to require domain name registrants to utilize circumlocutions like www.trademarksucks.com to designate a website for criticism of consumer commentary.').

the introduction of new gTLDs would not be a problem if those wishing to comment on trademark holders were required to insert qualifiers into their domain names like 'sucks'. Of course, this approach raises questions about the kind of power that might be achieved by any applicant who manages to secure the position as registry for any new '.sucks' gTLD that may be developed under ICANN's proposal to extend available gTLDs.

A zoning approach has a number of advantages for protecting online speech. For one thing, zoning would create clearer rules and hence greater certainty for courts and arbitrators. Such rules could cut cleanly across all trademark-based actions, including dilution, infringement, ACPA claims and UDRP disputes. Thus, if a domain name registrant had utilized an appropriate zone for her activities, there would be a presumption against any kind of trademark-based action.

Of course, creating free speech zones in cyberspace does not mean that utilizing a nondesignated zone would automatically result in a trademark action. Presumably, a registrant with the choice between a safe speech zone and a protected trademark zone who chose the latter could still argue non-infringement on the basis that she was not causing confusion or dilution, and had not registered the domain name in bad faith for a profit motive. For example, a registrant who chose 'nike.com' or 'nike.net' for a gripe site, as opposed to 'nike.sucks', or 'nikesucks.com', might still defend a trademark infringement action if she could establish that she was not confusing consumers or diluting Nike's brand, and had not registered the domain name in bad faith for a profit. However, in a system with protected speech zones, it might become more difficult for a defendant to establish these defenses. The presumption could arise that the decision by a registrant not to use a protected speech zone is prima facie evidence of a bad faith intent.

If a person registered a domain name in a protected speech zone, it would not be necessary for courts and arbitrators to make such complex determinations about bad faith profit motives or consumer confusion. The presumption would be that the use of the protected zone would negate these claims because consumers would not likely be confused by the use of a trademark in a commentary zone. Trademarks would not be diluted by their use in such a zone, and it would presumably be a showing of good faith, rather than bad faith, on the part of the registrant to utilize such a zone. Even if a registrant utilized the website in question for profit, such as referring to a preference for competitors of the targeted trademark holder, or operating a clickfarm from the website,[185] this should not be sufficient to show consumer confusion or dilution in a protected speech zone.

---

[185] See Lipton, *Clickfarming*, *supra* note 123, at 1.

However, the disadvantages of zoning might outweigh the advantages. For one thing, it seems somewhat distasteful to zone online speech at all. The Internet is an unparalleled global communications medium and, as such, regulators should be careful about creating rules in the basic framework of the domain system that might be regarded as forms of censorship. There is no obvious analog to the domain space in the physical world. Thus it is difficult to make real world analogies to zones for permitted and impermissible speech in the domain space. Of course, even in the real world, private property interests do not always trump speech interests, and courts have been careful to protect speech in the face of property ownership.[186]

The other obvious problem with zoning is that it is difficult to achieve such a system without relegating speech to lesser zones than trademark interests, presuming that trademark holders should be presumptively entitled to control 'trademark.com' domain names. Assuming that domain names will continue to have some use as search tools,[187] it is more likely that a user looking for information about a business will end up at the 'trademark.com' website, rather than at a speech zone commenting on the trademark holder. Thus, a commentator on a particular business is likely to receive a lesser audience if forced to use a speech zone than if she were allowed to use a standard gTLD version of the relevant mark, perhaps including the '.com' version.

One might also question whether this kind of system really adds much to the current state of affairs. It is arguably the case now that people wishing to parody or criticize trademark holders can use pejorative variations of marks in domain names, at least in existing domain spaces.[188] However, there has been some confusion in recent years as to whether

---

186 See, for example, *PruneYard Shopping Ctr. v Robins,* 447 U.S. 74 (1980); *Marsh v Alabama,* 326 U.S. 501 (1946); *State v Shack,* 277 A.2d 369 (N.J. 1971). These cases involve courts balancing rights to free speech in various contexts with private property rights in the physical world, with courts occasionally carving out exceptions to what otherwise might be thought of as almost absolute real property rights for purposes of expressing messages or accessing a particular audience for specific information.

187 Either as a direct search tool or because they are used by search engines as part of their search algorithms: Lastowka, *supra* note 27, at 1336–7.

188 See, for example, *Bally Total Fitness Holding Corp. v Faber,* 29 F.Supp.2d 1161 (C.D. Cal. 1998). In this case, the court found that a gripe site utilizing 'ballysucks' as part of its domain name did not infringe the plaintiff's mark. However, the domain name in question was not a direct transcription of the Bally mark with 'sucks' attached, rather, it was 'www.compupix.com/ballysucks', a subpage of a website with a domain name that did not correspond to Bally's mark.

registrants utilizing pejorative suffixes in domain names are free from trademark infringement liability. In a UDRP arbitration involving the Air France trademark, for example, a UDRP arbitration panel split on this question.[189] The majority panelists held that the domain name 'airfrance-sucks.com' for a complaint and commentary website was sufficiently confusing to consumers to justify an order for the name to be transferred to Air France.[190] The dissenting panelist disagreed on the consumer confusion point.[191]

3.5.2 Revising Trademark Law

3.5.2.1 Trademark infringement

Another approach to achieving a clearer balance of speech and trademark interests in the gripe site and parody context would be to clarify some of the current tests for infringement of trademark laws in these situations. This could be achieved concurrently with the zoning model described above,[192] or as a stand-alone approach. In fact, trademark infringement, dilution and ACPA actions have all created some challenges for the balance between speech and trademark interests. Perhaps some general guidelines might be developed that cut across the trademark-based actions in order to achieve a more appropriate balance.

A traditional trademark infringement action in the domain name context would require a domain name registrant to have created, or at least be creating a potential for, consumer confusion.[193] The problem in cyberspace is that it is often unclear, with respect to parody sites and gripe sites, how to determine whether consumer confusion is likely to exist as a result of a domain name registrant's activities. In *People for the Ethical Treatment of Animals v Doughney*,[194] for example, it would seem that consumers interested in PETA likely would not be confused by Doughney's peta.org website. That website contained a parody of PETA's activities, referring users to websites selling fur and meat products. Yet, the court found a likelihood of consumer confusion for trademark infringement purposes. This judicial practice has not been uncommon in domain

---

[189] *Société Air France v Virtual Dates, Inc.*, WIPO Arbitration and Mediation Center, Case No. D2005–0168 (May 24, 2005), available at www.wipo.int/amc/en/domains/decisions/html/2005/d2005-0168.html, last accessed March 16, 2010.

[190] *Id.* paras at 6–7.

[191] *Id.* dissent.

[192] See 3.5.1, *supra*.

[193] 15 U.S.C. §§ 1114(1), 1125(a)(1).

[194] 113 F.Supp.2d 915 (E.D. Va. 2000); *aff'd* 263 F.3d 359 (4th Cir. 2001).

name cases. Online, courts increasingly rely on notions of initial interest confusion,[195] even where consumers are not actually confused as to source of a product or service when making an ultimate purchasing decision.

In contrast to *Doughney*, the Fourth Circuit Court of Appeals in *Falwell*[196] found no trademark infringement when the defendant registered a domain name taking advantage of a deliberate misspelling of the plaintiff's surname to criticize the plaintiff's views on homosexuality. Although personal names in the domain space are considered in more detail in Chapter 4, the *Falwell* case was based on trademark infringement. The *Falwell* court accepted that the Reverend Jerry Falwell had a trademark in his personal name for the purposes of his trademark-based claims. The Fourth Circuit distinguished the *Doughney* decision in various ways. With respect to the ACPA claim, it noted that the defendant in *Doughney* had (a) suggested a willingness to sell the domain name to the plaintiff after the litigation commenced; and (b) registered some 50 to 60 other domain names corresponding with well-known trademarks.[197] The court held that these factors played into the bad faith intent to profit test for ACPA infringement.[198] For the purposes of trademark infringement, the *Falwell* court appears to distinguish *Doughney* on the basis that *Doughney* dealt with a constitutional parody defense to trademark infringement, while *Falwell* is a simple question of consumer confusion.[199]

Since parody might be regarded as a subclass of critical speech, it seems strange as a matter of policy to subject the two cases to different legal tests. There seems no clear policy reason why a consumer criticism site that is not a parody should be effectively subjected to a lower standard of constitutional scrutiny than a criticism site that takes the form of a parody. This is a peculiar result given that neither site likely confuses consumers for trademark purposes, and both sites involved links to other websites where

---

195 Eric Goldman, *Deregulating Relevancy in Internet Law*, 54 EMORY L.J. 507, 559 (2005) ('[Initial interest confusion] lacks a rigorous definition, a clear policy justification, and a uniform standard for analyzing claims. With its doctrinal flexibility, [it] has become the tool of choice for plaintiffs to shut down junior users who have not actually engaged in misappropriative uses.'). See also *Brookfield Commc'ns v Coast Entm't,* 174 F.3d 1036, 1054–64 (9th Cir. 1999); *Panavision Int'l v Toeppen,* 141 F.3d 1316 (9th Cir. 1998) (finding that consumers would not actually have been confused as to source by defendant's website, but may have been distracted from finding the plaintiff's actual web presence); *Playboy v Netscape*, 354 F.3d 1020, 1035(2004) *supra* note 87.

196 420 F.3d 309 (4th Cir. 2005).

197 *Id.* at 320–1.

198 *Id.* at 320.

199 *Id.* at 316–17.

goods and services could be commercially purchased.[200] It seems that, reading between the lines, maybe the answer lies in the subject matter of the relevant speech. Maybe the court felt that a somewhat clumsy parody of PETA's activities did not merit the same constitutional protection as a critical stance on the Reverend Jerry Falwell's views on homosexuality.

In any event, it may be necessary for the purposes of online trademark law to create some clearer presumptions about the use of particular gTLDs containing trademarks. In some ways, it may not matter what the presumptions are, as long as they can provide greater clarity for those registering and using Internet domain names. A presumption that 'trademark.com' names should be reserved to trademark holders and may not be used for gripe sites or parody sites would lessen some of the current confusion.[201] Of course, such a presumption would raise the criticisms identified above in relation to zoning speech in the domain space.[202]

Alternatively, a presumption that a commentator who registers a domain name corresponding with a trademark for speech purposes would not be liable for trademark infringement provided that the registrant included a disclaimer on the website could also lessen confusion. This would run counter to some existing judicial precedent,[203] so it may require congressional action. This approach might be criticized because it potentially cuts off rightful trademark holders from an obvious domain space. However, as the UDRP panel noted in *Bridgestone*, there are many permutations and combinations of relevant domain names that a rightful trademark holder can utilize.[204] Additionally, a rightful trademark holder

---

[200] In *Doughney*, the defendant's website contained links to organizations that sold fur and animal products, while in *Falwell*, the defendant's website contained a link to a particular book for sale on the Amazon.com website. See discussion in Lipton, *Commerce versus Commentary*, *supra* note 114, at 1366–7.

[201] Although such a presumption obviously would not help in the case of competing legitimate trademark holders, see discussion in Chapter 2.

[202] See 3.5.1, *supra*.

[203] *Planned Parenthood Federation of America Inc. v Bucci,* 42 U.S.P.Q.2d 1430, 1441 (S.D.N.Y. 1997).

[204] *Bridgestone*, WIPO Case No. D2000–0190, available at www.wipo.int/amc/en/domains/decisions/html/2000/d2000-0190.html ('Since there are now seven generic top level domains, with more in the process of being approved, as well as some 240 country top level domains, there are hundreds of domain name permutations available to complainants. Respondent's use of one of those permutations other than the principal ".com" domain name for purposes of critical commentary is a legitimate noncommercial and fair use.'). Obviously, the suggestion being made in this book is that it is possible to create a workable presumption that even a '.com' name might be registered and used legitimately by a nontrademark holder. This is taking the idea one step further than the arbitrator in *Bridgestone*, but the

could always bargain with the registrant for transfer of the name, provided that the current law was amended to ensure that such a bargain would not automatically be regarded as triggering the ACPA's bad faith intent to profit requirement.[205]

Either presumption might be justified on policy grounds, and either could create greater certainty for users of the domain name system. In fact, a mixture of the two could be created by following the suggestion of the panel in *Bridgestone* and reserving 'trademark.com' names for trademark holders while accepting that other gTLDs are open to anyone provided that disclaimers are utilized to avoid consumer confusion.[206] However, not all trademark holders will want to avail themselves of a '.com' presence, as they may feel that they are better described by a '.org' or a '.net' suffix. Some public interest groups may prefer a less commercial-looking online presence. In such cases, the trademark holders might defensively register the '.com' version of their name and redirect it to another website with a '.org' or '.net' suffix.

3.5.2.2 Trademark dilution

Dilution raises different concerns for free speech than infringement. As Judge Kozinski noted in *Mattel*, 'dilution injunctions . . . lack the built-in First Amendment compass of trademark injunctions'.[207] This is because dilution does not require a showing of consumer confusion. Thus, at least prior to the 2006 amendments to the dilution statute,[208] it was relatively easy for a plaintiff to satisfy the basic elements of a dilution claim with respect to gripe sites and parody sites. Prior to 2006, there was an accepted noncommercial use defense for a dilution action, but nothing dealing specifically with gripe sites or parody sites that may involve some commercial activity. Now, the dilution statute includes within the fair use defense:

(i) advertising or promotion that permits consumers to compare goods or services; or
(ii) identifying and parodying, criticizing, or commenting upon the famous mark owner or the goods or services of the famous mark owner.[209]

---

underlying notion of a variety of options available to the trademark holder is still valid.

[205] See discussion in Lipton, *Commerce versus Commentary*, *surpa* note 114, at 1367–8.

[206] *Bridgestone*, WIPO Case No. D2000–0190, available at www.wipo.int/amc/en/domains/decisions/html/2000/d2000-0190.html *supra* note 204.

[207] *Mattel, Inc. v MCA Records, Inc.*, 296 F.3d 894, 905 (9th Cir. 2002).

[208] Trademark Dilution Revision Act of 2006.

[209] 15 U.S.C. § 1125(c)(3)(A)(i) and (ii).

Under pre-2006 dilution law, courts attempting to protect free speech in the domain space were forced to focus predominantly on whether a given use might be excused as a noncommercial use even if the domain name registrant was engaged in some kind of commercial activity. Now, a court presumably has leeway to excuse even some commercial activity if it might be described as a fair use under the new provisions of the dilution statute.

To date, there has been little judicial guidance on the application of the new provisions of the fair use defense in the dilution statute. The first case interpreting the new parody/commentary aspect of the defense held that parody is not automatically a defense to a trademark dilution action in cases where the defendant is using the plaintiff's mark *as a trademark*.[210] Of course, in cases involving parody sites and gripe sites it is unlikely that the registrant is using the plaintiff's mark in a trademark sense – that is, as a source designator for her own products and services. A person running a gripe site or parody site is using the mark to draw eyeballs to a site that comments on a trademark holder, rather than a site where the registrant is attempting to pass off her own products or services as those of the trademark holder.

It may be that some guidance could be drawn from the book, song and movie title cases, even with respect to the new dilution statute. These cases basically relied on an interpretation of the noncommercial use defense that gave the defendant a little more leeway in cases where a mark was used as a descriptive identifier by way of a title for an underlying work. In *Mattel*, Judge Kozinski noted that the congressional purpose of the original dilution statute was clearly not to prohibit or threaten noncommercial speech, including 'parody, satire, editorial and other forms of expression that are not a part of a commercial transaction'.[211] Using evidence of this congres-

---

[210] *Louis Vuitton v Haute Diggity Dog*, 507 F.3d 252, 266 (2007) ('We begin by noting that parody is not automatically a complete *defense* to a claim of dilution by blurring where the defendant uses the parody as its own designation of source, i.e., *as a trademark*. Although the [Trademark Dilution Revision Act of 2006] does provide that fair use is a complete defense and allows that a parody can be considered fair use, it does not extend the fair use defense to parodies used as a trademark. As the statute provides:

The following shall not be actionable as dilution by blurring or dilution by tarnishment under this subsection: (A) Any fair use . . . *other than as a designation of source for the person's own goods or services*, including use in connection with . . . parodying . . . 15 U.S.C.A. § 1125(c)(3)(A)(ii) (emphasis added). Under the statute's plain language, parodying a famous mark is protected by the fair use defense only if the parody is *not* "a designation of source for the person's own goods or services"'.)

[211] See, for example, *Mattel, Inc. v MCA Records, Inc.*, 296 F.3d 894, 905 (9th Cir. 2002).

sional intent, he drew a distinction between speech that does no more than propose a commercial transaction – purely commercial speech – and other speech.[212] He favored full First Amendment protection for speech that does more than propose a commercial transaction.[213]

This seems a fitting analogy for most gripe sites and parody sites, given that the domain names in question will generally function much like a song or movie title and that the sites are being utilized for speech purposes. This reasoning could potentially encompass all domain names, including '.com' names, unless a presumption is to be created that would reserve '.com' names for trademark holders. Taking this approach, one avoids the potential difficulties in interpretation of the parody/commentary aspect of the fair use defense to dilution. Allowing full First Amendment protection for speech in the domain space that does more than propose a commercial transaction might also alleviate some of the problems of interpretation that have arisen thus far in the domain name context.

Existing dilution cases in the domain space have involved somewhat peculiar interpretations of the dilution statute. In *Doughney*, for example, the trial court regarded the following as supporting the plaintiff's dilution claim: (a) the defendant used PETA's trademark in its domain name; (b) this use caused actual economic harm to the mark by lessening its selling power; and (c) the defendant also linked his site to commercial enterprises engaged in conduct antithetical to the plaintiff's animal rights message.[214] It is difficult to see how these factors relate to the aims of the dilution statute, which are to protect the famous mark against 'companies who trade on the renown of the mark by selling unrelated goods, such as Kodak pianos or Buick aspirin'.[215]

The fact that a defendant uses a plaintiff's mark in its domain name is the very definition of a gripe site or parody site. Utilizing this factor to establish dilution, as in *Doughney*, would be tantamount to a presumption that gripe sites and parody sites must be relegated to lesser domains such as 'petasucks.org' or 'petaparody.org'. Further, the fact that the defendant promoted an anti-animal-rights message and linked to other sites selling fur and animal products is not the same as the defendant trading off the plaintiff's marks in an unrelated product market. The facts here do not support the purposes of a dilution claim. The Fourth Circuit Court of Appeals in *Doughney* subsequently chose not to rule on the dilution claim,

---

212 *Id.* at 906.

213 *Id.*

214 *People for the Ethical Treatment of Animals v Doughney,* 113 F.Supp.2d 915, 920 (E.D. Va. 2000), *aff'd* 263 F.3d 359 (4th Cir. 2001).

215 Lemley, *supra* note 14, at 1698.

having found trademark infringement and ACPA infringement made out on the facts.[216]

The solution to difficult dilution problems in the domain name space might be the creation of a judicial or legislative presumption that dilution actions are generally not intended to apply to cases involving trademarks in the domain space. The policy rationale for dilution does not fit the gripe site or parody site context particularly well. Other actions are available to protect trademark holders against unfair competition on the Internet. In the balance between speech and commerce online, it may be prudent to avoid regulations that generally favor commerce over commentary, particularly in cases where the policy bases for relevant rules are not clearly relevant to the domain name context.

3.5.2.3 The ACPA and the UDRP

The main technical difficulty with applying the ACPA and the UDRP in cases involving gripe sites and parody sites is that there is currently some confusion as to what constitutes bad faith for the purposes of these regulatory measures outside the traditional cybersquatting context.[217] This problem is exacerbated under the ACPA by the fact that the legislation is drafted in a way that disconnects the bad faith purpose from the actual registration.[218] Thus, any post-registration offer to sell the name to a trademark holder could theoretically constitute a bad faith intent that would trigger an ACPA action, even if such a sale was not the registrant's intent at the time of registration.[219] Additionally, some of the bad faith factors in the ACPA, although not mandatory in any given case, can be confusing when applied to gripe sites and parody sites. As noted above, the registration of multiple domain names is an example of this.[220] A traditional cybersquatter would generally register multiple names and not use them for anything in particular, whereas a gripe site or parody site developer may register multiple domain names, but will use at least some of them for expressive purposes.

The ACPA and the UDRP were not intended to curtail free expression in cyberspace. However, their drafting may lead to interpretations that do result in a chilling of online expression. They each contain strong protections for trademarks, while free speech is only protected, if at all, implicitly under the legitimate use defenses. Perhaps some revisions of the rules are

---

216 263 F.3d at 371, note 3.
217 See discussion at 3.4.1 and 3.4.2, *supra*.
218 See discussion at 3.4.1, *supra*.
219 See 3.4.1, *supra*.
220 15 U.S.C. § 1125(d)(1)(B)(i)(VIII).

now in order to clarify the fact that these regulations were presumably not intended to curb speech in the form of gripe sites or parody sites.

The ACPA might be revised to clarify what is meant by bad faith registration or acquisition of a domain name. Simply offering to sell a name to a rightful owner subsequent to the onset of a dispute should not necessarily be evidence of a bad faith intent to profit under the ACPA. Additionally, it is arguable whether the list of bad faith factors in the ACPA really adds anything significant to the notion of bad faith intent to profit from registration or use of the name. In the early days of the ACPA, these factors might well have given useful guidance to courts and litigants in outlining the kinds of conduct that traditionally went along with bad faith cybersquatting. Nevertheless, today the bad faith factors may be causing inconsistencies when applied outside the traditional cybersquatting context. The UDRP's bad faith factors are not as problematic as the ACPA's factors because they are more tightly limited to the prevention of cybersquatting and are not as broad as the bad faith factors in the ACPA.[221] Nevertheless, the UDRP might be revised to more clearly encompass free speech as a legitimate interest in the defenses to a UDRP claim.[222]

3.6 EMERGING FREE SPEECH ISSUES

New developments in the domain space are likely to implicate the balance between trademark interests and free speech in different ways to those that have previously arisen with respect to popular gTLDs like '.com'. One obvious example of an area likely to raise new concerns about balancing speech and trademark interests is in the current proposal by ICANN to allow registration of new gTLDs at the request of private applicants. New gTLDs will likely raise conflicts in the domain space that have not arisen before. For example, if there is to be a presumption that trademark holders have default rights in gTLDs that reflect their marks, then this might operate to the detriment of free speech.

For example, if the Nike corporation has rights in gTLDs that include its Nike mark, how many gTLDs will this include? It might be simple to say that Nike should own the '.nike' suffix, but what about '.nikeinfo', '.nikesucks' or '.nikeproducts'? One might even question whether the assumption that Nike should own '.nike' is valid. Part of the answer to this question will depend on how Internet usage norms and search engine

---

221 See discussion at 3.4.2, *supra*.

222 UDRP, para. 4(c).

algorithms develop over time with respect to these new gTLDs. If, for example, '.com' names retain their prominent place in online commerce, there may be no need to create special protections for trademark holders in the '.trademark' space. As with the UDRP, ICANN's current proposal for new gTLDs creates specific protections for trademark holders, while retaining only vague protections for speech and other competing interests.[223] Any final policies adopted by ICANN to resolve disputes between parties interested in new gTLDs should create a clearer balance between trademark rights and expressive rights.

Another area of emerging interest is that of the relatively new personalized Facebook URL program.[224] Facebook now allows its members to utilize identifying words and marks in their Facebook addresses.[225] Thus, Facebook users can now register pages with URLs like 'facebook.com/nike'. Companies and individuals may want to utilize this system to personalize their official Facebook pages. Businesses can utilize the service for advertising their products and communicating with their clients.[226] The system raises issues of who has better rights to trademarks utilized in Facebook URLs. Should those seeking to register a 'facebook.com/trademark' URL for expressive purposes have the right to do so, or should such URLs be reserved to trademark holders? And, of course, the problem of cybersquatting on potentially valuable Facebook URLs will linger and will not be covered by the UDRP, although it would be subject to domestic trademark laws.

Facebook maintains a private method of resolving disputes in relation to these URLs.[227] Facebook does not publicize the details of its grievance procedures, and presumably it is under no obligation to do so. It is a private company engaging in the provision of services to its members, and is not subject to the First Amendment in the United States because it is not a government actor. As the URLs including descriptive words and

---

223 See ICANN, New gTLD Program: Draft Applicant Guidebook (Draft RFP) (October 24, 2008), paras 3.5.2–3.5.3, available at www.icann.org/en/topics/new-gtlds/draft-rfp-24oct08-en.pdf, last accessed July 6, 2009.

224 Also known as 'usernames': see Facebook Help Center, Usernames: Intellectual Property Rights Holders, available at www.facebook.com/help.php?page=899, last accessed July 6, 2009.

225 *Id.*

226 See, for example,www.facebook.com/coca-cola, last accessed July 6, 2009.

227 Facebook's rights infringement complaint form is available at www.facebook.com/help/contact.php?show_form=username_infringement (rights infringement complaint form), last accessed July 6, 2009. Facebook also reserves the right to 'remove or reclaim any username at any time for any reason': www.facebook.com/help.php?page=899, last accessed July 6, 2009.

phrases are in reality subpages of the facebook.com website, some guidance may be drawn from previous case law that has considered the use of trademarks in subpages of existing domains.

One example is the *Faber* case in which the registrant of 'www.compupix.com' maintained a gripe site about Bally Total Fitness Corp. at 'www.compupix.com/ballysucks'.[228] The court in this case found no infringement or dilution largely because the site was intended as a purely expressive gripe site about the plaintiff. Traditional trademark infringement and dilution reasoning was applied by the court in coming to this conclusion. There is no reason why a similar approach could not be taken to Facebook subpages involving unauthorized use of trademarks. A court might simply apply provisions of domestic trademark law to ascertain whether an unacceptable trademark infringement, dilution or an ACPA infringement had taken place on Facebook. The potential for domestic trademark actions might encourage Facebook to err on the side of protecting trademark holders in its private dispute resolution procedures.

3.7 CHAPTER SUMMARY

This chapter has examined various difficulties of interpretation inherent in trademark law and policy in terms of finding an appropriate balance between protecting commercial trademark interests and facilitating free speech in domain names. This chapter has focused on the following.

(1) The nature of free speech rights in different jurisdictions, and difficulties inherent in accommodating free speech in the domain space.

(2) The ways in which American courts have attempted to balance free speech and trademark rights in the context of traditional trademark infringement and dilution actions.

(3) Ways in which courts and arbitrators have attempted to balance free speech and trademark interests in the domain space under the ACPA and the UDRP in the context of gripe sites and parody sites.

(4) The possibility of creating speech zones in cyberspace to better promote free speech, and the inherent advantages and disadvantages of such an approach.

(5) Suggestions for revising existing regulations (trademark infringement law, dilution law, the ACPA and the UDRP) to better accommodate free speech with respect to trademark holders.

---

228 *Bally Total Fitness Holding Corp. v Faber*, 29 F.Supp.2d 1161 (C.D. Cal. 1998).

(6) Emerging issues involving the balance between trademark interests and free speech in the domain space, including problems that may arise under ICANN's plans to introduce new gTLDs, as well as problems balancing speech and trademark interests in new personalized Facebook URLs.

The following chapters consider the protection of personal names, political, cultural and geographic identifiers in the domain space. Disputes involving these kinds of signifiers do not necessarily raise the same interests, or lend themselves to the same regulatory structures, as disputes involving trademarks.

4. Personal names in the domain space

4.1 DOMAIN NAMES AND PERSONAL NAMES

Personal names in the domain space raise some novel issues. For example, in the high profile UDRP dispute involving the domain name 'www.julia-roberts.com',[1] the popular Oscar™-winning actress, Julia Roberts, succeeded in gaining control of the name from someone who was apparently a good, old-fashioned cybersquatter.[2] However, this dispute, and others like it,[3] raises a number of questions about the application of the trademark-focused Uniform Domain Name Dispute Resolution Policy (UDRP)[4] and other trademark-based laws[5] to domain name disputes involving personal names. The issues raised by personal names include the extent to which individuals, even famous individuals, truly do have trademark rights in their personal names. Additionally, the question arises as to whether individual complainants are actually seeking to protect trademark-like attributes of their personal names, or rather using trademark-focused regulations to protect other aspects of their personas.

Not all disputed domain names correspond with trademarks.[6] Personal

---

1 *Julia Fiona Roberts v Russell Boyd*, WIPO Arbitration and Mediation Center, Case No. D2000–0210 (May 29, 2000), full text available at www.wipo.int/amc/en/domains/decisions/html/2000/d2000-0210.html, last accessed November 6, 2007.

2 ANNE GILSON LALONDE and JEROME GILSON, TRADEMARK PROTECTION AND PRACTICE para. 7A.06 ('Cybersquatters register trademarks in Internet domain names with no intention of developing a viable website but instead to hold the name for resale to either the trademark owner or a third party.'). For a discussion of this practice, see Jacqueline Lipton, *Beyond Cybersquatting: Taking Domain Name Disputes Past Trademark Policy*, 40 WAKE FOREST L. REV. 1361, 1369–77 (2005).

3 See also *Tom Cruise v Alberta Hot Rods*, WIPO Arbitration and Mediation Center, Case No. D2006–0560 (July 5, 2006), available at www.wipo.int/amc/en/domains/decisions/html/2006/d2006-0560.html, last accessed March 16, 2010.

4 The full text of the UDRP is available on ICANN's website at www.icann.org/udrp/udrp-policy-24oct99.htm, last accessed November 6, 2007.

5 See discussion in Chapter 1; Lipton, *Beyond Cybersquatting*, *supra* note 2.

6 *Id.* at 1363 (noting that a limitation of current approaches to the domain name dispute resolution system is that it is focused on trademark protection); Jacqueline

names may or may not be trademarked, depending on the circumstances.[7] Judges and arbitrators often have little guidance as to whether a particular name really operates a trademark. In order for a personal name to operate as a trademark it is necessary for it to have acquired secondary meaning as an indicator of the origin of goods or services.[8] While this is a well accepted trademark doctrine, judges and arbitrators have not been particularly clear or consistent in their application of the proposition to personal names in trademark-related actions.[9] This has led to inconsistent and arbitrary results in practice, particularly in some UDRP arbitrations. It is not immediately clear why Julia Roberts[10] and Tom Cruise[11] were regarded by UDRP arbitrators as having trademarks in their personal names when the same was not necessarily true for Bruce Springsteen[12] or the late Anna Nicole Smith.[13] It is not clear why Secretary of State Hillary

---

Lipton, *Celebrity in Cyberspace: A Personality Rights Paradigm for Personal Domain Name Dispute Resolution*, 65 WASHINGTON AND LEE L. REV. 1445, 1449 (2008) ('not all disputed domain names correspond with trademarks. Personal names, for example, may or may not be trademarked, depending on the circumstances').

7 Lipton, *Celebrity in Cyberspace*, *supra* note 6, at 1449.

8 GILSON, *supra* note 2, para. 2.03[4][d] ('Just as with descriptive terms, a trademark or trade name that consists of a personal name (first name, surname, or both) is entitled to legal protection only if it attains secondary meaning.').

9 Lipton, *Celebrity in Cyberspace*, *supra* note 6, at 1449–50.

10 *Julia Fiona Roberts*, WIPO Case No. D2000–0210, available at www.wipo.int/amc/en/domains/decisions/html/2000/d2000-0210.html.

11 *Tom Cruise*, WIPO Case No. D2006–0560, available at www.wipo.int/amc/en/domains/decisions/html/2006/d2006-0560.html.

12 *Bruce Springsteen v Jeff Burgar and Bruce Springsteen Club*, WIPO Arbitration and Mediation Center, Case No. D2000–1532 (January 25, 2001), para. 6 available at www.wipo.int/amc/en/domains/decisions/html/2000/d2000-1532.html, last accessed March 2, 2009 ('It appears to be an established principle from cases such as Jeanette Winterson, Julia Roberts, and Sade that in the case of very well known celebrities, their names can acquire a distinctive secondary meaning giving rise to rights equating to unregistered trade marks, notwithstanding the non-registerability of the name itself. It should be noted that no evidence has been given of the name "Bruce Springsteen" having acquired a secondary meaning; in other words a recognition that the name should be associated with activities beyond the primary activities of Mr. Springsteen as a composer, performer and recorder of popular music. In the view of this Panel, it is by no means clear from the UDRP that it was intended to protect proper names of this nature.').

13 *Anna Nicole Smith v DNS Research Inc.*, National Arbitration Forum, Claim No. FA0312000220007 (February 21, 2004) available at www.adrforum.com/domains/decisions/220007.htm, last accessed October 25, 2007 (involving annanicolesmith.com domain name) ('it is unlikely that the evidence submitted here by

Clinton's name,[14] or that of her husband former President William J. Clinton,[15] have been recognized as trademarks[16] when the same is not true for other politicians such as Kathleen Kennedy Townsend.[17]

One difficulty raised by personal names in the domain space is that complainants who are private individuals tend to prefer the UDRP as a dispute resolution mechanism over domestic litigation.[18] This is unsurprising given the time, cost and jurisdictional advantages inherent in the UDRP.[19] However, reliance on the UDRP to resolve personal domain name disputes raises two difficulties. The first is that the UDRP inadvert-

---

complainant of her career, in and of itself, is sufficient to establish common law trademark rights in the name, which is a requirement for complainant to prevail on this aspect of the case. While the UDRP does not require a *registered* trademark for protection of a trademark from a confusingly identical domain name, the mere fact of having a successful career as an actress, singer or TV program star does not provide exclusive rights to the use of a name under the trademark laws. The cases require a clear showing of high commercial value and significant recognition of the name as solely that of the performer. The *Humphrey Bogart* case cited by the complainant is a prime example of the type of case that would be expected to prevail, since virtually no one familiar with the movie industry would fail to recognize his name as that of a famous movie star. The Panel does not believe complainant's name has yet reached that level of fame.').

14 *Hillary Rodham Clinton v Michele Dinoia*, National Arbitration Forum, Claim No. FA0502000414641 (March 18, 2005), available at www.arb-forum.com/domains/decisions/414641.htm, last accessed March 2, 2009 (then Senator Clinton was regarded as having an unregistered trademark right in her personal name in connection with both her political activities and her career as an author of a number of books sold in commerce).

15 See *William J. Clinton and The William J. Clinton Presidential Foundation v Web of Deception*, National Arbitration Forum, Claim No. FA0904001256123 (June 1, 2009), available at http://domains.adrforum.com/domains/decisions/1256123.htm, last accessed July 10, 2009 (arbitrator 'reluctantly' concluded that former President Clinton had a trademark in his personal name, but the former president was unsuccessful in obtaining a transfer order for relevant domain names because he was unable to establish 'bad faith' registration and use on the part of the registrant).

16 *Hillary Rodham Clinton*, National Arbitration Forum, Claim No. FA0502000414641 available at www.arb-forum.com/domains/decisions/414641.htm.

17 *Kathleen Kennedy Townsend v Birt*, WIPO Arbitration and Mediation Center, Case No. D2002–0030 (April 11, 2002) available at www.wipo.int/amc/en/domains/decisions/html/2002/d2002-0451.html, last accessed March 16, 2010 (individual politician in state gubernatorial race held not to hold trademark rights in her personal name).

18 Lipton, *Celebrity in Cyberspace*, *supra* note 6, at 1448–9.

19 *Id.*

ently encourages the expansion of trademark law into questionable areas: for example, situations where an individual's name is *not* operating as a source indicator for products or services (that is, as a trademark or service mark). The second issue is that reliance on trademark-focused regulations for personal domain name disputes appears in practice to have stalled the development of legal rules more appropriately tailored for these disputes.

This chapter focuses on domain name disputes involving personal names. It commences by grouping personal domain name disputes into different categories involving celebrities, other public figures and private individuals, respectively. Even though the distinctions between these categories are not perfect, they serve to highlight the fact that different legal and policy interests might be raised by disputes involving different kinds of names. The discussion then turns to the limitations of existing domain name regulations for personal domain name disputes, with particular reference to the UDRP. It also examines the potential application to personal domain name disputes of regulations focused more squarely on the protection of personal names and identities. These regulations include the personality rights tort in the United States and the *sui generis* personal name protections in the federal cyberpiracy legislation.[20] The chapter also queries whether new approaches might be taken to personal domain name disputes under the UDRP, and particularly whether the UDRP might be revised to include specific provisions for personal names. Finally, some emerging issues are considered, including the implications of the development of new gTLDs and of personalized Facebook URLs on questions involving the regulation of personal names online.

4.2 CATEGORIZING PERSONAL DOMAIN NAME DISPUTES

Different classes of individuals have differing concerns about registration and use of their personal names in the domain space. The major classes of disputes arising to date might be divided into three subcategories, involving (a) celebrities' names, (b) politicians' and public figures' names, and (c) private individuals' names. These subcategories are considered below with particular reference to the limitations of existing regulations in each class of cases. Politicians' names are considered in further detail in Chapter

---

20 15 U.S.C. § 8131(1)(A).

5 which focuses on political, cultural and geographic identifiers in the domain space.

4.2.1 Celebrities' Names

The most prominent category of disputes involving personal names in the domain space has involved celebrities' names: that is, people who are famous for their professional activities in fields such as music,[21] television,[22] movies[23] and sports.[24] These people have the most commercially valuable personal names because they trade on their names for their livelihood.[25] However, the fact that celebrity names have commercial value does not necessarily mean that they automatically function as trademarks. Trademarks are defined in the Lanham Act to include 'any word, name, symbol, or device, or any combination thereof . . . used by a person . . . to

---

[21] See, for example, *Bruce Springsteen*, WIPO Case No. D2000–1532, available at www.wipo/int/amc/en/domains/decisions/html/2000/d2000-1532.html (involving 'brucespringsteen.com' domain name); *Madonna Ciccone v Dan Parisi,* WIPO Arbitration and Mediation Center, Case No. D2000–0847 (October 12, 2000), available at www.wipo.int/amc/en/domains/decisions/html/2000/d2000-0847.html, last accessed March 16, 2010 (involving 'Madonna.com' domain name); *Experience Hendrix LLC v Denny Hammerton,* WIPO Arbitration and Mediation Center, Case. No. D2000–0364 (August 2, 2000, *aff'd* August 15, 2000), available at www.wipo.int/amc/en/domains/decisions/html/2000/d2000-0364.html, last accessed March 16, 2010 (involving 'jimihendrix.com' domain name).

[22] *Anna Nicole Smith,* National Arbitration Forum, Claim No. FA0312000220007, available at www.adrforum.com/domains/decisions/220007.htm (involving 'annanicolesmith.com' domain name).

[23] *Julia Fiona Roberts*, WIPO Case No. D2000–0210, available at www.wipo.int/amc/en/domains/decisions/html/2000/d2000-0210.html (involving 'juliaroberts.com' domain name); *Tom Cruise*, WIPO Case No. D2006–0560, available at www.wipo.int/amc/en/domains/decisions/html/2006/d2006-0560.html (involving 'tomcruise.com' domain name); *Kevin Spacey v Alberta Hot Rods*, National Arbitration Forum, Claim No. 96937 (August 1, 2002), available at www.adrforum.com/domains/decisions/96937.htm, last accessed March 16, 2010 (involving the domain name 'kevinspacey.com').

[24] See, for example *Bjorn Borg v Miguel Garcia,* WIPO Arbitration and Mediation Center, Case No. D2007–0591 (June 21, 2007), available at www.wipo.int/amc/en/domains/decisions/html/2007/d2007-0591.html, last accessed March 16, 2010 (involving the domain name 'bjornborg.com').

[25] However, there is some dispute about the extent to which they trade on those names in a 'trademark sense'. For a general critique of this point in the domain name context, see Anthony Verna, www.whatsina.name, 14 SETON HALL J. SPORTS AND ENT. L. 153 (2004).

identify and distinguish his or her goods . . . from those manufactured or sold by others and to indicate the source of the goods'.[26]

A celebrity does not necessarily have a trademark or service mark in her personal name simply by virtue of being famous.[27] There must be products or services associated with the name, and the name must be used to distinguish her products or services from those of others. Nevertheless, celebrities have generally relied on the trademark-focused UDRP to bring complaints about unauthorized uses of their names in the domain space. This is largely because the UDRP is the simplest and most cost-effective avenue for personal name claimants,[28] even though it was never intended that the UDRP would inadvertently extend trademark protections to all personal names. While many UDRP arbitrators have accepted trademark claims in personal names,[29]

---

[26] 15 U.S.C. § 1127. 'Service marks' are similarly defined in 15 U.S.C. § 1127 ('The term "service mark" means any word, name, symbol, or device, or any combination thereof—(1) used by a person, or (2) which a person has a bona fide intention to use in commerce and applies to register on the principal register established by this chapter, to identify and distinguish the services of one person, including a unique service, from the services of others and to indicate the source of the services, even if that source is unknown. Titles, character names, and other distinctive features of radio or television programs may be registered as service marks notwithstanding that they, or the programs, may advertise the goods of the sponsor.').

[27] See, for example, *Chung, Mong Koo and Hyundai Motor Company v Individual*, WIPO Arbitration and Mediation Center, Case No. D2005–1068 (December 21, 2005), para. 6A, available at www.wipo.int/amc/en/domains/decisions/html/2005/d2005-1068.html, last accessed July 25, 2008 ('[T]he consensus view among UDRP panelists is that a complainant may show that his or her personal name has taken on such a *cachet* that it has become a trademark, but that to succeed in doing so the complainant will have to show that the name has actually been used in trade or commerce. It will instantly be seen that this is a considerable hurdle to vault and that the reason why some cases have failed to establish trademark rights in a personal name is that the evidence has shown only that the name is famous and not that it has been used in trade or commerce.').

[28] Costs of judicial proceedings can be prohibitive for private individuals: P. Landon Moreland and Colby Springer, *Celebrity Domain Names: ICANN Arbitration Pitfalls and Pragmatic Advice*, 17 Santa Clara Computer and High Tech L.J. 385 (2001) ('Prior to the establishment of ICANN Arbitration, recovery of celebrity domain names was an expensive and potentially lengthy process'); Jessica Litman, *The DNS Wars: Trademarks and the Internet Domain Name System*, 4 J Small and Emerging Bus. L. 149, 155 (2000) (noting the often prohibitive cost of trademark infringement and dilution litigation in early domain name disputes).

[29] See, for example, *Julia Fiona Roberts*, WIPO Case No. D2000–0210, para. 6, available at www.wipo.int/amc/en/domains/decisions/html/2000/d2000-0210.html; *Tom Cruise*, WIPO Case No. D2006–0560, available at www.wipo.int/

others have not.[30] Moreoever, it is difficult to ascertain a principled distinction between the different approaches.

It is possible that a Julia Roberts movie might be regarded as a product involving a 'Julia Roberts' trademark.[31] However, on closer inspection, this view may be difficult to sustain. Audiences may go to see a movie because Julia Roberts is in it, or they may associate a certain quality of performance with Ms Roberts. However, they are unlikely to think that Ms Roberts is the *source* of the movie in a trademark sense. The movie studio that produced the film is more likely to be regarded as the source of the movie. It is possible that Ms Roberts' name is a trademark or service mark when she offers her performance services to movie producers and movie studios. However, this is not the basis on which UDRP arbitrators have decided that she had trademark rights in her name.[32]

There was actually very little discussion of the trademark issue in the *Roberts* arbitration, other than an acknowledgment by the arbitrators that a mark does not have to be registered to be protected under the UDRP.[33]

---

amc/en/domains/decisions/html/2006/d2006-0560.html; *Kevin Spacey*, National Arbitration Forum, Claim No. FA020500096937, available at www.adrforum.com/domains/decisions/96937.htm.

[30] *Bruce Springsteen*, WIPO Case No. D2000–1532, para. 6 available at www.wipo.int/amc/en/domains/decisions/html/2000/d2000-1532.html; *Anna Nicole Smith*, National Arbitration Forum, Claim No. FA0312000220007, available at www.adr-forum.com/domains/decisions/220007.htm; *The Hebrew University of Jerusalem v Alberta Hot Rods,* WIPO Arbitration and Mediation Center, Case No. D2002–0616 (October 7, 2002), available at www.kipo.ke.wipo.net/amc/en/domains/decisions/html/2002/d2002-0616.html, last accessed March 16, 2010 (involving a complaint with respect to the domain name 'alberteinstein.com'); *Gordon Sumner aka Sting v Michael Urvan,* WIPO Arbitration and Mediation Center, Case No. D2000–0596 (July 20, 2000) para. 6.5, available at www.wipo.int/amc/en/domains/decisions/html/2000/d2000-0596.html, last accessed November 8, 2007 ('In the opinion of this Administrative Panel, it is doubtful whether the Uniform Policy is applicable to this dispute. Although it is accepted that the complainant is world famous under the name Sting, it does not follow that he has rights in Sting *as a trademark or service mark*.').

[31] Lipton, *Celebrity in Cyberspace*, *supra* note 6, at 1457–8.

[32] *Julia Fiona Roberts*, WIPO Case No. D2000–0210, para. 6, available at www.wipo.int/amc/en/domains/decisions/html/2000/d2000-0210.html.

[33] *Id.* ('A recent decision citing English law found that common law trademark rights exist in an author's name. The Policy does not require that the complainant should have rights in a registered trademark or service mark. It is sufficient that the complainant should satisfy the Administrative Panel that she has rights in common law trademark or sufficient rights to ground an action for passing off.')

There is a suggestion in the decision, and in other UDRP decisions involving personal names, that the name of an author of a creative work, such as the author of a book, may be regarded as a trademark.[34] However, even if this test for trademarkability is correct, an actor in a film is not the film's author.[35] Under this analysis, it would be more likely that the writer or director of the film was its author, and therefore it would be more sensible to regard their names as trademarks in relation to the film.[36]

Celebrities may have valid reasons for seeking to assert control over their names in the domain space, particularly in the 'name.com' space which is probably viewed by typical Internet users as the most likely site for a celebrity's authorized online presence. Celebrities may want to control this domain for their own commercial motives – which seems reasonable, particularly if this is in line with current Internet usage norms. For example, Tyra Banks' management company, Bankable Inc., appears to have registered the domain name 'tyrabanks.com' for this purpose.[37] It is an official website authorized and operated by Ms Banks, including details about her professional activities.[38] Another example is 'parishilton.com' which appears to be an authorized website for Paris Hilton, including details of her proposed appearances and her music career.[39]

Celebrities may also want to control some domain names to prevent unjust enrichment. In other words, celebrities who may not necessarily want to make their own commercial profits from personal domain names may nevertheless want to prevent others from profiting from their

---

[34] *Id.* See also *Hillary Rodham Clinton*, National Arbitration Forum, Claim No. FA0502000414641, available at www.arb-forum.com/domains/decisions/414641.htm *supra* note 14.

[35] Verna, *supra* note 25, at 162–3 ('If an author has trademark rights in his or her name, then it must come from the rather singular nature of a novel. Yes, there are editors in the writing process, however, editors do relatively little work compared to the author. A movie, on the other hand, has many other people involved in the process . . . Looking at the credits of any major motion picture, there are writers, assistant directors, and people who need to operate the microphone and the camera. There may be more than one scriptwriter. The actors and actresses are just a small part of the motion picture.')

[36] Although some people would disagree even with this analysis because of the collective creative nature of a motion picture. See Verna, *supra* note 25 at 162–3.

[37] See www.whois-search.com/whois/tyrabanks.com, last accessed November 7, 2007.

[38] See www.tyrabanks.com, last accessed November 7, 2007.

[39] See www.parishilton.com, last accessed November 7, 2007. Other examples of apparently official websites run by a famous notable personality are www.donaldtrump.com and www.trump.com for Donald Trump.

names online. The prevention of unjust enrichment may necessitate a presumption, similar to that discussed in the previous chapter about trademarks,[40] that 'name.com' versions of personal names should be reserved to the individuals whose names correspond with those domain names. There may be justifications for limiting such a presumption to celebrities' and public figures' names, rather than to private individuals' names. Private individuals' names are unlikely to raise the same potential for unjust enrichment as the commercially valuable names of celebrities and some other public figures. This would be similar to reserving rights in 'trademark.com' names to rightful trademark holders to prevent consumer confusion and unjust enrichment online. Of course, as with 'trademark.com' names, these kinds of presumptions do not work very well if multiple individuals have the same name. In such cases, maybe a 'first come, first served' approach or, in some situations, a domain name sharing approach would be preferable in practice.[41]

Celebrities may alternatively seek to control 'name.com' versions of their personal names in order to *avoid* the use of these names for any unauthorized purposes – somewhat like a privacy right. Some celebrities may wish to control these domain names to telegraph to the public that they have not authorized any official web content. Thus, Internet users will find nothing relating to the celebrity under the 'name.com' version of the name. This may support a presumption that any web content a user might find under other iterations of the celebrity's name is likely to be unauthorized content. In some ways, this analogizes to a privacy protection allowing the celebrity to communicate to the public a desire not to exploit her own image online, and perhaps implicitly requesting privacy considerations from others. An example of this is found in the *Julia Roberts*[42] scenario. After successfully obtaining a transfer of the 'juliaroberts.com' domain name, Ms Roberts has not utilized the name for an official website.

Reserving 'name.com' domain names to celebrities who do not desire any authorized online presence would not necessarily chill speech about celebrities online. Many other domain names are available for fans and critics who want to communicate about their idols. Search engines will

---

40 See 5.1, *supra*.

41 See 2.4, *supra*. See also discussion in Jacqueline Lipton, *A Winning Solution for Youtube and Utube: Corresponding Trademarks and Domain Name Sharing*, 21 HARVARD J. LAW AND TECHNOLOGY 509 (2008).

42 *Julia Fiona Roberts*, WIPO Case No. D2000–0210, available at www.wipo.int/amc/en/domains/decisions/html/2000/d2000-0210.html.

also help Internet users find unauthorized content about individuals posted under less intuitive domain names. However, the presumption may communicate something about how the celebrity feels about use of her name and persona online. If the 'name.com' version of a personal name is presumed always to be reserved for the authorized online space a celebrity is entitled to control as of right, then the celebrity can use this presumption to either disseminate authorized content to the public, or to telegraph a desire not to promulgate any authorized content online.

The interests identified above in both commercial control of 'name.com' domain names and in privacy protections of a celebrity persona match the emphases of the American right of publicity tort much more closely than trademark law. The right of publicity tort has been explained variously on the basis of economic property rights in an individual's name or likeness,[43] a

---

[43] Various justifications have been put forward for a property basis for personality rights, and have equally been criticized over the years. For a discussion of property theory in this context, see Stacey Dogan and Mark Lemley, *What the Right of Publicity Can Learn from Trademark Law*, 58 STANFORD L. REV. 1161, 1181–3 (2006) (critique of Lockean labor theory justifications for personality rights as property); Mark McKenna, *The Right of Publicity and Autonomous Self-Definition*, 67 U. PITT. L. REV. 225, 247 (2005) ('It might be true that identity is sufficiently similar to other objects the law regards as property and therefore deserves at least some of the sticks in the traditional bundle of property rights. But far too few courts and commentators have offered a theory as to why any of the traditional property justifications lead to that conclusion.'); 251–67 (critique of Lockean labor theory justifications for property rights in personal identity); Alice Haemmerli, *Whose Who? The Case for a Kantian Right of Publicity*, 49 DUKE L.J. 383, 388 (1999) ('Both proponents and critics of the right of publicity generally perceive it as a property claim grounded in Lockean labor theory'); 407–8 (noting dual property and privacy justifications for right of publicity actions); 412 ('To the extent that commentators specifically address publicity rights, they tend to do so within this property context, and to use Lockean labor theories of property to explain the assertion of a property right in identity or persona.'); Roberta Kwall, *Fame*, 73 INDIANA L.J. 1, 15 (1997) ('This article . . . contends that a property-based conception for publicity rights is the natural outgrowth of our cultural norms as well as our theoretical conceptions of property.'); David Westfall and David Landau, *Publicity Rights as Property Rights*, 23 CARDOZO ARTS AND ENT. L.J. 71 (2005) (examining property basis for rights of publicity); Eileen Rielly, *The Right of Publicity for Political Figures: Martin Luther King, Jr, Center for Social Change, Inc. v American Heritage Products*, 46 U. PITT. L. REV. 1161, 1165–9 (1985) (describing development of a property rights rationale for the right of publicity). See also Diane Zimmerman and Melissa Jacoby, *Foreclosing on Fame: Exploring the Uncharted Boundaries of the Right of Publicity*, 77 N.Y.U. L. REV. 1322 (2002).

need to prevent free-riding or unjust enrichment,[44] and the need to protect a person's privacy from unauthorized commercial interference.[45] Personality rights jurisprudence has also dealt with issues of balancing the public's interest in free speech about a celebrity with the celebrity's interest in controlling her public persona.[46] Although these are difficult issues that have

---

[44] Dogan and Lemley, *supra* note 43, at 1181–3 (critique of unjust enrichment explanation of rights of publicity); Sarah Konsky, *Publicity Dilution: A Proposal for Protecting Publicity Rights*, 21 SANTA CLARA COMPUTER AND HIGH TECH L.J. 347 (2005) (recognition of unjust enrichment, along with Lockean theory and several other theoretical justifications as explanations for the right of publicity); McKenna, *supra* note 43, at 247–8 (critique of unjust enrichment theories of the right of publicity); Michael Madow, *Private Ownership of Public Image: Popular Culture and Publicity Rights*, 81 CALIF. L. REV. 125, 196–204 (1993) (critique of unjust enrichment rationales for the right of publicity).

[45] Dogan and Lemley, *supra* note 43, at 1208–10 (critique of privacy based justifications for the right of publicity); Madow, *supra* note 44, at 167–8 (discussion of privacy rights basis for some early right of publicity cases); McKenna, *supra* note 43, at 285 ('Since all individuals share the interest in autonomous self-definition, every individual should be able to control uses of her identity that interfere with her ability to define her own public character.'); 286 ('Compelling a person to express a message herself presents a particular sort of threat to her freedom of belief: It threatens her ability to control what she tells the world about who she is and what she holds important'); Haemmerli, *supra* note 43, at 407–8 (describing theoretical muddle between property and privacy theory underlying rights of publicity claims); Rielly, *supra* note 43, at 1164–5 (description of privacy foundations of the right of publicity).

[46] Haemmerli, *supra* note 43, at 441–58 (analysis of First Amendment issues arising with respect to the right of publicity); Peter Felcher and Edward Rubin, *Privacy, Publicity, and the Portrayal of Real People by the Media*, 88 YALE L.J. 1577, 1590 (1979) ('The First Amendment inevitably defines the operation and extent of the right of publicity; once the defendant can establish that the expression in question is protected, he will almost invariably prevail'.); Roberta Kwall, *The Right of Publicity vs. the First Amendment: A Property and Liability Rule Analysis*, 70 INDIANA L.J. 47 (1994) (suggesting a property versus liability rule basis for balancing First Amendment concerns against right of publicity claims); Rielly, *supra* note 43, at 1172–4 (balancing First Amendment concerns with the publicity rights of public figures and politicians); Madow, *supra* note 44, at 140 (description of the role of the consumer as an active and creative participant in the creation of cultural commodities); Kwall, *Fame*, *supra* note 43, at 46–7 ('We do not deprive the owners of famous trademarks or the copyright owners of popular works of art or literature of their rights just because the public has played some role in placing a value on these works. Therefore, right-of-publicity critics must justify why the cachet of a person's fame should be treated differently.'). See also Diane Zimmerman, *Who Put the Right in the Right of Publicity?*, 9 DEPAUL-LCA J. ART AND ENT. L. 35 (1998).

not been definitively resolved even within the right of publicity, this body of law has at least grappled with these concerns and has attempted to develop responses to them. The right of publicity and its potential application to personal domain name disputes is considered in more detail below.[47]

While the above has suggested a presumption that 'name.com' versions of personal names should rightly belong to a person with the relevant name, it has said nothing about the '.name' gTLD that was introduced by ICANN as one of the seven gTLDs released in 2000.[48] The reason for the focus on the '.com' space is that, as with trademarks, there seem to be emerging norms that Internet users expect '.com' names to resolve to a business' or an individual's authorized online presence, despite the availability of other gTLDs. The fact that registrants, cybersquatters and Internet users alike still flock to '.com' names suggests that this gTLD has retained, and is likely to continue to retain, its popularity, despite the introduction of new gTLDs. In fact, it will be interesting to see if this continues to be the case when multiple new gTLDs are introduced under ICANN's new proposal to open up the gTLD space even further.[49]

4.2.2 Politicians' and Public Figures' Names

Politicians and other public figures may also have concerns about the use of their personal names in the domain space. These concerns may differ from those of celebrities. Disputes involving politicians' and public figures' names may, for example, raise free speech concerns more significantly than disputes involving celebrities' names.[50] Trademark law is

---

[47] See 4.4, *infra*.

[48] The other new gTLDs introduced in 2000 were '.biz', '.info', '.pro', '.name', '.aero', '.coop', and '.museum'. See MILTON MUELLER, RULING THE ROOT: INTERNET GOVERNANCE AND THE TAMING OF CYBERSPACE, 204 (2004).

[49] ICANN, New gTLD Program: Draft Applicant Guidebook (Draft RFP) (October 24, 2008), full text available at www.icann.org/en/topics/new-gtlds/draft-rfp-24oct08-en.pdf, last accessed December 11, 2008.

[50] See, for example, *New York Magazine v The Metropolitan Transit Authority and the City of New York*, 987 F. Supp. 254 (1997), *aff'd in part, vacated in part, New York Magazine v The Metropolitan Transit Authority and the City of New York*, 136 F.3d 123 (1998) (on balancing Mayor Rudolph Giuliani's rights of privacy and publicity against the First Amendment); Rielly, *supra* note 43, at 1172–4 (describing need to balance First Amendment interests in political debate against the publicity rights of politicians and public figures); *Wilson v Brown*, 73 N.Y.S.2d 587, 589 (Sup. Ct. Kings Co. 1947) ('One who takes an office, whether it is in government or in outside organizations, must be deemed to have agreed to any reasonable public use of, or reference to, his name . . . Persons who accept high

again a poor fit for balancing competing interests in such names. Even if some famous celebrities, such as authors,[51] have trademarks in their names, politicians are less likely to hold such rights.[52] Most politicians do not use their names as source indicators. [53] Rather, they use their names to raise public awareness about particular issues[54] and, in the case of politicians, often in the context of a political campaign. These names often have a temporal quality that is particularly significant to the democratic process. If, for example, electors are voting on a particular issue, a given domain name might be extremely valuable in the leadup to an election and much less valuable thereafter,[55] both in the hands of the person with whose name it corresponds, and in the hands of others.

The First Amendment is likely to be more significantly implicated in the

---

positions ought not to be so tender about the mention of their names; they must bear "the white light that beats upon a throne". If they want peace and privacy they should stay out of public life; if they object to having their names legitimately mentioned they need only to resign and they will quickly subside into happy obscurity.').

[51] Of course, where a politician is also an author, she may assert trademark rights in her name under this analysis. See, for example, *Hillary Rodham Clinton*, National Arbitration Forum, Claim No. FA0502000414641, available at www.arb-forum.com/domains/decisions/414641.htm (*supra* note 14)

[52] Jacqueline Lipton, *Who Owns 'Hillary.com'? Political Speech and the First Amendment in Cyberspace*, 49 Boston College L. Rev. 55 (2008); *Report of the Second WIPO Internet Domain Name Process* (September 3, 2001), para. 188, available at www.wipo.int/amc/en/process/process2/report/html/report.html#5, last accessed November 11, 2007 ('the names of political figures, religious leaders, scientists and historical persons may never have been used in commerce and, thus, are unlikely to have trademarks associated with them.'). However, some politicians have been regarded as having commercial trademark rights in their personal names in relation to certain commercial activities: *Hillary Rodham Clinton*, National Arbitration Forum, Claim No. FA 050200414641, available at www.arb-forum.com/domains/decisions/414641.htm (*supra* note 14).

[53] See definitions of 'trademark' and 'service mark' in 15 U.S.C. § 1127.

[54] That is not to say that celebrities do not also get involved in public interest issues – it is just more typical of politicians in their day-to-day activities.

[55] There can also obviously be temporal aspects to a celebrity's fame. However, the temporal issues can be more pronounced and more important in the leadup to an election where election day is effectively the deadline for a politician to get her message across to the electorate. The temporal issues in politics are also much more significant to the operation of a representative democracy than temporal issues relating to a celebrity's fame which are likely to have more to do with the creation and waning of public interest in cultural commodities at any given point in time.

political context than in the commercial context.[56] American personality rights jurisprudence may contribute some useful guidance to political domain name disputes because of its focus on protecting public figures against improper use of their personas, while at the same time attempting (at least in theory) to protect free speech.

Some concerns of politicians and public figures about their names in the domain space will mirror those of commercial celebrities. An obvious example is cybersquatting. A cybersquatter may register either a celebrity's name or a policitian's name in the hopes of making a commercial profit from its transfer. There may be situations in which cybersquatting is more serious for a politician than a celebrity in terms of practical consequences of failing to secure control of a given name. For example, in the leadup to an election, a politician will likely have a strong desire to control a domain name relating to her personal name, particularly the 'name.com' version, as the Internet has become a very important tool for communicating with the electorate and also for political fundraising.[57]

Like celebrities, politicians and public figures will also have concerns

---

56 *New York Magazine v The Metropolitan Transit Authority and the City of New York*, 987 F. Supp. 254, 262 (1997), *aff'd in part, vacated in part*, *New York Magazine v The Metropolitan Transit Authority and the City of New York*, 136 F.3d 123 (1998) (discussing continuum of protections available under the First Amendment for political versus commercial speech about politicians in the right of publicity context).

57 Most politicians now run websites where supporters can donate funds to their campaigns. See, for example, www.hillaryclinton.com, last accessed November 8, 2007, www.barackobama.com, last accessed November 8, 2007. Senator Obama's website has a rather sophisticated fundraising project where individuals can set up accounts and set fundraising goals that they plan to achieve to support the senator's campaign, see http://my.barackobama.com/page/outreach/login/main, last accessed November 8, 2007. Little has been written about the impact of the Internet on political fundraising to date. For a survey of Howard Dean's use of the Internet in his run for the 2004 presidential ticket, see Abigail Brown, *Politics, Innovation, and the Internet: A Source of Howard Dean's Fundraising Success?* (September 6, 2007), available at http://papers.ssrn.com/sol3/papers.cfm?abstract_id=1012481, last accessed November 8, 2007 (examining Dean's use of the Internet to set up town hall meetings for campaign and fundraising purposes). On domain name use in politics more generally, see Matthew Coleman, *Domain Name Piracy and Privacy: Do Federal Election Regulations Offer a Solution?*, 19 YALE L. AND POL'Y REV. 235 (2000); Jacqueline Lipton, *From Domain Names to Video Games: The Rise of the Internet in Presidential Politics,* 86 DENVER UNIVERSITY L. REV. 693, 697–8 (2009) (discussing importance of Internet domain names in political campaigns in the context of the 2004 presidential election in the United States).

about situations where a domain name registrant is not cybersquatting on a given name, but rather wants to use the name herself for some expressive or commercial purpose. Where the purpose is purely commercial, the right of publicity might sanction the conduct to the extent that this tort prohibits unauthorized commercial exploitations of a person's name or likeness.[58] Where the purpose is expressive, more difficult First Amendment concerns come into play.

An opposing party or candidate may be motivated to register a politician's name as a domain name in order to criticize the politician on the associated website. Because of the importance of free speech in the political process, these uses of a 'name.com' domain name raise important aspects of the speech-persona balance. On the one hand, if *all* political speech is to be protected, regardless of content or forum, then anyone should arguably be entitled to register and use such a name for any expressive purpose. On the other hand, if there is a social norm that 'name.com' domain names resolve to websites authorized by relevant individuals, it might be misleading to allow even purely expressive messages about a politician under those domain names without the politician's consent. Internet users could be misled in these cases as to the identity of the speaker, which could make it more difficult for them to locate authorized messages.

Two examples arose in state elections in Montana in recent years. One involved Bob Keenan, a Republican candidate running for the United States Senate. The domain name 'bobkeenan.com' had been registered by the Montana Democratic Party and hosted a website critical of Keenan's policies. The other involved a Democratic candidate for Montana Secretary of State, Linda McCulloch. The Montana Republican State Central Committee had registered the domain name 'lindamcculloch.com' and used it for a website critical of McCulloch. Given the lack of likely trademark interest in these politicians' names,[59] trademark law was not likely to help either candidate. The conduct would not even run afoul of the federal cyberpiracy statute (the provision that does not require a trademark interest) because § 8131 (1)(A) requires an attempt to sell a domain name for profit in order for liability

---

58 GILSON, *supra* note 2, para. 2B.01.

59 Often, local politicians, as compared with some federal politicians, are not regarded as having sufficient trademark interests in their names to support trademark-related actions. See, for example, *Kathleen Kennedy Townsend*, WIPO Case No. D2002–0030, available at www.wipo.int/amc/en/domains/decisions/html/2002/d2002-0451.html) (individual politician in state gubernatorial race held not to hold trademark rights in her personal name).

to attach.[60] The registrants in these scenarios were not attempting to sell the names. They were rather utilizing them to criticize politicians from opposing camps.

Some of the Californian state legislation discussed in Chapter 1[61] might indirectly cover these situations. California's Political Cyberfraud Abatement Act, for example, prohibits fraudulent and misleading conduct on the Internet in relation to a ballot measure.[62] This would catch some situations where domain name registrants mislead Internet users by registering a domain name based on a politician's name. However, this approach has not yet been adopted in other states, let alone at a more global level. The Californian provisions are also not targeted specifically at protecting individual names from unauthorized uses. Rather, the Act deals with ballot measures more generally.[63] It would therefore not apply outside the electoral context. As noted in Chapter 1,[64] there is additionally some Californian state legislation dealing more specifically with unauthorized registrations and uses of domain names corresponding with personal names.[65] The relevant provisions of California's Business and Professions Code cover all personal names, whether relating to politicians or public figures[66] or otherwise. However, again this is pure state law not yet mirrored in any other jurisdictions.

---

60 15 U.S.C. § 8131(1)(A) ('Any person who registers a domain name that consists of the name of another living person, or a name substantially and confusingly similar thereto, without that person's consent, with the specific intent to profit from such name by selling the domain name for financial gain to that person or any third party, shall be liable in a civil action by such person.').

61 See 1.6.1 and 1.6.2, *supra*.

62 Political Cyberfraud Abatement Act, Cal. Elections Code, §§ 18320–18323.

63 Cal. Elections Code, § 18320(c)(1) ('"Political cyberfraud" means a knowing and willful act concerning a political Web site that is committed with the intent to deny a person access to a political Web site, deny a person the opportunity to register a domain name for a political Web site, or cause a person reasonably to believe that a political Web site has been posted by a person other than the person who posted the Web site, and would cause a reasonable person, after reading the Web site, to believe the site actually represents the views of the proponent or opponent of a ballot measure.')

64 See 1.6.1 and 1.6.2, *supra*.

65 California Business and Professions Code, §§ 17525–17526. See, in particular, § 17525(a) ('It is unlawful for a person, with a bad faith intent to register, traffic in, or use a domain name, that is identical or confusingly similar to the personal name of another living person or deceased personality, without regard to the goods or services of the parties.').

66 In fact, there is specific mention of using a domain name corresponding with an individual person's name in bad faith to mislead electors: see California Business

4.2.3 Private Individuals' Names

Private individuals' names are much less likely to raise commercial problems of unjust enrichment and consumer confusion than more well-known names. Presumably they are also less likely to raise free speech concerns unless a private individual finds herself suddenly in the spotlight with respect to a matter of public interest. Unsurprisingly, there are fewer disputes involving unauthorized registration and use of private individuals' names on the Internet than celebrities' and public figures' names.[67] A number of disputes involving private individuals' names actually *do* relate to trademark uses of those names where a name has acquired secondary meaning[68] as being synonymous with a person's business activities.[69] Thus, trademark-focused laws, including the UDRP, are appropriate for dispute resolution in many of these cases.

Where a private individual's name is not operating as a trademark, it is unlikely to raise many conflicts in the 'name.com' space. There is less profit to be made by cybersquatting on nonfamous names, and little reason to set up gripe sites or parody sites about private individuals. However, one obvious example of where such a situation might arise would be where

---

and Professions Code, § 17526(j), including as a bad faith factor: 'The intent of a person alleged to be in violation of this article to mislead, deceive, or defraud voters'.

[67] Although there are some cases on record involving the names of private individuals: *Paul Wright v Domain Source Inc.*, 2002 U.S. Dist. LEXIS 16024 (2002); *Trudeau v Lanoue*, 2006 U.S. Dixt. LEXIS 7956 (2006); *Stephan Schmidheiny v Steven Weber*, 285 F.Supp.2d 613 (2003). All of these cases involved personal names used in conjunction with businesses conducted by the complainant.

[68] GILSON, *supra* note 2, para. 2.03[4][d] ('Just as with descriptive terms, a trademark or trade name that consists of a personal name (first name, surname, or both) is entitled to legal protection only if it attains secondary meaning.').

[69] Many businesses, in fact, use their chief officers' names as business names and trademarks: for example, The Trump Organization (owned by Donald Trump). See www.trump.com, last accessed January 23, 2008. Of course, because of his participation in the television show *The Apprentice*, it is possible that Trump's name also functions as a celebrity name. Nevertheless, due to his business activities (and perhaps also his authorship of several books), Trump's name is likely a trademark. Trump has also registered a variety of permutations of his personal name as registered marks with respect to particular goods and services: http://tess2.uspto.gov/bin/gate.exe (result of United States Patent and Trademark Office Search for 'Trump' trademark conducted on January 23, 2008).

more than one person shares the same personal name.[70] This situation is analogous to the case where more than one company legitimately shares the same or similar trademarks in different product or geographic markets.[71] In the absence of a domain name sharing strategy,[72] it may be that the 'first come, first served' rule has to apply here.[73]

---

[70] Ultimately, this was what happened in the paulwright.com dispute: *Paul Wright v Domain Source Inc.*, 2002 U.S. Dist. LEXIS 16024 (2002). Although the plaintiff was successful in an action to have the domain name 'paulwright.com' transferred back to him by a defendant cybersquatter, the order was conditional on no third party having acquired bona fide rights in the name. Another person called Paul Wright had the 'paulwright.com' domain name transferred to him before the court order went into effect so the plaintiff never regained control of the name.

[71] Stuart Weinstein, *The Cyberpiracy Prevention Act: Reconciling Real Space Sectoral and Geographic Distinctions in the Use of Internet Domain Names Under the Lanham Act,* 9 U. Miami Bus. L. Rev. 145, 158 (2001) ('an entity may use an identical mark as another, as long as he does not use that mark within the same sector or industry. As with geographical protection of a user's mark, the scope of protection is determined as an evidentiary matter, looking at the likelihood of consumer confusion.'); David Barrett, *The Future of the Concurrent Use of Trademarks Doctrine in the Information Age*, 23 Hastings Comm. and Ent. L.J. 687, 689–92 (2001) (examining American legislative history of the 'concurrent use' doctrine in trademark law which allows different trademark holders to use similar marks in different geographic areas); *Dawn Donut Co. v Hart's Food Stores, Inc.*, 267 F. 2d 358 (2d Cir. 1959) (holding no likelihood of confusion in case where plaintiff and defendant used similar marks in different product markets and different jurisdictions); *National Association for Healthcare Communications, Inc. v Central Arkansas Area Agency on Aging Inc.*, 257 F.3d 732 (8th Cir. 2001) (granting injunction against federal trademark owner in order to allow user of the same mark to use it in established six county area in California); Litman, *supra* note 28, at 152 ('Out here in meat space, we can have a whole bunch of different owners of Acme as a trademark – the last time I counted there were more than a hundred different trademark registrations, in addition to all the local unregistered Acme marks you can find by just looking in the telephone book. On the Internet, only one person can own acme.com.'); Lipton, *A Winning Solution, supra* note 41 (suggesting a domain name sharing mechanism for situations where two legitimate trademark holders are asserting rights in the same domain name simultaneously).

[72] Lipton, *A Winning Solution, supra* note 41; Eric Goldman, *Deregulating Relevancy in Internet Law*, 54 Emory L.J. 507, 546 (2005) ('some domain names resolve to a "gateway page" (also referred to as a "shared page" or "intermediate page") for the sole purpose of allowing multiple trademark owners or licensees to "share" the domain name through links on the page to their respective sites').

[73] Litman, *supra* note 28, at 151 ('Network Solutions registered .com domain names on a first-come first-served basis, just as all the Internet domain names

More relevant to this discussion would be the admittedly less usual case where someone registered one or more domain names relating to private individuals' names either in the hope of extracting money from those individuals for transfer of the names,[74] or, perhaps more likely, extracting money for offering web hosting services under the names. The first iteration of this conduct – the pure sale motive – sounds like cybersquatting, but probably is not covered by trademark law because private, noncommercial personal names will generally not be trademarked.[75] This conduct may be covered in the United States by 15 U.S.C. § 8131(1)(A). This provision does not require a trademark in a personal name.[76] The second iteration may or may not amount to cybersqsuatting depending on whether the registrant would be prepared to release the name to the relevant person without receiving a profit if the complainant did not want to accept the web hosting services. If the registrant is only holding the name in the hope of selling web hosting services and is prepared to give it up if the complainant does not agree, then the conduct may not be cybersquatting. However, if the registrant seeks a profit to transfer the name, it will run afoul of § 8131(1)(A).[77]

---

had always been allocated.'); Stephen Moccaldi, *Do Any Viable Solutions Exist to Prevent the Exploitation of Trademarks Used as Internet Domain Names?*, 21 SUFFOLK TRANSNAT'L L. REV. 179, 182–3 (1997) ('Network Solutions, Inc. (NSI), a United States business, controls the registration of internet domain names worldwide. Under the original registration policy, NSI simply registered domain names on a first-come, first-served basis with no requirement that the registrant actually intend to use the name in commerce. The method enabled domain name pirates to register famous trademarks as domain names without ever using them in commerce. Many pirates registered popular names and auctioned them off to the highest bidder. Trademark holders filed suits against the pirates for trademark infringement, and against NSI for contributory infringement.').

[74] See, for example, *Paul Wright v Domain Source Inc.*, 2002 U.S. Dist. LEXIS 16024 (2002) (involving the 'paulwright.com' domain name); *Stephan Schmidheiny v Steven Weber*, 285 F.Supp.2d 613 (2003) (involving the 'schmidheiny.com' domain name).

[75] GILSON, *supra* note 2, para. 2.03[4][d] ('Just as with descriptive terms, a trademark or trade name that consists of a personal name (first name, surname, or both) is entitled to legal protection only if it attains secondary meaning.').

[76] 15 U.S.C. § 8131(1) (A) ('Any person who registers a domain name that consists of the name of another living person, or a name substantially and confusingly similar thereto, without that person's consent, with the specific intent to profit from such name by selling the domain name for financial gain to that person or any third party, shall be liable in a civil action by such person.').

[77] One permutation of this conduct that is occurring with increasing frequency with respect to personal names and other names is where an individual

Another emerging issue that may implicate personal names is that of the recently adopted system by Facebook of personalized URLs or 'Facebook usernames'.[78] Because this is a social networking site, many private individuals will want personal usernames that correspond to their own names, such as 'www.facebook.com/johndoe'. As there are millions of individuals networking on Facebook, and many have the same names, conflicts will arise where someone wants a name that is already registered to someone else. Facebook may opt for a 'first come, first served' policy, or it may decide to implement other strategies, like username sharing. Alternatively, users could be encouraged to adopt variations of their names that identify them sufficiently for others to find them online, but that differ in some way from other Facebook usernames. Contrast, for example, 'www.facebook.com/johndoe' with 'www.facebook.com/jondoe' and 'www.facebook.com/jonathan.doe'. Despite the potential for multiple corresponding personal names, Facebook currently encourages users to choose usernames that identify them the most effectively.[79]

---

has registered his own name as a domain name and then accidentally lets the registration lapse. Some online businesses quickly register lapsed domain names of all kinds and then try to extort money from selling the names back to the original registrants or to someone else with an interest in the name. See, for example, *Paul Wright v Domain Source Inc.*, 2002 U.S. Dist. LEXIS 16024 (2002) (defendant registered plaintiff's domain name, 'paulwright.com', when plaintiff accidentally let it lapse and then attempted to resell it to plaintiff for almost US $2,000). This is basically a new form of cybersquatting that differs from traditional cybersquatting only in terms of timing. Traditional cybersquatters registered domain names in a more *anticipatory* way: that is, the cybersquatter would estimate what domain names would likely be valuable to 'rightful owners' in the future and would register those names in the hope of extorting money for their transfer. This new permutation relates to names that have been valuable to someone in the past, and the cybersquatter hopes that that person, or someone else with a competing interest in the name, will pay significant sums for transfer of the name, after its original registration has lapsed. This conduct will be caught by the anti-cybersquatting legislation assuming that second registrant (the cybersquatter) has no legitimate interest in the name other than seeking to make a profit from its sale back to the original owner or perhaps to someone else with an interest in the name.

[78] See, for example, discussion in Stoel Rives L.L.P., *Trademark Law Alert: New Personalized Facebook URLs May Infringe Your Trademarks and Brands* (June 11, 2009), full text available at www.stoel.com/showalert.aspx?Show=5515, last accessed July 6, 2009.

[79] See Facebook, Usernames: Facebook Pages available at www.facebook.com/help/search.php?hq=username&ref=hq, last accessed July 10, 2009 ('Your

4.3 PERSONAL DOMAIN NAMES: LIMITATIONS OF THE EXISTING REGULATORY FRAMEWORK

4.3.1 Trademark Infringement

The traditional trademark infringement action[80] protects a trademark holder against unauthorized uses of a mark in commerce that are likely to confuse consumers as to the source of a particular product or service.[81] It has been applied successfully in early domain name cases involving trademarks on the basis that unauthorized registration and use of domain names corresponding with someone else's trademark would likely confuse consumers.[82] Infringement actions have rarely been brought in the context of disputes involving personal names.[83] Perhaps potential complainants have not felt that they could support a trademark infringement action because of concerns that they might not be able to establish trademark interests in their names. The costs of trademark infringement proceedings may also be prohibitive for many individuals,[84] as compared with

---

username should be as close as possible to your true name (e.g. Jsmith or John. Smith). Names such as CoachJohn, BlondeJane, etc. don't clearly identify you as well as your true name.')

[80] 15 U.S.C. §§ 1114 (infringement of registered trademarks), 1125(a) (infringement of unregistered trademarks).

[81] Gilson, *supra* note 2, para. 5.01 (the general aim of trademark law is to prevent consumer confusion about the source of products or services).

[82] *Planned Parenthood Federation of America Inc. v Bucci*, 42 U.S.P.Q.2d 1430 (S.D.N.Y. 1997) (defendant's use of 'plannedparenthood.com' domain name for messages critical of the Planned Parenthood organization was likely to confuse consumers as to the source of various services provided by the plaintiff); *Brookfield Communications Inc. v West Coast Ent. Corp.*, 174 F.3d 1036 (9th Cir. 1999) (use of 'moviebuff.com' domain name by one video library was likely to confuse customers of one of its competitors where each had some association with an iteration of the term 'Movie Buff' in its trademark).

[83] There are some notable exceptions of cases that do involve personal names and have been litigated under trademark law largely on the basis of trademarks in personal names: *Lamparello v Falwell*, 420 F.3d 309, 320 (2005) (involving an intentional misspelling of the Reverend Falwell's name as a domain name); *Trudeau v Lanoue*, 2006 U.S. Dixt. LEXIS 7956 (2006) (involving Mr Kevin Trudeau's name as a domain name); *Stephan Schmidheiny v Steven Weber*, 285 F.Supp.2d 613 (2003).

[84] Costs of judicial proceedings can be prohibitive for private individuals: Moreland and Springer, *supra* note 28, at 385 ('Prior to the establishment of ICANN Arbitration, recovery of celebrity domain names was an expensive and

the cheaper and faster UDRP.[85] Trademark-based actions can also raise jurisdictional concerns that do not arise under the UDRP.[86] The actor Kevin Spacey, for example, failed to establish personal jurisdiction over a defendant in litigation for control of the domain name 'kevinspacey.com'.[87] He then went on to successfully obtain control of the name in a UDRP proceeding.[88]

Even in situations where the complainant is able to shoulder the burdens of trademark litigation, there will be the problem of satisfying the consumer confusion element of trademark infringement.[89] Consumer confusion is the key to a successful trademark infringement suit.[90] Many situations involving personal domain names will not raise consumer confusion concerns in the traditional trademark sense. It may be clear in many cases that the person making unauthorized commercial use of a given domain name does not represent the person whose name is used in the domain name.[91] This could happen where the registrant is simply using the name as a draw to attract unrelated commercial custom,[92]

---

potentially lengthy process.'); Litman, *supra* note 28, at 155 (noting the often prohibitive cost of trademark infringement and dilution litigation in early domain name disputes).

[85] Moreland and Springer, *supra* note 28, at 385 ('ICANN Arbitration provides an inexpensive and extremely quick means of recovering a domain name. In addition, celebrities have come to enjoy a very high success rate in arbitration.')

[86] See, for example, *Paul Wright v Domain Source Inc.*, 2002 U.S. Dist. LEXIS 16024, paras. 1–3 (2002) (discussion of jurisdictional issues raised in complaint against cybersquatter's registration of 'paulwright.com' domain name).

[87] Kieren McCarthy, *Kevin Spacey Loses Pivotal Cybersquatting Court Case*, The Register, November 26, 2001, available at www.theregister.co.uk/2001/11/26/kevin_spacey_loses_pivotal_cybersquatting/, last accessed November 8, 2007.

[88] *Kevin Spacey*, National Arbitration Forum, Claim No. FA0205000114437, available at www.adrforum.com/domains/decisions/96937.htm.

[89] Gilson, *supra* note 2, para. 5.01 (the general aim of trademark law is to prevent consumer confusion about the source of products or services).

[90] *Id.*

[91] There may be an argument that the right of publicity should not prohibit such conduct. However, if there is something significant about protecting the integrity of individual personas online, theories of personhood as well as property would come into play here, and they might support an argument for a right of publicity action here, even if such an action would not arise under trademark law. On personhood theories as a basis for the right of publicity, see generally Haemmerli, *supra* note 43; McKenna, *supra* note 43.

[92] Such conduct could amount to trademark infringement under the 'initial interest confusion' doctrine or perhaps to trademark dilution. However, both these

or perhaps where the individual is maintaining an unauthorized fan website.

There might be an open question in the celebrity cases as to whether the misleading use of the mark was in commerce in the sense required by trademark law. If the domain name registrant was not actually using the unauthorized website for commercial purposes in the sense of selling any goods or services, the use of the name purely to attract Internet users may not be sufficiently in commerce to support a trademark infringement action. There is some case law in the domain name context suggesting that any unauthorized use of a trademark as a domain name could be sufficiently in commerce for a trademark infringement action on the basis that the nature of the Internet itself is a global commercial communications medium.[93] On this reasoning, any use of a personal name in a domain name could potentially give rise to

---

approaches to domain name disputes under domestic trademark principles have come under attack for over-extending the boundaries of trademark law in cyberspace. On initial interest confusion see, for example, Greg Lastowka, *Google's Law*, 73 BROOKLYN L. REV. 1327, 1369–71 (2008) ('With respect to search engines . . . a . . . significant expansion of trademark law is the doctrine of initial interest confusion. Traditionally, and not surprisingly, most courts have focused analysis of consumer confusion on the time period proximate to consumer purchases. The doctrine of initial interest confusion shifts the focus of confusion analysis to a time prior to the time of purchase. Initial interest confusion can be found to exist even if that confusion was not present at the time of purchase.'); see also Jennifer Rothman, *Initial Interest Confusion: Standing at the Crossroads of Trademark Law*, 27 CARDOZO L. REV. 105 (2005); Goldman, *supra* note 72, at 559 ('[Initial interest confusion] lacks a rigorous definition, a clear policy justification, and a uniform standard for analyzing claims. With its doctrinal flexibility, [it] has become the tool of choice for plaintiffs to shut down junior users who have not actually engaged in misappropriative uses.').

93 *Planned Parenthood Federation of America Inc. v Bucci*, 42 U.S.P.Q.2d 1430, para. 11 (S.D.N.Y. 1997) ('Internet users constitute a national, even international, audience, who must use interstate telephone lines to access defendant's web site on the Internet. The nature of the Internet indicates that establishing a typical home page on the Internet, for access to all users, would satisfy the Lanham Act's "in commerce" requirement.') See also *American Libraries Association v Pataki*, 969 F.Supp. 160, 45 (S.D.N.Y. 1997) ('In addition, many of those users who are communicating for private, noncommercial purposes are nonetheless participants in interstate commerce by virtue of their Internet consumption. Many users obtain access to the Internet by means of an on-line service provider, such as America Online, which charges a fee for its services. "Internet service providers", including plaintiffs Panix, Echo, and NYC NET, also offer Internet access for a monthly or hourly fee. Patrons of storefront "computer coffee shops", such as New York's own CyberCafe, similarly pay for their access to the Internet, in addition to par-

a trademark infringement action, provided that the personal name was regarded as having sufficient secondary meaning to support a trademark interest.[94] However, it remains to be seen whether future courts would follow the line of reasoning that suggests that all online activities are sufficiently in commerce for trademark purposes.[95]

4.3.2 Trademark Dilution

Like the infringement action, trademark dilution[96] also has limited application to personal domain name disputes because of its requirement of a trademark interest in the personal name, and because of the time, cost and jurisdictional problems often associated with litigation. Dilution differs from infringement in that dilution is not premised on consumer confusion. Rather, it protects famous marks[97] from blurring[98] and tarnishment.[99] Dilution is designed to prevent blurring or tarnishment of a famous mark. The current statutory defenses to dilution include noncommercial use and fair use. The latter contemplates various forms of commentary on a trademark holder as a defense to a dilution action.[100]

Trademark dilution was used successfully by some trademark holders in the early days of the domain name system.[101] Early actions were par-

---

taking of food and beverages sold by the cafe. Dial-in bulletin board systems often charge a fee for access.')

[94] GILSON, *supra* note 2, para. 2.03[4][d] ('Just as with descriptive terms, a trademark or trade name that consists of a personal name (first name, surname, or both) is entitled to legal protection only if it attains secondary meaning.').

[95] Lastowka, *supra* note 92, at 1404 ('[I]t is not clear how *Bucci* had used the Planned Parenthood mark in commerce, given that he lacked any product or service. Those who advocate for an expansion of trademark use often criticize *Bucci* for this reason.').

[96] 15 U.S.C. § 1125(c).

[97] 15 U.S.C. § 1125(c)(2)(A) (statutory definition of 'famous mark' as inserted into the Lanham Act under the Trademark Dilution Revision Act, H.R. 683 of 2006).

[98] 15 U.S.C. § 1125(c)(2)(B) (defines 'blurring' as an 'association arising from the similarity between a mark or trade name and a famous mark that impairs the distinctiveness of the famous mark').

[99] 15 U.S.C. § 1125(c)(2)(C) (defines 'tarnishment' of a famous mark as an 'association arising from the similarity between a mark or trade name and a famous mark that harms the reputation of the famous mark').

[100] 15 U.S.C. § 1125(c)(3)(A)(ii).

[101] See, for example, *Panavision Int'l L.P. v Toeppen*, 141 F.3d 1316 (9th Cir. 1998) (successful trademark dilution action against cybersquatter who was not

ticularly effective in cases involving cybersquatters.[102] The use of someone else's trademark in a domain name for no particular purpose other than to sell the name to the trademark holder (or perhaps to a competitor of the trademark holder) was easily regarded by courts as creating noise around the mark in the dilution sense. Early courts held that a domain name corresponding to a trademark is integral to a business's ability to engage in commerce on the Internet. Thus, cybersquatting on the name would be prohibited as interfering with this practice.[103]

However, a dilution action requires that the plaintiff establish not only a trademark interest, but also that the mark is *famous*.[104] It has historically been reasonably easy in practice for commercial plaintiffs to establish that their mark is sufficiently famous to bring a dilution action.[105] However, this may not be the case with respect to personal names. Personal names are often not trademarks at all, even with respect to some rather well-known celebrities.[106] Recent amendments to the

---

using the name for any purpose other than attempting to sell it to the corresponding trademark holder).

102 *Id.*

103 *Id.* 1327 ('We reject [defendant's] premise that a domain name is nothing more than an address. A significant purpose of a domain name is to identify the entity that owns the website.'); 1327, ('[Defendant's] use of Panavision.com also puts Panavision's name and reputation at his mercy.').

104 15 U.S.C. § 1125(c)(1) ('Subject to the principles of equity, the owner of a famous mark that is distinctive, inherently or through acquired distinctiveness, shall be entitled to an injunction against another person who, at any time after the owner's mark has become famous, commences use of a mark or trade name in commerce that is likely to cause dilution by blurring or dilution by tarnishment of the famous mark, regardless of the presence or absence of actual or likely confusion, of competition, or of actual economic injury.'). 'Famous mark' is now defined for these purposes in 15 U.S.C. § 1125(c)(2)(A).

105 Mark Lemley, *The Modern Lanham Act and the Death of Common Sense*, 108 YALE L. J. 1687, 1698–9 (1999). However, since the enactment of the TDRA in 2006, it may be more difficult to establish that a mark is famous than in the past due to the new definition of 'famous mark' now inserted into 15 U.S.C. § 1125(c)(2)(A). At least courts may have to undertake an analysis of whether a mark is famous or not with regard to this provision.

106 See, for example, Moreland and Springer, *supra* note 28, at 390 (comparing UDRP arbitrations where celebrities have not been able to establish trademark rights in their personal names); *Bruce Springsteen*, WIPO Case No. D2000–1532, para. 6, available at www.wipo.int/amc/en/domains/decisions/html/2000/d2000-1532.html (*supra* note 12); *Anna Nicole Smith*, National Arbitration Forum, Claim No. FA0312000220007, available at www.adr-forum.com/domains/decisions/220007.htm (*supra* note 13); *Gordon Sumner aka Sting*, WIPO Case No. D2000–0596, para. 6.5, available at www.wipo.int/amc/en/domains/decisions/html/2000/d2000-0596.

federal dilution statute may make it more difficult for individuals, even famous individuals, to establish that their personal names operate as famous marks.

The definition of famous mark inserted into the Lanham Act in 2006 contemplates the notion of a famous mark in very consumer-oriented terms with respect to the source of goods or services.[107] Many famous individual's names will not operate in this way. Thus, it may now be more difficult for a plaintiff to establish trademark dilution with respect to a personal name than to establish trademark infringement. Celebrities to one side, presumably most politicians, public figures and private individuals will not be able to show marks at all, or at least marks with sufficient fame, to bring a successful dilution action. This coupled with the costs of litigation make a trademark dilution action an unlikely avenue for the resolution of many personal domain name disputes.

4.3.3 The Anti-Cybersqsuatting Consumer Protection Act and California's Business and Professions Code

As discussed in Chapter 1,[108] the ACPA was enacted in 1999 to address some of the concerns of trademark holders about the then-burgeoning practice of cybersquatting. It focused on protecting trademarks against cybersquatting, and it originally included a provision for the protection of personal names which has now been revised and moved to another section of Title 15 of the United States Code: 15 U.S.C. § 8131. The ACPA inserted

---

html ('In the opinion of this Administrative Panel, it is doubtful whether the Uniform Policy is applicable to this dispute. Although it is accepted that the complainant is world famous under the name Sting, it does not follow that he has rights in Sting *as a trademark or service mark*. Unlike the personal names in issue in the cases *Julia Fiona Roberts v Russell Boyd*, *Jeannette Winterson v Mark Hogarth*, and *Steven Rattner v BuyThisDomainName (John Pepin)*, the personal name in this case is also a common word in the English language, with a number of different meanings.').

[107] 15 U.S.C. § 1125(c)(2)(A) ('For purposes of paragraph [15 U.S.C. § 1125(c)(1)], a mark is famous if it is widely recognized by the general consuming public of the United States as a designation of source of the goods or services of the mark's owner. In determining whether a mark possesses the requisite degree of recognition, the court may consider all relevant factors, including the following: (i) the duration, extent, and geographic reach of advertising and publicity of the mark, whether advertised or publicized by the owner or third parties; (ii) the amount, volume, and geographic extent of sales of goods or services offered under the mark; (iii) the extent of actual recognition of the mark').

[108] See 1.4, *supra*.

two new provisions into the Lanham Act, one directed at the prevention of cybersquatting with respect to trademarks,[109] and the other directed at the prevention of cybersquatting with respect to personal names.[110] Both provisions prohibited the registration of a domain name with a bad faith profit motive[111] where there is no other legitimate purpose for using the name.[112]

The trademark-focused provision is of limited use to personal name holders because many personal names will not function as trademarks.[113] However, the personal name provision[114] is available to people who are concerned about cybersquatters registering their names as domain names regardless of a trademark interest in the name.[115] This latter provision provides some comfort to those concerned about having to pay exorbitant sums of money for return of a name that corresponds with their own name. Interestingly, this provision has not been utilized much in practice, particularly in comparison with the UDRP.[116] This is because the UDRP

---

[109] 15 U.S.C. § 1125(d).

[110] 15 U.S.C. § 1129(1); see now 15 U.S.C. § 8131.

[111] 15 U.S.C. § 1125(d)(1)(A)(ii) prohibits registering, trafficking or using a domain name in bad faith for a profit while § 1129(1)(A), now § 8131(1)(A) contemplates an attempted sale of the name in bad faith.

[112] 15 U.S.C. §§ 1125(d)(1)(A)(i), 1129(1)(A); see now § 8131(1)(A).

[113] Gilson, *supra* note 2, para. 2.03[4][d] ('Just as with descriptive terms, a trademark or trade name that consists of a personal name (first name, surname, or both) is entitled to legal protection only if it attains secondary meaning.').

[114] 15 U.S.C. § 8131(1)(A).

[115] Examples of cases where this section was argued in situations involving cybersquatting on personal names include *Paul Wright v Domain Source Inc.*, 2002 U.S. Dist. LEXIS 16024 (2002) (successful action under 15 U.S.C. § 1129(1)(A), precursor to § 8131, with respect to the 'paulwright.com' domain name); *Stephan Schmidheiny v Steven Weber*, 285 F.Supp.2d 613 (2003) (successful action under 15 U.S.C. § 1129(1) for transfer of the 'schmidheiny.com' domain name to the plaintiff, Mr Schmidheiny, and injunction against the defendant registering any further iterations of the plaintiff's name as a domain name). Note also discussion of these provisions by UDRP arbitrator in *Kathleen Kennedy Townsend*, WIPO Case No. D2002–0030 available at www.wipo.int/amc/en/domains/decisions/html/2002/d2002-0451.html ('The Panel finds that the protection of an individual politician's name, no matter how famous, is outside the scope of the Policy since it is not connected with commercial exploitation as set out in the Second WIPO Report. This does not mean that complainant is without remedy. The ACPA contains express provisions protecting the rights in personal names. Complainant is free to pursue her claims in that forum. And, as mentioned, the committee may have rights in the marks that are sufficiently commercial as to entitle the committee to protection under the Policy.')

[116] Moreland and Springer, *supra* note 28, at 386 (noting high success rate of celebrities in personal domain name disputes under the UDRP, and citing

is faster and cheaper,[117] despite being premised on the protection of a trademark interest.

A significant limitation of the federal anti-cybersquatting and anti-piracy legislation is that it does not cover situations where the registrant is not a cybersquatter, but is using a domain name for some other purpose. This purpose may be commercial, or may be expressive, or may be a combination of the two.[118] Some registrants of 'name.com' names will use them to attract commercial custom through advertising.[119] If they can make more money by doing this than by selling the name, they will not be cybersquatting under § 8131(1)(A). Unauthorized uses of personal domain names for purely expressive purposes raise more difficult policy considerations. Should there be an overriding presumption that 'name.com' domain names belong to people with corresponding names, regardless of the use a registrant is making of the domain name? Such a presumption may well trample on First Amendment concerns where the registrant's use of the name is purely expressive.[120]

Issues of the First Amendment versus the rights of trademark holders have arisen already in trademark disputes that do not involve personal names: for example, some UDRP arbitrators have suggested that legitimate commentary about a trademark holder should be protected on the Internet.[121] This might include allowing an unauthorized use of a domain name that corresponds in some way with a registered trademark for, say, a

---

Statistical Summary for Proceedings under the Uniform Domain Name Dispute Resolution Policy (February 26, 2001), 394 ('A plethora of disputes involving personal names have been submitted to ICANN Arbitration.').

117 Moreland and Springer, *supra* note 28, at 385 ('ICANN Arbitration provides an inexpensive and extremely quick means of recovering a domain name.').

118 Miriam Claire Beezy, *Good Marksmanship*, 29 Los Angeles Lawyer 20, 24 (2006) ('the distinction between cybersquatter and cybergriper – that is, the difference between bad faith registration and use of a domain name that incorporates another's mark and permissible registration and use, albeit unauthorized, of another's mark – will become difficult to discern.').

119 Jacqueline Lipton, *Clickfarming: The New Cybersquatting?*, 12 J. Internet Law 1, 16 (2008).

120 See 4.2.2, *supra*.

121 *Bridgestone Firestone*, WIPO Arbitration and Mediation Center, Case No. D2000–0190 (July 6, 2000), available at www.wipo.int/amc/en/domains/decisions/html/2000/d2000-0190.html, last accessed March 2, 2009 ('Although free speech is not listed as one of the [UDRP's] examples of a right or legitimate interest in a domain name, the list is not exclusive, and the Panel concludes that the exercise of free speech for criticism and commentary . . . demonstrates a right or legitimate interest in the domain name under Paragraph 4(c)(iii). The Internet is above all a

gripe site about the trademark holder.[122] However, judges and arbitrators in the trademark context have not generally accepted that commentators should be allowed to utilize the most intuitive domain name corresponding to the trademark – that is, the 'trademark.com' version of the name.[123] Commentators have generally been relegated to lesser forms of the domain name, such as those using a different gTLD such as '.org' or '.net', or those using a qualifier at the end of the domain, such as 'trademarksucks.com'.[124] On this analogy, there perhaps should be a presumption that well-known individuals have default rights to the 'name.com' versions of their names.

Interestingly, one state, California, has experimented with legislation directed at personal name cybersquatting. The relevant provisions can be found in §§ 17525–17526 of California's Business and Professions Code.[125] Section 17525(a) provides that:

---

framework for global communication, and the right to free speech should be one of the foundations of Internet law.').

[122] *Id.* There is some judicial authority suggesting the same thing: *Bosley v Kremer*, 403 F.3d 672, 679–80 (9th Cir. 2005) ('Kremer is not Bosley's competitor; he is their critic. His use of the Bosley mark is not in connection with a sale of goods or services – it is in connection with the expression of his opinion about Bosley's goods and services. The dangers that the Lanham Act was designed to address are simply not at issue in this case. The Lanham Act . . . does not prohibit all unauthorized uses of a trademark . . . Any harm to Bosley arises not from a competitor's sale of a similar product under Bosley's mark, but from Kremer's criticism of their services. Bosley cannot use the Lanham Act either as a shield from Kremer's criticism or as a sword to shut Kremer up.').

[123] *Bridgestone*, WIPO Case No. D2000–0190, available at www.wipo.int/amc/en/domains/decisions/html/2000/d2000-0190.html ('In the cybersquatting cases, the domain names in question generally were www.trademark.com domain names, which prevented the trademark holder from utilizing the customary commercial domain name for its "official" site . . . Here, however, the domain name registrant has not usurped the ".com" domain, but has utilized only the ".net" domain, has posted disclaimers on the website homepage, and has included criticism or commentary on the site so that a reasonably prudent Internet user can tell that the site is not the trademark holder's "official" site.').

[124] Although, some arbitrators have held that even domain names employing pejorative qualifiers should be in the control of the trademark holder rather than anyone else. See, for example, *Société Air France v Virtual Dates, Inc.*, WIPO Arbitration and Mediation Center, Case No. D2005–0168 (May 24, 2005), available at www.wipo.int/amc/en/domains/decisions/html/ 2005/d2005-0168.html, last accessed March 16, 2010 (majority panelists decided that 'airfrancesucks.com' domain name should be transferred to the trademark holder and ought not be controlled by a gripe site operator).

[125] See also discussion at 1.6.1, *supra*.

> It is unlawful for a person, with a bad faith intent to register, traffic in, or use a domain name, that is identical or confusingly similar to the personal name of another living person or deceased personality, without regard to the goods or services of the parties.

This legislation is broader than 15 U.S.C. § 8131(1)(A) in that it contemplates deceased as well as living persons. It also contains a list of bad faith factors that includes an intention on the part of the registrant to 'mislead, deceive, or defraud voters'.[126] This may be relevant to situations where a politician complains about unauthorized use of her name in a corresponding domain name, at least if the use of the name is misleading or fraudulent.[127] However, it is an open question as to whether the legislation would, or indeed should, cover pure political gripe sites, such as the 'bobkeenan.com' and 'lindamcculloch.com' examples described at 4.2.2, *supra*. This is because a legitimate criticism of a politician may not be regarded as misleading, deceptive or fraudulent, provided it is clear from the context that the website in question has not been endorsed by the politician. On the other hand, if the view is taken that 'name.com' domain names should be reserved for authorized websites, then arguably any unauthorized use of such a domain name could be regarded as misleading, deceptive or fraudulent.

4.3.4 Uniform Domain Name Dispute Resolution Policy

As noted previously, the UDRP is the most popular avenue for personal domain name disputes.[128] It is global in scope because of its incorpora-

---

[126] California Business and Professions Code, § 17526(j).

[127] On this point, see also Cal. Elections Code, § 18320 which prohibits certain activities described as 'political cyberfraud'. This legislation, although not specifically targeted at personal name protection, may have the same results in practice as the Business and Professions Code with respect to some uses of politicians' names in the leadup to elections. For a more general discussion of the operation of both Californian statutes in the political domain name context, see Lipton, *Who Owns 'Hillary.com', supra* note 52.

[128] Beezy, *supra* note 118, at 23–4 (noting high success rate of celebrities in personal domain name proceedings under the UDRP and surveying some of the recent decisions); Moreland and Springer, *supra* note 28, at 386 (noting high success rate of celebrities in personal domain name disputes under the UDRP, and citing Statistical Summary for Proceedings under the Uniform Domain Name Dispute Resolution Policy (February 26, 2001), 394 ('A plethora of disputes involving personal names have been submitted to ICANN Arbitration.')).

tion into relevant[129] domain name registration agreements.[130] It thus does away with the jurisdictional problems inherent in both trademark and personality rights-based litigation.[131] Again, the UDRP is aimed at preventing cybersquatting on trademarks.[132] The two major hurdles for personal domain name complainants are that (a) a trademark must be established in the personal name,[133] and (b) the UDRP will only apply to cybersquatting.[134] As noted in previous chapters, the UDRP contains a defense for

---

[129] ICANN, UDRP Notes, Note 2, available at www.icann.org/udrp/udrp-policy-24oct99.htm, last accessed November 10, 2007 ('This policy has been adopted by all accredited domain-name registrars for domain names ending in .com, .net, and .org. It has also been adopted by certain managers of country-code top-level domains (e.g., .nu, .tv, .ws).').

[130] UDRP, para. 1 ('This Uniform Domain Name Dispute Resolution Policy (the "Policy") has been adopted by the Internet Corporation for Assigned Names and Numbers ("ICANN"), is incorporated by reference into your Registration Agreement, and sets forth the terms and conditions in connection with a dispute between you and any party other than us (the registrar) over the registration and use of an Internet domain name registered by you.').

[131] See, for example, *Paul Wright v Domain Source Inc.*, 2002 U.S. Dist. LEXIS 16024, paras. 1–3 (2002) (discussion of jurisdictional issues raised in complaint against cybersquatter's registration of 'paulwright.com' domain name). The movie actor Kevin Spacey was also initially unsuccessful in a cybersquatting claim against the registrant of 'kevinspacey.com' on jurisdictional grounds, but later succeeded in a UDRP proceeding: Kieren McCarthy, *Kevin Spacey Loses Pivotal Cybersquatting Court Case*, THE REGISTER, November 26, 2001 available at www.theregister.co.uk/2001/11/26/kevin_spacey_loses_pivotal_cybersquatting/, last accessed November 8, 2007. For completeness, it should also be noted that the ACPA contains some *in rem* provisions to simplify jurisdictional issues for actions taken under 15 U.S.C. § 1125(d)(1). See 15 U.S.C. § 1125(d)(2).

[132] UDRP, para. 4(a)(i) ('You are required to submit to a mandatory administrative proceeding in the event that a third party (a "complainant") asserts to the applicable Provider, in compliance with the Rules of Procedure, that (i) your domain name is identical or confusingly similar to a trademark or service mark in which the complainant has rights').

[133] UDRP, para. 4(a)(i).

[134] Beezy, *supra* note 118, at 24 ('the distinction between cybersquatter and cybergriper – that is, the difference between bad faith registration and use of a domain name that incorporates another's mark and permissible registration and use, albeit unauthorized, of another's mark – will become difficult to discern.'); Moreland and Springer, *supra* note 28, at 390–2 (noting that the UDRP will not assist a complainant where a domain name registrant is using a domain name for commentary or otherwise to refer to the complainant in a legitimate manner).

domain name registrants making a 'legitimate noncommercial or fair use of the relevant domain name'.[135]

It has not been clear what will constitute a fair use in this context, although noncommercial use should be relatively easy to identify in practice. Further, it is unclear whether the UDRP is intended to cover personality rights in individual names.[136] A World Intellectual Property Organization (WIPO) Report on the subject specifically suggested that personality rights are not covered under the UDRP.[137] However, some UDRP arbitrators have felt that in the absence of a specific prohibition on the protection of such rights, they are covered.[138] Thus, to the extent that complainants are specifically basing claims on personality interests rather than trademark rights, there is some confusion as to whether they might be successful in the absence of a trademark right.[139]

The current application of the UDRP to personal domain name dis-

---

[135] UDRP, para. 4(c)(3).

[136] Moreland and Springer, *supra* note 28, at 394–5 (citing WIPO report to the effect that personality rights were never intended to be covered by the UDRP).

[137] Second WIPO Internet Domain Name Process, (September 3, 2001), available at www.wipo.int/amc/en/processes/process2/report/html/report.html#5, last accessed November 11, 2007, para. 199 ('It is clear that many sensitivities are offended by the unauthorized registration of personal names as domain names. It is clear also that UDRP does not provide solace for all those offended sensitivities, nor was it intended to do so, as originally designed. The result is that there are some perceived injustices. Persons who have gained eminence and respect, but who have not profited from their reputation in commerce, may not avail themselves of the UDRP to protect their personal names against parasitic registrations. The UDRP is thus perceived by some as implementing an excessively materialistic conception of contribution to society. Furthermore, persons whose names have become distinctive in countries that do not recognize unregistered trademark rights are unlikely to find consolation in the UDRP in respect of bad faith registration and use of their personal names as domain names in those countries.'); para. 202 ('It is recommended that no modification be made to the UDRP to accommodate broader protection for personal names than that which currently exists in the UDRP.').

[138] *Id.* paras 181–4 (surveying decisions in which UDRP arbitrators have ordered transfers of domain names based on personal names); *Kevin Spacey*, National Arbitration Forum, Claim No. 114437, available at www.arb-forum.com/domains/decisions/114437.htm ('Respondent has argued that the Final Report of the WIPO Internet Domain Name Process reveals that "personality" disputes are outside the scope of the Policy. We would find the report persuasive on this issue as "legislative history" if we found some ambiguity in the Policy itself. Because the Policy does not purport to exclude the category of disputes involving "personality rights", we join the many other Panels that have recognized that the Policy does, indeed, protect such interests.').

[139] See, for example, *Kevin Spacey*, National Arbitration Forum, Claim No.

putes is arbitrary and inconsistent. Some arbitrators are more prepared to recognize protectable interests in personal names than others, usually on the basis of an unregistered trademark interest. Julia Roberts[140] and Tom Cruise[141] were found to have trademark interests in their personal names, but a majority panel of UDRP arbitrators felt that Bruce Springsteen did not likely have such rights.[142] A UDRP arbitrator also held that the late Anna Nicole Smith was not sufficiently famous to assert a trademark interest in her personal name.[143] In the political context, Secretary of State Hillary Clinton's name has been recognized as a trademark under the UDRP,[144] along with that of her husband former President William J Clinton.[145] However, Maryland gubernatorial candidate Kathleen Kennedy Townsend was not so lucky.[146]

Although one could attempt some factual distinctions, it appears that Roberts, Cruise, Springsteen and the late Anna Nicole Smith are all basically entertainers who do not sell products or services under their names in a trademark sense – unless one considers their names to be marks for the

---

96937, available at www.arb-forum.com/domains/decisions/96937.htm (*supra* note 138).

140 *Julia Fiona Roberts*, WIPO Case No. D2000–0210, available at www.wipo.int/amc/en/domains/decisions/html/2000/d2000-0210.html.

141 *Tom Cruise*, WIPO Case No. D2006–0560, available at www.wipo.int/amc/en/domains/decisions/html/2006/d2006-0560.html.

142 *Bruce Springsteen*, WIPO Case No. D2000–1532, para. 6, available at www.wipo.int/amc/endomains/decisions/html/2000/d2000-1532.html (*supra* note 12).

143 *Anna Nicole Smith*, National Arbitration Forum, Claim No. FA0312000220007, available at www.adrforum.com/domains/decisions/220007.htm (*supra* note 13).

144 *Hillary Rodham Clinton*, National Arbitration Forum, Claim No. FA0502000414641, available at www.arb-forum.com/domains/decisions/414641.htm (Senator Clinton was regarded as having an unregistered trademark right in her personal name in connection with both her political activities and her career as an author of a number of books sold in commerce).

145 *William J. Clinton*, National Arbitration Forum, Claim No. FA0904001256123, available at http://domains.adrforum.com/domains/decisions/1256123.htm (arbitrator 'reluctantly' concluded that former President Clinton had a trademark in his personal name, but the former president was unsuccessful in obtaining a transfer order for relevant domain names because he was unable to establish 'bad faith' registration and use on the part of the registrant).

146 *Kathleen Kennedy Townsend*, WIPO Case No. D2002–0030, available at www.wipo.int/amc/en/domains/decisions/html/2002/d2002-0451.html (individual politician in state gubernatorial race held not to hold trademark rights in her personal name).

movies or television shows they appear in, or the songs they perform.[147] If the marks work in this way, it is not clear why Bruce Springsteen would not be a mark in the same way as Julia Roberts or Tom Cruise. A UDRP arbitrator recognized a trademark interest in then-Senator Hillary Clinton's name partly on the basis that she had authored books under her name.[148] If this is the basis for a trademark interest in a personal name, shouldn't Bruce Springsteen's name also be a trademark as the writer and performer of songs?

Rules relating to the protection of trademark interests are not automatically geared towards protecting personal names, although they may cover personal names in some situations.[149] It may be possible to create regulations that better protect personal names in the domain space. The following discussion suggests one avenue for revising the UDRP in a way that better protects personal names by drawing on some of the personality rights jurisprudence in the United States. It starts with a consideration of how existing personality rights law might apply to personal domain name disputes. It then moves to a consideration of ways in which personality rights theory could be incorporated into a revised UDRP.

4.4 PERSONALITY RIGHTS

4.4.1 Right of Publicity and Personal Name Disputes

Personality rights law – or the right of publicity – is a subset of tort law unique to the United States. Even within the United States it is a disharmonized pastiche of state common law and legislation. This discussion is focused on the extent to which some of the, admittedly disharmonized, theory surrounding the right of publicity in the United States might be applied in an attempt to create a regulatory structure that better suits the

---

147 Verna, *supra* note 25 (questioning why certain famous personalities are able to establish trademark rights in their personal names for UDRP purposes while others are not).

148 *Hillary Rodham Clinton*, National Arbitration Forum, Claim No. FA0502000414641, available at www.arb-forum.com/domains/decisions/414641.htm.

149 The obvious case is where the personal name is, in fact, used as a trademark in a business context. See, for example, *Trudeau v Lanoue*, 2006 U.S. Dixt. LEXIS 7956 (2006) (involving Mr Kevin Trudeau's name as a domain name); *Stephan Schmidheiny v Steven Weber*, 285 F.Supp.2d 613 (2003).

needs of personal name claimants in the domain space. The main advantage of an approach based on the right of publicity is that the right focuses on the protection of individual names and personas rather than on trademarks. Scholars have debated the relationship between personality rights and trademarks, but there is no denying that there are distinct differences between the two.[150]

The right of publicity is effectively the right of an individual to control the commercial use of his or her name, likeness, signature or other personal characteristics.[151] It derives originally from the right of privacy.[152] This genesis has caused some confusion about the scope of the modern day tort which covers both privacy and some property-like aspects of an individual's persona.[153] Over the years, the right has developed in different states, sometimes as a matter of common law[154] and sometimes under state legislation.[155] High profile examples include unauthorized uses of Elvis Presley's name and likeness after his death,[156] John Wayne's likeness on greeting cards,[157] Martin Luther King's likeness on unauthorized plastic

---

150 Dogan and Lemley, *supra* note 43.

151 GILSON, *supra* note 2, para. 2B.01.

152 Haemmerli, *supra* note 43, at 406 ('It is worth asking why we are here, why the doctrinal confusion is so extreme. One reason is that the doctrine [of the right of publicity] may have taken a wrong turn forty-six years ago, when Second Circuit Judge Jerome Frank severed the right of publicity from the right of privacy.'); Madow, *supra* note 44, at 167 ('As Thomas McCarthy tells the story, the right of publicity was "carved out of the general right of privacy" – "like Eve from Adam's rib". In my view, this simile is . . . misleading. The right of publicity was created not so much from the right of privacy as from frustration with it.').

153 Haemmerli, *supra* note 43, at 407–8 ('The doctrine . . . developed in a schizoid manner: publicity rights were purely economic property rights, as distinct from "personal" privacy rights (thereby enabling publicity rights to become transferable and descendible); but publicity rights, even though economic in nature, were also part of the tort of invasion of privacy, thereby implying that they should be viewed as a species of personal privacy rights, and as such nonassignable and nondescendible.'); Dogan and Lemley, *supra* note 43, at 1208–9 (noting that privacy based justifications for right of publicity are legitimate and are different from economic trademark rationale for publicity rights).

154 Kentucky, for example, has a common law basis for the right of publicity: see discussion in GRAEME DINWOODIE AND MARK JANIS, TRADEMARKS AND UNFAIR COMPETITION LAW AND POLICY 823–7 (2004).

155 See, for example, Indiana Code Title 32 (property), art. 36 (publicity), chap. 1 (rights of publicity).

156 *Estate of Elvis Presley v Russen*, 513 F. Supp. 1339 (1981).

157 See discussion in Madow, *supra* note 44, at 141–3.

busts,[158] Rosa Parks' name as a song title,[159] Arnold Schwarzenegger's likeness as a bobblehead doll,[160] and Rudolph Giuliani's likeness on an advertisement run on city buses in New York City.[161]

Because the right is based both on aspects of property theory[162] and

---

[158] *Martin Luther King Jr, Center for Social Change Inc. v American Heritage Products*, 694 F. 2d 674 (11th Cir. 1993) (the estate of Martin Luther King, Jr sought an injunction to prevent the defendant from selling plastic busts of Dr King).

[159] *Rosa Parks v LaFace Records*, 329 F.3d 437 (2003) (involving publicity rights of Rosa Parks in the context of a song title using her name in relation to a hip hop recording that had nothing in particular to do with her or her work)

[160] Charles Harder and Henry L. Self. III, *Schwarzenegger vs. Bobbleheads: The Case for Schwarzenegger*, 45 SANTA CLARA L. REV. 557 (2005); William Gallagher, *Strategic Intellectual Property Litigation, the Right of Publicity, and the Attenuation of Free Speech: Lessons from the Schwarzenegger Bobblehead Doll War (and Peace)*, 45 SANTA CLARA L. REV. 581 (2005); David Welkowitz and Tyler Ochoa, *The Terminator as Eraser: How Arnold Schwarzenegger Used the Right of Publicity to Terminate Non-Defamatory Political Speech*, 45 SANTA CLARA L. REV. 651 (2005).

[161] *New York Magazine v The Metropolitan Transit Authority of the City of New York*, 987 F. Supp. 254 (1997); *aff'd in part, vacated in part, New York Magazine v The Metropolitan Transit Authority and the City of New York*, 136 F.3d 123 (1998). Mayor Giuliani ultimately failed in his appeal on free speech grounds. The right of publicity tort has also been extended to 'lookalikes' and 'soundalikes' of famous people, notably the use of a Vanna White lookalike robot in a television commercial (*Vanna White v Samsung Electronics America Inc.*, 971 F. 2d (9th Cir. 1992); *cert denied*, 508 U.S. 951 (1993)), and the use of imitators of Bette Midler's and Tom Waits' distinctive singing voices in advertising campaigns: *Bette Midler v Ford Motor Co.*, 849 F. 2d 460 (1988); *Tom Waits v Frito-Lay Inc.*, 978 F. 2d 1093 (1992).

[162] Various justifications have been put forward for a property basis for personality rights, and have equally been criticized over the years. For a discussion of property theory in this context, see Dogan and Lemley, *supra* note 43, at 1181–3 (critique of Lockean labor theory justifications for personality rights as property); McKenna, *supra* note 43, at 247 ('It might be true that identity is sufficiently similar to other objects the law regards as property and therefore deserves at least some of the sticks in the traditional bundle of property rights. But far too few courts and commentators have offered a theory as to why any of the traditional property justifications lead to that conclusion.'); 251–67 (critique of Lockean labor theory justifications for property rights in personal identity); Haemmerli, *supra* note 43, at 388 ('Both proponents and critics of the right of publicity generally perceive it as a property claim grounded in Lockean labor theory'); 407–8 (noting dual property and privacy justifications for right of publicity actions); 412 ('To the extent that commentators specifically address publicity rights, they tend to do so within this property context, and to use Lockean labor theories of property to explain the assertion of a property right in identity or persona.'); Kwall, *supra* note 43, at 15

of personhood,[163] it can arguably protect individual personas in ways that trademark law cannot. Personality rights claims do not require the establishment of a trademark in a person's name or likeness. The interests individuals have wanted to protect in their personal names in the domain space roughly correspond to the kinds of interests people have sought to protect under the right of publicity more generally.[164]

Personality rights theory can be a useful avenue for addressing online conflicts that fall somewhere in between privacy, defamation, copyright

---

('This Article . . . contends that a property-based conception for publicity rights is the natural outgrowth of our cultural norms as well as our theoretical conceptions of property.'); Westfall and Landau, *supra* note 43, at 1165–9 (examining property basis for rights of publicity); Rielly, *supra* note 43, at 1165–9 (describing development of a property rights rationale for the right of publicity). See also Zimmerman and Jacoby, *supra* note 43.

[163] See, for example, McKenna, *supra* note 43, at 285 ('Since all individuals share the interest in autonomous self-definition, every individual should be able to control uses of her identity that interfere with her ability to define her own public character.'; 286 ('Compelling a person to express a message herself presents a particular sort of threat to her freedom of belief: It threatens her ability to control what she tells the world about who she is and what she holds important'); Haemmerli, *supra* note 43, at 390 ('Viewing the right of publicity as an extension of human worth and autonomy, rather than as a purely economic interest, also changes the nature of the exercise that balances the right against competing social claims . . . [A] Kantian grounding is preferable to a Lockean justification not only because a Kantian foundation forces the realization that the balancing challenge is complex, but because it more accurately reflects the value of the human being behind the persona at issue.'); Rielly, *supra* note 43, at 1164–5 (description of privacy foundations of the right of publicity).

[164] Haemmerli, *supra* note 43, at 407–8 (see *supra* note 153); Dogan and Lemley, *supra* note 43, at 1208–9 (noting that privacy based justifications for right of publicity are legitimate and are different from economic trademark rationale for publicity rights); Kwall, *supra* note 43, at 36–7 ('[Other than economic harm], the right of publicity protects another type of incentive, one that focuses on moral rather than economic concerns. For most celebrities, the cachet of fame is attributed to an image that the publicity plaintiff has a reputational interest in controlling. The author has argued elsewhere that "the unauthorized use of an individual's persona potentially poses the maximum harm [to that individual] when the persona is being appropriated in an objectionable context or for an objectionable purpose". Although some celebrities still might want to pursue the limelight even if the law sanctioned such unauthorized appropriations, other celebrities, particularly those with strong moral philosophies, might not. The impact of the decisions regarding the use of a celebrity's persona are felt more directly by the celebrity since it is the celebrity, rather than anyone in the celebrity's entourage, whose reputation is at stake.')

and trademark law. Consider, for example, a case where a person manufactures and sells an unauthorized coffee mug bearing a photograph of Britney Spears. It may be difficult for Ms Spears to bring an invasion of privacy action when her persona has been developed largely for public consumption.[165] In other words, it is hard to claim invasion of privacy for something that she herself has put into public view (her image and likeness)[166] unless the image on the coffee mug was taken in an unauthorized private context: for example, by a photographer using a telephoto lens to shoot her in the privacy of her own home. [167] Further, if the coffee mug does not suggest anything defamatory about Ms Spears, there will be no remedy in defamation law.[168] Copyright, also, will be an unlikely avenue for Ms Spears unless she can bring a copyright infringement action with respect to the photograph.[169] She does not hold a copyright interest in her own persona, although she may own copyright in a particular photograph.

---

165 Madow, *supra* note 44, at 168 ('Claims of . . . emotional injury [under privacy law] were not nearly as convincing when they came from celebrities . . . After all, how could a movie star or professional athlete, who had deliberately and energetically sought the limelight, complain of embarrassment or hurt feelings when an advertiser or merchandiser simply gave his face some *additional* publicity?').

166 *Id*; Kwall, *supra* note 43, at 36 ('Some courts . . . hold that celebrities cannot maintain right-of-privacy actions, although this view is not universal.'); Dogan and Lemley, *supra* note 43, at 1171 (noting that privacy actions were not generally much use to celebrities because they were regarded as having purposely sought out the limelight so there was no obvious invasion of privacy).

167 For a summary of the genesis of privacy rights based on media intrusion into personal space, see, for example, Madow, *supra* note 44, at 167–70.

168 Kwall, *supra* note 43, at 36 ('Another significant disadvantage [for celebrities protecting their personality rights] derives from the law of defamation, under which celebrities enjoy less protection than other citizens. Defendants in defamation actions involving public officials and public figures must meet the higher, "actual malice" standard of liability that requires knowledge of falsity as to the libelous statement or reckless disregard as to its truth.')

169 Copyright generally subsists in the author of an original work, which would typically include a photographer in the case of a photograph, or the person who hired the photographer to take the photograph under the 'works for hire' doctrine. See 17 U.S.C. § 201(a) ('Copyright in a work protected under this title vests initially in the author or authors of the work'); § 201(b) ('In the case of a work made for hire, the employer or other person for whom the work was prepared is considered the author for purposes of this title, and, unless the parties have expressly agreed otherwise in a written instrument signed by them, owns all of the rights comprised in the copyright.').

Trademark law may not help Ms Spears either. The goal of trademark law is to protect source indicators of products and services to prevent consumer confusion[170] and to encourage investment in developing those products and services.[171] Thus, if Ms Spears could establish trademark rights in her image, and could establish that the coffee mugs in question were confusing consumers as to source, origin or affiliation with her, she may be able to establish trademark infringement. Alternatively, if she could establish a trademark in her image, and also that the coffee mugs were blurring or tarnishing the mark, she may be able to sustain a claim in trademark dilution.[172] However, it is not clear whether Ms Spears actually has a trademark in her name or image.[173] Even if she could establish such a mark, it may not be sufficiently connected to the sale of merchandise, like coffee mugs, to support a successful trademark infringement action. It would seem more likely that any mark that did exist would relate to concerts and music products and not to merchandising of coffee mugs and associated products.[174]

With respect to the possibility of a dilution action, Ms Spears would have to establish a trademark right in her image, as well as establishing that the use of the picture on the coffee mug blurred or tarnished the mark. By increasing circulation of her image in the marketplace, it may actually

---

170 GILSON, *supra* note 2, para. 5.01 (the general aim of trademark law is to prevent consumer confusion about the source of products or services); DINWOODIE AND JANIS, *supra* note 154, at 16–17 (citing S. Rep. No. 1333, 79th Cong., 2d Sess. 3 (1946)) ('In the United States, two primary justifications have traditionally been offered in support of trademark protection: to "protect the public so that it may be confident that, in purchasing a product bearing a particular trademark which it favorably knows, it will get the product which it asks for and which it wants to get"; and to ensure that "where the owner of a trademark has spent energy, time and money in presenting to the public the product, he is protected in his investment from its appropriation by pirates and cheats".').

171 DINWOODIE AND JANIS, *supra* note 154, at 16–17 (citing S. Rep. No. 1333, 79th Cong., 2d Sess. 3 (1946)) (see *supra* note 170).

172 15 U.S.C. § 1125(c).

173 A search of the United States Patent and Trademark Office's Trademarks Database as of November 11, 2007 shows that Britney Spears has, in fact, registered her name as a trademark for various products and services. However, the mere fact of registration does not prove that a trademark is valid: DINWOODIE AND JANIS, *supra* note 154, at 315 ('Trademark registration . . . does not create rights; it only confirms the existence of rights.').

174 The search, *id.*, shows that Britney Spears has registered her name as a mark for a variety of products including arts and craft kits, desk organizers and backpacks. However, there does not appear to be a registration specifically for coffee mugs.

enhance the value of her mark rather than blurring or tarnishing it.[175] Additionally, the dilution action is limited to famous marks as defined in the dilution statute.[176] The name of a famous person is not necessarily a famous *mark*.

People other than athletes and entertainers may have greater difficulties with trademark focused laws. A politician, public figure or private individual may have more trouble establishing trademark rights in her name or likeness than a celebrity.[177] Thus, if the above hypothetical involved Rudolph Giuliani coffee mugs, rather than Britney Spears coffee mugs,

---

[175] Madow, *supra* note 44, at 168 ('Claims of . . . emotional injury [under privacy law] were not nearly as convincing when they came from celebrities . . . After all, how could a movie star or professional athlete, who had deliberately and energetically sought the limelight, complain of embarrassment or hurt feelings when an advertiser or merchandiser simply gave his face some *additional* publicity?'). There is also some debate about whether increased circulation of a name or image actually increases or rather decreases the value of the celebrity identity: McKenna, *supra* note 43, at 269–70 ('Landes and Posner argue that overgrazing on identity leads to "face wearout", a reduction in the value of one's persona due to declining interest in the person as her persona is increasingly used. Their argument is at odds with the well-known maxim that "all publicity is good publicity", though both sentiments are oversimplifications of the phenomenon of fame. Publicity tends to feed off of itself and, as a result, many uses actually increase the value of a celebrity's identity, whatever the character of those uses. But additional publicity will increase the value of an individual's identity only until a certain point, after which interest may wane, along with the value of the identity. In other words, early additional uses may create "network effects" that increase the value of an identity, but at some point the number of uses will lead consumers to tire of the identity and it no longer will capture their attention. In most cases, consumers lose interest in particular cultural objects simply because something has come along that better defines them at that point in time. The point of tedium, however, may be accelerated, at least in terms of chronological time, as a result of overexposure. Some celebrities have more enduring cultural significance than others and, as a result, almost every aspect of an identity's long-term value will vary from individual to individual: the rate at which value is added by early uses, the point at which additional uses begin to erode value and the value of the persona at that point, and the rate at which the value will decline beyond the wearout point.').

[176] 15 U.S.C. § 1125(c)(2)(A) (statutory definition of 'famous mark' as inserted into the Lanham Act under the Trademark Dilution Revision Act, H.R. 683 of 2006).

[177] *Report of the Second WIPO Internet Domain Name Process* (September 3, 2001), para. 188, available at www.wipo.int/amc/en/processes/process2/report/html/report.html#5, last accessed November 11, 2007 ('the names of political figures, religious leaders, scientists and historical persons may never have been used in commerce and, thus, are unlikely to have trademarks associated with them.').

Giuliani may have much more trouble establishing a trademark interest in his name or likeness, simply because he does not sell any goods or services in connection with his name or likeness in the trademark sense.

These are the kinds of situations where personality rights theory may be helpful. Personality rights naturally cover celebrities.[178] However, they can also cover politicians,[179] public figures[180] and private individuals.[181] These rights can provide remedies for unauthorized commercial uses of anyone's persona. Although generally regarded as an economic tort focusing on commercial harms,[182] the tort also comprises distinct moral elements.[183] The key moral harm protected by the right of publicity is more

---

178 Gilson, *supra* note 2, para. 2B.01.

179 *New York Magazine v The Metropolitan Transit Authority and the City of New York*, 987 F. Supp. 254 (1997), *aff'd in part, vacated in part, New York Magazine v The Metropolitan Transit Authority and the City of New York*, 136 F.3d 123 (1998) (action with respect to then Mayor Rudolph Giuliani's personality rights).

180 *Rosa Parks v LaFace Records*, 329 F.3d 437 (2003) (involving publicity rights of Rosa Parks in the context of a song title using her name in relation to a hip hop recording that had nothing in particular to do with her or her work); *Martin Luther King Jr, Center for Social Change Inc. v American Heritage Products*, 694 F. 2d 674 (11th Cir. 1993) (the estate of Martin Luther King, Jr sought an injunction to prevent the defendant from selling plastic busts of Dr King).

181 *Tellado v Time-Life Books, Inc.*, 643 F. Supp 904 (D.N.J. 1986) (unauthorized use of image of private individual plaintiff in Vietnam war for book and advertising materials relating to book); see also discussion in Kwall, *First Amendment, supra* note 46, at 96–100.

182 Haemmerli, *supra* note 43, at 392 ('The right of publicity is traditionally formulated as the right to exploit the commercial value of personal identity.'); Kwall, *supra* note 43, at 15 ('a property-based conception for publicity rights is the natural outgrowth of our cultural norms as well as our theoretical conceptions of property'); Dogan and Lemley, *supra* note 43, at 1172–4 (note growth of the right of publicity as an economic right); Konsky, *supra* note 44, at 349 ('most courts and commentators now ground the right of publicity in property rationales'); McKenna, *supra* note 43, at 226 ('Because the right of publicity has focused entirely on the economic value of a celebrity's identity, courts considering claims have no basis to differentiate among the variety of ways in which others might exploit that value.').

183 McKenna, *supra* note 43, at 231 ('All individuals have a legitimate interest in autonomous self-definition, and celebrities deserve protection against uses of their identities that implicate that interest.'); Haemmerli, *supra* note 43, at 390 ('Viewing the right of publicity as an extension of human worth and autonomy, rather than as a purely economic interest, also changes the nature of the exercise that balances the right against competing social claims . . . [A] Kantian grounding is preferable to a Lockean justification not only because a Kantian foundation forces the realization that the balancing challenge is complex, but because it more accurately reflects the value of the human being behind the persona at issue.');

like a privacy protection than a property protection. The obvious example is where unauthorized commercial use is made of an individual's name or likeness in circumstances where that individual wants to maintain privacy of her image, rather than control commercial profits. Another advantage of a right of publicity framework is that courts have already engaged in balancing exercises between personality rights and the First Amendment in a variety of contexts.[184] Such jurisprudence is more relevant to the personal domain name dispute context than cases balancing *trademark rights* against the First Amendment.

As with trademark law, questions have arisen as to how the right of publicity should impact, if at all, on the free speech rights of others. In *Rogers v Grimaldi*,[185] for example, expressive conduct was not compensable under trademark law or under the right of publicity.[186] In *Rogers*, the defendant had used the title 'Ginger and Fred' in a film about a cabaret act that impersonated Ginger Rogers and Fred Astaire.[187] The court held that the defendants had used no more of Ms Rogers' identity than was neces-

Kwall, *First Amendment, supra* note 46, at 50 ('In evaluating the nature of the harm to the plaintiff, this article asserts that economic harms are typically far less onerous than nonmonetizable harms which derive from uses the plaintiff would never have condoned. These nonmonetizable, or morally based, harms can include reputational damage, distasteful associations, or uses which advance a substantive argument the plaintiff finds objectionable. In addition, the potential for consumer deception is particularly strong where the use is one to which the plaintiff would never have consented.').

184 Haemmerli, *supra* note 43, at 441–58 (analysis of First Amendment issues arising with respect to the right of publicity); Felcher and Rubin, *supra* note 46, at 1590 ('The First Amendment inevitably defines the operation and extent of the right of publicity; once the defendant can establish that the expression in question is protected, he will almost invariably prevail.'); Kwall, *First Amendment, supra* note 46 (suggesting a property versus liability rule basis for balancing First Amendment concerns against right of publicity claims); Rielly, *supra* note 43, at 1172–4 (balancing First Amendment concerns with the publicity rights of public figures and politicians); Madow, *supra* note 44, at 140 (description of the role of the consumer as an active and creative participant in the creation of cultural commodities); Kwall, *supra* note 43, at 46–7 ('We do not deprive the owners of famous trademarks or the copyright owners of popular works of art or literature of their rights just because the public has played some role in placing a value on these works. Therefore, right-of-publicity critics must justify why the cachet of a person's fame should be treated differently.'). See also Zimmerman, *supra* note 46.

185 875 F. 2d 994 (1988).

186 *Id.*

187 *Id.* 996–7.

sary for expressive artistic purposes.[188] Ms Rogers was therefore unsuccessful in her claims under trademark law and personality rights law.

In the Internet context, one analog to the *Rogers* facts might be the use of a personal domain name resolving to a website that comments on the person in question. The commentary could be a fan website, a parody, or a website critical of the person. Assuming the domain name registrant did not receive any commercial profit from the use of the domain name, the right of publicity may not provide any compensation to the plaintiff. However, if the registrant was attempting to make a profit from the name either by selling the name itself (that is, cybersquatting) or by using the name to attract customers to the website for commercial purposes, a right of publicity claim would more likely be successful.

4.4.2 Personality Rights versus the UDRP

Most personal name disputes are currently brought under the UDRP,[189] despite the potential for actions under personality rights law in jurisdictions where the action is available. There are a number of reasons why the UDRP has been the favored avenue of recourse for personal name

---

188 *Id.* 1005 ('[W]e hold that section 43(a) of the Lanham Act does not bar a minimally relevant use of a celebrity's name in the title of an artistic work where the title does not explicitly denote authorship, sponsorship, or endorsement by the celebrity or explicitly mislead as to content. Similarly, we conclude that Oregon law on the right of publicity, as interpreted by New York, would not bar the use of a celebrity's name in a movie title unless the title was "wholly unrelated" to the movie or was "simply a disguised commercial advertisement for the sale of goods or services".').

189 There are only a small handful of cases where the right of publicity has been argued in the domain name context. See, for example, *Kevin Trudeau v George Lanoue*, 2006 U.S. Dist. LEXIS 7956 (2006) (in which a right of publicity claim was made, amongst other unfair competition claims, in a dispute involving a domain name corresponding with the plaintiff's personal name); *Paul Wright v Domain Source Inc.*, 2002 U.S. Dist. LEXIS 16024 (2002) (plaintiff brought a claim under Californian Business and Professions Code, § 17525 which is a cyberspace analog to right of publicity law in some respects as it protects personal names in the domain space against certain unauthorized uses); Beezy, *supra* note 118, at 23–4 (noting high success rate of celebrities in personal domain name proceedings under the UDRP and surveying some of the recent decisions); Moreland and Springer, *supra* note 28, at 386 (noting high success rate of celebrities in personal domain name disputes under the UDRP, and citing Statistical Summary for Proceedings under the Uniform Domain Name Dispute Resolution Policy (February 26, 2001), 394 ('A plethora of disputes involving personal names have been submitted to ICANN Arbitration.')).

complainants. These reasons relate to the cost, time and jurisdictional advantages of the UDRP compared with litigation under either trademark or personality rights law.[190] Judicial proceedings will be more costly and time/resource intensive than online arbitration.[191] Compared even with federal trademark law, the right of publicity has a number of procedural disadvantages. For one thing, it is state law that is not harmonized nationally within the United States,[192] let alone globally. This potentially causes conflicts of law issues, including problems of asserting jurisdiction over an out-of-state defendant,[193] and choice of law issues.[194]

It is also likely that complainants are more focused on the UDRP for *any* domain name dispute than with any domestic law. When complainants and their lawyers think about personal domain name disputes, they probably instinctively categorize them as 'domain name disputes', rather than 'personal name disputes'. Thus, they would tend to focus on the set of rules geared towards resolving domain name disputes.[195] In many ways, this is a problem of categorization. If one classifies a given dispute as a

---

[190] Moreland and Springer, *supra* note 28, at 395 ('ICANN Arbitration offers celebrities and their lawyers a quick, cost effective and usually successful means to recover domain names registered by third parties that incorporate the celebrity's name.').

[191] *Id.*

[192] Haemmerli, *supra* note 43, at 389 ('Existing practice [under the right of publicity] is . . . confused, with fifty state regimes protecting differing aspects of identity, for varied terms, and with disparate remedies.'); *Rogers v Grimaldi*, 875 F. 2d 994, 1002–4 (1988) (court discussing problems of applying Oregon's right of publicity law in a New York forum).

[193] This has been an issue with respect to personal domain name disputes in the past. See *Paul Wright v Domain Source Inc.*, 2002 U.S. Dist. LEXIS 16024, paras 1–3 (2002) (discussion of jurisdictional issues raised in complaint against cybersquatter's registration of 'paulwright.com' domain name). The movie actor Kevin Spacey was also initially unsuccessful in a cybersquatting claim against the registrant of 'kevinspacey.com' on jurisdictional grounds, but later succeeded in a UDRP proceeding: Kieren McCarthy, *Kevin Spacey Loses Pivotal Cybersquatting Court Case*, The Register, November 26, 2001, available at www.theregister.co.uk/2001/11/26/kevin_spacey_loses_pivotal_cybersquatting/, last accessed November 8, 2007.

[194] See, for example, *Rogers v Grimaldi*, 875 F. 2d 994, 1002–4 (1988) (court discussing problems of applying Oregon's right of publicity law in a New York forum).

[195] Of course, there are some legislative provisions that could be categorized as aimed at both domain name disputes and personal names: for example, 15 U.S.C. § 8131(1)(A). However, these laws require expensive domestic litigation as opposed to inexpensive online arbitration.

'domain name dispute' rather than as a 'dispute to protect the integrity of an individual's persona', one will tend to think of domain name focused rules, rather than personal identity rules.

The following discussion considers the possibility of combining the substance of personality rights with the procedural advantages of the UDRP to arrive at potentially better targeted solutions for personal domain name disputes. The idea would be to achieve the time, cost and jurisdictional benefits of the UDRP, but with a clearer focus on the aspects of an individual's persona that should be protected in the domain space as a matter of policy. Another advantage of this approach would be that it could avoid undesirable expansions of trademark law into matters involving personal names. There would be less pressure on arbitrators to accept trademarks in personal names if an effective alternative was available for protecting personal names under the UDRP.

In cybersquatting cases, a personality rights framework might improve on the UDRP in several ways. It would not require the complainant to establish a trademark right in her personal name.[196] Thus, it would apply equally to celebrities,[197] politicians,[198] other public

---

[196] Of course, infringement under legislative provisions such as 15 U.S.C. § 8131(1)(A) does not require establishment of a trademark in a personal name, but it does require often expensive litigation.

[197] The right of publicity has its most obvious applications in the case of celebrity personas: GILSON, *supra* note 2, para. 2B.01 ('The right of publicity, a developing common law right of great value to the celebrity'); Dogan and Lemley, *supra* note 43, at 1164 (conceiving right of publicity in terms of protecting celebrities' names and likenesses); *Bette Midler v Ford Motor Co.*, 849 F. 2d 460 (1988) (right of publicity action involving Bette Midler's distinctive singing voice); *Tom Waits v Frito-Lay Inc.*, 978 F. 2d 1093 (1992) (right of publicity action involving Tom Waits' distinctive singing voice); *Rogers v Grimaldi*, 875 F. 2d 994 (1988) (right of publicity action involving Ginger Rogers' name); Michael Carrier, *Cabining Intellectual Property Through a Property Paradigm*, 54 DUKE L.J. 1, 141–2 (2004) ('Celebrities play a central role in discourse today . . . In a world of increasing fragmentation, references to celebrities are essential for dialogue on issues such as culture and values . . . By putting alternative conceptions of celebrity off limits, the right of publicity . . . threatens to suppress expression and to give celebrities the power to censor alternative versions of their images that are, for example, iconoclastic or irreverent.'); McKenna, *supra* note 43, at 226 (conceiving of the right of publicity as being focused 'entirely on the economic value of a celebrity's identity'); Madow, *supra* note 44 (critiquing the right of publicity in the celebrity context).

[198] Rielly, *supra* note 43, at 1169–72 (discussing the application of the right of publicity to political figures); *New York Magazine v The Metropolitan Transit Authority and the City of New York*, 987 F. Supp. 254 (1997), *aff'd in part, vacated in part, New York Magazine v The Metropolitan Transit Authority and the City of*

figures[199] and private individuals.[200] It would cover all cybersquatting involving personal names regardless of the trademarkability of the name.[201] Outside of cybersquatting, a personality rights-based dispute resolution procedure might more effectively deal with cases where a domain name registrant does not want to *sell* the name for a profit, but rather wants to *use* it herself for some reason.

These situations arguably boil down into two subcategories which can overlap: commerce and commentary. Some unauthorized uses of a personal domain name will be commercial and some will be for expressive purposes, whether it be idolatry, parody, criticism or a combination. A website may contain elements of both commerce and commentary simultaneously. For example, an unauthorized fan website may charge a subscription fee and may at the same time be selling unauthorized celebrity merchandise. A website criticizing a particular individual may equally sell merchandise supporting opposing views.[202] Even a parody website may advocate the sale of merchandise critical of the person or

---

New York, 136 F.3d 123 (1998) (on Mayor Rudolph Giuliani's rights of privacy and publicity); Charles Harder and Henry L. Self III, *Schwarzenegger vs. Bobbleheads: The Case for Schwarzenegger*, 45 SANTA CLARA L. REV. 557 (2005); William Gallagher, *Strategic Intellectual Property Litigation, the Right of Publicity, and the Attenuation of Free Speech: Lessons from the Schwarzenegger Bobblehead Doll War (and Peace)*, 45 SANTA CLARA L. REV. 581 (2005); David Welkowitz and Tyler Ochoa, *The Terminator as Eraser: How Arnold Schwarzenegger Used the Right of Publicity to Terminate Non-Defamatory Political Speech*, 45 SANTA CLARA L. REV. 651 (2005); Lipton, *Who Owns 'Hillary.com?', supra* note 52.

199 *Rosa Parks v LaFace Records*, 329 F.3d 437 (2003) (involving publicity rights of Rosa Parks in the context of a song title using her name in relation to a hip hop recording that had nothing in particular to do with her or her work); *Martin Luther King Jr, Center for Social Change Inc. v American Heritage Products*, 694 F. 2d 674 (11th Cir. 1993) (the estate of Martin Luther King, Jr sought an injunction to prevent the defendant from selling plastic busts of Dr King).

200 *Kevin Trudeau v George Lanoue*, 2006 U.S. Dist. LEXIS 7956 (2006) (in which a right of publicity claim was made, amongst other unfair competition claims, in a dispute involving a domain name corresponding with the plaintiff's personal name); *Paul Wright v Domain Source Inc.*, 2002 U.S. Dist. LEXIS 16024 (2002) (plaintiff brought a claim under Californian Business and Professions Code, § 17525 which is a cyberspace analog to right of publicity law in some respects as it protects personal names in the domain space against certain unauthorized uses).

201 Of course, 15 U.S.C. § 8131 would also cover the same conduct. However, that would require litigation as opposed to inexpensive online arbitration.

202 See, for example, *Lamparello v Falwell*, 420 F.3d 309 (2005) (gripe site contained links to Amazon.com webpage selling a book critical of the Reverend Jerry Falwell's views on homosexuality).

institution being parodied.[203] These cases raise difficult questions of the balance between rights to free expression and rights in an individual's persona. Personality rights theory has dealt with these issues in a way that trademark law has not, because balancing speech against personal integrity is a different question to balancing speech against trademark rights.

4.5 A PERSONALITY RIGHTS VERSION OF THE UDRP

Even if a personality rights-based version of the UDRP were adopted by ICANN, personality rights actions under domestic law would still be available to complainants in jurisdictions where such actions are currently available.[204] As we saw previously, dispute resolution procedures such as the UDRP cannot, and are not intended to, oust the jurisdiction of domestic courts.[205] As noted above, most domain name disputes, including those involving personal names, arise in the '.com' domain space.[206]

---

203 *People for the Ethical Treatment of Animals v Doughney*, 113 F.Supp.2d 915 (2000); *aff'd* 263 F.3d 359 (2001) (parody site linking to websites where fur and animal products antithetical to plaintiff's views were available for sale).

204 It has, in fact, been argued in several domain name cases involving personal domain names to date: *Kevin Trudeau v George Lanoue*, 2006 U.S. Dist. LEXIS 7956 (2006) (in which a right of publicity claim was made, amongst other unfair competition claims, in a dispute involving a domain name corresponding with the plaintiff's personal name); *Paul Wright v Domain Source Inc.*, 2002 U.S. Dist. LEXIS 16024 (2002).

205 This is expressly recognized currently in UDRP, para. 4(K): 'The mandatory administrative proceeding requirements set forth in Paragraph 4 shall not prevent either you or the complainant from submitting the dispute to a court of competent jurisdiction for independent resolution before such mandatory administrative proceeding is commenced or after such proceeding is concluded.'

206 See, for example, *Julia Fiona Roberts*, WIPO Case No. D2000–0210, available at www.wipo.int/amc/en/domains/decisions/html/2000/d2000-0210.html (involving 'juliaroberts.com' domain name); *Tom Cruise*, WIPO Case No. D2006–0560, available at www.wipo.int/amc/en/domains/decisions/html/2006/d2006-0560.html) (involving 'tomcruise.com' domain name); *Kevin Spacey*, National Arbitration Forum, Claim No. 96937, available at www.adrforum.com/domains/decisions/96937.htm (involving the domain name 'kevinspacey.com'); *Anna Nicole Smith*, National Arbitration Forum, Claim No. FA0312000220007, available at www.adrforum.com/domains/decisions/220007.htm (involving 'annanicolesmith.com' domain name); *Bjorn Borg*, WIPO Case No. D2007–0591, available at www.wipo.int/amc/en/domains/decisions/html/2007/d2007-0591.html

Thus, it may be wise to limit any new arbitral approach to this space until a clearer personal domain name jurisprudence emerges. Limiting a new dispute resolution policy effectively to 'name.com' cases would also go some way towards alleviating concerns about the potential chilling effect on free speech.

There would likely be no need to extend any new dispute resolution policy to the '.name' gTLD. There are already other effective protections within that gTLD that might assist people in the protection of their personal names.[207] A new personal domain name policy could clearly fit into the basic structure of the UDRP as currently drafted. Many of the current provisions could apply to personal domain name disputes, including representations and warranties made by the registrant,[208] orders that could be made by arbitrators,[209] and procedural matters such as how to lodge communications relating to a dispute.[210] As with the current drafting of the UDRP, a person who has registered a 'name.com' domain

(involving the domain name 'bjornborg.com'); *Hillary Rodham Clinton*, National Arbitration Forum, Claim No. FA0502000414641, available at www.arb-forum.com/domains/decisions/414641.htm (involving 'hillaryclinton.com' domain name); *Bruce Springsteen*, WIPO Case No. D2000–1532, available at www.wipo.int/amc/en/domains/decisions/html/2000/d2000-1532.html.

207 Lipton, *Beyond Cybersquatting*, *supra* note 2, at 1420–1 (describing domain name 'watch' service and 'defensive registration' service; the former allows individuals to be notified if anyone else attempts to register a given domain name without having to register it herself, while the latter allows a person with a legitimate interest in a domain name to register it without having to actively use it in order to maintain the registration).

208 UDRP, para. 2 ('By applying to register a domain name, or by asking us to maintain or renew a domain name registration, you hereby represent and warrant to us that (a) the statements that you made in your Registration Agreement are complete and accurate; (b) to your knowledge, the registration of the domain name will not infringe upon or otherwise violate the rights of any third party; (c) you are not registering the domain name for an unlawful purpose; and (d) you will not knowingly use the domain name in violation of any applicable laws or regulations. It is your responsibility to determine whether your domain name registration infringes or violates someone else's rights.').

209 *Id.* para. 4(i) ('The remedies available to a complainant pursuant to any proceeding before an Administrative Panel shall be limited to requiring the cancellation of your domain name or the transfer of your domain name registration to the complainant.').

210 See Rules for Uniform Domain Name Dispute Resolution Policy, available at www.icann.org/udrp/udrp-rules-24oct99.htm, last accessed November 23, 2007.

name[211] would be required to submit to a mandatory arbitration proceeding if a complainant with a relevant personal name established the matters set forth in the policy.

To establish a complaint under the new policy, a complainant might be required to establish that (a) the registrant's domain name corresponds letter for letter with the complainant's personal name (that is, a 'name.com' version of the complainant's name); (b) the registrant has no legitimate interests in the domain name; and (c) the registrant has registered or used the name for an unauthorized commercial purpose. This would be the personal name analog to paragraph 4(a) of the UDRP.[212] Rather than establishing a trademark interest, the complainant would only have to establish what her own name is – this should be easier than establishing a trademark right in a personal name for obvious reasons. The provision might cover a complainant's actual personal name, as well as a name by which she is commonly known. Thus, it would cover 'Cher' for 'Cheryl Sarkisian LaPiere' and 'Madonna' for 'Madonna Louise Veronica Ciccone'.[213] It could also potentially cover 'Tyra' for 'Tyra Banks' and 'Trump' for 'Donald Trump'.[214]

---

[211] And perhaps ultimately some other iterations of the name if there was ever a need to extend the policy more broadly.

[212] UDRP, para. 4(a) (requiring a domain name registrant to submit to mandatory arbitration under the UDRP when (i) the registrant's domain name is identical or confusingly similar to a trademark or service mark in which the complainant has rights; and (ii) the registrant has no rights or legitimate interests in respect of the domain name; and (iii) the registrant's domain name has been registered and is being used in bad faith).

[213] This would accord with the way in which the right of publicity currently works. See, for example, Indiana Code Title 32 (property), art. 36 (publicity), chap. 1 (rights of publicity), § 32–36–1-3 (defining 'name' for the purposes of the statute as including 'the actual or assumed name of a living or deceased natural person that is intended to identify the person').

[214] It may or may not cover intentional misspellings of complainants' names such as 'Tom Kruse' for 'Tom Cruise'. See, for example, *Lamparello v Falwell*, 420 F.3d 309 (2005) (involving an intentional misspelling of the Reverend Falwell's name as a domain name). However, perhaps such names should not be covered in the first instance of the policy in the interests of avoiding the chilling of speech. This may be a little like the 'lookalike' and 'soundalike' cases under the right of publicity in the 'real world' which have been criticized for extending the right too far. See, for example, William Heberer, *The Overprotection of Celebrity: A Comment on White vs Samsung Electronics America Inc.*, 22 HOFSTRA L. REV. 729 (1994); Steven Clay, *Starstruck: The Overextension of Celebrity Publicity Rights in State and Federal Courts*, 79 MINN. L. REV. 485 (1994).

The requirement of showing that the registrant has no legitimate interests in the domain name would be necessary to cover cases where, for example, the registrant happens to have the same personal name as a complainant. In cases of competing legitimate interests in the same name, probably a 'first come, first served' rule, subject to private negotiation between the parties, is preferable to a dispute resolution mechanism in which the arbitrators have little to go on as to who has the best interest in a given domain name. This accords with the way the UDRP currently operates in the case of competing trademark interests.[215]

With respect to the unauthorized commercial use requirement, a new policy might either give specific examples of such uses or could leave the wording vague and allow arbitrators to develop relevant policies on a case by case basis. If the policy were to be drafted more comprehensively to include examples of unauthorized commercial use, these could be drawn from current right of publicity statutes. For example, the Indiana statute[216] defines 'commercial purpose' in the context of the right of publicity as:

> the use of an aspect of a personality's right of publicity . . .
> (1) On or in connection with a product, merchandise, goods, services, or commercial activities.
> (2) For advertising or soliciting purchases of products, merchandise, goods, services, or for promoting commercial activities.
> (3) For the purpose of fundraising.[217]

The incorporation of such a definition would give arbitrators some guidance and may be helpful at least in the early days of such a dispute resolution policy. It would also allow disputing parties and arbitrators to draw on existing personality rights jurisprudence to help inform initial determinations under a new policy. Although this test does reflect some concepts traditionally associated with trademark law, it is also broader with its inclusion of uses such as the promotion of commercial activities for fundraising purposes.

It may be a good idea for a new policy to include a defense such as that found in paragraph 4(c) of the UDRP. This would give the registrant some guidance on how to establish a legitimate interest in a domain name. The

---

[215] See discussion in Lipton, *A Winning Solution*, *supra* note 41.

[216] Indiana Code Title 32 (property), art. 36 (publicity), chap. 1 (rights of publicity).

[217] *Id.* § 32–26–1-2.

indicia of a legitimate interest in the current UDRP largely relate to good faith uses of the domain name in commerce in connection with the registrant's own commercial or non-commercial endeavors.[218] Any legitimate interest provision for personal domain names should be drafted in a different way because presumably the policy might prohibit some unauthorized commercial uses of a name even if they are associated with a bona fide business plan of the registrant.

The UDRP, for example, currently excuses a registrant's use, or demonstrable preparation to use, a relevant domain name in connection with a bona fide offering of goods or services.[219] This makes sense in a trademark-based system because it amounts to two competing legitimate interests in using the mark in a domain name, presumably in different areas of commerce.[220] For example, if the complainant has registered the trademark 'Hypo' for medical syringes and I have registered the domain name, 'hypo.com' for a business involving the sale of practice law exam questions, and I have registered the domain name in good faith for these purposes, I should be entitled to use it.[221]

---

218 UDRP, para. 4(c) which gives examples of legitimate use as including the registrant's ability to establish: '(i) before any notice to [the registrant] of the dispute, [the registrant's] use of, or demonstrable preparations to use, the domain name or a name corresponding to the domain name in connection with a bona fide offering of goods or services; or (ii) [the registrant] (as an individual, business, or other organization) [has] been commonly known by the domain name, even if [she has] acquired no trademark or service mark rights; or (iii) [the registrant is] making a legitimate noncommercial or fair use of the domain name, without intent for commercial gain to misleadingly divert consumers or to tarnish the trademark or service mark at issue'.

219 *Id.* para. 4(c)(i).

220 The issues arising in relation to two competing trademark interests with one corresponding domain name are taken up in more detail in Lipton, *A Winning Solution*, *supra* note 41.

221 If such a case was brought under domestic trademark law, I may have some difficulties under the 'initial interest confusion' doctrine. The medical supply company might argue in a court proceeding for trademark infringement that, even though consumers are not confused about the source of the products when they get to my website, I am potentially diverting custom from them by attracting consumers to my website by using a similar online address. It may be that consumers who assume that 'hypo.com' is the website of the medical supply company would accidentally access my website and then cease looking for the other company on the basis that it is too difficult to find. Regardless of what view a court would take of this argument under domestic trademark law, the UDRP currently has no 'initial interest confusion' doctrine built into it in this sense and seems to allow as a defense that the registrant was using, or plan-

In contrast, if the policy behind the right of publicity is to prevent anyone from making any kind of unjust profit from another person's name or likeness, new arbitration procedures might not always permit registration of a person's name as a domain name even for bona fide offering of goods or services. In any event, it is difficult to think of a situation in which someone would register someone else's name as a domain name with such an intent. Why would anyone register, say, 'tomcruise.com' for the sale of goods or services completely unrelated to Tom Cruise unless they wanted to use the name to attract attention to their own goods, services or advertising?[222] This would not be a good faith registration if we accept the presumption that individuals have a right to prevent unauthorized commercial profits being made from their online personas, at least in 'name.com' spaces. Even if Tom Cruise himself has no intention of using 'tomcruise.com' to sell particular goods or services, the unauthorized registrant has interfered with his ability to control his persona in commerce which may be prohibited under a personality rights framework.[223]

Difficulties may arise under a new personality rights framework where a personal name truly is a trademark, as where the individual in question runs a business under her own name. In these cases, arguably trademark-based laws should apply with respect to the trademarked version of the

---

ning to use, the relevant domain name in a bona fide trademark manner. On the initial interest doctrine in trademark law generally, see Lastowka, *supra* note 92, at 1369–70 ('With respect to search engines . . . a . . . significant expansion of trademark law is the doctrine of initial interest confusion. Traditionally, and not surprisingly, most courts have focused analysis of consumer confusion on the time period proximate to consumer purchases. The doctrine of initial interest confusion shifts the focus of confusion analysis to a time prior to the time of purchase. Initial interest confusion can be found to exist even if that confusion was not present at the time of purchase.'); see also Jennifer Rothman, *Initial Interest Confusion: Standing at the Crossroads of Trademark Law*, 27 CARDOZO L. REV. 105 (2005); Goldman, *supra* note 72, at 559 ('[Initial interest confusion] lacks a rigorous definition, a clear policy justification, and a uniform standard for analyzing claims. With its doctrinal flexibility, [it] has become the tool of choice for plaintiffs to shut down junior users who have not actually engaged in misappropriative uses.').

[222] This appears to have been the strategy utilized by the domain name registrant of 'tomcruise.com' under discussion in *Tom Cruise*, WIPO Case No. D2006–0560, available at www.wipo.int/amc/en/domains/decisions/html/2006/d2006-0560.html.

[223] Tom Cruise, in fact, did set up an official website for the first time in 2008 under 'tomcruise.com' to celebrate the 25th anniversary of the release of his movie, *Risky Business*. See www.tomcruise.com, last accessed June 2, 2008.

name. Of course, this happens routinely in judicial proceedings under trademark law. In such cases, courts have the power to determine trademark-based claims and right of publicity claims in the alternative in the same proceedings.[224] It may be that a new personal name policy should include some provision for joining trademark and personal name complaints in the same arbitration. This would allow arbitrators to hear the entire dispute and decide whether the name in question is being used by the registrant in a trademark sense or in a personal name sense.

There may also be situations in which a domain name registrant simply happens to have the same name as a complainant and has registered the domain name for her own personal use: for example, to set up her own webpage. These situations may be more difficult than they first appear as a matter of policy. It may be that a complainant is actually harmed in a right of publicity sense even where the registrant herself has a legitimate interest in the name by virtue of having a similar name to the complainant. As the right of publicity has no consumer confusion requirement, it may be that simply using the complainant's name in a domain name on a personal website might contravene the right in some cases, particularly if the website contains commercial advertising. This may be one area in which personality rights theory needs to be pared down to meet the realities of the Internet age. In most cases, it would probably be best to excuse, as a legitimate interest, the conduct of a person who has been commonly known by the relevant name and is only using it for her own personal website, even if there is some commercial activity taking place on the website. Of course, if the registrant were not making *any* commercial use of the name in question, there would be no basis for a complaint in the first place.

A personal name dispute resolution policy should, like the current UDRP, be limited in terms of remedies to a transfer or cancellation order.[225] In most personal domain name disputes under the UDRP to date, the registrant has sought a transfer,[226] even where she does not intend to use the name herself, presumably in order to maintain control over the most intuitive version of her online persona – the 'name.com' version

---

[224] See, for example, *Kevin Trudeau v George Lanoue*, 2006 U.S. Dist. LEXIS 7956 (2006); *Rogers v Grimaldi*, 875 F. 2d 994 (1988).

[225] See UDRP, para. 4(i) ('The remedies available to a complainant pursuant to any proceeding before an Administrative Panel shall be limited to requiring the cancellation of your domain name or the transfer of your domain name registration to the complainant.').

[226] See, for example, *Julia Fiona Roberts*, WIPO Case No. D2000–0210, available at www.wipo.int/amc/en/domains/decisions/html/2000/d2000-0210.html.

of her name. Because of these limitations on remedies, a personality rights-based policy may have less of a chilling effect on speech than the threat of litigation under the right of publicity. Although the usual remedy in a right of publicity action is an injunction,[227] which, in the domain name case, may be tantamount to a cancellation or transfer order, courts can award other remedies for infringement of personality rights.

Other remedies include damages based on injury to a plaintiff's feelings,[228] damages based on unjust enrichment,[229] and accounts of profits.[230] Additionally, even an injunction may be tailored to a given case more broadly than a mere transfer or cancellation order. For example, an injunction may prohibit the defendant from engaging in any commerce online utilizing the name or likeness of a plaintiff, regardless of the domain name used by the defendant. Thus, even though personality rights actions are rare in practice, the threat of broader remedies under such actions may chill speech to a greater extent than the threat of a personality rights-based arbitration.

One contentious issue that has arisen under personality rights law is the appropriate duration of those rights.[231] Related questions are whether the rights are transferable or descendible.[232] This discussion has presumed protection for a personal domain name during the course of a complainant's lifetime and has not focused on issues of transferability or descendibility. This is implicit in the suggestion that a new personality rights-based arbitration mechanism should require the complainant to establish that the domain name in question corresponds with her personal name, rather than with a name in a deceased estate that she may control.

There have been some arbitrations under the UDRP involving the unauthorized registration and use of names of deceased persons.[233] Thus, there is perhaps a plausible argument that a framework should be developed to assist assignees and beneficiaries of personality rights to protect those rights in the domain space. If this were to be done, the arbitration

---

227 GILSON, *supra* note 2, para. 2B.08.

228 *Id.*

229 *Id.*

230 *Id.*

231 In particular, there has been some disagreement as to whether personality rights should survive a person's death: *id.* para. 2B.04[3]; Kwall, *First Amendment, supra* note 46, at 81–6.

232 GILSON, *supra* note 2, para. 2B.04 [3].

233 See discussion in Lipton, *Celebrity in Cyberspace*, *supra* note 6, at 1523–4.

policy would need to provide for a complainant to establish that she controls personality rights relating to a person with the relevant name. It may be difficult for arbitrators to determine the validity of such claims in practice. Thus, it might be wise to leave such determinations for a later iteration of a personal domain name arbitration policy, at least in the first instance.

In any event, such issues may not arise very often in practice. The estates of many deceased famous people currently hold the domain names corresponding with the relevant names.[234] At the same time, today's celebrities and politicians are getting better about aggressively fighting for control of relevant domain names during their lifetimes.[235] The question of post-mortem personal domain name disputes may therefore have minimal practical importance. If a policy is established now to help those who want to assert interests in relevant domain names to obtain those names, those people can presumably hold on to the names and pass them to their estates in the future as a matter of contract law. It is a simple matter for a successful complainant to transfer the domain name to anyone she wants, either during her lifetime or presumably post mortem if she executes the transfer formalities prior to her death.

4.6 EMERGING ISSUES INVOLVING PERSONAL DOMAIN NAMES

As we saw in previous chapters, there are some new developments in the domain space that may implicate a variety of issues about the regulation of domain names. In particular, ICANN is currently working on a system to introduce new gTLDs.[236] Additionally, Facebook has recently adopted a system that allows personalized usernames for its members.[237] Both of these moves may lead to disputes involving personal names. If ICANN

---

[234] See, for example, www.marlonbrando.com, www.johnwayne.com, www.marilynmonroe.com, last accessed November 24, 2007.

[235] See, for example, discussion in Moreland and Springer, *supra* note 28; Beezy, *supra* note 118.

[236] ICANN, New gTLD Program: Draft Applicant Guidebook (Draft RFP) (October 24, 2008), full text available at www.icann.org/en/topics/new-gtlds/draft-rfp-24oct08-en.pdf, last accessed December 11, 2008.

[237] See, for example, discussion in Stoel Rives L.L.P., *Trademark Law Alert: New Personalized Facebook URLs May Infringe Your Trademarks and Brands*, (June 11, 2009), available at www.stoel.com/showalert.aspx?Show=5515, last accessed July 6, 2009.

receives an application for registration of a new gTLD that involves a person's name, ICANN will need to have policies in place to determine whether such a move may lead to unauthorized uses of the name that might implicate existing legal rights in the name. ICANN will need to consider whether private individuals should be given an opportunity to oppose the approval of a gTLD that implicates their personal name. Currently, the opposition procedures contemplated by ICANN focus more on protecting trademarks in the new gTLD space than in protecting other interests like personal names.[238]

Additionally, some thought may need be given to policies that might apply to registration of individual domain names within a new gTLD that implicates an individual's name. For example, a registry might apply for the rights to administer a '.smith' gTLD with a view to providing vanity domains involving people's names such as 'john.smith'. Questions may arise as to whether ICANN would require, as a condition of approving the '.smith' gTLD that the registry adopt a policy along the lines discussed above that would protect personality interests in cases where a registrant has a bad faith motive of making an unauthorized commercial profit from someone else's name. An example of this might be if someone registered 'annanicole.smith' in order to draw custom to a website unrelated to the late Anna Nicole Smith for the registrant's own commercial advantage. ICANN perhaps should require registries approved to administer gTLDs incorporating common last names to adopt dispute resolution policies that protect personal interests in those names.

Facebook personalized URLs are described in some detail above.[239] They may be less problematic in this context than domain names and gTLDs involving individuals' names because, at least at the present time, Facebook is more of a social networking service than a commercial medium. Having said this, Facebook is likely to deal with problems where multiple individuals claim the same Facebook usernames on the basis of each having a corresponding personal name. As Facebook is a private service, it has the right to create whatever policies it likes to regulate these disputes – 'first come, first served' being the most obvious. It may also want to facilitate private negotiations between individuals to share or transfer usernames in some way.

---

238 ICANN, New gTLD Program: Draft Applicant Guidebook (Draft RFP) (October 24, 2008), para. 3.5.2, available at www.icann.org/en/topics/new-gtlds/draft-rfp-24oct08-en.pdf, last accessed December 11, 2008.

239 See 4.2.3, *supra*.

4.7 CHAPTER SUMMARY

This chapter has considered how overreliance on trademark focused rules, such as the UDRP, to resolve personal domain name disputes can lead to inconsistent and arbitrary results. It has suggested that other models focused more squarely on protecting personal names per se might ultimately be preferable to maintaining the focus on protecting trademarks in the domain space. In particular, it has addressed the following.

(1) Different ways in which personal domain name disputes may be categorized, and different rights and interests typically implicated within each classification.

(2) The limitations of existing trademark focused laws in relation to personal domain name disputes.

(3) The limitations of existing personality focused laws in relation to personal domain name disputes.

(4) The possibility of developing a revised UDRP that draws on personality rights theory to better focus on the kinds of interests individuals may wish to protect in their personal names in the domain space.

(5) Emerging issues in the domain space that may implicate interests in personal names, including the adoption of new gTLDs,[240] and Facebook's recent creation of personalized usernames.[241]

The following chapter covers some more interests that may be implicated in the domain space. It focuses on the protection of political, cultural and geographic signifiers.

---

240 ICANN, New gTLD Program: Draft Applicant Guidebook (Draft RFP) (October 24, 2008), available at www.icann.org/en/topics/new-gtlds/draft-rfp-24oct08-en.pdf, last accessed December 11, 2008.

241 See, for example, discussion in Stoel Rives L.L.P., *Trademark Law Alert: New Personalized Facebook URLs May Infringe Your Trademarks and Brands* (June 11, 2009), full text available at www.stoel.com/showalert.aspx?Show=5515, last accessed July 6, 2009.

5. Political, cultural and geographic identifiers in the domain space

5.1 POLITICS, CULTURE AND GEOGRAPHY IN THE DOMAIN SPACE

While the previous chapters focused respectively on protecting free speech and personal identity in the domain space, this chapter examines more specific instances of political, cultural and geographic identifiers in cyberspace. It focuses on domain names in politics because this is one of the more developed areas of domain name regulation to date. However, some comment is also made about attempts to balance other kinds of cultural and geographic interests against trademark interests online. Such interests include religious terminology like 'Madonna', 'Christ' or 'God' and geographic identifiers like 'Uluru', 'Ubuntu' or 'Amazon'. Even the word 'Obama' denotes both the President of the United States and a city in Japan. Some of these signifiers will compete with existing trademarks in the domain space. Madonna, for example, is the registered trademark of the popular singer known as 'Madonna'. Amazon is the trademark of 'Amazon.com', the popular online store.

Because domain name regulations developed with a focus on trademarks, little thought was initially given to protecting these other interests. To the extent that discussion has focused on other cultural interests in the domain space, little clear progress has been made. There are a number of reasons for this, including (a) lack of lobbying power of groups with interests in such names; (b) lack of clarity over who should have the rights to protect these terms; (c) lack of legal and technological sophistication of groups with interests in such terms; and (d) disharmonization of legal rules relating to the protection of such terms. Some attempts have been made by the Internet Corporation for Assigned Names and Numbers (ICANN) and the World Intellectual Property Organization (WIPO) to create processes for protecting political, cultural and geographic indicators in the domain space.[1]

[1] See, for example, discussion in David Lindsay, International Domain Name Law: ICANN and the UDRP 117–20 (2007).

However, these approaches are still in their infancy compared with the relatively sophisticated protections for trademarks.

This chapter focuses on the protection of politically significant domain names. It commences by dividing political domain name disputes into two distinct categories. These categories may overlap in practice depending on the actions and motivations of an individual registrant. The categories are (a) political cyberfraud and (b) political cybersquatting. Political cyberfraud connotes activities that are likely to confuse voters as to the source of a given political message. Political cybersquatting, on the other hand, is more akin to traditional cybersquatting.[2] It connotes the registration of a domain name corresponding with a political term or politician's name in order to profit from sale of the name.

This chapter also examines a potential third category of cases involving political names: situations where a legitimate trademark interest may compete with a political name. These cases are likely to be few and far between, although they are not outside the bounds of possibility. For example, a software corporation with the name 'Hillary Software' has registered the 'hillary.com' domain name, even though some people might automatically associate this name with the Secretary of State, Hillary Clinton.[3] Presumably, any contests arising between politicians or political organizations and trademark holders will raise different policy issues to the cases involving cyberfraud or cybersquatting. This chapter concludes by considering approaches to protecting other culturally significant words and phrases in the domain space, outside of the political process. It also examines the relevance of ICANN's new gTLD proposals on the balance between culturally significant terms and other interests in relevant domain names.

5.2 DOMAIN NAMES IN POLITICS

5.2.1 Categorizing Political Domain Name Disputes

Since the dawn of the millennium, politicians have increasingly become aware of the importance of securing an online presence, utilizing their

---

2 Anne Gilson Lalonde and Jerome Gilson, Trademark Protection and Practice, para. 7A.06 ('Cybersquatters register trademarks in Internet domain names with no intention of developing a viable website but instead to hold the name for resale to either the trademark owner or a third party.').

3 Jacqueline Lipton, *Who Owns 'Hillary.com'? Political Speech and the First Amendment in Cyberspace*, 49 Boston College L. Rev. 55, 56 (2008).

own names and those of their political parties as domain names.[4] More recently, politics online has become much more sophisticated than it was earlier in the millennium. Today's politicians routinely utilize social networking sites, email, Twitter and various other digital media to garner support and communicate with the electorate.[5] However, most uses of the Internet by politicians and political parties at some level involve control of intuitive domain names. This means that politicians and political parties must often take defensive measures to ensure that intuitive domain names are not taken by opposing parties[6] or cybersquatters.[7]

None of this is to say that politicians do, or indeed should, control all online content about them. In fact, it is unlikely that politicians could control all content, even if they were able to secure all of the most intuitive domain names. What is lacking in our current regulations is a methodology for distinguishing between appropriate and inappropriate uses of a politician's or political party's name in the domain space. Such a methodology could assist the democratic process by ensuring that domain names are used in ways that further the benefits of democracy, and that minimize voter fraud.

As most politicians and political parties have come to understand in recent years, Internet domain names are an important tool to help Internet users identify political websites. These websites can be utilized both for fundraising purposes, and to disseminate information about policy issues. An Internet presence is invaluable for a politician. Political websites have become increasingly sophisticated over the years, as evidenced by the phenomenal success of the Obama campaign in the 2008 presidential election.[8] The Internet can be used to reach an audience on a scale never before possible for a fraction of the cost of other media conduits. In some respects, this potentially levels the playing field for politicians and political commentators alike. A sophisticated and interactive Internet presence can also encourage debate and support in ways never before imaginable.

---

[4] Jacqueline Lipton, *From Domain Names to Video Games: The Rise of the Internet in Presidential Politics*, 86 DENVER UNIVERSITY L. REV. 693, 697–9 (2009).

[5] *Id*; JOE TRIPPI, THE REVOLUTION WILL NOT BE TELEVISED: DEMOCRACY, THE INTERNET, AND THE OVERTHROW OF EVERYTHING (2008).

[6] Jacqueline Lipton, *Celebrity in Cyberspace: A Personality Rights Paradigm for Personal Domain Name Disputes*, 65 WASHINGTON AND LEE L. REV. 1445, 1466–7 (2008).

[7] See, for example, *Hillary Rodham Clinton v Michele Dinoia*, National Arbitration Forum, Claim No. FA0502000414641 (March 18, 2005), full text available at www.arb-forum.com/domains/decisions/414641.htm, last accessed March 2, 2009.

[8] Lipton, d*omain names to video games*, *supra* note 4.

However, an Internet presence with an intuitive domain name can cause problems for politicians. Many of these problems stem from the fact that current domain name regulations are largely premised on protecting trademarks,[9] and not on protecting political interests.[10] There are significant regulatory gaps when it comes to the use of domain names in politics. Particularly during a political campaign, it is important that those wishing to use available media to discuss candidates and their views should be able to do so. However, there are currently few clear rules about how domain names, particularly those corresponding with politicians' names, may be legitimately used in the political process.

Application of current regulations to prevent misleading or wasteful registrations and uses of political domain names is limited in two ways. The first is that current regulations will predominantly protect trademarked (and therefore trademarkable) domain names. The second limitation is that the regulations focus on bad faith cybersquatting. These are potentially significant limitations in the political context. Many policiticans' names will not be registrable as trademarks.[11] They may not even attain common law trademark status if used in a purely political, as opposed to a commercial, context.[12] Further, much of the abusive conduct that arises

---

[9] Jacqueline Lipton, *Beyond Cybersquatting: Taking Domain Names Past Trademark Policy*, 40 Wake Forest L. Rev. 1361, 1363 (2005) ([T]he current dispute resolution mechanisms [for domain name disputes] are focused on the protection of commercial trademark interests, often to the detriment of other socially important interests that may inhere in a given domain name.').

[10] *Id.* 1425–31 (discussion of the gaps in current regulations in the political context).

[11] Generally, personal names are not registrable as trademarks: 15 U.S.C. § 1052 (c). See also Gilson, *supra* note 2, para. 2.03[d]. Although a personal name may be registrable on the federal trademark register with the consent of the person whose name it is, in order to *maintain* registration, the name must function as a trademark: in other words, it must be able to distinguish the goods of the applicant for registration from the goods of others: 15 U.S.C. § 1052. If it serves purely political purposes and does not distinguish goods or services in commerce, it is unlikely to retain its registration. Thus, some politicians could choose to register their names as trademarks in order to protect them from unauthorized use, but the registration would only be valid in the commercial trademark context and not necessarily in the noncommercial speech or political context.

[12] See, for example, *Friends of Kathleen Kennedy Townsend v Birt*, WIPO Arbitration and Mediation Centre, Case No. D2002–0451, available at www.wipo.int/amc/en/domains/decisions/html/2002/d2002-0451.html, last accessed March 14, 2007 (UDRP panel suggesting that the politician Kathleen Kennedy Townsend would not have a common law trademark in her personal name used for purely political purposes).

in the electoral context involves misleading content on a political website, rather than an attempt to sell a domain name for a profit.

This discussion sets out a tripartite categorization of political domain name disputes involving (a) political cybersquatting; (b) political cyberfraud; and (c) competitions between politicians and trademark holders. 'Political cybersquatting' might be defined as a situation in which a registrant with no personal connection to a relevant name has registered it in order to sell it for profit. 'Political cyberfraud' involves situations where an individual or political group registers a relevant domain name to promulgate a misleading message about a politician. This category of conduct may coincide with cybersquatting in some contexts, but the legal issues raised by the two categories of conduct are different.

The third category involves the more unusual situation of a competition between a legitimate trademark holder and a politician or political party with a similar name. The example noted above is that of the software company with the 'Hillary' trademark, and the personal name of the Secretary of State, Hillary Clinton. Each of these situations is discussed below with reference to existing regulations. The overarching message is that in the absence of a clear categorization scheme, it has not been possible to comprehensively and clearly develop a regulatory approach that facilitates political discourse in the most effective way possible.

5.2.2 Political Cybersquatting

5.2.2.1 Politicians' names and the Anti-Cybersquatting Consumer Protection Act

Political cybersquatting is the political analog to traditional cybersquatting. It involves registration and use of a domain name corresponding with a politician's name with the intent to sell the domain name for a profit.[13] While the conduct is similar, and similarly motivated, in both the trademark and the political contexts, different legal and policy issues arise. Traditional cybersquatting involves people registering often multiple domain names corresponding with registered trademarks with the intent to profit from selling the names to the relevant trademark holders or to a third party.[14] This conduct was originally prohibited under trademark infringement[15] and

---

[13] Gilson, *supra* note 2, para. 7A.06

[14] *Id.*

[15] 15 U.S.C. §§ 1114(1)(a), 1125(a)(1): statutory prohibitions against trademark infringement at the federal level for registered and common law marks respectively, premised on creation of consumer confusion as to source of relevant goods or services. See also *Planned Parenthood Federation of America*

dilution[16] law. Later, additional regulatory measures were implemented to control this conduct. In the United States, the Anti-Cybersquatting Consumer Protection Act (ACPA) was inserted into the Lanham Act[17] in 1999 to combat cybersquatting. This legislation prohibits cybersquatting and sets out a number of bad faith factors to guide courts in determining whether or not particular conduct falls within the notion of a bad faith intent to profit from registration of a relevant domain name.[18]

At roughly the same time, ICANN adopted the Uniform Domain Name Dispute Resolution Policy (UDRP) to achieve similar ends.[19] The UDRP has a number of time, cost and jurisdictional advantages over domestic legislation. UDRP arbitrations are fast,[20] inexpensive [21] and largely online procedures[22] that can result in transfer of a domain name[23] if the complainant can establish that the registration or use of the domain name was in bad faith[24] and the registrant had no legitimate purpose for registering the name.[25]

Political cybersquatting is not always covered by these rules, par-

---

Inc. v Bucci, 42 U.S.P.Q.2d 1430 (S.D.N.Y.1997) (for an example of the use of traditional trademark infringement law to prohibit unauthorized bad faith registration and use of a domain name corresponding with someone else's registered trademark).

16 15 U.S.C. §§ 1125(c); *Panavision Int'l v Toeppen*, 141 F.3d 1316 (9th Cir. 1998) (an example of a successful trademark dilution action against cybersquatting).

17 15 U.S.C. §§ 1125(d). See also 15 U.S.C. § 8131(1)(A).

18 15 U.S.C. § 1125(d)(1)(B)(i). See also discussion at 1.4.1, *supra*.

19 See discussion at 1.5, *supra*.

20 A domain name arbitration will generally take less time than judicial proceedings, typically taking around two months for a decision to be issued. See *InterNic FAQs on the Uniform Domain Name Dispute Resolution Policy (UDRP)*, available at www.internic.net/faqs/udrp.html, last accessed March 14, 2007.

21 The range of fees for an arbitration will be around US$1,000–2,000 for a single arbitrator panel and a little more for a larger panel. See *InterNic FAQs on the Uniform Domain Name Dispute Resolution Policy (UDRP)*, *id.*

22 Rules for Uniform Domain Name Dispute Resolution Policy, available at www.icann.org/udrp/udrp-rules-24oct99.htm, last accessed March 14, 2007: rule 3(b) (complaint to be submitted in hard copy and electronic format); rule 5(b) (response to be submitted in hard copy and electronic format); rule 13 (no in-person hearings); rule 16(b) (Panel decisions to be posted on panel website).

23 UDRP, para. 4(i) ('The remedies available to a complainant pursuant to any proceeding before an Administrative Panel shall be limited to requiring the cancellation of your domain name or the transfer of your domain name registration to the complainant.').

24 *Id.* para 4(b).

25 *Id.* para 4(c).

ticularly if the political name or phrase is not trademarked or trademarkable.[26] While some additional anti-cybersquatting laws deal specifically with the protection of individuals names against bad faith cybersquatting even in the absence of a trademark interest in the name,[27] they can be limited in application. The obvious example of an anti-cybersquatting law that protects non-trademarked personal names is 15 U.S.C. § 8131(1)(A).

> Any person who registers a domain name that consists of the name of another living person, or a name substantially and confusingly similar thereto, without that person's consent, with the specific intent to profit from such name by selling the domain name for financial gain to that person or any third party, shall be liable in a civil action by such person.

---

[26] This may be the case at both common law and under trademark legislation, despite the recognition of some common law marks in personal names. In terms of federal trademark registration, personal names are not often not registrable as trademarks: 15 U.S.C. § 1052(c). See also GILSON, *supra* note 2, para. 2.03[d], and see *supra* note 11. Personal names may receive some common law protection as common law marks: *Julia Fiona Roberts v Russell Boyd*, WIPO Arbitration and Mediation Center, Case No. D2000–0210 (May 29, 2000) available at www.wipo.int/amc/en/domains/decisions/html/2000/d2000-0210.html, last accessed March 14, 2007 (UDRP arbitrators accepting that the movie actress Julia Roberts does have common law trademark rights in her personal name for the purposes of a UDRP proceeding). However, this may well be limited more to celebrity names that function similarly to trademarks because of their commercial value, as opposed to politicians' names that may well be used more in the political arena than the commercial arena: *Friends of Kathleen Kennedy Townsend*, WIPO Case No. D2002–0451, available at www.wipo.int/amc/en/domains/decisions/html/2002/d2002-0451.html (UDRP panel suggesting that the politician Kathleen Kennedy Townsend would not have a common law trademark in her personal name used for purely political purposes). Additionally, not all famous celebrities are regarded as unquestionably holding common law trademark rights in their personal names: *Bruce Springsteen*, WIPO Case No. D2000–1532, available at www.wipo.int/amc/en/domains/decisions/html/2000/d2000-1532.html (UDRP panel failed to unanimously agree that the singer Bruce Springsteen did have a common law trademark right in his name for UDRP arbitration purposes, but decided the matter on other grounds). That may be one reason for the growing popularity of the right of publicity tort to protect personal names against unauthorized commercial uses. For a discussion of modern applications of that right and a critique of tort theory underlying the right, see Sarah Konsky, *Publicity Dilution: A Proposal for Protecting Publicity Rights*, 21 SANTA CLARA COMPUTER AND HIGH TECH L.J. 347 (2005); Mark McKenna, *The Right of Publicity and Autonomous Self-Definition*, 67 U. PITT. L. REV. 225 (2005); Stacey Dogan and Mark Lemley, *What the Right of Publicity Can Learn from Trademark Law*, 58 STANFORD L. REV. 1161 (2006).

[27] 15 U.S.C. § 8131 (this section protects personal names against cybersquatting and is not limited to trademark, or trademarkable, interests in personal names).

This provision would cover some political cybersquatting, but not all cases. In the leadup to the 2004 presidential election, for example, the domain name 'kerryedwards.com' was registered to a Mr Kerry Edwards who tried to auction it off to the highest bidder after the democratic Presidential nominee, Senator John Kerry, named then-Senator John Edwards as his running mate.[28] Regardless of whether one regards this as the kind of conduct that should be proscribed by trademark law, the domain name was effectively a wasted resource during that presidential campaign. The registrant did not use it for any particular expressive purpose. It nevertheless remained unavailable to any of the political parties, as no one was prepared to pay a fee that would satisfy the registrant.

Section 8131(1)(A), or its predecessor § 1129(1), may not have been much help if the democratic party had been minded to litigate for control of the name. The registrant, Kerry Edwards, may have been in a position to raise several viable defenses to such a challenge. He might have argued that the domain name did not correspond with the name of another living person on the basis that Kerry Edwards was not the name of either Senator Kerry or Senator Edwards, but was rather an amalgam of both of their names. He might also have argued that, even if the name in question did consist of the name of another living person, it also consisted of his own personal name, Kerry Edwards, and that his own right to a domain name corresponding with his personal name must equally be protected.

With respect to the first argument, the defense might fail on the basis that § 8131 protects complainants against bad faith registrations of domain names that are 'substantially and confusingly similar' to their own personal names. Arguably, the amalgam of the names Kerry and Edwards in 'kerryedwards.com' would be considered a registration of a name 'substantially and confusingly similar' to the senators' respective personal names. The second potential defense may be more problematic. However, a court may have found that the use of the name for a presidential campaign would have been less socially and economically wasteful than the use of the name by a person trying to make a profit from selling the name.

There were two additional unusual factors about the 'kerryedwards.com' scenario that are not likely to be repeated in many future cases. Mr Kerry Edwards happened fortuitously to have registered the domain name several years before the presidential campaign.[29] Thus, in this particular

---

[28] Lipton, *Who Owns 'Hillary.com'?*, *supra* note 3, at 55–6.
[29] *Id.* at 64–5.

case, had the senators brought an action against the registrant, they may well have failed on the basis that he had not actually *registered* the domain name with the intent to profit from its sale as required by then-§ 1129(1).[30] The other factor, which is of course related to this first factor, is that Mr Kerry Edwards happened to have a personal name that corresponded with the names on the presidential ticket. This is unlikely to happen in many future cases. However, it is possible that a private individual might have a personal name corresponding with an individual politician's name in a future case and this could raise many of the difficulties that could have arisen had 'kerryedwards.com' been litigated.

Other than the relatively unusual situations where a private individual's name corresponds with a politician's name, there are a few other practical problems with § 8131(1) in the political context. One is that it does not have global reach, although at least a federal statute has advantages over often-piecemeal state laws.[31] The other problem with § 8131 is arguably general lack of familiarity with its provisions, partly perhaps because the provisions have been overshadowed in practice by the UDRP. Since the introduction of both the ACPA and the UDRP in 1999, many more complaints have been brought under the UDRP than the ACPA, even with respect to names of private individuals.[32]

---

[30] 15 U.S.C. § 1129(1)(A), now see § 8131(1)(A), ('Any person who *registers* a domain name that consists of the name of another living person, or a name substantially and confusingly similar thereto, without that person's consent, *with the specific intent to profit* from such name by selling the domain name for financial gain to that person or any third party, shall be liable in a civil action by such person.') (emphasis added). 15 U.S.C. § 1125(d) would not have applied here because the 'Kerry Edwards' name was not trademarked, nor was it likely trademarkable in the electoral context. Generally, personal names are not registrable as trademarks: 15 U.S.C. § 1052(c). See also Gilson, *supra* note 2, para. 2.03[d].

[31] See discussion of some relevant Californian state laws at 1.6.1, 1.6.2, *supra*.

[32] For example, *Julia Fiona Roberts*, WIPO Case No. D2000–0210, available at www.wipo.int/amc/en/domains/decisions/html/2000/d2000-0210.html, last accessed March 14, 2007 (involving the Julia Roberts name); *Bruce Springsteen*, WIPO Case No. D2000–1532, available at www.wipo.int/amc/en/domains/decisions/html/2000/d2000-1532.html, last accessed March 14, 2007 (involving Bruce Springsteen's name); *Rita Rudner v Internetco Corp.*, WIPO Arbitration and Mediation Center, Case No. D2000–0581 (August 3, 2000), available at www.wipo.int/amc/en/domains/decisions/html/2000/d2000-0581.html, last accessed March 14, 2007 (involving Rita Rudner's personal name); *Helen Folsade Adu, known as Sade v Quantum Computer Services Inc.*, WIPO Arbitration and Mediation Center, Case No. D2000–0794 (September 26, 2000), available at www.wipo.int/amc/en/domains/decisions/html/2000/d2000-0794.html, last accessed March 14, 2007 (involving Sade's stage name); *Friends of Kathleen Kennedy Townsend*, WIPO Case No. D2002–0451, available at www.wipo.int/amc/en/domains/decisions/html/2002/

Much of this discussion so far could be criticized for being premised on the assumption that a given politician or political party should have de facto rights in a domain name corresponding with her personal name or party affiliation. It could be argued that politicians and political parties should be more savvy about registering intuitive domain names and that they deserve what they get if they fail to be proactive in this respect. In fact, in the leadup to the 2008 presidential election, most presidential candidates had registered their names as domain names well before they announced their bids for the presidency.[33] In fact, many people considering a presidential bid will already have secured a relevant domain name for a prior political career.[34] Thus, political cybersquatting is less likely to be a problem in the future, at least in high-profile presidential elections, than it has been in the past.

Nevertheless, there are still areas where political cybersquatting may continue to be problematic. In smaller elections involving local politicians who are less experienced and have less access to sophisticated campaign machinery, candidates may be slower to secure their names as domain names. They may end up fighting with cybersquatters or others who have beat them to registration.[35] Also, many presidential-vice presidential nominee combinations will not be so obvious for registration prior to the announcement of a vice presidential nominee. For example, in the leadup to the announcements of the vice-presidential nominees for both the Republicans and the Democrats in the 2008 presidential election, much political cybersquatting was apparent on various name combinations in

---

d2002-0451.html, last accessed March 14, 2007 (involving Kathleen Kennedy Townsend's name); *Madonna Ciccone v Parisi*, WIPO Arbitration and Mediation Center, Case No. D2000–0847 (October 12, 2000), available at www.wipo.int/amc/en/domains/decisions/html/2000/d2000-0847.html, last accessed March 16, 2010 (involving the singer Madonna's stage name); *Hillary Rodham Clinton*, National Arbitration Forum, Claim No. FA0502000414641, available at www.arb-forum.com/domains/decisions/414641.htm, last accessed March 14, 2007 (involving the domain name 'hillaryclinton.com'). A comparison of these disputes suggests that it is far from clear that UDRP arbitrators will always find the existence of a trademark corresponding with a famous personal name.

33 See discussion in Lipton, *Domain Names to Video Games*, *supra* note 4.

34 For example, Secretary of State Hillary Clinton had secured the domain name 'hillaryclinton.com' when she was the junior senator for New York, well before her failed presidential bid in the 2008 presidential election. See *Hillary Rodham Clinton*, National Arbitration Forum, Claim No. FA0502000414641, available at www.arb-forum.com/domains/decisions/414641.htm.

35 Lipton, *Celebrity in Cyberspace*, *supra* note 6, at 1466–7 (examples of cyberfraud conduct in state political races).

the domain space.[36] One high profile example was that the domain name 'obamaclinton.com' was registered to a business selling Obama-Clinton T-shirts at a time when there was still some speculation that then-Senator Obama would choose then-Senator Clinton as his running mate.[37]

It is clearly desirable in a democracy that no one politician or political party is able to dominate all possible permutations of his or her name or party's name in the domain space. There must be room for competing discussion about a politician and her policies online. Search engines will naturally play a role here. In the 2008 presidential election, for example, the democratic ticket did not register all possible permutations of then-Senator Obama's and Biden's names in the domain space. In fact, the domain name 'josephbiden.com', as opposed to 'joebiden.com', was registered to Republican supporters as a gripe site against the democratic nominees.[38] However, it seems reasonable that regulations should protect perhaps one or two intuitive spaces for a politician or political party, at least in the leadup to an election when political discourse is particularly important in communicating with voters. Such protection should likely extend to cybersquatting and cyberfraud, but it should not chill legitimate political discourse. Drawing these lines will not always be easy in practice, and may vary from culture to culture. This discussion is intended to at least stimulate some debate as to where lines might be drawn, and to identify some of the existing gaps in the regulatory structure.

5.2.2.2 Politicians' names and the Uniform Domain name Dispute Resolution Policy

For those concerned about cybersquatting, including cybersquatting on personal names, the UDRP offers clear time, cost and jurisdictional advantages.[39] Its major limitation for any names, including politicians' names, is that it does not specifically protect such names unless the name in question is operating as a trademark.[40] Thus, to the extent that a personal name is trademarked, or that a political party's or action group's name is trademarked, and the registrant otherwise meets the bad faith criteria of the UDRP without a legitimate use defense, the UDRP will apply. Many individuals have successfully established trademarks in their

---

36 Lipton, *Domain Names to Video Games*, *supra* note 4, at 706 (description of uses of obamaclinton.com domain name in the leadup to the 2008 presidential election).

37 *Id.*

38 *Id.* at 702–3.

39 Lipton, *Celebrity in Cyberspace*, *supra* note 6, at 1448–9.

40 See discussion at 4.3.4, *supra*.

personal names under the UDRP, and have satisfied the other factors of a UDRP claim. Even some politicians have established trademarks in their names for UDRP purposes.[41] However, as a general proposition, politicians' names do not easily support trademark interests. That is not to say that there is anything particularly *wrong* with the UDRP. Its purpose was to protect trademarks online. Its application to politics is problematic precisely because it was not drafted with political domain names in mind. The question is whether something more is needed to protect political domain names and, if so, what form such regulations should take.

If another avenue was available for politicians seeking to protect their names in the domain space, it would lessen pressure on UDRP arbitrators to attempt to fit a square peg into a round hole when approaching domain name disputes involving politics and politicians. In the context of a UDRP arbitration involving several domain names corresponding to former President William J. Clinton's personal name, the UDRP arbitrator expressed some discomfort with the way in which the UDRP has been applied to politics by too easily recognizing trademarks in politicians' names.[42] This case, in fact, did not involve political cybersquatting in the strict sense because the registrant was prepared to return the name without making a profit[43] and was not otherwise offering the name for sale.[44] The website was actually being used for expressive purposes as it resolved to the Republican National Convention website.[45] Nevertheless, the arbitrator's approach to the case is instructive because it emphasizes the fact that the UDRP is not a great fit for disputes involving names of politicians.

---

41 *Hillary Rodham Clinton*, National Arbitration Forum, Claim No. FA0502000414641, available at www.arb-forum.com/domains/decisions/414641.htm (then-Senator Clinton was regarded as having an unregistered trademark right in her personal name in connection with both her political activities and her career as an author of a number of books sold in commerce); see *William J. Clinton and The William J. Clinton Presidential Foundation v Web of Deception*, National Arbitration Forum, Claim No.: FA0904001256123 (June 1, 2009), available at http://domains.adrforum.com/domains/decisions/1256123.htm, last accessed July 10, 2009 (arbitrator 'reluctantly' concluded that former President Clinton had a trademark in his personal name, but the former president was unsuccessful in obtaining a transfer order for relevant domain names because he was unable to establish 'bad faith' registration and use on the part of the registrant). See also discussion at 4.1, *supra*.

42 *William J. Clinton*, National Arbitration Forum, Claim No. FA0904001256123 available at http://domains.adrforum.com/domains/decisions/1256123.htm.

43 *Id.*

44 *Id.*

45 *Id.*

5.2.2.3 Application of cyberfraud legislation to political cybersquatting

Politicians concerned about political cybersquatting might, in appropriate cases, avail themselves of some relevant state legislation. For example, California's Political Cyberfraud Abatement Act (PCAA),[46] prohibits engaging in acts of 'political cyberfraud'. 'Political cyberfraud' is defined to include conduct concerning a political website 'that is committed with the intent to deny a person access to a political Web site, deny a person the opportunity to register a domain name for a political Web site, or cause a person reasonably to believe that a political Web site has been posted by a person other than the person who posted the Web site'.[47] Some aspects of this may cover political cybersquatting, even though the legislation is expressly directed at *cyberfraud*.[48]

The third statutory prohibition on cyberfraud would likely be of little relevance to political cybersquatting: that is, causing a person reasonably to believe that a political website has been posted by a person other than the person who posted the website. The aim of cybersquatting is to sell the name for a profit, rather than to make misleading use of the site. It is possible that a registrant could use a domain name for both purposes simultaneously: that is, disseminating misleading information about a politician while at the same time offering to sell the domain name. However, the 'misleading information' part of the conduct is categorized here as 'political cyberfraud', rather than 'political cybersquatting'. It is important to appreciate the distinction between the two classes of conduct, even though they may occur simultaneously in some cases. This is because, at least individually, they raise different policy imperatives in terms of regulation.

It is possible that the first two prohibitions in the PCAA would cover political *cybersquatting*. Cybersquatting may fall within the class of conduct described as conduct that is intended to deny a person access to a political website or to deny a person the opportunity to register a domain name for a political website. Although cybersquatting generally refers to a bad faith profit motive, it also involves use of a domain name to which

---

46 Cal. Elections Code, §§ 18320–18323.

47 *Id.* § 18320(c)(1).

48 'Political cyberfraud' is defined in California Elections Code, § 18320(c)(1) rather broadly as 'a knowing and willful act concerning a political Web site that is committed with the intent to deny a person access to a political Web site, deny a person the opportunity to register a domain name for a political Web site, or cause a person reasonably to believe that a political Web site has been posted by a person other than the person who posted the Web site, and would cause a reasonable person, after reading the Web site, to believe the site actually represents the views of the proponent or opponent of a ballot measure'.

another person may have a more obvious claim. Subsection 18320(c)(1) of the PCAA further defines political cyberfraud as including, but not being limited to:

> (A) Intentionally diverting or redirecting access to a political Web site to another person's Web site by the use of a similar domain name . . ..[49]
> (C) Registering a domain name that is similar to another domain name for a political Web site.[50]
> (D) Intentionally preventing the use of a domain name for a political Web site by registering and holding the domain name or by reselling it to another with the intent of preventing its use, or both.[51]

Subparagraph (D) seems the most obvious fit for conduct traditionally regarded as cybersquatting. It contemplates registering the political domain name most obviously associated with someone else and potentially reselling it. Of course, the focus in the PCAA is on preventing the use of the name by the 'rightful' owner as opposed to selling the name for a bad faith profit, the latter being the typical motivation underlying cybersquatting.

A person who engages in political cybersquatting might not necessarily be regarded as having 'intentionally diverted or redirected access to a political website to another website by the use of a similar domain name' as contemplated in subparagraph (A). In situations where a politician has not registered a domain name corresponding with her name, for example, it would be difficult to argue that access was being 'diverted' or 'redirected' from her website. Similar comments may be made about subparagraph (C). 'Registering a domain name that is similar to another domain name for a political website' will not likely include situations where the politician in question has not yet registered a domain name corresponding with her personal name.

However, where the politician in question already does have a web presence, this subprovision may be more useful than subsection (A) because it does not require the complainant to establish an intent to divert or redirect access to the website. It only requires registration of a name that is similar to an existing political domain name. Subparagraph (D) likewise does not appear to require the politician in question to have already registered any domain name. It would cover a situation where a politician was prevented from registering a name she wanted as a domain name by a registrant who

---

49 *Id.*, § 18320(c)(1)(A).
50 *Id.*, § 18320(c)(1)(C).
51 *Id.*, § 18320(c)(1)(D).

either holds on to the name and does not resell it, or by a registrant who sells the name with the intent to prevent its use by the politician.

All of these subparagraphs may have limited application in the political cybersquatting context. For one thing, the provision does not cover situations where the registrant of the domain name is prepared to sell the domain name to the politician for a profit. It is only expressed to cover situations where the registrant is attempting to prevent a politician from using the name. Thus, it would cover the situation where the registrant of a 'politician.com' name either wasted an important political resource by holding it and not using it, or where the registrant attempted to sell it to someone else who might prevent its use by the relevant politician or political party. The statute does not expressly contemplate a situation where the registrant specifically attempts to sell the name to the politician or political party for a profit.

As compared with the UDRP, the PCAA also raises significant jurisdictional limitations. Currently, California is the only state with such legislation. It is not clear whether this legislation would apply in situations where neither the politician nor the domain name registrant is located in California. It is possible that the ability of web users to access the website in California would be a sufficient connection with California for the Californian law to apply.[52] Additionally, it is possible that if the domain name was registered in California, this would be sufficient grounds for Californian law to apply.[53] However, if this was the case, most domain name cybersquatters would simply select a domain name registrar not situated in California.[54]

Maybe if political cybersquatting is ultimately regarded as worthy of

---

[52] Although some case law suggests that the mere ability to access a website within a jurisdiction, without more, is insufficient basis at least for the assertion of personal jurisdiction against a defendant website operator. See, for example, *Bensusan Restaurant Corp. v King*, 937 F. Supp. 295 (S.D.N.Y. 1996), *aff'd* 126 F.3d 25 (2d Cir. 1997) (the defendants who operated a jazz club in Missouri could not be subject to personal jurisdiction in New York by the owners of a jazz club with the same name in New York City in the absence of conduct greater than advertising their Missouri club on their website that was accessible in New York City, although not specifically directed to New York City residents).

[53] The ACPA, for example, is a domain name law that includes *in rem* jurisdiction provisions in the case of domain names registered in a particular jurisdiction where the plaintiff is not otherwise able effectively to assert personal jurisdiction over the defendant domain name registrant: 15 U.S.C. § 1125(d)(2)(A).

[54] For example, a list of ICANN-accredited domain name registries from all over the world is available at www.icann.org/registrars/accredited-list.html, last accessed March 14, 2007.

federal or global regulation, ideas might be drawn from the PCAA and incorporated into federal legislation or a global dispute resolution procedure. Domain name registrants might be asked to agree on registration that they would submit to an arbitration procedure not unlike the UDRP if a politician, or political party,[55] complained about registration of the relevant name, particularly in the context of an election. Such regulations should also cover situations where the registrant attempts to sell the domain name to either the politician or a third party. This approach would be quicker, cheaper and more efficient than a legislative approach.

Any approach taken along these lines risks chilling political speech. Regulations developed with respect to political domain names should not quell important competing viewpoints. Rather, they should be aimed at ensuring that more viewpoints are made available to Internet users in the most intuitively accessible manner possible. In fact, some may suggest that even California's PCAA raises First Amendment concerns. This has yet to be judicially tested. However, implementing similar policy initiatives in private arbitration processes like the UDRP might be less open to constitutional challenge because ICANN and private parties will not be subject to First Amendment guarantees in the same way as federal and state legislatures within the United States.

5.2.2.4 Political cybersquatting, defamation law and the right of publicity

(a) Defamation Another potential avenue of legal recourse for political cybersquatting arises from the torts that protect individual reputations from harmful conduct. These include defamation law, the right of publicity,[56] and some *sui generis* legislation such as California's Business

---

55 Political parties may, in fact, be in a better position than politicians under the UDRP as currently drafted. See *Friends of Kathleen Kennedy Townsend*, WIPO Case No. D2002–0451, para. 6 available at www.wipo.int/amc/en/domains/decisions/html/2002/d2002-0451.html ('Here, the claim for the domain names is brought by the individual politician, and not by the political action committee actively engaged in the raising of funds and promotion of complainant's possible campaign. Had the claim been brought in the name of the Friends of Kathleen Kennedy Townsend, the result might well have been different. But it was not.').

56 Michael Madow, *Personality as Property: The Uneasy Case for Publicity Rights* in Peter Yu (ed.), Intellectual Property and Information Wealth: Issues and Practices in the Digital Age, vol. 3, Trademark and Unfair Competition 345(2007) (the right to publicity 'gives a celebrity a legal entitlement to the commercial value of her identity, and thereby enables her to determine the extent, manner, and timing of its commercial exploitation.').

and Professions Code.[57] The most obvious tort that deals with a person's reputation is defamation. Defamation generally refers to false statements which damage an individual's reputation.[58] Although defamation may be relevant to *political cyberfraud*,[59] it likely has little to no application to political *cybersquatting*. This is because cybersquatting does not deal with statements that might damage an individual politician's reputation. Rather, it removes from a politician's reach a domain name that she might desire for her own use. Thus, defamation need not be discussed further with respect to political cybersquatting.

(b) Right of publicity The right of publicity, on the other hand, may apply to some political cybersquatting. The right of publicity is the right of an individual to control the commercial use of her name, likeness, signature or other personal characteristics.[60] It has been likened to a trademark right in the sense that it protects the goodwill inherent in a person's commercial persona.[61] The right of publicity operates much like a trademark in the sense that it reserves to an individual celebrity the exclusive right to the commercial exploitation of her name, likeness, signature or product endorsement.[62] To determine whether the right of publicity may apply to political cybersquatting, two fundamental questions must be answered. The first is whether the registration of a domain name corresponding with a politician's name for the purposes of commercial profit amounts to a commercial exploitation of the name for purposes of the tort. The second is whether politicians are protected by the right of publicity. Neither question has been definitively answered.

It is not clear whether the sale or attempted sale of a domain name that corresponds with a politician's name is the kind of conduct generally contemplated within the right of publicity. Usually, actions brought under this tort are concerned with the sale of specific items (photographs, T-shirts, magazines, toys, and the like) that contain, or are based on, an unauthorized likeness of a famous celebrity.[63] Could the sale of an un-

---

57 See discussion at 1.6.1, *supra*.

58 JANET L. SILVERBERG, BUSINESS TORTS 1–6, para. 6.01; Arlen Langvardt, *Section 43(a), Commercial Falsehood, and the First Amendment: A Proposed Framework*, 78 MINN. L. REV. 309, 334 (1993) ('the common law defines defamation as the publication of a false and defamatory statement about the plaintiff. Defamatory statements, by definition, tend to harm the plaintiff's reputation.').

59 See 5.2.1, *supra*.

60 GILSON, *supra* note 2, para. 2B.01.

61 *Id.*

62 *Id.*

63 *Winterland Concessions Co. v Creative Screen Design Ltd*, 210 U.S.P.Q. 6 (N.D. Ill 1980) (dealing with rock star names on T-shirts); *Allen v Men's World*

authorized photograph, T-shirt or coffee mug bearing the name or likeness of, say, Britney Spears, really be likened to the sale of a blank webpage with the domain name 'britneyspears.com'? In the case of the physical goods, it would seem more plausible that consumers would be confused as to whether or not the singer, Britney Spears, had authorized the product line, than in the case of a blank webpage utilizing a domain name that corresponds with her name. This is because the goods in question might constitute a line of products that collectors may want to purchase, whereas a blank webpage (or a webpage that is obviously for sale to the highest bidder) is unlikely to attract consumers in this way.

Even if this analysis is incorrect, there is still the question as to when the right of publicity will protect politicians, as opposed to celebrities. The fame of celebrities is generally based on commercial, rather than political, aspects of their personas.[64] The commercially-oriented right of publicity seems a much more natural fit for celebrities than for politicians. This issue was discussed by commentators in the context of a case that eventually settled out of court involving Governor Arnold Schwarzenegger suing the manufacturer of bobblehead dolls bearing his name and likeness.[65] Although the case was settled, it raised many legal and policy issues about the application of the right of publicity to politicians.

Governor Schwarzenegger's persona raises particularly thorny issues because he has, over the course of his career, gained notoriety through

---

Outlet Inc., 679 F. Supp. 360, U.S.P.Q.2d 1850 (use of Woody Allen lookalike for clothing store advertisements); *Hoffman v Capital Cities/ABC Inc.,* 255 F.3d 1180, 59 U.S.P.Q.2d 1363 (9th Cir. 2001) (use of digitally manipulated image of Dustin Hoffman in magazine).

64 See, for example, *Martin Luther King, Jr Center for Social Change, Inc. v American Heritage Products, Inc.,* 508 F.Supp. 854 (N.D. Ga. 1981), *rev'd per curiam*, 694 F.2d. 674 (11th Cir. 1983) (holding that the right of publicity extends to 'public figures who are not public officials' in the sense of holding public office); *New York Magazine v The Metropolitan Transit Authority*, 987 F.Supp. 254 (1997) (holding that then-Mayor Rudolph Guiliani could not succeed in a right of publicity with respect to advertisements for the *New York Times* that depicted him in a less than complimentary light, and that an attempt to prevent display of the advertisements on public buses in New York City was an infringement of the *New York Times*' First Amendment rights); *New York Magazine v The Metropolitan Transit Authority*, 987 F.Supp. 254, 269 (1997) ('Though the ad as a whole is commercial speech, the advertisement undeniably includes an element of political commentary. It would be anomalous indeed to permit a reprint of a caricature of Guiliani that had appeared in the magazine, but prohibit the Ad at issue which includes speech of public interest.').

65 *See* discussion in Tyler Ochoa, *The Schwarzenegger Bobblehead Case: Introduction and Statement of Facts*, 45 SANTA CLARA L. REV. 547 (2005).

sports, film, and political careers. Had the matter been judicially decided, the court may have had to decide specifically whether the bobblehead dolls were commenting on the Governor's political persona – in which case they may have been protected by the First Amendment – or were purely usurping the Governor's commercial interests in his persona and likeness, in which case he may have claimed greater protection under the right of publicity.[66] In the course of debates over the dolls, commentators noted how few right of publicity actions had been brought by sitting politicians in the past.[67] Various suggestions were raised as to why this might be the case. They included (a) politicians are often not

[66] Charles Harder and Henry Self III, *Schwarzenegger vs Bobbleheads: The Case for Schwarzenneger*, 45 SANTA CLARA L. REV. 547, 557 (2005) (noting that there is a public affairs exception to the right of publicity in California, but that it would not likely apply to the Schwarzenegger bobblehead dolls because they contained no discernable political slogans or messages, but were merely a depiction or imitation of Schwarzenegger in the form of a doll); William Gallagher, *Strategic Intellectual Property Litigation, the Right of Publicity, and the Attenuation of Free Speech: Lessons from the Schwarzenegger Bobblehead Doll War (and Peace)*, 45 SANTA CLARA L. REV. 581, 597–8 (2005) ('[T]he Schwarzenegger likeness was not being used to sell other products but was the product itself, albeit in a creative expression of that image. The Schwarzenegger image was thus part of the "raw materials" or the medium that the bobblehead doll's creators used to convey the multivocal messages the doll communicated. This message invariably comments, at least in part, on the Schwarzenegger political image and persona even if it also simultaneously comments on the Schwarzenegger Hollywood movie star persona. The governor himself, after all, has certainly made effective use of his Hollywood tough-guy, "Terminator" image in political life. Schwarzenegger, now the governor, has become the "Governator", a play on words that evokes the dual personas of the current Schwarzenegger image. This image is also used extensively in political cartoons commenting on Schwarzenegger's new status as a politician. It would be disturbing for a court to hold that the right of publicity should trump the . . . defendants' right to sell a doll that similarly comments on the Schwarzenegger image. Such a decision would also be incongruous because it would permit Schwarzenegger to monopolize his image as the "Governator" for both political and private profit.').

[67] Gallagher, *supra* note 66, at 597–8 ('[I]t was virtually unprecedented for a sitting politician to sue in order to control the use of his or her image in similar circumstances [to the Schwarzenegger litigation]. The . . . defendants sold an entire series of bobbleheads depicting both living and deceased politicians; yet they had never previously been subject to legal threats of proceedings to prevent the sales of these dolls. In fact, as many news reports gleefully explained the [defendants] had previously sent copies of dolls to several politicians who apparently appreciated (or, perhaps, acquiesced to) having their likeness made into a bobblehead doll.'); Harder and Self, *supra* note 66, at 567 ('Few courts have had an opportunity to rule on an unauthorized commercial use of a political figure's name or likeness. Politicians typically do not pursue such claims').

generally concerned with commercial use of their image 'because it is not their typical business';[68] (b) politicians do not wish to invest resources into such claims;[69] (c) politicians want to avoid negative publicity that may arise from such claims[70] partly because they do not want to appear 'humorless or soft-skinned';[71] and (d) politicians are aware that the sale of products bearing their name or likeness might be protected by the First Amendment.[72]

Arguments in favor of extending the right of publicity to politicians include the fact that in cases of pure commercial use of a politician's name or likeness, there seem to be no good policy reasons for differentiating between politicians and other well-known figures, like sports and entertainment stars.[73] Assuming that First Amendment concerns can effectively be dealt with on a case-by-case basis,[74] there seems to be no good policy reason why politicians who have spent time and effort developing their images should not be protected from unauthorized commercial, as opposed to political, exploitations of those images.[75] This would appear to

---

[68] Harder and Self, *supra* note 66, at 567–8.

[69] *Id.* 568.

[70] *Id.*

[71] Gallagher, *supra* note 66, at 583.

[72] *Id.*

[73] Harder and Self, *supra* note 66, at 565 ('The notion that political figures have no right to control the commercial use of their names and images contradicts both the letter and purpose of right of publicity laws. If the law did not apply to political figures, companies could freely exploit politicians' names and images in advertising for their products, or on the products themselves, with impunity. George W. Bush toothbrushes and Dick Cheney laundry detergent, for example, could pervade our supermarkets and households.').

[74] Harder and Self, *supra* note 66, at 557, Gallagher, *supra* note 66, at 59–8. Even prior to the Schwarzenegger bobblehead doll controversy, suggestions had been made that it would not be an impossible task to differentiate free speech concerns from purely commercial concerns in many right of publicity cases involving political figures: Eileen Rielly, *The Right of Publicity for Political Figures: Martin Luther King, Jr., Center for Social Change, Inc. v American Heritage Products*, 46 U. PITT. L. REV. 1161, 1174 (1985) ('Where no legitimate First Amendment purpose is served by the product, the manufacturer or advertiser should be required to pay for the privilege of using the political figure's name or face to sell it. As an example, even though commemorative items may deserve protection in some instances, it is hard to image [*sic*] that such items as "plastic toy pencil sharpeners, soap products, target games, candy dispensers and beverage stirring rods" are a form of expression. An advertiser should not be able to hide behind the First Amendment simply because he has chosen to exploit a political figure.').

[75] Rielly, *supra* note 74, at 1170 ('Political figures have usually invested much time, money, and effort in building up a public image, just as entertainers have. Few people are simply thrust into the political arena. By their own labors, in a very

be the case whatever the theoretical basis for the right of publicity, which is still a matter of some debate even in traditional celebrity focused cases.[76] Additionally, in response to the concern that allowing political right of publicity actions would be opening the floodgates to frivolous litigation, many politicians have been, and will continue to be, deterred from action because of concerns about public perception and about wasting valuable campaign resources.

In the electoral context, political cybersquatting may chill political speech. This is an undesirable and wasteful outcome. It is difficult to imagine that political cybersquatting could result in *more* or *more useful* political discourse if the conduct in question is purely holding a domain name for ransom in the hope of profiting from its sale. This conduct effectively makes political discourse more expensive online, in a medium where we might hope that political speech would be less expensive and more readily available to a more global audience. Political cybersquatting might thus chill protected First Amendment speech in the absence of some accessible remedy. It may be that the right of publicity is a plausible possibility. If indeed there is no reason not to extend the right to politicians, at least in contexts where the defendant's use of a politician's name or likeness is for purely commercial purposes, then there should be no objection to developing the right of publicity in this context.

Of course, right of publicity actions have significant limitations, including the disadvantages of reliance on costly and time-consuming litigation based on an action that is not even federally harmonized within the United States, and is not available at all outside the United States. There may also be some question as to whether the action would provide appropriate remedies for political cybersquatting. Generally, in a traditional right of publicity case, a plaintiff will want an injunction to prevent the sale of the products in question as well as perhaps an account of profits or some other kind of monetary damages. In the political cybersquatting case, the politician in question will more than likely desire transfer of the name, rather than an injunction or monetary compensation. Thus, the remedies for right of publicity actions are not necessarily a good fit for cybersquatting. UDRP remedies, like cancellation or transfer of the domain name, would be much more appropriate. Perhaps the simplest and most effective

---

competitive field, political figures have created publicity value in their names and faces.').

[76] For a summary of the various theoretical arguments posited to support the right of publicity, see Madow, *supra* note 56, at 535–61 (describing moral, economic and consumer protection-focused theories underlying the right of publicity); McKenna, *supra* note 26; Dogan and Lemley, *supra* note 26.

solution for political cybersquatting would be to include political names as protected under the UDRP.

(c) California's Business and Professions Code California's Business and Professions Code[77] was revised early in the new millennium to deal with certain kinds of cybersquatting activities. Section 17525(a) of the Code now provides that:

> It is unlawful for a person, with a bad faith intent to register, traffic in, or use a domain name, that is identical or confusingly similar to the personal name of another living person or deceased personality, without regard to the goods or services of the parties.

California's Code extends protection to a deceased personality as well as to a living person. The Code's bad faith factors are relatively broad In particular, § 17526(j) of the Code includes as a bad faith factor: 'The intent of a person . . . to mislead, deceive, or defraud voters'.

At first glance, the Code's provisions seem to apply to political cybersquatting in the sense that the registrant in question has registered a domain name that corresponds with the name of another person without regard to the goods or services of the parties. The real question is whether the registrant had an intent to 'mislead deceive or defraud voters'. A political cybersquatter who is not using the domain name to promulgate any message about the relevant politician, other than that the domain name is available for sale, probably has not engaged in such conduct. Unlike a person engaging in political cyberfraud, a pure political cybersquatter is trying to profit from registration of the name without disseminating any message to voters.

It is possible that a political cybersquatter might infringe § 17525(a) regardless of a failure to satisfy the bad faith test in § 17526(j). There are other bad faith factors that may apply to political cybersquatting. The bad faith factors set out in § 17526 are not intended to be an exhaustive list.[78] Additionally, some of the express bad faith factors in § 17526 may apply to political cybersquatting. For example:

> (e) The intent of a person . . . to divert consumers from the person's . . . online location to a site accessible under the domain name that could harm the

---

[77] See discussion at1.6.1, *supra*.

[78] The wording of § 17526 itself makes this clear by stating that: 'In determining whether there is a bad faith intent pursuant to Section 17525, a court may consider factors, including, but not limited to, the following . . .'.

goodwill represented by the person's . . . name either for commercial gain or with the intent to tarnish or disparage the person's . . . name by creating a likelihood of confusion as to the source, sponsorship, affiliation, or endorsement of the site.

(f) The offer by a person . . . to transfer, sell, or otherwise assign the domain name to the rightful owner or any third party for substantial consideration without having used, or having an intent to use, the domain name in the bona fide offering of any goods or services. . .

(h) The registration or acquisition by the person . . . of multiple domain names that are identical or confusingly similar to names of other living persons or deceased personalities.

(i) Whether the person . . . sought or obtained consent from the rightful owner to register, traffic in, or use the domain name.

Subsections (e) and (f) are borrowed relatively directly from the policies and principles underlying both the ACPA and the UDRP. While they appear to apply to political cybersquatting, they both rely on trademark concepts: likelihood of confusion[79] in subsection (e), and bona fide offering of goods or services[80] in subsection (f). Courts interpreting these provisions in the political cybersquatting context might take the view that these bad faith factors are related to situations more akin to traditional trademark infringement or trademark focused cybersquatting than to political cybersquatting.

Subsection (h) is borrowed directly from the ACPA,[81] which in turn was drafted in response to cases where cybersquatters registered multiple domain names corresponding with well-known trademarks.[82] It may or may not apply to political cybersquatting, depending on the circumstances. In both the commercial and political contexts, it is possible for an alleged

---

[79] 15 U.S.C. §§ 1114(1)(a) (requiring consumer confusion for registered trademark infringement action), 1125(a)(1)(A) (requiring consumer confusion for common law trademark infringement action).

[80] 15 U.S.C. §§ 1114(1)(a) (requiring commercial exploitation of relevant goods or services for registered trademark infringement action), 1125(a)(1)(A) (requiring commercial exploitation of relevant goods or services for common law trademark infringement action).

[81] 15 U.S.C. § 1125(d)(1)(B)(i)(VIII) (contemplating as a 'bad faith factor' under the trademark-based provisions of the ACPA the defendant's 'registration or acquisition of multiple domain names which the person knows are identical or confusingly similar to marks of others that are distinctive at the time of registration of such domain names, or dilutive of famous marks of others that are famous at the time of registration of such domain names, without regard to the goods or services of the parties').

[82] Such as the conduct of Mr Dennis Toeppen in the early days of Internet domain name disputes. See Lipton, *Beyond Cybersquatting*, *supra* note 9, at 1370–1.

cybersquatter not to register multiple domain names, hoping instead to make a profit from the sale of just one particularly promising name.

Subsection (i) might be the most fruitful avenue for a politician concerned about cybersquatting. The main problem with the section is that it is not clear who is a 'rightful owner' of a relevant domain name and on what theoretical basis. Under modern trademark law it has been assumed in many circumstances that a trademark holder is the rightful owner of a corresponding domain name, at least in the '.com' space, and at least as against bad faith cybersquatters. However, the same may not hold true for politicians' names or the names of political parties or action groups who do not otherwise hold trademarks in those names. On the other hand, if one takes the view that any form of cybersquatting, including political cybersquatting, is inherently wasteful, then it might be easier to argue that a politician or political group is the rightful owner of a corresponding domain name in this context. Section 17526(i) might therefore prove useful to political actors who are the victims of political cybersquatting, depending on how courts interpret the scope of this bad faith factor.

California's Business and Professions Code shares some potential practical limitations with the PCAA. It is untested state legislation which has not been adopted in other jurisdictions. It may serve as a useful 'legislative laboratory'[83] on many issues related to cybersquatting. However, it may not yet be of much assistance to politicians concerned about this conduct. Additionally, it has not been tested against any potential First Amendment challenges as an impermissible burden on speech in the domain space. It is possible that the approach taken in the Code may be more fruitfully adopted in a private dispute resolution context than in legislation in the face of free speech concerns.

5.2.2.5 Summary: political cybersquatting

There are various avenues available to politicians and political groups concerned about cybersquatting. If a politician can establish trademark rights in her name, like Secretary of State Hillary Clinton[84] and her

---

[83] *Report to Congress: The Anticybersquatting Consumer Protection Act of 1999, section 3006 concerning the abusive registration of domain names*, para. IV, available at www.uspto.gov/web/offices/dcom/olia/tmcybpiracy/repcongress.pdf, last accessed March 14, 2007 ('California may serve as a legislative "laboratory" on [the issue of use of personal names in domain names]').

[84] *Hillary Rodham Clinton*, National Arbitration Forum, Claim No. FA0502000414641, available at www.arb-forum.com/domains/decisions/414641.htm) ('The Panel finds that complainant's uncontested allegations establish common law rights in the Hillary Clinton mark sufficient to grant standing under

husband former President Clinton,[85] that politician has a number of trademark-based alternatives. With a trademark, a politician or political group could potentially take advantage of the trademark-based provisions of the ACPA[86] or the UDRP, as well as some of the other trademark-oriented remedies. Trademark infringement may be possible if consumer confusion can be proven.[87] Trademark dilution might also be available in some cases. For politicians' names, there are also some actions available under federal legislation,[88] as well as potentially under the right of publicity or various state cyberfraud[89] and cybersquatting legislation[90] where applicable.

However, the current regulatory framework is piecemeal and context-specific. A complainant's chances of success will ultimately depend on factors such as the jurisdiction in which the politician and registrant are located or in which the domain name was registered, as well as on whether the politician can establish a trademark right. The system is neither nationally nor globally harmonized. Whatever view one takes of cybersquatting generally, political cybersquatting in particular adds costs to an electoral system without providing any specific benefits. Creating markets for valuable political domain names and effectively holding the names hostage awaiting the highest bidder can be wasteful, particularly in the electoral context which is time-sensitive. If this is the only purpose of the conduct – as opposed to facilitating political speech – it arguably should be proscribed.

One obvious answer to this problem, and to some other associated problems, would be to legislatively ban *all* forms of cybersquatting. In other words, a general rule could be adopted at the national or global level prohibiting all speculative registrations of domain names where

---

the UDRP. Complainant alleges that the Hilary Clinton mark has become distinctive through complainant's use and exposure of the mark in the marketplace and through use of the mark in connection with complainant's political activities, including a successful Senate campaign.').

85 *William J. Clinton*, National Arbitration Forum, Claim No: FA0904001256123, available at http://domains.adrforum.com/domains/decisions/1256123.htm (arbitrator 'reluctantly' concluded that former President Clinton had a trademark in his personal name, but the former president was unsuccessful in obtaining a transfer order for relevant domain names because he was unable to establish 'bad faith' registration and use on the part of the registrant).

86 15 U.S.C. § 1125(d)(1).

87 15 U.S.C. § 1125(a).

88 15 U.S.C. § 8131.

89 For example, California's PCAA: Cal. Elections Code, §§18320–18323.

90 For example, California's Business and Professions Code, § 17525(a).

the sole intent is to profit from selling the name. This would overlap with the current trademark-based regulations, but would not be limited to trademarks. It would potentially prohibit political cybersquatting as well as other conduct that wastes a valuable resource. However, such an approach would impact negatively on less objectionable domain name markets, such as those involving purely generic terms in the domain space. A narrower alternative would be to simply outlaw political cybersquatting. In this context, political cybersquatting might be defined as purely speculative registration of politicians' names in the domain space with no purpose other than to profit from the sale of the names. Regulations could be limited to the 'name.com' space or could apply more broadly to the registration of any domain name involving a politician's name where the motive was purely to profit from sale of the name.

There are likely to be many other potential solutions to problems of political cybersquatting – and political cyberfraud for that matter. At least one commentator has suggested a zoning approach to political speech.[91] This could be achieved by setting aside a dedicated official political gTLD for official political speech, such as a '.pol' gTLD.[92] One shortcoming of this approach might be that many politicians and political groups would likely still gravitate towards '.com' names because they have become so popular as the generic space for any web presence, commercial or otherwise.[93] It may prove difficult in practice to move official political speech to an authorized '.pol' zone.

Even if politicians and political groups were prepared to utilize such a space, their audiences may still be more attuned to the '.com' presence, and there may not be sufficient incentives for this to change. For example, why should politicians waste often scarce campaign resources on educating potential supporters to go to a '.pol' space, when they could just be vigilant and register the '.com' version of their name before running for office? Of course, another answer to the cybersquatting problem in politics may simply be that politicians and political organizations become better over time at defensively registering names they might want to use in the future. The cybersquatting problem would become less of an issue as a result.

---

[91] Matthew Sanderson, *Candidates, Squatters, and Gripers: A Primer on Political Cybersquatting and a Proposal for Reform*, 8 ELECTION L. J. 3 (2009).

[92] *Id.* at 26–8.

[93] See, for example, discussion at 4.2.1, *supra*.

5.2.3 Political Cyberfraud

5.2.3.1 Cyberfraud versus cybersquatting

In contrast to cybersquatting, political cyberfraud involves registration of a domain name corresponding with a politician's or political organization's name in order to misdirect or defraud people seeking the official presence of the relevant politician or group. It differs from cybersquatting in that it looks to the substantive content of the relevant website in association with the domain name, rather than a simple attempt to sell the domain name. Examples of cyberfraud would include publishing misleading or damaging information on a website about a politician, or fraudulently raising funds in the name of the politician under a domain name corresponding with her name.

This definition of cyberfraud begs an important question. Is there anything necessarily wrong with registering a domain name such as, say, 'johnkerry.com' and using it for a website critical of Senator Kerry and his views? In other words, is there – or should there be – a presumption that domain names corresponding with names of politicians and political organizations actually default to websites authorized by those entities? This is not unlike the question whether 'trademark.com' names are presumed to resolve to official websites administered by the relevant trademark holder.[94] However, the First Amendment might be less significantly impacted in the trademark context than in the political context. The First Amendment might appropriately protect those who register domain names corresponding with the names of politicians or political organizations in order to criticize them, even if it would not come into play in an analogous trademark situation.

Presumably, it would be difficult to support a rule that *any* domain name comprising a politician's or political group's name should be reserved to that politician or group. However, perhaps the '.com' version should be reserved in this way.[95] Under this reasoning, there is a colorable argument that *anyone* registering a '.com' version of a politician's or political organization's name may be liable for cyberfraud, even if the purpose is purely expressive. It would follow that the 'johnkerry.com' domain name rightly belongs to Senator Kerry, provided that people who want to criticize the senator online can utilize other domains such as 'johnkerrysucks.com' or 'johnkerry.net'.

---

[94] See, for example, discussion at 3.4.2, *supra*.

[95] Sanderson, *supra* note 91, at 26–8 (suggesting the alternative that a '.pol' gTLD should be developed for this purpose).

A domain name registrant engaging in cyberfraud might simultaneously propose to sell the domain name and thus may also be a cybersquatter. However, the basic conduct comprising cyberfraud raises distinct policy and regulatory issues. Cyberfraud raises more difficult issues of subjective judgment than cybersquatting. It is generally going to be much easier to determine whether someone is seeking to profit from selling a name, than to evaluate the content on the associated website in terms of whether it should be regarded as fraudulent. This is why pure cybersquatting is theoretically easier to regulate than cyberfraud. It is easier to work out whether a domain name registrant has registered a domain name with a sale-for-profit motive. Further, cybersquatting in and of itself does not implicate free speech in the same way as cyberfraud. Any regulation of cyberfraud needs to be as minimally invasive of speech as possible without allowing the electorate to be defrauded by bad faith domain name registrants.

Some cyberfraud may already be covered by specifically targeted local laws.[96] Additionally, some aspects of cyberfraud may be defamatory and subject to liability on that basis. For example, the registrant of a 'john-kerry-is-a-pedophile' domain name might be subject to a defamation suit. Attempting to defraud the public and raise money fraudulently under, say, 'johnkerry.com' for a Republican group would presumably contravene various criminal statutes.[97] Interestingly, however, the use of domain names corresponding with former President William J. Clinton's name to resolve to a Republican website was found by a UDRP arbitrator not to be bad faith conduct under the UDRP.[98] This does not necessarily mean the conduct would not run afoul of, say, California's political cyberfraud legislation[99] if the former President brought a claim under Californian

---

[96] See, for example, discussion at 1.6.1 and 1.6.2, *supra*.

[97] The Federal Department of Justice has defined 'Internet fraud' as follows: 'The term "Internet fraud" refers generally to any type of fraud scheme that uses one or more components of the Internet – such as chat rooms, e-mail, message boards, or Web sites – to present fraudulent solicitations to prospective victims, to conduct fraudulent transactions, or to transmit the proceeds of fraud to financial institutions or to other connected with the scheme' (see Department of Justice, *Internet Fraud*, available at www.usdoj.gov/criminal/fraud/Internet.htm) last accessed March 14, 2007. While the Department of Justice does not appear to be actively focusing on political fraud at this time, it appears to be increasingly concerned with criminal prosecutions for Internet fraud generally.

[98] *William J. Clinton*, National Arbitration Forum, Claim No. FA0904001256123, available at http://domains.adrforum.com/domains/decisions/1256123.htm.

[99] See, for example, discussion at 1.6.2, *supra*.

law. The UDRP is currently premised on protecting trademarks against cybersquatting.[100] It is not intended to control noncommercial messages promulgated under political domain names, even if those messages are fraudulent or misleading in some way.

5.2.3.2 California's political cyberfraud legislation

California's Political Cyberfraud Abatement Act (PCAA)[101] may prove to be a good legislative model for the kinds of conduct described here as political cyberfraud. This legislation prohibits (a) attempts to deny a person access to a political website;[102] (b) attempts to deny a person the opportunity to register a domain name for a political website;[103] and (c) activities concerning a website that would cause a person to believe that the website actually represents the views of a proponent or opponent of a ballot measure.[104]

Class (a) may be limited in operation. If a person registers a domain name corresponding with a politician's name to promulgate a misleading or deceptive message about the politician, the registrant may not have actually denied the person access to a political website as contemplated by the PCAA. The access question would depend upon whether the politician in question still had access to *any* relevant domain names for her own political message. If the domain name registrant had registered multiple domain names corresponding to the politician's name and had cut off access to all obvious iterations of the name, such as 'name.com', 'name.org' and 'name.net', this might be an example of cutting off access to a political website as contemplated in class (a). Of course, it may be increasingly difficult to satisfy this aspect of the legislation after ICANN introduces its proposed new gTLD program under which the number of available gTLDs for any given name is effectively limitless. Of course, then disputes may arise about the registration and use of gTLDs themselves that correspond with the names of politicians or political organizations.[105]

Class (b) would cover situations where a person registers a domain name corresponding with a politician's name with a view to denying her the opportunity to register the domain name. It is arguable that class (b)

---

[100] See discussion at 1.5.1, *supra*.

[101] Cal. Elections Code, §§ 18320–18323.

[102] *Id.*, § 18320(c)(1).

[103] *Id.*

[104] *Id.*

[105] For example, if a registry applied for the registration rights to, say, a '.clinton' gTLD.

conduct may not be judicially interpreted this broadly under the PCAA if the provision were read as prohibiting attempts to deny a person the opportunity to register *any* domain name, as opposed to a particular domain name. In other words, it is not clear on the face of the statute whether the prohibition applies only to situations where the domain name registrant has effectively cut off access to *any* relevant web presence via her registration of relevant domain names, or has cut off access to *one specific* domain name. The legislative phrase 'to deny a person the opportunity to register a domain name for a political Web site' is ambiguous.[106] It is unclear whether the indefinite article refers to one or many domain names. Again, one might need to consider precisely *which* iterations of the politician's name had been registered. The unavailability of 'name.com' names should perhaps raise more red flags than, say, 'namesucks.com' or even the less pejorative, but also less intuitive, 'nameinfo.com' or even 'name.info'. Again, ICANN's plans to increase the scope of the gTLD space may confuse matters even further in interpretation of this kind of legislative provision.

Class (c) may be more promising for victims of political cyberfraud. This class refers to conduct that causes an Internet user to believe that a website has been posted by someone other than the person who posted it. This would contemplate conduct of a person who has registered a domain name corresponding with a politician's name for the purposes of promulgating a misleading message about the politician. Some of these situations may also be caught by defamation law, depending on the content of the website. However, the PCAA may well cast a broader net here and be cheaper and easier to litigate than defamation. All that a victim of class (c) conduct would have to prove is that the website in question has been used to suggest an affiliation with the relevant politician that does not exist. This could be established by proving that the defendant had registered a domain name corresponding with the politician's name to provide messages about the politician regardless of whether the messages were defamatory or not. The misleading conduct would simply be using the politician's name in the domain name for an unauthorized website about the politician.[107]

The PCAA could be a useful model for more global protections against

---

[106] Cal. Elections Code, § 18320(c)(1).

[107] There may be some First Amendment concerns here as to whether, in this context, this provision, or any similar provision that may ever be debated at the federal level, would survive judicial scrutiny as a content-based restriction on First Amendment freedoms. At the date of writing, there is, as yet, no judicial interpretation on relevant issues, such as whether such a provision could be regarded

political cyberfraud. Of course, the PCAA and any approach like it may raise First Amendment concerns. To the extent that the legislation is regarded as an unacceptable burden on core political speech, it risks First Amendment challenge. Questions about where lines should be drawn between conduct that amounts to cyberfraud and protected comment about a politician or political organization will require further thought.

5.2.3.3 Laws protecting personal reputation

Some of the laws that protect personal reputation (discussed with respect to political cybersquatting)[108] may apply to political cyberfraud. Defamation is a possibility, although it has limited reach in the political context for public figures.[109] The right of publicity tort might also apply but only if there was a commercial profit motive on the part of the registrant. Thus, for example, if someone registered 'johnkerry.com' and sought financial contributions for a cause allegedly spearheaded by Senator Kerry, this might be an infringement of the right of publicity, albeit of an unconventional kind. Additionally, it is likely to infringe various criminal prohibitions on fraudulent conduct.

Legislation such as California's Business and Professions Code may have some application to cyberfraud, although it is more clearly directed to cybersquatting. As described above, § 17525(a) of the Code prohibits the bad faith registration, trafficking or use of a domain name that is identical or confusingly similar to the personal name of another person.[110] This would cover the registration or use of a domain name corresponding with a politician's name for bad faith purposes which likely include promulgating a misleading message about the politician. Three of the bad faith factors set out in the Code may be relevant to political cyberfraud, as described below.

Subsection 17526(e) contemplates as a bad faith factor: 'The intent of a person . . . to divert consumers from the person's . . . online location to a site accessible under the domain name that could harm the goodwill represented by the person's . . . name either for commercial gain or with the intent to tarnish or disparage the person's . . . name by creating a likelihood of confusion as to the source, sponsorship, affiliation, or endorsement of the

---

as a content-based restriction on speech and, if so, whether it would survive strict scrutiny.

[108] See 5.2.2, *supra*.

[109] See, for example, Jan Christie, *The Public Figure Plaintiff v the Nonmedia Defendant in Defamation Law: Balancing the Respective Interests*, 68 IOWA L. REV. 517, 517–18 (1983) (describing limited recourse to defamation actions in the United States for public figure plaintiffs against media defendants).

[110] See 5.2.2.4(c), *supra*.

site'. This provision is drafted in trademark focused terms – consider, for example, the references to goodwill and likelihood of confusion. However, it is possible that in some cases it might apply to political names. Consider, for example, the hypothetical registration of 'johnkerry.com' for a website that attempts to tarnish Senator Kerry's reputation by confusing Internet users into thinking it is an official website, but that actually contains information contrary to the senator's views. This would presumably amount to an attempt to divert customers[111] from the senator's online location to a site that could tarnish or disparage the senator's reputation by creating a likelihood of confusion as to the source of the website.

Subsection 17526(i) of the Code contemplates consideration of whether a domain name registrant 'sought or obtained consent from the rightful owner to register, traffic in, or use the domain name'. If we presume a politician is the rightful owner of a domain name corresponding with her personal name, this provision would cover some cyberfraud. The question will always be context-specific with respect to the domain name actually registered. While we may accept a presumption that the Secretary of State, Hillary Clinton, is the rightful owner of 'hillaryclinton.com', it is not necessarily true that she is also the rightful owner of variations such as 'hillaryclintonsucks.com', 'hillarycriticism.com' or even 'whyhillary.com'.

Finally, subsection 17526(j) of the Code contemplates as a bad faith factor the intent of a domain name registrant 'to mislead, deceive, or defraud voters'. This provision may be particularly relevant to political cyberfraud because of its focus on the use of the name to interfere with the electoral process. In other words, it appears to be aimed squarely at conduct of a domain name registrant who registers a domain name corresponding with, say, a politician's name with an intent to mislead Internet users as to the politician's message.

The Californian Code may have a significant role to play in developing a framework for regulating political cyberfraud. As with provisions of the PCAA, it may be worth watching the interpretation of this legislation and treating California as a laboratory for testing how courts interpret this legislation with respect to both political cybersquatting and political cyberfraud. Obviously, state legislation that has no, or few, analogs in other states can only provide a limited testing ground for the development of relevant principles. It may be desirable for more states to experiment with such laws in the interests of developing clearer principles about the appropriate boundaries of domain name use in the electoral context.

---

111 Of course, the term 'customers' suggests more of a trademark-protecting legislative intention than a speech-protection.

5.2.3.4 Political cyberfraud and anti-cybersquatting regulations

Some of the anti-cybersquatting regulations may incidentally catch some aspects of political cyberfraud. Even though regulations like the ACPA and the UDRP are premised on domain name registration or use with a bad faith profit motive,[112] they may apply to cases of cyberfraud where the profit motive overlaps with misleading or deceptive use of a domain name in a political website. Of course, neither of these measures is likely to apply in the absence of a trademark interest in the name of a politician or political organization. The one exception to this general limitation is 15 U.S.C. § 8131(1) which protects personal names (including names of politicians)[113] against cybersquatting.[114]

The main problem with § 8131in the ACPA is that it will not apply to any kind of cyberfraud unless there is a corresponding cybersquatting motive. In other words, if there is no bad faith intent to sell the domain name in question, § 8131 will not apply. Thus, if a registrant utilized a domain name corresponding with a politician's name to make comments about the politician, no action would lie unless the registrant had also at some point attempted to sell the domain name to the politician or to someone else. Section 8131 is limited to cases involving cybersquatting, even if they also involve cyberfraud. As such, the second does not add much to a discussion of pure cyberfraud that does not involve this kind of bad faith profit motive.

The UDRP may be different in this respect. Although, like the ACPA, the UDRP is premised on notions of bad faith cybersquatting, it is a little broader in its drafting. Under the UDRP, a complainant must establish that the registrant (a) has a domain name that is identical or confusingly similar to a trademark in which the complainant has rights;[115] (b) has no

---

[112] 15 U.S.C. § 1125(d)(1)(a)(i) ('a person shall be liable in a civil action by the owner of a mark, including a personal name which is protected as a mark under this section, if, without regard to the goods or services of the parties, that person . . . has a *bad faith intent to profit* from that mark').

[113] *Friends of Kathleen Kennedy Townsend*, WIPO Case No. D2002–0451, para. 6, and available at www.wipo.int/amc/en/domains/decisions/html/2002/d2002-0451.html ('This does not mean that complainant is without remedy. The ACPA [then 15 U.S.C. § 1129] contains express provisions protecting the rights in personal names.').

[114] 15 U.S.C. § 8131(1)(A) ('Any person who registers a domain name that consists of the name of another living person, or a name substantially and confusingly similar thereto, without that person's consent, with the specific intent to profit from such name by selling the domain name for financial gain to that person or any third party, shall be liable in a civil action by such person.').

[115] UDRP, para. 4(a)(i).

rights or legitimate interests in the name;[116] and (c) has registered and used the domain name in bad faith.[117] An attempt to actually sell the name[118] (or make some other form of profit from the name in bad faith)[119] is not necessary for a successful UDRP arbitration. The main problem under the UDRP will be for a politician to establish trademark rights in her personal name.[120] If she can establish such rights, then it may be possible to bring a cyberfraud claim under the UDRP if she can prove that the registrant has no legitimate interest in the name and has used it in bad faith.[121]

The next problem is to ascertain the bounds of legitimate interest and bad faith in this context. The UDRP itself gives little guidance here. Some arbitrators have recognized free speech as a legitimate interest,[122] in both the trademark context and the political context,[123] even though free speech is not expressly mentioned in the UDRP. The arbitrators who have accepted free speech as a legitimate interest have generally assumed

---

116 *Id.* para. 4(a)(ii).

117 *Id.* para. 4(a)(iii).

118 As required by 15 U.S.C. § 8131(1)(A) with respect to personal names.

119 As required by 15 U.S.C. §1125(d)(1)(A)(i) with respect to trademark-based protections.

120 See, for example, *Friends of Kathleen Kennedy Townsend*, WIPO Case No. D2002–0451, available at www.wipo.int/amc/en/domains/decisions/html/2002/d2002-0451.html (UDRP panel suggesting that the politician Kathleen Kennedy Townsend would not have a common law trademark in her personal name used for purely political purposes).

121 See, for example, *Hillary Rodham Clinton*, National Arbitration Forum, Claim No. FA0502000414641, available at www.arb-forum.com/domains/decisions/414641.htm (*supra* note 84).

122 The UDRP 'legitimate use' factors do not contemplate free speech per se and are limited to the various legitimate commercial uses set out in para. 4(c) of the UDRP. This list is not exclusive so arbitrators have had some leeway to extend on it. This occurred in *Bridgestone-Firestone v Myers*, WIPO Arbitration and Mediation Center, Case No. D2000–0190 (July 6, 2000), para. 6, available at www.wipo.int/amc/en/domains/decisions/html/2000/d2000-0190.html, last accessed March 14, 2007 ('The question presented in this case is whether fair use and free speech are defenses to a claim for transfer of a domain name under the Policy. Under Paragraph 4 (c)(iii) of the Policy, noncommercial fair use is expressly made a defense, as noted above. Although free speech is not listed as one of the Policy's examples of a right or legitimate interest in a domain name, the list is not exclusive, and the Panel concludes that the exercise of free speech for criticism and commentary also demonstrates a right or legitimate interest in the domain name under Paragraph 4 (c)(iii). The Internet is above all a framework for global communication, and the right to free speech should be one of the foundations of Internet law.').

123 *Id.*; *William J. Clinton*, National Arbitration Forum, Claim No. FA0904001256123 available at http://domains.adrforum.com/domains/decisions/1256123.htm, last accessed July 10, 2009.

that the speech on the website associated with the domain name is itself legitimate – usually a legitimate critique of the trademark holder or person whose name appears in the domain name.[124] In the commercial context, these cases have generally involved straightforward speech such as gripe sites about a trademark holder.[125] At least one arbitrator has held that the use of a series of political domain names, derived from former President William J. Clinton's name, was not in bad faith for UDRP purposes despite the fact that the registrant had directed the names to a Republican website.[126]

One problem with reliance on the UDRP and the ACPA in political cyberfraud cases is that those regulations are not drafted with politics in mind. Thus, it was probably appropriate for the UDRP arbitrator to hold against former President Clinton in the above case. UDRP arbitrators are trained to make trademark focused determinations and should not be burdened with questions about appropriate contours of political discourse online, at least unless clearer guidelines for such conduct can be developed for them. On the one hand, it is a positive development that some UDRP arbitrators are realizing that the UDRP is a poor fit for political disputes.[127] On the other hand, the fact that political domain name disputes are brought repeatedly under the UDRP suggests that there are currently gaps in domain name regulations as far as political speech is concerned. If more appropriate guidelines could be developed for political speech in the domain space, and more cost-effective avenues could be available for resolving political domain name disputes, less pressure would be put on UDRP arbitrators to find trademark interests in political names. Of course, to the extent that a political name (such as the name of a political party or organization) actually *is* a trademark, the application of trademark focused regulations is appropriate. But disputes involving names of politicians, in particular are not generally based on trademarks.

---

[124] *Id.*

[125] *Bridgestone*, WIPO Case No. D2000–0190, available at www.wipo.int/amc/en/domains/decisions/html/2000/d2000-0190.htm, last accessed March 14, 2007.

[126] *William J. Clinton*, National Arbitration Forum, Claim No. FA0904001256123 available at http://domains.adrforum.com/domains/decisions/1256123.htm, last accessed July 10, 2009.

[127] *Id.*; *Friends of Kathleen Kennedy Townsend*, WIPO Case No. D2002–0451, available at http://www.wipo.int/amc/en/domains/decisions/html/2002/d2002-0451.html, last accessed March 14, 2007 (UDRP panel suggesting that the politician Kathleen Kennedy Townsend would not have a common law trademark in her personal name used for purely political purposes).

5.2.4 Politicians' Names versus Trademarks

There is another category of political domain name conflicts that involves neither cybersquatting nor cyberfraud. It is the relatively rare situation that involves a coincidental cross-over between politics and the trademark system. It encompasses situations in which a trademark interest happens to correspond with the name of a politician or political organization, and both parties seek to use a corresponding domain name. This is another example of a situation involving multiple competing legitimate interests in a given domain name.[128] An obvious example might theoretically arise with respect to the domain name 'hillary.com', currently registered to the Hillary Software corporation.[129] Many Internet users might assume that typing this name into a web browser would take them to the official website of the Secretary of State, Hillary Clinton.

While this may be confusing for some Internet users looking for the website of the Secretary of State, it is apparently not an attempt to hijack her name in the domain space or to extort money for transfer of the name. The Hillary Software website does not provide any information about the Secretary of State. It is, of course, possible that if she wanted that domain name for herself she might make an offer to Hillary Software, but the company would be under no legal obligation to sell it to her. It appears to have legitimately registered the domain name for its own businesses purposes. As long as no attempt is made by the company to sell the name to the Secretary of State or anyone else for a profit, the company does not appear to be contravening any provisions of the ACPA or 15 U.S.C. § 8131. Likewise, there appears to be no obvious UDRP violation as the company appears to be using the name in good faith for legitimate purposes.

For similar reasons, it is unlikely that Hillary Software has run afoul of California's laws relating to unfair business practices[130] or political cyberfraud,[131] assuming of course these laws have jurisdictional reach between the Secretary of State and a software corporation headquartered in New Jersey. If there is no bad faith for the purposes of the unfair business laws[132] and no willful intent to deceive electors under the cyber-

---

128 See generally discussion in Chapter 2, for consideration of competing legitimate trademark interests in the same domain name.

129 See www.hillary.com, last accessed on July 15, 2009.

130 California's Business and Professions Code, § 17525(a).

131 Cal. Elections Code, §§ 18320–23.

132 California's Business and Professions Code, § 17525(a).

fraud legislation,[133] these laws would not be available even if the Secretary of State was minded to bring a claim.

It is theoretically possible that the Secretary of State could bring a trademark dilution action,[134] presuming she has a famous trademark interest in her own name.[135] Such an action is premised on the notion of tarnishment or blurring of a mark.[136] The problem with dilution is that it is premised on the notion that the underlying mark be famous[137] and be used in connection with the sale of goods or services.[138] It is not clear that Hillary Clinton's first name would qualify on either count, although it is possible. In any event, it is unclear that the software company's use of the name would, in fact, be regarded as blurring or tarnishing any such mark.

Is there an obvious solution to these kinds of admittedly rare problems? Some form of domain name sharing is theoretically possible along the lines described in previous chapters if there is sufficient incentive built into the system to facilitate such an arrangement.[139] Sufficiently powerful politicians may have enough caché, or simply enough cash, to gain control of names from small corporations. In fact, a similar situation has recently played out with respect to President Obama's name in the domain space. During the presidential campaign, the domain name 'obama.com' was registered in Japan for a Japanese language website about the city of Obama. It was subsequently transferred to the President for his official website.

Another possibility is the creation of a '.pol' space for authorized political discourse.[140] Thus, the Secretary of State could utilize 'hillary.pol' while the software corporation retained 'hillary.com'. The President might be relegated to 'obama.pol' while the city in Japan retained 'obama.

---

133 Cal. Elections Code, §§ 18320–18323.

134 15 U.S.C. § 1125(c)(1).

135 Although personal names are not generally trademarkable (GILSON, *supra* note 2, para. 2.03[d]), a UDRP panel did find the senator to have a common law trademark interest in 'Hillary Clinton': *Hillary Rodham Clinton*, National Arbitration Forum, Claim No. FA0502000414641 (March 18, 2005). It is not clear whether this would extend to protection of 'Hillary' as a mark per se. Further, the UDRP panel's comments would not be binding on a domestic court or even a later arbitration panel. There may also be questions as to whether the mark is sufficiently 'famous' to support a trademark dilution action under 15 U.S.C. § 1125(c)(1).

136 15 U.S.C. § 1125(c)(1).

137 *Id.*

138 *Id.*

139 See 2.4, *supra*. See also Jacqueline Lipton, *A Winning Solution for Youtube and Utube: Corresponding Trademarks and Domain Name Sharing*, 21 HARV. J. LAW AND TECH. 509, 519–24 (2008).

140 Sanderson, *supra* note 91, at 26–8.

com'. Of course, the creation of an official political speech gTLD would necessitate the development of its own regulations and guidelines to ensure that it was not misused by cybersquatters and those intending to commit forms of cyberfraud. Even the creation of such a zone would do little in and of itself to combat the current preference of most Internet users and domain name registrants to gravitate towards the '.com' space. This may or may not change in the wake of ICANN's proposed process to open up the gTLD space to new gTLDs proposed by private applicants.[141]

5.3 CULTURAL AND GEOGRAPHICAL IDENTIFIERS

Another potentially problematic category of domain name disputes involves domain names that correspond to more miscellaneous subjects, such as culturally and geographically significant words and phrases. These are difficult considerations because social and cultural norms relating to rights in such terms are more difficult to establish and more globally disharmonized even than rights relating to free speech in the political process. It is also difficult to establish precisely who should have the strongest claims to rights in various culturally and geographically significant terms. These difficulties were recognized in the Report of the Second WIPO Internet Domain Name Process.[142] WIPO specifically recommended leaving these issues for further consideration.[143] With respect to names of indigenous people in particular, WIPO suggested that further consideration could take place, including through WIPO's process of investigating intellectual property and genetic resources, traditional knowledge and folklore.[144]

Rights in cultural and geographic terms may well conflict with other rights deriving from corporate and personal domain names. Thus, the matrix for resolving domain name disputes becomes even more complex when cultural and geographical indicators are added to the mix. One high profile example is the correspondence of the name of the city of Obama in Japan with the personal name of the American president. Another

---

[141] See ICANN, New gTLD Program: Draft Applicant Guidebook (Draft RFP) (October 24, 2008), available at www.icann.org/en/topics/new-gtlds/draft-rfp-24oct08-en.pdf, last accessed July 6, 2009.

[142] See *Second WIPO Internet Domain Name Process, Final Report* (September 3, 2001), full text available at www.wipo.int/amc/en/processes/process2/report/html/report.html, last accessed July 17, 2009.

[143] *Id.* para. 297.

[144] *Id.*

example could arise with respect to a domain name like 'madonna.com'. This domain name is currently registered to the popular entertainer who goes by the name of Madonna. She has registered 'Madonna' as a trademark.[145] She therefore has trademark interests in the name by virtue of the trademark registration, as well as probably through common law trademark rights and, perhaps, through personality rights in the name. However, the name clearly corresponds with other cultural interests, especially religious and artistic representations of the mother of Christ.

To date, disputes involving the 'madonna.com' domain name have revolved around competing trademark interests in the name, rather than cultural or religious interests.[146] The 'madonna.com' domain name was originally registered to a Dan Parisi in New York who had registered the trademark 'Madonna' under Tunisian law, expressly to defend against any challenge by the singer to his domain name registration.[147] Parisi admitted during the course of the UDRP proceedings that he only obtained the Tunisian trademark in order to protect his interests in the domain name.[148] He was not located in Tunisia at the time, nor did he register the mark for the purpose of making any bona fide use of the mark in commerce in Tunisia.[149] Parisi presumably chose Tunisia because registration of trademarks there proceeds without any substantive examination.[150] Thus, it would not have mattered for registration purposes that Parisi was not using the name in connection with a bona fide offering of goods or services in Tunisia or anywhere else.

Madonna, the singer, successfully obtained a transfer order for the domain name under the UDRP on the basis that Parisi had registered the mark in bad faith and had no legitimate interest in it.[151] However, Madonna was in an unusually strong position because of her registered trademark in the term 'Madonna'. Many other famous figures have been less fortunate in attempts to defend their names in the domain space because of failure to establish a trademark interest in their personal names.[152] In the entertain-

---

145 See U.S. Trademark No. 1,473,554 (registered January 18, 1989), at http://tess2.uspto.gov/bin/showfield?f=doc&state=ctbup4..2.1; U.S. Trademark No. 1,463,601 (registered November 3, 1987), at http://tess2.uspto.gov/bin/showfield?f=doc&state=ctbup4.3.

146 *Ciccone v Parisi*, WIPO Case No. D2000–0847, paras 4–5, available at http://arbiter.wipo.int/domains/decisions/html/2000/d2000-0847.html.

147 *Id.* para. 4.

148 *Id.* para. 6.

149 *Id.*

150 *Id.*

151 *Id.* para. 7.

152 *Id.*

ment sphere, Bruce Springsteen and Anna Nicole Smith are obvious examples.[153] There are also examples of politicians and other public figures who have not been able to establish trademarks in their personal names for UDRP purposes.[154] Of course these examples relate only to personal

---

153 *Bruce Springsteen*, WIPO Case No. D2000–1532, para. 6 available at www.wipo.int/amc/en/domains/decisions/html/2000/d2000-1532.html ('It appears to be an established principle from cases such as Jeanette Winterson, Julia Roberts, and Sade that in the case of very well known celebrities, their names can acquire a distinctive secondary meaning giving rise to rights equating to unregistered trade marks, notwithstanding the non-registerability of the name itself. It should be noted that no evidence has been given of the name "Bruce Springsteen" having acquired a secondary meaning; in other words a recognition that the name should be associated with activities beyond the primary activities of Mr. Springsteen as a composer, performer and recorder of popular music. In the view of this Panel, it is by no means clear from the UDRP that it was intended to protect proper names of this nature.'); *Anna Nicole Smith v DNS Research Inc.*, National Arbitration Forum, Claim No. FA0312000220007, February 21, 2004) available at www.adrforum.com/domains/decisions/220007.htm, last accessed October 25, 2007(involving 'annanicolesmith.com' domain name) ('it is unlikely that the evidence submitted here by complainant of her career, in and of itself, is sufficient to establish common law trademark rights in the name, which is a requirement for complainant to prevail on this aspect of the case. While the UDRP does not require a *registered* trademark for protection of a trademark from a confusingly identical domain name, the mere fact of having a successful career as an actress, singer or TV program star does not provide exclusive rights to the use of a name under the trademark laws. The cases require a clear showing of high commercial value and significant recognition of the name as solely that of the performer. The *Humphrey Bogart* case cited by the complainant is a prime example of the type of case that would be expected to prevail, since virtually no one familiar with the movie industry would fail to recognize his name as that of a famous movie star. The Panel does not believe complainant's name has yet reached that level of fame.'). Note, however, that the *Springsteen* arbitration was decided on other grounds so the failure to find a common law mark in Springsteen's name was not determinative of the issue in the decision.

154 *Kathleen Kennedy Townsend*, WIPO Case No. D2002–0451, available at www.wipo.int/amc/en/domains/decisions/html/2002/d2002-0451.html (individual politician in state gubernatorial race held not to hold trademark rights in her personal name); *The Hebrew University of Jerusalem v Alberta Hot Rods*, WIPO Arbitration and mediation Center, Case No. D2002–0616, (October 7, 2002) available at www.Kip.Ke.wipo.net/amc/en/domans/decisions/html/2002/d2002–0616.html, last accessed March 16, 2010 (involving a complaint with respect to the domain name 'alberteinstein.com'); *Gordon Sumner aka Sting v Michael Urvan,* WIPO Arbitration and mediation center Case No. D2000–0596, (July 20, 2000), para. 6.5, available at www.wipo.int/amc/en/domains/decisions/html/2000/d2000-0596.html, last accessed November 8, 2007 ('In the opinion of this Administrative Panel, it is doubtful whether the Uniform Policy is applicable to this dispute. Although it is accepted that the complainant is world famous under

names of well-known figures. Considering how difficult it can be for even well-known figures to establish marks in their personal names, these difficulties may be exponentially increased for those asserting interests in other cultural and geographic indicators.

WIPO was probably correct in 2001 when it suggested that some of the more complex domain name issues require further scrutiny, consideration and comment before any decisive legal and policy rules are formulated. Geographical indicators and cultural references are the most obvious candidates for further consideration, along with political names and affiliations. However, it is important that consideration is given sooner, rather than later, to these issues. Otherwise, we risk the very real possibility that commercial interests, and trademarks in particular, will come to dominate law and policy in the domain name context. It is possible that important interests are currently being overlooked and will continue to be overlooked, unless the debate is refocused to take account of some of these issues. The problems are likely to be multiplied when ICANN introduces its new gTLD process. The possibility to have cultural, geographic and political terms accepted as gTLDs in their own right will raise more issues relating to competing interests in those terms online.[155]

Various possibilities for legal reform exist to ensure a more balanced approach to competing interests in the domain space, in order to accommodate not only trademark interests, but also political, cultural and geographical interests. Some of these options have been discussed in relation to trademark interests in previous chapters. They include the following.

(a) Generic Top Level Domains might be zoned so that speech related to one area of social, cultural or economic activity is presumptively zoned into a particular gTLD space, such as '.pol' for politics.[156]

(b) As a corollary to the previous point, gTLD rules might be developed to ensure that one person or organization is limited in the number of gTLD variations on the same term that can be registered. This would prevent one person or entity from monopolizing all gTLD spaces relating to the one term. Thus, for example, the online store Amazon.com may be entitled to the domain name 'Amazon.com' and potentially also 'Amazon.biz', but other gTLDs relating to, say, the Amazon River, would be reserved to other gTLD spaces, such as '.geo'.

---

the name Sting, it does not follow that he has rights in Sting *as a trademark or service mark*'.).

[155] See discussion at 5.4, *infra*.

[156] Sanderson, *supra* note 91, at 26–8.

(c) Domain name sharing systems may be developed in appropriate cases, allowing two or more individuals or entities with legitimate competing interests in the same domain name jointly to host the relevant website containing hyperlinks to their respective main webpages on a permanent or temporary basis.[157]

(d) Defensive registration or veto systems could be adopted to protect interests in domain names where an interested person or entity does not want anyone to use the most intuitive form of a particular name for personal or cultural reasons, but does not necessarily desire to use the name herself. An obvious example of this would be allowing famous individuals to defensively register – but not be required to actually use – relevant domain names. Alternatively, they might be allowed to veto others' registration of '.com' and maybe also '.name' versions of their personal names. This system might also allow objection to registration of any new gTLD corresponding with a famous person's name.

(e) Some of the domain name watch services, and exclusion mechanisms developed previously by the WIPO Arbitration and Mediation Center, may be extended.[158] These procedures would also allow those with personal, political, cultural or geographic interests in a given term, who do not themselves want to use the term in the domain space, to monitor proposed uses of relevant domain names. This kind of service could also potentially be extended to new gTLDs.

5.4 EMERGING ISSUES

Issues about protecting political, cultural and geographic identifiers in the domain space will likely emerge in relation to ICANN's new gTLD process.[159] Thus, any procedures developed to protect these kinds of terms in the context of existing gTLDs should also be extended to (a) protect the terms in the context of new gTLDs and (b) protect the terms *as* new gTLDs. For example, consider a term like 'Jehovah'. If we want to ensure an appropriate balance of uses of the term that protects free speech, religion, and any commercial interests that might inhere in the term, we would have to consider how the term is used in existing gTLDs (for example, 'Jehovah.com' and 'Jehovah.org'). We would also have to consider how

---

157 See discussion at 2.4.2, *supra*.

158 See discussion in Lipton, *Beyond Cybersquatting*, *supra* note 9, at 1438.

159 See ICANN, New gTLD Program: Draft Applicant Guidebook (Draft RFP) (October 24, 2008), available at www.icann.org/en/topics/new-gtlds/draft-rfp-24oct08-en.pdf, last accessed July 6, 2009.

the term might be permitted to be used in any new gTLDs (for example, 'Jehovah.religion'), *and* how or whether the term might be permitted to be used *as* a new gTLD (for example, '.jehovah').

Other online mnemonic systems, like Facebook's personalized username program,[160] might raise similar issues. Facebook is entitled to make its own decisions, based on its own policies, as to what entities can register terms as personalized URLs. So it will be interesting to see what kinds of terms Facebook ultimately allows to be used in this context, and what kinds of policies it applies, if any, to protect cultural, geographic and political terms. The Facebook URL program also raises potentially interesting questions about the application of § 230 of the Communications Decency Act (CDA) in the United States. This provision generally immunizes providers of Internet services against liability for the speech of others on their services.[161] This has had a very broad reach in the context of online defamation.[162] However, previous case law has not considered the application of the section with respect to the domain space or other aspects of a URL. Section 230 immunizes service providers from liability for content posted by their members. However, if Facebook itself provides the personalized usernames at the request of its member, a court might find Facebook to be the publisher or speaker of the relevant content.[163] Facebook might therefore not be immunized from any otherwise applicable tortious liability by § 230.

5.5 CHAPTER SUMMARY

This chapter has examined some of the intricacies of balancing interests in political, cultural and geographic terms in the domain space against other competing interests. It has noted that there are no clear guidelines for protecting these kinds of interests against commercial or other uses of relevant domain names. In particular, the chapter has addressed the following.

---

[160] See, for example, discussion in Stoel Rives L.L.P., *Trademark Law Alert: New Personalized Facebook URLs May Infringe Your Trademarks and Brands* (June 11, 2009), full text available at www.stoel.com/showalert.aspx?Show=5515, last accessed on July 6, 2009.

[161] 47 U.S.C. § 230(c)(1) ('No provider or user of an interactive computer service shall be treated as the publisher or speaker of any information provided by another information content provider.').

[162] See, for example, *Zeran v America Online*, 129 F.3d 327 (4th Cir. 1997); *Blumenthal v Drudge*, 992 F. Supp. 33 (D.D.C. 1998).

[163] See discussion in *Fair Housing Association v Roommates.com*, 521 F.3d 1157 (9th Cir. 2008).

(1) The protection of political discourse online with respect to the names of politicians and political organizations in the domain space.

(2) The lack of clear guidelines for political speech in the domain space, and the possibility that developing categories of political conduct in the domain space (such as political cyberfraud and political cybersquatting) might assist with the development of appropriate regulatory structures.

(3) Approaches to regulation of different categories of political conduct in the domain space.

(4) The protection and regulation of other culturally and geographically significant terms in the domain space.

(5) The implications for balancing political, cultural and geographical interests in the context of new gTLDs and personalized Facebook URLs.

The following chapter considers the regulation of conduct often described as clickfarming and typosquatting. It considers whether, and to what extent, clear rules can or should be developed for regulating such conduct and the extent to which these practices raise – or should raise – a presumption of bad faith on the part of a domain name registrant. In this context, it examines the various motivations of people engaged in such conduct involving trademarks, personal names and generic words and phrases.

6. The boundaries of bad faith in the domain space

6.1 CLICKFARMING, TYPOSQUATTING AND BAD FAITH

The discussion in Chapters 2 through 5 highlighted conduct in the domain space that is problematic because it relates to balancing competing legitimate interests in particular words or phrases. Balancing rights in competing trademarks, free speech, personal names, and political, cultural and geographic signifiers are difficult challenges in the face of rivalrous online property like domain names. This chapter turns the focus to the appropriate boundaries of domain name regulation, with particular emphasis on conduct that might more readily be described as being in bad faith. The discussion focuses on case studies involving clickfarming and typosquatting. Clickfarming is the registration and use of a domain name corresponding with another person's trademark (or perhaps some other interest) for the purposes of raising advertising revenues from click-through advertisements on the associated webpage.[1] Typosquatting refers to a domain name registrant taking advantage of common misspellings of trademarks – or other legitimate interests by registering those misspellings as domain names, usually for financial benefit.[2]

Clickfarming and typosquatting may occur simultaneously, depending on the circumstances. In other words, a clickfarmer may elect to register a common misspelling of a trademark as a domain name in order to use the associated website as a clickfarm. Additionally, clickfarmers may also engage in traditional cybersquatting.[3] A clickfarmer may attempt to make money utilizing someone else's trademark, or a common misspelling of

---

[1] Jacqueline Lipton, *Clickfarming: The New Cybersquatting?*, 12. J. INTERNET LAW 1 (2008).

[2] DAVID LINDSAY, INTERNATIONAL DOMAIN NAME LAW: ICANN AND THE UDRP 259 (2007).

[3] Jonathan Nilsen, *Mixing Oil with Water: Resolving the Differences Between Domain Names and Trademark Law*, 1 J. HIGH TECH. L. 47, 51 (2002) ('Cybersquatting has been defined several ways. The most general definition of a

the mark, in the domain name, and may at the same time be prepared to sell the domain name for a profit.[4] If the registrant's motive is maximizing profit, she will likely calculate whether she can make the most profit from selling the name or running a clickfarm on the associated website.[5] Thus, the lines between clickfarming, cybersquatting and typosquatting are not always clear in any given case. However, the common thread is some evidence of a bad faith profit motive utilizing another person's trademark.

Naturally, there may be circumstances in which a domain name registrant is using a clickfarm without infringing anyone else's interests. It is possible to register valuable generic words as domain names (for example, 'love.com' or 'hope.com') and run a clickfarm in the hope of generating revenues from Internet users typing the generic word into a URL bar or search engine. A secondary hope may be that someone else will offer money to buy a popular generic word as a domain name. This is unlikely to be regarded as bad faith conduct in the absence of a trademark interest. There are currently no regulations that would prohibit a commercial use of a common term in the domain space. In any event, this chapter focuses on conduct that may be described as bad faith, involving unauthorized use of someone else's trademark or other interest. However, it is important to recognize that not all clickfarmers and typosquatters are engaged in bad faith conduct. Where their conduct revolves around generic terms, there is presumably no bad faith inherent in clickfarming or typosquatting.

Many domain name regulations are premised on notions of bad faith conduct that interferes with the rights of a trademark holder, or in some cases with other legitimate interests, such as rights in a personal name.[6] The Anticybersquatting Consumer Protection Act (ACPA) expressly contemplates bad faith as a requisite element of a claim,[7] as does the Uniform Domain Name Dispute Resolution Policy (UDRP).[8] The more traditional trademark actions, infringement and dilution, do not expressly require bad faith, although it is implied in many of the judicial decisions involving

---

cybersquatter is a person who registers a domain name that matches a well-known company for the purpose of ransoming it to that company.').

4 Lipton, *Clickfarming*, *supra* note 1, at 16 (noting that some clickfarmers are also prepared to sell the name to a rightful trademark holder).

5 *Id.* (recognizing that clickfarmers may not want to sell domain names if they can make more money from advertising on the associated website).

6 See, for example, 15 U.S.C. § 8131(1)(A) (protecting personal names against cybersquatting regardless of a trademark right in the name).

7 15 U.S.C. § 1125(d)(1)(A)(i) (requiring bad faith). See also 15 U.S.C. § 8131(1)(A) (bad faith required for personal name cybersquatting).

8 UDRP, para. 4(a)(iii), 4(b).

domain names.[9] This chapter examines the various domain name regulations as they might apply to clickfarming and typosquatting. One important question considered in the chapter is whether it is possible to identify clear rules about precisely what type of conduct should be proscribed in the domain space as being in bad faith. This chapter considers the application of current domain name regulations first to clickfarming and then to typosquatting.

6.2 CLICKFARMING

6.2.1 Trademark Infringement

Trademark infringement is premised on consumer confusion about the source of products or services.[10] In the domain name context, successful trademark infringement actions have generally involved uses of a trademark in a domain name that might confuse consumers about the source of a product or service marketed on the associated website.[11] Commentators have criticized the application of trademark infringement law to the domain space in cases involving what has come to be described as initial interest confusion.[12] These are cases in which an Internet user may have ended up on the registrant's website by mistake (due to reliance on a domain name, meta-tag[13] or search engine keyword[14] similar to another person's mark) but when a purchasing decision is ultimately made, the user is not confused as to the source of the product or service purchased.[15]

---

[9] Jacqueline Lipton, *Beyond Cybersquatting: Taking Domain Name Disputes Past Trademark Policy*, 40 Wake Forest L. Rev. 1361, 1370–71 (2005).

[10] 15 U.S.C. § 1114(1)(a) (requiring consumer confusion in an action for infringement of a registered trademark), § 1125(a)(1)(A) (requiring consumer confusion in an action for infringement of an unregistered trademark).

[11] See, for example, *Brookfield Communications v West Coast Ent. Corp.*, 174 F.3d 1036 (9th Cir.1999).

[12] Eric Goldman, *Deregulating Relevancy in Internet Law*, 54 Emory L.J. 507, 559 (2005) ('[Initial interest confusion] lacks a rigorous definition, a clear policy justification, and a uniform standard for analyzing claims. With its doctrinal flexibility, [it] has become the tool of choice for plaintiffs to shut down junior users who have not actually engaged in misappropriative uses.')

[13] *Brookfield Communications v West Coast Ent. Corp.*, 174 F.3d 1036 (9th Cir.1999); *Playboy v Terri Welles*, 279 F.3d 796 (2002).

[14] *Playboy v Netscape*, 354 F.3d 1020 (2004).

[15] Greg Lastowka, *Google's Law*, 73 Brooklyn L. Rev.1327, 1369–71 (2008) (providing a recent critique of the doctrine of initial interest confusion which extends the reach of trademark infringement online).

Nevertheless, courts hearing cases of online trademark infringement have been relatively ready to find consumer confusion made out in these kinds of scenarios.[16]

The question now arises as to whether the operator of a clickfarm that utilizes someone else's trademark as its domain name, or that utilizes a very similar term as the domain name, could be liable for trademark infringement. A clickfarmer may display click-through advertisements that relate in some way to the domain name. An example of this would be a clickfarmer who hypothetically registered 'mcdonalds.org' and used the domain name for a clickfarm that displayed click-through advertisements for various fast food outlets other than the McDonalds burger franchise. In contrast, the advertisements available on a clickfarm may have nothing to do with the domain name in question. In other words, the domain name might be used to draw custom for a clickfarm that displayed advertisements unrelated to the domain name. Thus, a clickfarmer might hypothetically register the name 'mcdonalds.org' for a website that contained a variety of advertisements that had nothing to do with McDonalds itself or any other fast food. In this latter situation, the McDonalds mark is still arguably used to mislead Internet users into thinking that the website has something to do with McDonalds. Thus, the clickfarmer is using the trademark to gain custom that she otherwise would not have attracted without unauthorized use of the mark. However, in this situation, the clickfarmer is not likely confusing consumers as to the source of any advertised products or services.

It is equally possible in the first scenario (where the clickfarm advertisements actually relate to fast food) that customers are not truly confused at the time they click on an advertisement. This may amount to a case of initial interest confusion. The Internet user is attracted to the website by mistake, but is then diverted to information about another fast food service (not McDonalds) in full knowledge that she is not dealing with McDonalds. Thus, she may end up ordering a product or service, or

---

16 *Playboy v Netscape*, 354 F.3d 1020, 1035 (2004) ('I do not think it is reasonable to find initial interest confusion when a consumer is never confused as to source or affiliation, but instead knows, or should know, from the outset that a product or web link is not related to that of the trademark holder because the list produced by the search engine so informs him. There is a big difference between hijacking a customer to another website by making the customer think he or she is visiting the trademark holder's website (even if only briefly), which is what may be happening in this case when the banner advertisements are not labeled, and just distracting a potential customer with another *choice*, when it is clear that it is a choice.').

information about a product or service, that competes with McDonalds. This is similar to the well-known *Brookfield* case.[17] In that case, Internet users initially arriving at the defendant's website due to technological misdirection involving the plaintiff's mark might ultimately decide to deal with the defendant in full knowledge that they were not dealing with the plaintiff. Thus, the defendant obtained the benefits of the initial consumer confusion even though consumers were not confused at the time a purchasing decision was made.

The clickfarm scenario, however, is different from *Brookfield* in that the clickfarmer herself is not directly competing with the plaintiff trademark holder, but is rather facilitating competitors of the plaintiff in directing custom away from the plaintiff's website. Arguably, to the extent that this conduct implicates trademark infringement, it may be better described as a case of indirect liability on the part of the clickfarmer, rather than direct liability.[18] While clickfarm cases have not been at the forefront of online trademark litigation, it is possible that this will happen in the future, and that questions will arise as to whether these cases are properly considered as involving direct or indirect liability for trademark infringement.

6.2.2 Trademark Dilution

Trademark dilution differs from infringement in that it does not require a showing of consumer confusion by the plaintiff.[19] Instead, the holder of a famous mark[20] must establish that the mark has been diluted by the defendant. Dilution comes in two forms: blurring and tarnishment.[21] Blurring involves the defendant creating noise around a mark such that it cannot function as effectively as a mark.[22] Tarnishment involves creating

---

17 *Brookfield Communications v West Coast Ent. Corp.*, 174 F.3d 1036 (9th Cir.1999).

18 See, for example, *Tiffany v eBay*, 576 F. Supp. 2d 463 (2008) (discussing secondary trademark infringement liability for Internet intermediaries in the context of the popular online auction service, eBay).

19 15 U.S.C. § 1125(c)(1) (dilution does not require consumer confusion).

20 15 U.S.C. § 1125(c)(1), (2)(A) (definition of 'famous mark' for dilution purposes).

21 15 U.S.C. § 1125(c)(1), (2)(B) (definition of dilution by blurring); § 1125(c)(2)(C) (definition of dilution by tarnishment).

22 15 U.S.C. § 1125(c)(2)(B) ('"dilution by blurring" is association arising from the similarity between a mark or trade name and a famous mark that impairs the distinctiveness of the famous mark.').

unsavory associations with the defendant's mark.[23] As with infringement, the defendant's use of the mark must take place in commerce to support a dilution action.[24]

Dilution actions have been successfully argued by trademark holders in the cybersquatting context.[25] For example, the *Panavision* court held that an unauthorized use of a mark in a domain name for purposes unrelated to the trademark holder's product or service market is dilutive of the mark.[26] The reasoning was that such a use interferes with the trademark holder's ability effectively to use its mark to attract online custom.[27] Similar reasoning might be applied to clickfarming. If a clickfarmer utilized another person's mark in its domain name to attract advertising revenues through its clickfarm, this arguably interferes with the trademark holder's ability to utilize the mark itself. Even an intentional misspelling of the mark by the clickfarmer would likely be captured by dilution on this reasoning. Blurring and tarnishment actions require the plaintiff to establish that the defendant's mark is similar to its mark.[28] The domain name would not have to be *identical* to the plaintiff's mark to support a dilution action.

The *Panavision* court additionally held that a cybersquatter's activities are in commerce for dilution purposes because the cybersquatter is in the business of registering domain names with the intention of selling them. This was the case in *Panavision* despite the fact that the defendant was not conducting any commercial activity on the relevant website.[29] A clickfarmer, on the other hand, is clearly conducting commercial activity on the relevant website because she makes money from the click-through advertisements associated with the defendant's mark. If registering a domain name with a sale motive is sufficiently in commerce for trademark dilution, then presumably using the domain name with a commercial profit motive related to advertising on the underlying website would satisfy this test.

The question of dilution by tarnishment may be less clear than that of

---

23 15 U.S.C. § 1125(c)(2)(C) ('"dilution by tarnishment" is association arising from the similarity between a mark or trade name and a famous mark that harms the reputation of the famous mark.').

24 15 U.S.C. § 1125(c)(1) (including 'in commerce' requirement for dilution action).

25 *Panavision Int'l L.P. v Toeppen*, 141 F.3d 1316 (9th Cir. 1998).

26 *Id.*

27 *Id.* at 1326–27.

28 15 U.S.C. § 1125(c)(2)(B), (2)(C).

29 *Panavision Int'l L.P. v Toeppen*, 141 F.3d 1316, 1325 (9th Cir. 1998) ('Toeppen made a commercial use of Panavision's trademarks. It does not matter that he did not attach the marks to a product. Toeppen's commercial use was his attempt to sell the trademarks themselves.').

blurring. Tarnishment requires damage to the reputation of the mark.[30] The mere act of diverting customers to a clickfarming website, without more, would probably not damage the mark's reputation in a tarnishment sense. However, diverting customers to a website hosting lewd or obscene content that also hosts a clickfarm may support a tarnishment action. Of course, in order to mount a successful dilution action, a plaintiff must establish that its mark is sufficiently famous under the statutory definition of famous mark.[31]

The dilution action may provide some comfort for trademark holders against clickfarmers, but only in the case of famous marks, and only if courts accept that clickfarming amounts to a commercial use of a mark that may blur or tarnish the mark. It will not apply to nonfamous marks, and will not apply to designators that do not actually operate as marks at all, such as some personal names, and some culturally and geographically significant terms. However, where a mark is sufficiently famous, it is likely that a clickfarmer will be liable for dilution by blurring in situations where he or she uses the mark, or an intentional misspelling of the mark, in a domain name. Depending on the content of a relevant website, dilution by tarnishment may also be available in some cases.

6.2.3 Anti-Cybersquatting Consumer Protection Act

6.2.3.1 Trademarks

The ACPA creates a civil action against a person who 'registers, traffics in or uses a domain name', with a bad faith profit motive, where the domain name is identical or confusingly similar to a distinctive or a famous mark, or where the domain name is dilutive of a famous mark.[32] The legislation includes a list of bad faith factors that courts may consider in determining whether the defendant has infringed the legislation.[33] Thus, unlike trademark infringement and dilution actions, the ACPA expressly contemplates bad faith as an element of the action.

If we assume that most clickfarming conduct (at least clickfarming that involves trademarks) is in bad faith, the ACPA action may be a logical first step for trademark holders concerned about unauthorized uses of their marks in the domain space. Of course, one might argue that clickfarming does not necessarily involve a bad faith profit motive in the same way that,

---

30 15 U.S.C. § 1125(c)(2)(C).
31 15 U.S.C. § 1125(c)(2)(A).
32 15 U.S.C. § 1125(d)(1)(A).
33 15 U.S.C. § 1125(d)(1)(B)(i).

say, cybersquatting has been regarded as being in bad faith. However, if courts and Congress have been prepared to proscribe cybersquatting on the basis that it interferes with a trademark holder's ability to effectively utilize its mark online, there is at least a strong argument that clickfarming on a trademark should be covered for the same reasons.

Although there is no necessary *trafficking* motive on the part of a clickfarmer, in contrast with the typical cybersquatter, the clickfarmer does *register* and *use* a domain name as contemplated by the ACPA.[34] The trademark protections in the ACPA only require the plaintiff to show that the defendant registered, trafficked in or used the relevant domain name for a bad faith profit purpose.[35] A clickfarmer that uses trademarks in its domain names is clearly registering and using those marks with a profit motive.

For a successful action, the plaintiff must also establish that the defendant's domain name is identical or confusingly similar to a distinctive or famous mark, or dilutive of a famous mark.[36] Thus, as with infringement and dilution actions, typosquatting for the purposes of a clickfarm would also be covered here. If the clickfarmer has registered a deliberate misspelling of a mark for her clickfarm, the ACPA would reach this conduct provided that the domain name is sufficiently similar to the mark in question.

6.2.3.2 Personal names

Domain names corresponding with nontrademarked personal names will not be covered by the trademark protections in the ACPA. Nontrademarked personal names will also not be covered by trademark infringement or dilution actions.[37] The question thus arises as to whether the one federal statutory provision that protects personal names against cybersquatters may apply to clickfarmers. 15 U.S.C. § 8131(1)(A) provides that:

> Any person who registers a domain name that consists of the name of another living person, or a name substantially and confusingly similar thereto, without that person's consent, with the specific intent to profit from such name by selling the domain name for financial gain to that person or any third party, shall be liable in a civil action by such person.

---

34 15 U.S.C. § 1125(d)(1)(A).

35 *Id.*

36 15 U.S.C. § 1125(d)(1)(A)(ii)(I), (II).

37 ANNE GILSON LALONDE AND JEROME GILSON, TRADEMARK PROTECTION AND PRACTICE para. 2.03[4][d] ('Just as with descriptive terms, a trademark or trade name that consists of a personal name (first name, surname, or both) is entitled to legal protection only if it attains secondary meaning.').

Unlike the provisions of the ACPA, the personal name cyberpiracy law requires a bad faith intent to *sell* the domain name. Many clickfarmers are not in the business of selling the names. They would prefer to earn money from operating the clickfarm under the name. There may be situations in which a domain name registrant has a dual purpose and may operate a clickfarm with the hope that she could later sell the name. If she does then attempt to sell the name, § 8131(1)(A) may come into play.

6.2.4 State Cybersquatting Laws

Some state laws may have a bearing on conduct involving unauthorized use of trademarks and personal names in the domain space. They include the right of publicity, which is a combination of state legislation and common law, as well as *sui generis* legislation that includes provisions of California's Business and Professions Code,[38] as well as California's Political Cyberfraud Abatement Act (PCAA).[39]

The right of publicity prohibits making an unauthorized commercial profit from the use of someone else's name or likeness.[40] Thus, if a click-farmer was to register another person's name as a domain name to attract custom for a clickfarm the conduct could presumably run afoul of the right of publicity in jurisdictions where it is available. Of course, this action is a creature of disharmonized state law and it raises significant time, cost and jurisdictional challenges for individual litigants, particularly where the parties are located in different jurisdictions. It may not be a particularly practical avenue for individuals concerned about unauthorized use of their names in domain names associated with clickfarms.

Sections 17525–17526 of California's Business and Professions Code also have some bearing on domain name conflicts involving personal names. Section 17525(a) provides that:

> It is unlawful for a person, with a bad faith intent to register, traffic in, or use a domain name, that is identical or confusingly similar to the personal name of another living person or deceased personality, without regard to the goods or services of the parties.

The structure of the anti-cybersquatting provisions of the Code are more like the trademark focused provisions in § 1125(d) of the ACPA than the personal name provisions of § 8131(1)(A). The main prohibition in the

---

38 California Business and Professions Code, §§ 17525–17526.

39 California Elections Code, § 18320.

40 GILSON, *supra* note 37, para. 2B.01.

Code is on bad faith conduct relating to the registration, trafficking or use of a domain name.[41] That provision is followed by a nonexclusive list of bad faith factors that a court may consider in determining a defendant's liability.[42] Most of the bad faith factors set out in the Code are not directly applicable to clickfarming.[43] The factor most relevant to clickfarming is found in § 17526(e). It allows the court to consider:

> The intent of a person . . . to divert consumers from the person's or deceased personality's name [*sic*] online location to a site accessible under the domain name that could harm the goodwill represented by the person's or deceased personality's name either for commercial gain or with the intent to tarnish or disparage the person's or deceased personality's name by creating a likelihood of confusion as to the source, sponsorship, affiliation, or endorsement of the site.

This looks like a combination of the policies underlying trademark infringement and dilution, but applied here to personal names. A click-farmer might be liable under this provision if she has (a) confused an Internet user about an association between the plaintiff and the clickfarm, or (b) tarnished the plaintiff's name. Confusion may arise if the clickfarm contains advertisements relating to people or products that Internet users might believe to have some association with the plaintiff. An example might arise if a clickfarmer registered a domain name like 'davidbeckham.org' and used it for a clickfarm for products relating to soccer. It is also arguable that even a clickfarm relating to nonsoccer-related products under a name like 'davidbeckham.org' may cause consumer confusion if Internet users are led to believe that the well-known soccer player, David Beckham, has endorsed those products. Thus, using 'davidbeckham.org' for a clickfarm with advertisements for random products or services might satisfy the consumer confusion requirements of the Code.

The tarnishment requirement of the Code may be more difficult to satisfy with respect to a clickfarm unless the clickfarm contains advertisements for products or services that may be demeaning to the plaintiff in some way. For example, if a clickfarmer registered 'davidbeckham.org' for a clickfarm that contained advertisements for pornography, that might be an example of a situation where David Beckham's name is disparaged in the tarnishment sense. It is also worth remembering that the bad faith factors in the Code are not intended as an exclusive list,

---

41 Cal. Business and Professions Code, § 17525(a).

42 *Id.* § 17526.

43 See discussion at 1.6.1, *supra.*

so the mere fact of running a clickfarm in association with a website relating to a person's name, without that person's authorization, may in itself satisfy a court of bad faith conduct. Of course, the Code is Californian state law. Its provisions will be available only in very limited circumstances where a plaintiff can satisfy a court of a sufficient connection with California.

The PCAA prohibits engaging in acts of 'political cyberfraud'. This term is defined to include an act concerning a political website: 'that is committed with the intent to deny a person access to a political Web site, deny a person the opportunity to register a domain name for a political Web site, or cause a person reasonably to believe that a political Web site has been posted by a person other than the person who posted the Web site'.[44] 'Political website' is defined as 'a Web site that urges or appears to urge the support or opposition of a ballot measure'.[45] The PCAA gives further guidance on the nature of 'political cyberfraud' in terms that contemplate:

(a) intentionally diverting or redirecting access to a political website to another person's website by the use of a similar domain name, meta-tags or other electronic measures;[46]
(b) intentionally preventing or denying exit from a political website by the use of frames, hyperlinks, mousetrapping, popup screens or other electronic measures;[47]
(c) registering a domain name that is similar to another domain name for a political website;[48] and,
(d) intentionally preventing the use of a domain name for a political website by registering and holding the domain name or by reselling it to another with the intent of preventing its use, or both.[49]

This legislation may be relevant to a small category of clickfarms that utilize political names as domain names. In this context, the legislation would cover uses of politicians' names and names of political organizations. Clickfarmers who utilize such terms as domain names and thereby deny politicians and political organizations access to the names, particularly in the electoral context, might run afoul of this legislation. However,

---

44 *See* Cal. Elections Code, § 18320(b), (c)(1).
45 Cal. Elections Code, § 18320(b), (c)(3).
46 *Id.* at § 18320(c)(1)(A).
47 *Id.* at § 18320(c)(1)(B).
48 *Id.* at § 18320(c)(1)(C).
49 *Id.* at § 18320(c)(1)(D).

as with the Business and Professions Code, this legislation is only available in California so has very limited jurisdictional reach.

6.2.5 Uniform Domain Name Dispute Resolution Policy

Unlike the federal and state laws discussed above, the UDRP is a private contractual online dispute resolution procedure. It is incorporated by reference into registration agreements for domain names ending in '.com', '.net' and '.org', amongst others.[50] It requires the registrant to submit to a mandatory arbitration proceeding if a trademark holder lodges a complaint about registration or use of a domain name. The UDRP has a variety of advantages over trademark-based litigation in terms of time, cost and jurisdictional scope.[51] Remedies under the UDRP are limited to transfer or cancellation orders.[52]

The UDRP was not drafted with clickfarming in mind. Its aim was to provide an efficient and inexpensive solution for cybersquatting problems that began to arise in the mid-to-late 1990s.[53] Nevertheless, clickfarming may be covered under the terms of the UDRP as currently drafted. A UDRP complainant must establish (i) that the registrant's domain name is identical or confusingly similar to the complainant's trademark or service mark;[54] (ii) that the registrant has no rights or legitimate interests in the domain name;[55] and (iii) that the domain name has been registered and is being used in bad faith.[56]

The complainant must have a trademark to support a UDRP action. However, there is no requirement that the mark be particularly distinctive or famous, nor that it be registered.[57] Thus, many personal names and

---

[50] See UDRP, Note 2, available at www.icann.org/en/udrp/udrp-policy-24 oct99.htm, last accessed July 24, 2009.

[51] Jacqueline Lipton, *Celebrity in Cyberspace: A Personality Rights Paradigm for Personal Domain Name Disputes*, 65 Washington and Lee L. Rev. 1445, 1448–9 (2008).

[52] UDRP, para 4(i) ('The remedies available to a complainant pursuant to any proceeding before an Administrative Panel shall be limited to requiring the cancellation of your domain name or the transfer of your domain name registration to the complainant.').

[53] See 1.4.1, *supra*.

[54] UDRP, para. 4(a)(i).

[55] *Id.* para. 4(a)(ii).

[56] *Id.* para. 4(a)(iii).

[57] *Bruce Springsteen v Jeff Burgar and Bruce Springsteen Club*, WIPO Arbitration and Mediation Center, Case No. D2000–1532 (January 25, 2001), para. 6 available at www.wipo.int/amc/en/domains/decisions/html/2000/d2000-1532.html, last accessed March 2, 2009 ('It appears to be an established

generic terms will be covered by the UDRP if they have acquired secondary meaning. Like the ACPA, the UDRP is premised on bad faith conduct in the domain space.[58] Thus, to the extent that clickfarming is automatically presumed to be in bad faith, this presumption would support a UDRP action in cases where the clickfarmer is making unauthorized use of a trademark or a deliberate misspelling of a trademark.[59]

The UDRP's conception of bad faith includes circumstances indicating that (i) the registrant has acquired a domain name primarily for the purpose of transferring it to the complainant for a profit;[60] (ii) the registrant has registered the name in order to prevent the trademark holder from reflecting the mark in a corresponding domain name where the registrant has engaged in a pattern of such conduct;[61] (iii) the registrant has registered the name primarily to disrupt the business of a competitor;[62] and (iv) the registrant has used the domain name to attract Internet custom for commercial gain by creating a likelihood of confusion with the complainant's mark.[63] Of these factors, probably factor (iv) is the most directly relevant to clickfarming. A clickfarmer will generally use a domain name to attract custom to its website for commercial gain by attracting customers presumably seeking the trademark holder's products or services. The elements the complainant has to establish here resemble those necessary to support a trademark infringement action.[64]

As with trademark infringement, there may be an open question as to whether a clickfarm that contains advertisements unrelated to the complainant's products or services would be causing the requisite kind of consumer confusion. Even in the case of products or services advertised on a clickfarm that are in similar markets to those of the complainant, there may be an open question as to whether consumer confusion is present. This is really an initial interest confusion issue. If Internet users are not confused at the time they purchase an online product or service, but were

---

principle from cases such as Jeanette Winterson, Julia Roberts, and Sade that in the case of very well known celebrities, their names can acquire a distinctive secondary meaning giving rise to rights equating to unregistered trade marks, notwithstanding the non-registerability of the name itself.').

58 UDRP, para. 4(a)(iii), (b).

59 The UDRP would cover deliberate misspellings because it provides relief where a registrant uses a domain name that is identical *or confusingly similar to* a trademark: UDRP, para. 4(a)(i).

60 *Id.* para. 4(b)(i).

61 *Id.* para. 4(b)(ii).

62 *Id.* para. 4(b)(iii).

63 *Id.* para. 4(b)(iv).

64 See 6.2.1, *supra*.

initially confused by the misleading domain name, it is not immediately clear whether this should amount to consumer confusion for trademark infringement or UDRP purposes. To date, courts have been relatively sympathetic to plaintiffs running initial interest confusion arguments in infringement actions involving online conduct.[65] However, commentators and some judges have begun to raise concerns that initial interest confusion should not be applied too broadly for fear of chilling online commerce and competition.[66] UDRP arbitrators are not bound by judicial precedents on this issue, but they may find judicial determinations of the boundaries of online consumer confusion persuasive in applying the bad faith factors of the UDRP.

6.3 TYPOSQUATTING

6.3.1 Trademark Infringement

As with clickfarming, typosquatting is conduct that may relatively readily be presumed to be in bad faith in most cases.[67] It generally arises when a domain name registrant registers a name that is a common misspelling of a trademark or personal name in order to attract custom to her website.[68] Of course, the content of the website may vary from typosquatter to typosquatter. Some registrants may be using the name to attempt to extort money from the trademark holder for transfer of the name. Others may be using the name for a gripe site or parody site about the trademark holder. Nevertheless, the typical case involves an attempt to attract Internet custom to a website for commercial purposes by taking advantage of Internet users who accidentally misspell the trademark holder's name in a URL search or into a search engine.[69]

To the extent that making unauthorized commercial use of a domain name corresponding with another person's trademark might be regarded as trademark infringement,[70] the same would be true for a common misspelling of the mark. Trademark infringement actions require consumer confusion and, in most typosquatting cases, consumers would be confused by a typosquatter's use of a domain name that is confusingly similar to

---

65 Goldman, *supra* note 12, at 559.
66 *Id.*; *Playboy v Netscape*, 354 F.3d 1020, 1035 (2004) (*supra* note 16).
67 See, for example, discussion in LINDSAY, *supra* note 2, at 259–60.
68 *Id.*
69 *Id.*
70 See 6.2.1, *supra*.

the mark,[71] provided that the other elements of the infringement action are satisfied.[72] There may be no infringement in cases where a deliberate misspelling of a mark is used in a domain name for purely expressive purposes, rather than commercial purposes. Thus, if a typosquatter was using a deliberate misspelling of a mark in a domain name for a gripe site about the trademark holder, this may not amount to infringement provided there is no commercial activity on the associated website.

6.3.2 Trademark Dilution

Even though the dilution action does not require consumer confusion, there may be circumstances in which the deliberate misspelling of a trademark in a domain name for commercial purposes might amount to trademark dilution. The prerequisite for a dilution action is that the trademark holder owns a 'famous mark' as defined in the Lanham Act.[73] Assuming the mark is sufficiently famous and the defendant is making an unauthorized use of a misspelling of the mark in its domain name, it is possible that the defendant has engaged in dilution by blurring. The Lanham Act defines dilution by blurring as 'association arising from the similarity between a mark or trade name and a famous mark that impairs the distinctiveness of the famous mark'.[74] If the domain name is sufficiently similar in its spelling to the famous mark, blurring may be established. So again, this will be a question of how close the misspelling is to the spelling of the original mark.

Dilution by tarnishment is less likely in a typosquatting case unless the material on the associated website might in some way tarnish the trademark holder's reputation. Thus, for example, a typosquatter using a domain name for a clickfarm containing advertisements for pornographic products and services might run into tarnishment issues. Deliberate misspellings of a mark are likely covered by tarnishment because the Lanham Act definition of tarnishment describes tarnsihment as 'association arising from the similarity between a mark or trade name and a famous mark that

---

[71] LINDSAY, *supra* note 2, at 259 (noting that in ACPA cases, courts have held deliberate misspellings of trademarks to be 'confusingly similar' to the marks for the purposes of ACPA infringement).

[72] *Planned Parenthood Federation of America Inc. v Bucci*, 42 U.S.P.Q.2d 1430, 1434 (S.D.N.Y. 1997) (holding that Internet users constitute a national, if not international, audience who must use interstate telephone lines to access the Internet, and the nature of the Internet itself satisfies the in commerce requirement).

[73] 15 U.S.C. §1125(c)(2)(A).

[74] 15 U.S.C. § 1125(c)(2)(B).

harms the reputation of the famous mark'.[75] Provided the misspelling of the famous mark is sufficiently *similar* to the mark, and that the domain name could properly be described as a 'mark or trade name' in the hands of the typosquatter, a tarnishment action would be possible where the domain name is used in a way that harms the reputation of the plaintiff's mark. Again, the mark must be used by the defendant in commerce to support a tarnishment action.[76] Thus, a purely expressive use of the misspelling in the domain space would not likely amount to tarnishment. A gripe site or parody site would be an obvious example here.

6.3.3 Anti-Cybersquatting Consumer Protection Act

6.3.3.1 Trademarks

As noted above, the ACPA provisions relating to trademarks are premised more expressly on notions of bad faith than the infringement and dilution provisions. The ACPA creates civil liability for a person who 'registers, traffics in or uses a domain name', with a bad faith profit motive, where the domain name is identical or confusingly similar to a distinctive or a famous mark, or where the domain name is dilutive of a famous mark.[77] The legislation includes a list of bad faith factors that courts may consider in determining whether the defendant has infringed the legislation.[78] Because of the joint requirements of bad faith and the use of a domain name that is identical *or confusingly similar* to a mark, the section would seem well suited to typosquatting cases. As the ACPA does not require an intent to *sell* the name for a profit,[79] it will likely apply to typosquatting where the defendant's intent is to use the domain name for any commercial purpose, regardless of an intent to sell.

While there is no requirement that the plaintiff establish any particular bad faith factor set out in § 1125(d)(1)(B)(i), as the factors are nonexclusive, subparagraph 1125(d)(1)(B)(i)(V) may be particularly relevant to typical typosquatting situations. It sets out as a bad faith factor 'the [registrant's]

---

[75] 15 U.S.C. § 1125(c)(2)(C).
[76] 15 U.S.C. § 1125(c)(1).
[77] 15 U.S.C. § 1125(d)(1)(A).
[78] 15 U.S.C. § 1125(d)(1)(B)(i).
[79] However, an intent to sell is listed as one of the bad faith factors a court may consider for the purposes of a determination of infringement of § 1125(d)(1)(A). See 15 U.S.C. § 1125(d)(1)(B)(i)(VI) (a court may consider 'the [registrant's] offer to transfer, sell, or otherwise assign the domain name to the mark owner or any third party for financial gain without having used, or having an intent to use, the domain name in the bona fide offering of any goods or services, or the person's prior conduct indicating a pattern of such conduct.').

intent to divert consumers from the mark owner's online location to a site accessible under the domain name that could harm the goodwill represented by the mark, either for commercial gain or with the intent to tarnish or disparage the mark, by creating a likelihood of confusion as to the source, sponsorship, affiliation, or endorsement of the site'. The drafting conflates elements typically associated with dilution by tarnishment with elements typically associated with trademark infringement by marrying consumer confusion to tarnishment within the same provision. However, this drafting irregularity is not particularly important in the typosquatting situation provided that the plaintiff can establish a use in commerce and consumer confusion by the defendant. Most typosquatting cases will lend themselves to this kind of analysis by definition.[80]

6.3.3.2 Personal names

With respect to personal names, 15 U.S.C. § 8131 will have little application to cases involving intentional misspellings of names in domain names in order to attract custom to associated websites. As noted above, this provision specifically protects personal names against cybersquatting, but only in situations where the cybersquatter is attempting to sell the name in bad faith. The provision will have no application where the domain name registrant is using the name for some other unauthorized commercial purpose, such as a clickfarm. While § 8131(1)(A) does effectively contemplate actions against people who register deliberate misspellings of personal names as domain names,[81] it will only apply to typosquatters who attempt to sell the domain names for a profit, not those who intend to use the names for their own commercial purposes.

6.3.4 State Cybersquatting Laws

The most obvious state laws that may apply to typosquatting involving trademarks or personal names are the right of publicity tort as well as some *sui generis* Californian laws: relevant provisions of the Business and

---

[80] See, for example, *Shields v Zuccarini*, 254 F.3d 476, 483 (3d Cir. 2001) in which the court held that the defendant's use of a domain name that was an intentional misspelling of the plaintiff's mark would be 'confusingly similar' to the misspelled mark for ACPA purposes.

[81] 15 U.S.C. § 8131(1)(A) ('Any person who registers a domain name that consists of the name of another living person, *or a name substantially and confusingly similar thereto*, without that person's consent, with the specific intent to profit from such name by selling the domain name for financial gain to that person or any third party, shall be liable in a civil action by such person.') (emphasis added).

Professions Code[82] and the PCAA.[83] As the right of publicity relates to unauthorized commercial uses of a personal name, it would at first glance appear to be applicable to typosquatting involving an individual's name. However, the availability of the tort in any given state will depend on the way the tort is structured within that state. For example, most state right of publicity statutes only contemplate unauthorized commercial use of a person's name, voice, signature, image, etc.[84] There is no express provision for the unauthorized use of a *misspelling* of the name that may be confusingly similar to the name. Thus, typosquatting cases involving personal names may fall through the cracks of the legislation in these states.

The anti-cybersquatting provisions of California's Business and Professions Code provide an alternative for personal name complainants, but only if they can prove a sufficient nexus with California. As noted above, § 17525(a) states that 'It is unlawful for a person, with a bad faith intent to register, traffic in, or use a domain name, that is identical or confusingly similar to the personal name of another living person or deceased personality, without regard to the goods or services of the parties'. Unlike many right of publicity statutes, the Code contemplates unauthorized bad faith use of a domain name that is *confusingly similar* to a personal name. Thus, the Code would cover typosquatting on a personal name, while California's right of publicity statute would be limited to unauthorized commercial use of the name itself.

The Code requires bad faith as a constituent element,[85] and contains a nonexclusive list of bad faith factors.[86] If we assume that most typosquatting, at least commercially motivated typosquatting, is presumptively in bad faith, this will not be a difficult element to satisfy. Additionally, two of the bad faith factors in the Code may be particularly relevant to typosquatting in circumstances where the domain name registrant is either (a) attempting to use a deliberate misspelling of the name to divert commercial custom to its own website;[87] or (b) is attempting to sell the domain name for a profit.[88] Of course, where a typosquatter is not utilizing the domain name for a commercial purpose, but is using it purely expressively

---

82 Cal. Business and Professions Code, §§ 17525–17526.

83 Cal. Elections Code, § 18320.

84 See, for example, N.Y. C.L.S Civ. R. § 50 (criminal right of publicity law), § 51 (civil right of publicity action) (2000).

85 Cal. Business and Professions Code, § 17525(a).

86 *Id.* § 17526.

87 *Id.* § 17526(e).

88 *Id.* § 17526(f).

as in the context of a gripe site, she is unlikely to have infringed the Code's anti-cybersquatting provisions.

California's PCAA, on the other hand, may prohibit some purely expressive uses of deliberate misspellings of names and marks in the political context. As we have seen previously,[89] the PCAA prohibits engaging in acts of 'political cyberfraud' defined in terms of denying a person 'access to a political Web site, deny[ing] a person the opportunity to register a domain name for a political Web site, or caus[ing] a person reasonably to believe that a political Web site has been posted by a person other than the person who posted the Web site'.[90] 'Political website' is defined as 'a Web site that urges or appears to urge the support or opposition of a ballot measure'.[91]

Further indications of political cyberfraud include (a) intentionally diverting or redirecting access to a political website to another person's website by the use of a similar domain name, meta-tags or other electronic measures;[92] (b) registering a domain name that is similar to another domain name for a political website;[93] and (c) intentionally preventing the use of a domain name for a political website by registering and holding the domain name or by reselling it to another with the intent of preventing its use, or both.[94]

At least two of these provisions contemplate the registration of a name that is similar to that of a political candidate, organization or ballot measure.[95] Presumably, this would cover registering deliberate misspellings of such words and phrases for the proscribed purposes. It is less clear whether the third provision would apply to typosquatting. It contemplates preventing a rightful owner from using a political domain name by registering it and either holding or reselling it.[96] It does not specifically contemplate typosquatting. The only way typosquatting would be covered would be by adopting a presumption of a default right in, say, a politician or political organization with respect to a domain name containing a deliberate misspelling of the person's or organization's name or mark. It is not likely to be the case that Internet users would assume all variations of a politician's or political organization's name in the domain space, including deliberate

---

89 See, for example, discussion at 6.2.4, *supra*.
90 *See* Cal. Elections Code, § 18320(b), (c)(1).
91 *Id.* § 18320(b), (c)(3).
92 *Id.* § 18320(c)(1)(A).
93 *Id.* § 18320(c)(1)(C).
94 *Id.* § 18320(c)(1)(D).
95 *Id.* § 18320(c)(1)(A), (C).
96 *Id.* § 18320(c)(1)(D).

misspellings, automatically belong to the politician or political organization.

In any event, assuming that much typosquatting is for commercial, rather than political, purposes, this particular provision of the PCAA may have limited application. Where a typosquatter is using a deliberate misspelling of a political name in the domain space for, say, a clickfarm or other commercial enterprise unassociated with the political entity in question, she is unlikely to be regarded as 'intentionally preventing the use of the domain name for a political Web site'.[97] In other words, if the typosquatter's motives are not to prevent political speech, but rather to make commercial profit, there would be an argument that her motives do not satisfy the intent requirements of the PCAA. Of course, a complainant may prove a dual intent on the part of the typosquatter, and a PCAA infringement may be found on the basis of the political intent. That determination would have to be made on a case-by-case basis by a court with appropriate jurisdiction.

6.3.5 Uniform Domain Name Dispute Resolution Policy

The UDRP is a private contractual online dispute resolution procedure incorporated by reference into registration agreements for domain names ending in '.com', '.net' and '.org', amongst others.[98] It imposes a mandatory arbitration proceeding on the registrant if a trademark holder lodges a complaint about registration or use of the domain name. The UDRP has a variety of advantages over trademark-based litigation in terms of time, cost and jurisdictional scope.[99] As previously stated, remedies under the UDRP are limited to transfer or cancellation orders.[100] A UDRP complainant must establish (i) that the registrant's domain name is identical or confusingly similar to the complainant's trademark or service mark;[101] (ii) that the registrant has no rights or legitimate interests in the domain name;[102] and (iii) that the domain name has been registered and is being used in bad faith.[103]

UDRP panels have historically been prepared to grant relief in

[97] *Id.*

[98] UDRP, Note 2, available at www.icann.org/en/udrp/udrp-policy-24oct99.htm, last accessed July 24, 2009.

[99] Lipton, *Celebrity in Cyberspace*, *supra* note 51, at 1448–9.

[100] UDRP, para. 4(i).

[101] *Id.* para 4(a)(i).

[102] *Id.* para 4(a)(ii).

[103] *Id.* para 4(a)(iii).

typosquatting cases.[104] UDRP panelists have regarded deliberate misspellings of famous marks in the domain space as satisfying the 'confusing similarity' requirements of the UDRP.[105] Thus, provided that a complainant can satisfy the other requirements of a complaint (bad faith conduct on the part of the registrant and lack of legitimate interest defense) a transfer or cancellation order should be forthcoming. In typical typosquatting scenarios where a domain name registrant is purposely using a deliberate misspelling of a complainant's mark in order to either attract customers or to force a sale of the name, bad faith has been relatively readily inferred by UDRP arbitrators.[106]

6.4 EMERGING ISSUES

Previous chapters examined the introduction of new gTLDs by ICANN and the introduction of personalized usernames by Facebook as issues meriting further consideration in the context of balancing trademark, personal name, privacy, speech and other interests online.[107] Those new developments are less relevant to the clickfarming and typosquatting conduct discussed in this chapter. While applicants seeking to register a new gTLD under ICANN's new application procedure may well come up with a gTLD that is a deliberate misspelling of someone's trademark or famous personal name, hopefully ICANN's processes will be tailored to catch this kind of conduct at the application stage.

Even if a new gTLD is accepted that is a deliberate misspelling of, say, a famous mark, it may not cause the same problems in practice as typosquatting in the '.com' space, assuming, of course, that customers will still perceive the '.com' space as the prime online real estate for commercial activities. This has certainly been the experience when new gTLDs have

---

104 Lindsay, *supra* note 2, at 259–61.

105 UDRP, para. 4(a)(i); see also *Marriott International v Seocho*, NAF Case No. FA149187 (April 28, 2003) ('Respondent's efforts constitute "typosquatting", whereby a registrant deliberately introduces slight deviations into famous marks in order to commercially benefit. Respondent's typosquatting, by its definition, renders the domain name confusingly similar to the complainant's mark.').

106 Lindsay, *supra* note 2, at 362 (noting that evidence of typosquatting is a common circumstance that results in findings of 'bad faith' in UDRP arbitrations); 380 ('In *Wal-Mart Stores, Inc. v Longo*, for example, the combination of typosquatting, the fame of the complainant's mark and an offer of sale indicated that the "www-wal-mart.com" domain was registered and was being used in bad faith.').

107 See 2.6, 3.6, 4.6 and 5.4, *supra*.

been introduced in the past. Thus, the acceptance by ICANN of a '.nkie' new gTLD may not cause the Nike Corporation much concern in practice. Likewise, the acceptance of a '.macdonalds' gTLD may not cause the senior management of the McDonalds fast food franchise to lose too much sleep.

Clickfarming issues are unlikely to raise any particularly different issues under new gTLDs as they currently do under existing gTLDs. Of course, for new gTLDs that adopt different dispute resolution procedures to the UDRP, complainants would have to proceed under those mechanisms rather than the UDRP. It remains to be seen what kinds of dispute resolution procedures will be established for new gTLDs. Other protective measures could include defensive registration procedures[108] and domain name registration watch services.[109] Additionally, trademark holders may be given early registration privileges in certain new gTLDs, as has been the case in the past with the introduction of gTLDs like '.eu'.[110]

Presumably it would be difficult to typosquat on a personalized Facebook username, provided that Facebook is vigilant about responding to complaints by trademark holders under its current online procedure.[111] Personal name typosquatting in Facebook may be more problematic. However, it is difficult to see why anyone would want to engage in such conduct on Facebook, at least with respect to traditional typosquatting which tends to involve a commercial motive. Facebook usernames are nontransferable[112] so a typosquatter would not be able to profit from offering to sell the name to a rightful owner.

Typosquatters are unlikely to be able to make any other kinds of commercial profits from Facebook pages because it is a predominantly social networking service and is not traditionally used for commercial

---

108 See, for example, discussion in Lipton, *Beyond Cybersquatting*, *supra* note 9, at 1438.

109 *Id.*

110 See, for example, .eu registrar, *EU Domain Names*, available at www.africaregistry.com/domain-names/europe/eu-domain-registration.html, last accessed July 24, 2009 ('The Sunrise period allows those with specific rights to a given Domain Name to obtain a name that *exactly* matches their trademark or company name before the Registry opens up for *all* applications.')

111 See Facebook's Username Infringement Form, available at www.facebook.com/help/contact.php?show_form=username_infringement, last accessed July 24, 2009.

112 Facebook, Usernames: General Information, available at www.facebook.com/help/search.php?hq=usernames&ref=hq, last accessed July 24, 2009 (noting that Facebook usernames are not transferable to other accounts).

activities.[113] Likewise, it is difficult to conceive of a clickfarmer being able to make use of a personalized Facebook URL. For one thing, a clickfarmer who cannot establish an intellectual property right in a relevant username is unlikely to be able to secure registration and, if registration is secured, it may easily be lost on the receipt by Facebook of a complaint by a trademark holder.[114] In any event, Facebook pages do not lend themselves to clickfarming. Their purpose is social and they are not technologically set up or formatted to accommodate click farms.

6.5 THE BOUNDARIES OF BAD FAITH IN THE DOMAIN SPACE

One question worth considering before concluding the discussion of clickfarming and typosquatting is whether these activities illuminate our thinking about the concept of bad faith in the domain space more generally. Most of the regulations aimed specifically at regulating conduct in the domain space were adopted with reference to cybersquatting which, in the mid-to-late 1990s, was the paradigmatic example of bad faith conduct involving domain names. At the time the UDRP and the ACPA were adopted, no one was thinking about the future of the domain space, or about developing a concept of bad faith that would apply readily to new online situations.

The question for today is how to determine the boundaries of bad faith conduct in the face of new practices involving unauthorized commercial uses of trademarks in various domain spaces. The most obvious examples of potentially bad faith conduct today are the iterations of clickfarming and typosquatting described above. Again, that is not to say that all clickfarms are in bad faith. Some may use generic words and phrases rather than trademarks and thus not infringe anyone's rights. Some typosquatting also may be for expressive rather than commercial purposes, and so may, in that sense, not be in bad faith. So the question is whether anything

---

[113] At the time of writing, businesses like Pepsi, Coca-Cola and McDonalds had Facebook pages, although other well-known businesses like Nike, Burger King and the Disney Corporation did not have a Facebook presence.

[114] Although Facebook's intellectual property rights infringement forms seems only to contemplate protecting registered trademark holders: See Facebook's Username Infringement Form, available at www.facebook.com/help/contact.php?show_form=username_infringement, last accessed July 24, 2009. It is not clear whether an unregistered trademark holder would be protected uner Facebook's current policies and procedures.

can be gleaned from this chapter that in some sense provides greater guidance as to how the regulation of the domain space should proceed in the face of these new classes of conduct that typically, but not always, involve bad faith.

This issue is further complicated by the fact that conduct such as clickfarming, typosquatting and cybersquatting can occur simultaneously or separately, depending on the circumstances. It is possible to register a deliberately misspelled trademark as a domain name with an intent to sell it to the highest bidder. One might even operate a clickfarm from it in the meantime. Thus, it is not always possible in practice to distinguish a cybersquatting case from a clickfarming case or a typosquatting case. However, it is useful to consider these three practices separately in an attempt to determine the extent to which they may involve bad faith practices that should be regulated by legislation or private arbitration mechanisms such as the UDRP.

It may be useful to think about these classes of conduct in the context of the relationship between the domain name chosen by a registrant and the registrant's motivations for registering the name. This could be represented in tabular form as set out in Table 6.1. In Table 6.1, the columns represent the potential motivations of a domain name registrant, while the rows represent the kinds of domain names that might be registered.

Looking at where regulations currently apply, it seems fairly clear that expressive use for the most part is not proscribed conduct in most situations. This is an appropriate outcome if we assume that Internet policy should facilitate the development of the Internet as an unparalleled global communications medium. What is more problematic is delineating a clear set of guidelines from situations where a registrant registers different categories of domain names for either sale or clickfarming purposes. These situations are currently subject to a disharmonized and somewhat unprincipled set of regulations. So far this discussion has predominantly focused only on American law and the UDRP. The regulatory framework likely becomes even more complex when other countries' laws are added to the mix.

It does appear to be the case that most typosquatting conduct is potentially regulated as bad faith conduct under existing cybersquatting regulations, provided that the registrant's purpose is not predominantly expressive (see the last two rows of Table 6.1). Additionally, most clickfarming conduct seems to be subject to regulation as potentially bad faith conduct, provided that it does not involve generic words or phrases (see column 2 in Table 6.1). Likewise, cybersquatting is generally proscribed, again provided that it does not use a generic word or phrase (see column 1 in Table 6.1). This is not surprising, given that the purpose of the existing

Table 6.1 Relationship between registrant's motivations and categories of domain name registered

	Sale motive	*Clickfarming motive*	*Expressive use*
Trademarks	Traditional cybersquatting	Potentially cybersquatting	Usually legitimate, particularly if the registrant does not use the '.com' version of the name
Personal names	Traditional cybersquatting (if name is trademarked) and 15 U.S.C. § 8131(1)(A) liability (regardless of trademark)	Potentially cybersquatting (if name is trademarked); little recourse if no trademark	Usually legitimate use, particularly if registrant does not use '.com' version of trademarked personal name
Generic words and phrases	Presumptively legitimate use	Presumptively legitimate use	Presumptively legitimate use
Deliberate misspellings of trademarks	Cybersquatting	Potentially cybersquatting	Presumptively legitimate use
Deliberate misspellings of personal names	Cybersquatting (if name is trademarked); and 15 U.S.C. § 8131(1)(A) regardless of trademark	Potentially cybersquatting (if name is trademarked); little recourse if no trademark	Presumptively legitimate use

cybersquatting regulations was to protect trademark owners against cybersquatters. No one seems to have objected to the development of a robust market in domain names that do not infringe others' trademark rights.[115]

From Table 6.1, it is arguably possible to discern a general guideline that cybersquatting and clickfarming are bad faith conduct that is appro-

[115] See, for example, DAVID KESMODEL, THE DOMAIN GAME: HOW PEOPLE GET RICH FROM INTERNET DOMAIN NAMES 193 (2008) (table of 25 largest reported sales of domain names as at the end of 2007 which includes mostly generic terms).

priately subject to regulation, except where generic nontrademarked words and phrases are concerned. Additionally, a rule might be accepted that typosquatting should generally be proscribed unless the registrant's purpose is purely expressive. This does leave difficult cases where, say, a typosquatter's purpose is both expressive and commercial as, for example, where a typosquatter uses clickthrough advertisements to gain some revenue from a site intended predominantly as a gripe site or parody site. These situations may need to be determined on a case-by-case basis with judges and arbitrators considering the significance of the commercial activity to the overall endeavor of the registrant. However, at least the development of these relatively simple guidelines gives judges and arbitrators a starting point. The guidelines drawn largely from current practice might ultimately lead to some streamlining of laws and policies relating to domain name regulation. They might prove particularly useful if some of the suggestions in previous chapters are ever developed by domestic courts and legislatures or by ICANN. In other words, if greater protections are ever adopted for personal names, political, cultural or geographic indicators in the domain space, the above guidelines might help to determine the boundaries of bad faith in situations involving those kinds of words and phrases.

6.6 CHAPTER SUMMARY

This chapter has identified and examined conduct typically described as bad faith registration and use of domain names, with particular emphasis on clickfarming and typosquatting. It has considered the application of current regulations to situations involving both clickfarming and typosquatting on trademarks and personal names in the domain space. It has also considered whether this discussion can illuminate anything more generally about the concept of bad faith in the domain space. In particular, the chapter has addressed the following.

(1) The nature of conduct typically described as clickfarming and cybersquatting.

(2) The application of existing trademark and cybersquatting regulations to clickfarming involving uses of trademarks and personal names.

(3) The application of existing trademark and cybersquatting regulations to typosquatting conduct involving deliberate misspellings of trademarks and personal names.

(4) The impact of the development of new gTLDs by ICANN and new personalized usernames by Facebook on the regulation of clickfarming and typosquatting.

(5) The question whether an examination of the regulation of click-farming, typosquatting and cybersquatting conduct more generally might illuminate concepts of bad faith in the domain space and whether more general principles for future domain name regulation may be developed on the basis of this discussion.

The following chapter considers whether it is now necessary to develop theories for domain name regulation outside of traditional trademark laws to cover conduct that ought to be proscribed in the domain space. The discussion is based on taking a bottom up look at existing domain name regulations, arbitrations and cases, and drawing from a mixture of trademark policy, property and restitution theory.

7. Domain name theory

7.1 THEORIES OF DOMAIN NAME REGULATION

Previous chapters have examined the existing regulatory matrix for domain name disputes, which is focused largely on the protection of trademarks and some other interests (such as personal names) in the domain space. It has become apparent that there are limitations within the current regulations both in terms of scope and in terms of focus. While the regulations have focused predominantly on trademarks, little thought has been given to the protection of other competing interests in the domain space, such as free speech and other cultural and geographic interests in particular words and phrases.

There are other limitations inherent in current domain name regulations, several of which are beyond the scope of this text. One of the limitations arises from the question of who, if anyone, has constitutional power to make general policy for the domain space. While ICANN administers the technical side of the domain name system, its bylaws limit its policy-making role to 'policy development reasonably and appropriately related to [its] technical functions'.[1] Domestic legislatures and courts can only reach disputes within their jurisdictional competence.

In the absence of a central policy-making body, each entity dealing with domain name conflicts can only address a small piece of a much larger puzzle. This can easily result in a domain name market that is regulated inconsistently, often leading to wasteful uses of potentially valuable online assets. The domain space potentially becomes clogged with registrations of multiple domain names by speculators who, more often than not, will park websites under those names and fail to use them for any particularly useful purpose, in the hope that someday they may sell the names for a profit.[2] In the meantime, they may derive revenue from click-through

---

[1] Bylaws for Internet Corporation for Assigned Names and Numbers, art. I, section 1(3). Full text available at www.icann.org/en/general/bylaws.htm, last accessed August 10, 2009.

[2] David Kesmodel, The Domain Game: How People Get Rich from Internet Domain Names 136–8 (2008) (describing the practice of domain name 'parking').

advertising.[3] Domain name speculators often now focus their activities on registering personal names, geographical and cultural indicators, and generic words and phrases in the domain space.[4] This is because many of the trademark issues have now been resolved under existing regulations such as trademark infringement and dilution, the Anti-Cybersquatting Consumer Protection Act (ACPA), and the Uniform Domain Name Dispute Resolution Policy (UDRP).

In many ways, the practice of domain name speculating has moved away from trademark policy, while the regulatory system has not. This creates an inconsistency between the often overly robust protection of trademarks in the domain space and the lack of regulation over other kinds of conduct. There is a need to develop a coherent theory for domain name regulation, outside of pure trademark policy. Domain name conflicts are not likely to diminish in quantity in the near future.[5] The development of a more comprehensive domain name theory outside of the trademark arena is necessary for the future development of the domain name system.

The creation of a coherent theory for domain name regulation may also play an important role in the new generic Top Level Domain (gTLD) application process soon to be rolled out by ICANN.[6] The identification of coherent theoretical principles governing the domain space will be imperative for the release of new gTLDs.[7] The fact that ICANN may not have the constitutional power to implement all relevant policies itself, and that implementation may ultimately fall to a combination of domestic courts, legislators and private arbitrators, means that relatively quick work may be needed to create the theoretical groundwork. If multiple bodies need

---

[3] *Id.* at 68–73 (describing the development of pay-per-click advertising systems).

[4] *Id.* at 24–33 (noting use of generic and other terms in the domain space by domain name speculators).

[5] See WIPO, *Record Number of Cybersquatting Cases in 2008, WIPO Proposes Paperless UDRP* (March 16, 2009), available at www.wipo.int/pressroom/en/articles/2009/article_0005.html, last accessed on August 10, 2009.

[6] Christine Haight Farley, *Convergence and Incongruence: Trademark Law and ICANN's Introduction of New Generic Top-Level Domains*, 25 J. Computer and Information Law 625 (2008), at 626 (noting that ICANN has accredited 15 gTLDs to date including '.com', '.net', and '.edu'), at 626 (noting that ICANN is now considering a new system to approve new gTLDs in the hundreds or thousands).

[7] *Id.*, describing the mismatch between trademark policy and domain name regulation and the implications of the current inconsistencies for the proposed new gTLD process.

to work together to create a workable regulatory matrix, then the earlier appropriate policies can be identified, the better.

This chapter attempts to identify some possibilities for at least the basis for a more comprehensive approach to domain name regulation. It starts by extrapolating from past practice three theoretical justifications for domain name regulation: property theory, trademark policy and restitution or unjust enrichment. These three justifications may have to be developed simultaneously to create a useful framework for domain name regulation. The discussion then surveys some of the current regulatory inconsistencies in the domain space, a number of which have been developed in more detail in previous chapters. It suggests ways in which the theoretical models identified in this chapter might assist in the development of more robust and consistent policy determinations going forwards. The discussion then turns to the position of domain name registrars in terms of potential liability for bad faith activities of their registrants under the various theories of domain name regulation canvassed here. The chapter concludes by making more general suggestions for future directions in domain name regulation.

7.2 THREE THEORIES OF DOMAIN NAME REGULATION

7.2.1 Extrapolating Theory from Practice

As noted in previous chapters, early cybersquatting cases tended to be decided on the basis of trademark infringement and dilution law.[8] Infringement requires the trademark holder to establish a likelihood of consumer confusion as to the source of products or services.[9] Dilution has no consumer confusion requirement and is limited to the protection of famous marks.[10] The dilution action comes in two forms: blurring and tarnishment.[11] Blurring relates to the creation of noise around a mark that interferes with its capacity to operate as a mark.[12] Tarnishment relates to the creation of unsavory associations with a mark.[13]

---

[8] See 1.1, *supra*; KESMODEL, *supra* note 2, at 23–4 (noting how early trademark law dealt effectively with cybersquatters).

[9] 15 U.S.C. §§ 1114(1)(a), 1125(a)(1).

[10] 15 U.S.C. §§ 1125(c)(1), 1125(c)(2)(A).

[11] 15 U.S.C. § 1125(c)(1).

[12] 15 U.S.C. § 1125(c)(2)(B).

[13] 15 U.S.C. § 1125(c)(2)(C).

Despite the early focus on trademark policy, the basis for applying trademark doctrines to cybersquatting was sometimes unclear, suggesting that a pure trademark-based policy model was insufficient for the domain space. For example, the Ninth Circuit struggled to explain why a cybersquatter who conducted no commercial activities on his website was acting *in commerce* as required by the Lanham Act.[14] A trial judge in the Southern District of New York likewise struggled to explain why a domain name registrant who was not conducting any significant commercial activities on his website was nevertheless potentially confusing consumers in commerce as required for a successful infringement action.[15] While traditional trademark policy had its uses, the awkwardness of applying existing trademark doctrines to cybersquatting soon prompted action by the United States Congress and ICANN. They adopted the ACPA and the UDRP respectively.[16]

While still expressly based on trademark policy, the new regulations focused narrowly on specific conduct: cybersquatting. Both the ACPA and the UDRP prohibit registration of a domain name corresponding with someone else's trademark[17] with a bad faith profit motive.[18] Both contain nonexhaustive lists of bad faith factors to guide courts and arbitrators.[19] Both contain defenses for a person who has registered a domain name for a legitimate purpose.[20] Neither is focused on conflicts in the domain space outside of cybersquatting on other people's trademarks. However, federal cyberpiracy law involving personal names is somewhat broader in this respect than the ACPA and the UDRP in that it contains an additional *sui generis* protection for personal names regardless of their trademark status.[21]

The fact that the congress extended protection to nontrademarked personal names suggests a broader regulatory impulse than that stemming solely from trademark policy. While trademark policy obviously has a significant role to play, there must be other regulatory justifications that come into play in relation to the protection of personal names. The statu-

---

14 *Panavision v Toeppen*, 141 F.3d 1316, 1324–6, (9th Cir. 1998).

15 *Planned Parenthood Federation of America Inc. v Bucci*, 1997 U.S. Dist. LEXIS 3338 at 13–15.

16 See 1.4, 1.5, *supra*.

17 Note that neither set of rules expressly requires the mark to be registered; thus each will protect unregistered marks.

18 15 U.S.C. § 1125(d)(1)(A)(i); UDRP, para. 4(a)(iii).

19 15 U.S.C. § 1125(d)(1)(B)(i); UDRP, para. 4(b).

20 15 U.S.C. § 1125(d)(1)(B)(ii); UDRP, para. 4(c).

21 See 1.4.3, *supra*; 15 U.S.C. § 8131(1)(A).

tory concern with bad faith intent to profit perhaps suggests an underlying unjust enrichment – or restitutionary – rationale as an alternative policy basis for the legislation.

One major limitation of both the ACPA and the UDRP in modern domain name practice is that many of today's disputes do not involve traditional trademark cybersquatting. More recent conflicts raise issues not so neatly resolved by trademark policy. Thus, there is a need to find other theoretical justifications for domain name policy that could work alongside the existing, but limited, trademark policy bases. Current regulations such as the ACPA implicitly suggest at least two distinct, but sometimes overlapping, policy justifications for domain name regulation: trademark policy and restitution or unjust enrichment. To this, we might usefully add a property rights justification for regulation in some circumstances, particularly those involving generic words and phrases in the domain space.[22]

7.2.2 Property Theory, Restitution and Trademark Policy

Of the three theoretical justifications for domain name regulation, a property rights justification may at first glance appear to be the most intuitively appealing. The domain name market involves routine trading of domain names as assets.[23] Since the early days of the commercial Internet, domain names have been equated with property in a variety of contexts.[24] Real world property analogies can easily be made with domain names, although each analogy has limitations. It is easy to think about bad faith conduct involving domain names in terms of trespass or conversion.[25] One might describe cybersquatting as a form of trespassing, or squatting, on someone else's virtual property. Generally, a property holder in the real world can remove a trespasser if the trespasser has not used the property for long enough to raise a plausible adverse possession claim.[26]

Trespass is not the only property analogy that can be made with

---

22 See, for example, *Kremen v Cohen*, 337 F.3d 1024 (9th Cir. 2003) (finding domain name to be property for the purposes of the Californian statutory tort of conversion).

23 For a general discussion of modern domain name markets, see KESMODEL, *supra* note 2.

24 See, for example, *Kremen v Cohen*, 337 F.3d 1024 (9th Cir. 2003)

25 *Id.*

26 Walter Quentin Impert, *Whose Land is it Anyway? It's Time to Reconsider Sovereign Immunity from Adverse Possession*, 49 U.C.L.A. L. REV. 447, 448 (2001) ('People are often surprised to learn that a trespasser may take title to land from a true owner under certain conditions and that such theft is authorized by the government under laws of adverse possession.').

cybersquatting. Early cybersquatters did not regard themselves as trespassers. Some thought of themselves as property speculators.[27] They took a gamble that certain pieces of virtual real estate (domain names corresponding with other people's trademarks) would be more valuable to the trademark holders than to anyone else. Thus, a cybersquatter who could beat a trademark holder to registration could make a handsome profit. In the real world, there is nothing wrong with this entrepreneurial impulse. If I buy property adjacent to your land in the hope of selling it to you for a profit because I have speculated that you may want to expand your business onto the land, I am within my rights to charge whatever price I want for it.

The problem is that real property analogies do not perfectly fit the virtual world. The speculating analogy ultimately falls short because a trademark holder does have some rights in a domain name corresponding with her trademark as a matter of trademark policy.[28] A real property holder, on the other hand, has no pre-existing rights in adjacent land. The trespass analogy is also problematic because it is only possible in the real world to trespass on land that another person legally owns. Even though a trademark holder may have some interest in a domain name corresponding with her mark, she does not *own* the domain name unless she has registered it.

Under current regulations like the ACPA and the UDRP, there is an implicit assumption that a trademark holder has property rights in corresponding domain names. However, the full extent of those rights is unclear. Some judges and arbitrators have suggested that those rights might extend to 'trademark.com' domain names, but not necessarily to other iterations of the trademark in the domain space.[29] Nevertheless, this

---

[27] See www.toeppen.com, last accessed August 10, 2009 ('In 1995, I registered about 200 domain names. Some were generic English words, like hydrogen.com. Others corresponded with trademarks that were shared by more than one company, like americanstandard.com. And some corresponded with trademarked coined words, like panavision.com. It was clear to me at the time that domain names were valuable, undeveloped virtual real estate. There was absolutely no statutory or case law regarding trademarks in the context of Internet domain names at the time. It seemed to be an excellent opportunity to do the virtual equivalent of buying up property around a factory – eventually the factory owner would realize that he needed the scarce resource which I possessed.').

[28] This is evidenced by the availability of trademark infringement and dilution actions in early cyberqsuatting cases: KESMODEL, *supra* note 2, at 23–4.

[29] See, for example, discussion in Jacqueline Lipton, *Commerce versus Commentary: Gripe Sites, Parody, and the First Amendment in Cyberspace*, 84 WASHINGTON UNIVERSITY L. REV. 1327, 1359–61 (2006).

view is not universally accepted.[30] Thus, while a property rights rationale for domain name regulation is useful, what is currently missing is guidance as to the nature and scope of any property rights that may be protected in the domain space. This issue becomes even more complex when one departs from the more familiar trademark territory and turns to consideration of property rights in personal names, geographic and cultural indicators, and generic terms in the domain space. Applying the property rights rationale, we might argue that a person has property rights in her name that could be protected against those seeking to profit from the name in the domain space. However, many commentators reject property rights in a personal name.[31]

The property rights rationale may nevertheless be useful in some admittedly limited circumstances involving generic domain names. There have been a few cases where a domain name 'thief' has fraudulently secured a transfer of a generic domain name initially registered to another person.[32] The obtaining of the fraudulent transfer by the wrongdoer has been likened by some commentators to theft or conversion of physical property.[33] The willingness to attach a property label to the virtual property in these cases has enabled at least one court to attach secondary liability to a domain

---

30 For example, the majority panelists in *Bruce Springsteen v Jeff Burgar*, WIPO Arbitration and Mediation Center, Case, No. D2000–1532 (January 25, 2001), available at www.wipo.int/ame/endomains/lecisions/html/2000/12000-1532.html, last accessed March 2, 2009 were prepared to allow an unauthorized use of the 'brucespringsteen.com' domain name by a fan who had registered it, on the basis that Bruce Springsteen had his own web presence under 'brucespringsteen.net'. The majority panelists accepted a trademark in Springsteen's name with some reservations, but decided the case on other grounds.

31 Mark McKenna, *The Right of Publicity and Autonomous Self-Definition*, 67 U. PITT. L. REV. 225, 247 (2005) ('It might be true that identity is sufficiently similar to other objects the law regards as property and therefore deserves at least some of the sticks in the traditional bundle of property rights. But far too few courts and commentators have offered a theory as to why any of the traditional property justifications lead to that conclusion. Such approaches are reflective of the general imprecision that has plagued the right of publicity.').

32 *Kremen v Cohen*, 337 F.3d 1024 (9th Cir. 2003) (involving 'sex.com'). See also Purva Patel, *Not Masters of their (Web) Domains After All: Stolen Internet Names Difficult to Track*, HOUSTON CHRONICLE, August 5, 2009, available at www.chron.com/disp/story.mpl/tech/news/6560302.html, last accessed August 10, 2009 (involving 'p2p.com' domain name).

33 *Kremen v Cohen*, 337 F.3d 1024 (9th Cir. 2003) (holding fraudulently obtained transfer of 'sex.com' domain name to be conversion under Californian tort statute).

name registrar where the fraudulent transferee could not be located.[34] Thus, the property rights rationale for domain name regulation may have a place in a broader theoretical justification for domain name law.

The trademark policy rationale obviously has had a more pronounced place in the regulatory matrix. The trademark-focused UDRP has become the most popular avenue for cybersquatting disputes, while trademark infringement and dilution actions and some ACPA cases still filter through domestic courts, all protecting trademark rights in the domain space.[35] A third policy rationale for domain name regulation that may explain the bleeding of UDRP policy outside of clear trademark doctrine into some other areas, such as personal name protections, may be found in restitution, or unjust enrichment. Restitution is less well developed in the United States than in some other countries.[36] Nevertheless, the basic premise is that a defendant has been unjustly enriched at the expense of a complainant, and the plaintiff is entitled to a remedy.[37] The advantage of restitution is that it does not require a property right in the hands of

---

[34] *Id.* at 1030 ('Property is a broad concept that includes "every intangible benefit and prerogative susceptible of possession or disposition." . . . We apply a three-part test to determine whether a property right exists: "First, there must be an interest capable of precise definition; second, it must be capable of exclusive possession or control; and third, the putative owner must have established a legitimate claim to exclusivity". . . . Domain names satisfy each criterion. Like a share of corporate stock or a plot of land, a domain name is a well-defined interest. Someone who registers a domain name decides where on the Internet those who invoke that particular name – whether by typing it into their web browsers, by following a hyperlink, or by other means – are sent. Ownership is exclusive in that the registrant alone makes that decision. Moreover, like other forms of property, domain names are valued, bought and sold, often for millions of dollars . . . and they are now even subject to in rem jurisdiction . . . Finally, registrants have a legitimate claim to exclusivity. Registering a domain name is like staking a claim to a plot of land at the title office. It informs others that the domain name is the registrant's and no one else's. Many registrants also invest substantial time and money to develop and promote websites that depend on their domain names. Ensuring that they reap the benefits of their investments reduces uncertainty and thus encourages investment in the first place, promoting the growth of the Internet overall . . . Kremen therefore had an intangible property right in his domain name, and a jury could find that Network Solutions "wrongfully disposed of" that right to his detriment by handing the domain name over to Cohen.')

[35] See, for example, *Bosley v Kremer*, 403 F.3d 672 (2005); *People for the Ethical Treatment of Animals v Doughney*, 263 F.3d 359 (2001).

[36] The American law on restitution is currently stated in the RESTATEMENT OF THE LAW, RESTITUTION (1937).

[37] *Id.* para. 1 ('A person who has been unjustly enriched at the expense of another is required to make restitution to the other.').

the complainant.[38] Thus, it might explain domain name conflicts where a domain name registrant has taken advantage of the goodwill a complainant has built up in a word or phrase regardless of whether the complainant has a trademark, or other proprietary or quasi-proprietary interest in that word or phrase.

This might occur in the case of personal names that have not acquired trademark status, or in the context of geographical terms where, say, a local tourist board has built up some goodwill in the name of a city, but not in a trademark sense.[39] To support an unjust enrichment approach, the domain name registrant must have been *enriched* at the expense of the plaintiff. Thus, a restitutionary rationale for domain name regulation will be limited to situations where a registrant has profited unjustly from a domain name in which the complainant has legitimate, although potentially nonproprietary or nontrademark, interests. An example might be where the defendant operates a clickfarm from a domain name in which the plaintiff has some legitimate interests. The identification of these three distinct, albeit sometimes overlapping, theoretical justifications might assist in resolving some of the current gaps and inconsistencies inherent in domain name regulation.

7.3 EXISTING REGULATORY INCONSISTENCIES

7.3.1 General Inconsistencies

The current state of domain name regulation might be summarized as set out in Table 7.1. This table matches the various motivations for domain name registration against the most obvious categories of words and phrases that are commonly registered as domain names. The individual cells within the table identify the extent to which each pairing of market motivations with word type is regulated under existing rules. The results

---

38 *Id.* Comment b ('A person confers a benefit upon another if he gives to the other possession of or some other interest in money, land, chattels, or choses in action, performs services beneficial to or at the request of the other, satisfies a debt or a duty of the other, or in any way adds to the other's security or advantage. He confers a benefit not only where he adds to the property of another, but also where he saves the other from expense or loss. The word "benefit," therefore, denotes any form of advantage.').

39 GILSON ON TRADEMARKS, para. 2.03[4][d] ('Just as with descriptive terms, a trademark or trade name that consists of a personal name (first name, surname, or both) is entitled to legal protection only if it attains secondary meaning.').

Table 7.1 Relationship between registrants' motivations and categories of domain name registered

	Sale motive	*Clickfarming motive*	*Expressive use*	*Legitimate commercial use*
Trademarks	Traditional cybersquatting	Potentially cybersquatting	Usually legitimate, particularly if the registrant does not use the '.com' version of the name	Competing trademark interests: first come, first served
Personal names	Traditional cybersquatting (if name is trademarked) *and* 15 U.S.C. § 8131(1)(A) liability (regardless of trademark)	Potentially cybersquatting (if name is trademarked); little recourse if no trademark	Usually legitimate use, particularly if registrant does not use '.com' version of trademarked personal name	Competing personal names: first come first served
Cultural and geographic indicators	No regulation unless name is trademarked	No regulation unless term is trademarked	Presumptively legitimate use	Presumptively legitimate use
Generic words and phrases	Presumptively legitimate use	Presumptively legitimate use	Presumptively legitimate use	Presumptively legitimate use
Deliberate misspellings of trademarks	Cybersquatting	Potentially cybersquatting	Unclear: potentially legitimate use	No legitimate use
Deliberate misspellings of personal names	Cybersquatting (if name is trademarked); and U.S.C. § 8131(1)(A) regardless of trademark	Potentially cybersquatting (if name is trademarked); little recourse if no trademark	Unclear: potentially legitimate use	No legitimate use
'trademarksucks' names	Unclear	Unclear: potentially trademark infringement, dilution or cybersquatting	Generally legitimate use	No legitimate use

evidence an inconsistent and unpredictable pastiche of regulations. There is no clear or consistent underlying theoretical basis for domain name regulation.

The only conduct that is clearly sanctioned under current regulations is traditional cybersquatting, represented in the first, fifth, and sixth rows of column 1 in Table 7.1. The regulation of other conduct is largely unclear. It is possible to discern some general principles about domain name regulation from this table, but at a fairly high level of abstraction. For example, purely expressive uses of domain names are for the most part regarded as being legitimate, regardless of the type of word or phrase registered (see column 3). Even expressive uses of trademarks (column 3, row 1) and of deliberate misspellings of trademarks (column 3, row 5) may be legitimate uses if the associated website is used for commentary, rather than commercial purposes.

Another general principle that may be derived from Table 7.1 is that registration of a deliberate misspelling of another person's trademark is presumptively illegitimate, at least if undertaken for a commercial purpose. In fact, it is difficult to conceive of a situation where someone registers a deliberate misspelling of another person's trademark for a purely expressive purpose, although it is possible that the operator of a purely expressive gripe site or parody site may want to engage in this conduct.[40] In any event, the fifth, sixth and, seventh rows of column 4 in Table 7.1 are shaded out because it is difficult, if not impossible, to conceive of any legitimate *commercial* purpose for registering a deliberate misspelling of another's mark or name.

Table 7.1 also illustrates the confusion inherent with respect to 'sucks'-type domain names.[41] These are names that use a trademark with a pejorative word or phrase attached: for example 'nikesucks.com'. Typically, these domains are used for gripe sites, websites that include critical commentary about a trademark holder.[42] However, these kinds of names are sometimes used for commercial purposes such as cybersquatting or click-farming.[43] Where pejorative domain names are used for commercial purposes, they are sometimes referred to as 'sham speech' domain names.[44] There is currently no clear regulatory approach to 'sucks'-type domain

---

40 See discussion at 6.3, *supra*.

41 David Lindsay, International Domain Name Law: ICANN and the UDRP 262 (2007).

42 *Id.*

43 *Id.*

44 *Id.*

names.[45] Most commercial uses of such names are colorably illegitimate as they take advantage of the goodwill in a trademark to draw custom for a nonrelated commercial purpose.[46] However, some uses are legitimately expressive and others combine expressive and commercial elements. The development of a more coherent theoretical framework for domain name regulation might assist in ascertaining what kinds of conduct concerning 'sucks'-type domain names should be proscribed, and on what basis. A theoretical framework based on both trademark policy and unjust enrichment may be useful to separate legitimate expressive uses of 'sucks'-type domain names from bad faith commercial uses.

Another notable feature of Table 7.1 is that it highlights the position of clickfarming in the context of current domain name regulations. Most clickfarming involving trademarks or deliberate misspellings of trademarks is potentially regulated as a form of cybersquatting.[47] This is because clickfarms that utilize other people's trademarks essentially use the marks for bad faith commercial profit motives. The commercial profit motive in clickfarming is different from traditional cybersquatting. For clickfarmers, the profit is not derived from a sale of the name, but rather from using the name to generate revenue from click-through advertisements.[48] Nevertheless, most cybersquatting regulations are broad enough to encompass this kind of conduct. In the ACPA, for example, the notion of a bad faith intent to profit from a mark is not inextricably linked to a sale motive.[49] The bad faith factors in the UDRP are likewise not limited to a sale motive. The intention to sell the domain name is only one of four nonexclusive bad faith factors in the UDRP.[50]

Clickfarming involving words and phrases other than trademarks has a less clear regulatory rationale. Personal names and cultural and geographic terms that operate as registered or unregistered marks will likely be protected from clickfarming in the same way as other trademarks.[51] However, nontrademarked names, words and phrases are more troublesome. While various individuals and entities may have legitimate interests

---

45 *Id.*

46 This is why the last cell at the bottom of column 4 in Table 7.1 is shaded out.

47 See discussion at 6.2.3.1, *supra*.

48 Jacqueline Lipton, *Clickfarming: The New Cybersquatting?*, 12 J. INTERNET LAW 1 (2008).

49 15 U.S.C. § 1125(d)(1)(A)(i).

50 UDRP, para. 4(b)(i).

51 GILSON, *supra* note 39, para. 2.03[4][d] ('Just as with descriptive terms, a trademark or trade name that consists of a personal name (first name, surname, or both) is entitled to legal protection only if it attains secondary meaning.').

in these terms, in the absence of a trademark they have little recourse against clickfarmers. Even the federal personal name cyberpiracy provisions will not cover clickfarming because those provisions are limited to prohibiting registrations of personal names as domain names with a sale motive.[52]

There is nothing necessarily wrong with these outcomes if the regulatory policy is that clickfarming is problematic only in trademark cases. The rationale for distinguishing nontrademarked personal names, cultural and geographic indicators and generic terms here would be that the people and entities with interests in those terms have not necessarily put the same resources into developing goodwill in relevant words as the trademark holder. However, this rationale may not bear close scrutiny.

Even an individual with no trademark interest in her personal name may have spent time and resources on building up a public persona. Politicians, for example, may not have commercial trademark interests in their names, but may nevertheless have spent much time, effort and resources building up their professional reputations. The ability of a clickfarmer to take unfair advantage of that reputation should arguably be sanctioned on the same basis as the regulation of clickfarming that utilizes trademarks. Likewise, local city councils may spend significant time and effort building up a reputation for their city to attract tourism or business. It is not clear why those entities should be denied protection against clickfarmers trading on their geographical reputations while trademark holders are protected.

The failure to develop any regulations that prevent the monopolization of different classes of words and phrases by clickfarmers creates a situation in which the Internet potentially becomes clogged with clickfarms. Words and phrases that could be used for more useful expressive or commercial purposes are effectively monopolized by clickfarmers or held to ransom by domain name speculators. The way in which one responds to this state of affairs depends on the view one has of the domain name market more generally. Free market advocates may well support domain name speculators including those who run clickfarms. Others may be disappointed that the Internet will likely be unable to reach its full potential as a global communications medium if more and more of its online addresses are taken up by poorly maintained clickfarms advertising products that few people want.[53]

---

52 15 U.S.C. § 8131(1)(A). See also discussion at 6.2.3.2, *supra*.

53 KESMODEL, *supra* note 2, at 138 ('Although domain parking clearly has been good for investors and networks, the level of value the sites offer to consumers has been hotly debated. Some critics say the proliferation of the bare-bones [clickfarms] has sullied the Internet. Some liken the millions of ad-bloated sites to an endless stream of billboards along a highway, distracting drivers and ruining the scenery.').

Nevertheless, even those who support regulation to preserve the potential of the Internet by reining in clickfarming face the problem of identifying (a) a theoretical rationale for regulation; (b) an entity with constitutional competence to regulate; and (c) an effective enforcement mechanism for any regulations that may be developed. These are extremely difficult questions. This chapter focuses predominantly on the first. Without a clear theoretical basis for regulating, the succeeding questions are moot. With no clear theoretical idea of the basis for regulations, it does not matter who theoretically *might* regulate or how those regulations might be enforced.[54]

7.3.2 Specific Inconsistencies and Possible Solutions

7.3.2.1 Personal names

The following discussion surveys some examples of the various regulatory inconsistencies identified in the previous section. It focuses on certain kinds of words and phrases commonly registered in modern domain name markets. Current domain name disputes often involve nontrademarked words and phrases. One obvious example is personal names. Personal names have come to the forefront of many modern domain name battles because of their obvious commercial value and their uncertain trademark status. Some famous people cannot successfully assert trademarks in their personal names. This is especially true of famous people who do not use their names in commerce: for example, politicians and some other public figures.[55]

Domain name speculators often register personal names as domain

---

[54] This is a bit of an oversimplification, because in reality the three regulatory questions overlap to some extent. One might argue that in the absence of a competent regulating entity, the idea of formulating theory is arguably moot because no body could meaningfully implement relevant policies. Even if there is a competent entity (or entities) that might implement policy in new regulations, the regulations will be meaningless if aggrieved persons either do not have standing or do not have sufficient access to dispute resolution forums to enforce them. Nevertheless, there is some value in focusing on theory of regulation as an initial matter. There are currently bodies who implement regulations, albeit in a piecemeal way. They include ICANN, UDRP arbitrators and domestic courts. The increasing pace of UDRP arbitrations over the year also suggests that there is a significant body of complainants with sufficient standing to enforce existing regulations, even if they are currently obliged to frame their complaints in trademark terms.

[55] Jacqueline Lipton, *Celebrity in Cyberspace: A Personality Rights Paradigm for Personal Domain Name Disputes*, 65 WASHINGTON AND LEE L. REV. 1445, 1462–8 (2008) (describing mismatch between trademark law and the status of the personal names of politicians and public figures). See also Jacqueline Lipton, *Who Owns 'hillary.com'? Political Speech and the First Amendment in Cyberspace*, 49 BOSTON COLLEGE L. REV. 55 (2008).

names with the aim of defending against any subsequent complaints on the basis of either a lack of a trademark interest in the hands of the complainant, or possibly a lack of bad faith conduct on the part of the registrant.[56] It is usually relatively easy for domain name speculators to beat famous people to registration of their names because many famous individuals, unlike trademark holders, do not necessarily plan for, or even desire, an Internet presence.[57] Thus, many valuable personal names are not initially registered by the people to whom the names relate. The failure by those individuals to register the names leaves ample opportunity for cybersquatters, clickfarmers and others to profit from the names. The failure to register is also understandable because a name is supposed to be used once it is registered. A registrant has to do something with the associated website. Many famous people do not want to use their names at all. They simply do not want other people to register them.[58]

As noted in previous chapters,[59] personal name conflicts in the domain space have involved all kinds of people: actors,[60] singers,[61]

---

[56] *William J. Clinton v Web of Deception*, National Arbitration Forum, Claim No. FA0904001256123 (June 1, 2009), available at http://domains.adrforum.com/domains/decisions/1256123.htm, last accessed August 10, 2009. Registrant of 'williamclinton.com', 'williamjclinton.com' and 'presidentbillclinton.com', argued that the complainant had no trademark rights in his personal name, and that the registrant had not registered and was not using the names in bad faith. Although the former President established trademark rights in his personal name, the registrant's bad faith argument was successful and the arbitrator did not order transfer of the names to the former President.

[57] See discussion of the dispute involving the name 'juliaroberts.com' in Jacqueline Lipton, *Beyond Cybersquatting: Taking Domain Name Disputes Past Trademark Policy*, 40 WAKE FOREST L. REV. 1361, 1414–15 (2005).

[58] *Id.*

[59] See, in particular, Chapter 4 and Chapter 5.

[60] *Julia Fiona Roberts v Russell Boyd*, WIPO Arbitration and Mediation Center, Case No. D2000–0210 (30 May, 2000), available at www.wipo.int/amc/en/domains/decisions/html/2000/d2000-0210.html, last accessed November 6, 2007 (involving 'juliaroberts.com' domain name); *Tom Cruise v Alberta Hot Rods*, WIPO Arbitration and Mediation Center, Case No. D2006–0560 (July 5, 2006), available at www.wipo.int/amc/en/domains/decisions/html/2006/d2006-0560.html, last accessed March 16, 2010 (involving 'tomcruise.com' domain name); *Kevin Spacey v Alberta Hot Rods*, National Arbitration Forum, Claim No. 114437 (August 1, 2002), available at www.adrforum.com/domains/decisions/96937.htm, last accessed March 16, 2010 (involving the domain name 'kevinspacey.com').

[61] See, for example, *Bruce Springsteen*, WIPO Case No. D2000–1532, available at www.wipo.int/amc/en/domains/decisions/html/2000/d2000-1532.html, last accessed March 2, 2009 (involving 'brucespringsteen.com' domain name); *Madonna Ciccone v Dan Parisi,* WIPO Arbitration and Mediation Center, Case No. D2000–0847 (October 12, 2000), available at www.wipo.int/amc/en/domains/decisions/

athletes,[62] politicians,[63] prominent business people,[64] and other public figures.[65] Additionally, some disputes have involved the names of private individuals, although these are less common because nonfamous names are less valuable to domain name speculators.[66] The recorded conflicts evidence a variety of motivations for registration, including commercial and expressive purposes, and combinations of both. For example, a private individual registered the domain name 'brucespringsteen.com' for an unauthorized fan site about the popular singer, Bruce Springsteen.[67] This is by and large an expressive purpose, although it is also possible for fan site operators to make commercial profits by charging fees to join a fan club or to subscribe to a newsletter, or by operating a clickfarm on the website.[68]

---

html/2000/d2000-0847.html, last accessed March 16, 2010 (involving 'Madonna.com' domain name); *Experience Hendrix LLC v Denny Hammerton,* WIPO Arbitration and Mediation Center, Case. No. D2000–0364 (August 2, 2000, *aff'd* August 15, 2000), available at www.wipo.int/amc/en/domains/decisions/html/2000/d2000-0364.html, last accessed March 16, 2010 (involving 'jimihendrix.com' domain name).

[62] See, for example *Bjorn Borg v Miguel Garcia,* WIPO Arbitration and Mediation Center, Case No. D2007–0591 (June 21, 2007), available at www.wipo.int/amc/en/domains/decisions/html/2007/d2007-0591.html, last accessed March 16, 2010 (involving the domain name 'bjornborg.com').

[63] *William J. Clinton*, Claim No. FA0904001256123, National Arbitration Forum, available at http://domains.adrforum.com/domains/decisions/1256123.htm; *Hillary Rodham Clinton v Michele Dinoia*, National Arbitration Forum, Claim No. FA0502000414641 (March 18, 2005), available at www.arb-forum.com/domains/decisions/414641.htm, last accessed March 2, 2009; *Kathleen Kennedy Townsend v Birt*, WIPO Arbitration and Mediation Center, Case No. D2002–0451 (April 11, 2002), available at www.wipo.int/amc/en/domains/decisions/html/2002/d2002-0451.html, last accessed March 16, 2010.

[64] *Trudeau v Lanoue*, 2006 U.S. Dixt. LEXIS 7956 (2006); *Stephan Schmidheiny v Steven Weber*, 285 F.Supp.2d 613 (2003).

[65] *Anna Nicole Smith v DNS Research Inc.*, National Arbitration Forum, Claim No. FA0312000220007 (February 21, 2004), available at www.adrforum.com/domains/decisions/220007.htm, last accessed October 25, 2007 (involving 'annanicolesmith.com' domain name); *The Hebrew University of Jerusalem v Alberta Hot Rods,* WIPO Arbitration and Mediation Center, Case No. D2002–0616 (October 7, 2002), available at www.kipo.ke.wipo.net/amc/en/domains/decisions/html/2002/d2002-0616.html, last accessed March 16, 2010 (involving a complaint with respect to the domain name 'alberteinstein.com').

[66] *Paul Wright v Domain Source Inc.*, 2002 U.S. Dist. LEXIS 16024 (2002).

[67] *Bruce Springsteen*, WIPO Case No. D2000–1532, available at www.wipo.int/amc/en/domains/decisions/html/2000/d2000-1532.html.

[68] Lipton, *Clickfarming*, *supra* note 48, at 16 (describing the practice of clickfarming on personal names).

As this book is focused on the extent to which a more comprehensive theory of domain name regulation could help with current domain name problems, the question clearly arises as to whether such a theory could help with personal names. Existing regulations have been premised on trademark policy which does not always provide the best protection for personal names. A pure trademark focus, for example, fails to explain the regulatory impulse behind 15 U.S.C. § 8131(1)(A), the *sui generis* personal name protections against cybersquatting. Clearly, the legislature saw a need to protect personal names. However, Congress's actions cannot be explained solely with respect to trademark policy. There must be some other theoretical justification.

The unjust enrichment model might help with personal names. Unjust enrichment theory does not require a trademark or even a generic property right to ground a claim for relief. Box 7.1 contains examples of five hypothetical scenarios involving personal names. The subsequent discussion illustrates how the adoption of a clearer policy basis for the domain space – potentially based on unjust enrichment – might help to resolve the conflicts arising in these scenarios.

It is difficult to apply existing domain name regulations to these scenarios. The first hurdle in all five scenarios is that the complainant needs a trademark in his or her personal name for the most affordable avenue of recourse, a UDRP arbitration.[69] This may be difficult to establish even in the case of famous names.[70] With respect to Scenario 5, for example, an unknown politician would not likely be successful. However, an unknown politician who later became famous and used his name in commerce (for example, by selling campaign merchandise relating to his name) might

---

69 UDRP, para. 4(a)(i).

70 *Bruce Springsteen*, WIPO Case No. D2000–1532, para. 6 available at www.wipo.int/amc/en/domains/decisions/html/2000/d2000-1532.html ('It appears to be an established principle from cases such as Jeanette Winterson, Julia Roberts, and Sade that in the case of very well known celebrities, their names can acquire a distinctive secondary meaning giving rise to rights equating to unregistered trade marks, notwithstanding the non-registerability of the name itself. It should be noted that no evidence has been given of the name 'Bruce Springsteen' having acquired a secondary meaning; in other words a recognition that the name should be associated with activities beyond the primary activities of Mr. Springsteen as a composer, performer and recorder of popular music.

In the view of this Panel, it is by no means clear from the UDRP that it was intended to protect proper names of this nature. As it is possible to decide the case on other grounds, however, the Panel will proceed on the assumption that the name Bruce Springsteen is protected under the policy; it then follows that the domain name at issue is identical to that name.').

BOX 7.1 HYPOTHETICAL SCENARIOS INVOLVING PERSONAL NAMES IN THE DOMAIN SPACE

Scenario 1. An individual registers a domain name corresponding with the name of an internationally famous Democrat ex-President with a view to illuminating the lack of regulation for cybersquatting on personal names. Ultimately, he directs the domain name to a website containing information posted by the Republican National Committee. He makes no attempt to sell the name to the ex-President or to anyone else.[a]

Scenario 2. An individual registers a domain name corresponding with the name of a minor celebrity known mainly for her reality TV show. She rose to fame as a model with a weight problem who married a wealthy millionaire. She does not use her name to sell any particular products or services. The registrant would be prepared to sell the domain name to her for an acceptable fee.[b]

Scenario 3. An individual registers a domain name corresponding with the name of a famous movie star for an unauthorized fan site containing click-through advertisements. It is clear from the content of the website that it is not the official, authorized fan site for the movie star. The click-through advertisements on the website are unrelated to any of the movie star's professional activities. The registrant makes no attempt to sell the name, although she would be prepared to consider an offer if it was forthcoming.[c]

Scenario 4. An individual registers a domain name corresponding with the name of a famous movie star. She puts minimal content on the associated website – a two paragraph plain text description of the actor's movies. She conducts no commercial activities from the website and makes no offer to sell the name.

Scenario 5. A young, little known junior senator from the midwest makes a speech at the Democratic National Convention. It becomes a major media sensation. The next day the newspapers are abuzz with speculation that the senator is going to be the next major star of the Democratic Party and may even run for president some day. A domain name entrepreneur registers the senator's name as a domain name, thinking that it may be valuable one day.

[a] This hypothetical is based on *William J. Clinton*, National Arbitration Forum, Claim No. FA0904001256123, available at http://domains.adrforum.com/domains/decisions/1256123.htm.
[b] This hypothetical is based on *Anna Nicole Smith*, National Arbitration Forum, Claim No. FA0312000220007, available at www.adrforum.com/domains/decisions/220007.htm.
[c] This hypothetical is based on *Tom Cruise*, WIPO Case No. D2006–0560, available at www.wipo.int/amc/en/domains/decisions/html/2006/d2006-0560.html.

later succeed in a UDRP arbitration. In this scenario, he would need to establish that the registrant was using the name in bad faith and not for any legitimate purpose.[71] An attempt to sell the name for a profit in the course of a subsequent presidential election campaign may satisfy this requirement.

The overall problem here is that there is no clear principle to guide registrants on what conduct is legitimate in these cases. The reliance on the trademark policy rationale underlying the UDRP creates uncertainty in relation to its application to personal name disputes. Unjust enrichment theory, on the other hand, might support rules to ensure return of a domain name to a rightful owner (or at least cancellation of the registration) in cases where a registrant had taken unfair commercial advantage of the name. This approach would not interfere with free speech as it would be based on unjust *commercial* enrichments, not on use of another's name for expressive purposes.

Applying an unjust enrichment approach to Scenario 1 in Box 7.1, for example, we might find that a registrant who has used a politician's name for purely expressive and non-commercial purposes should not be subject to a transfer or cancellation order. While at least one UDRP decision supports this result, the underlying theoretical rationale for the decision is trademark policy. In other words, applying the UDRP as written, an arbitrator found that, although former President William J. Clinton did have a trademark in his personal name, the registrant was not acting in

[71] UDRP, para. 4(b) and (c).

bad faith in registering the name for an expressive purpose.[72] It would make more sense as a matter of theory and practice for such disputes to be decided not on the grounds of trademark policy, but on the grounds of unjust enrichment. An unjust enrichment rationale would support the development of new regulations that do not require individuals to rely on trademarks in their personal names. An unjust enrichment rationale may lead to a similar result in the case of President Clinton, but on a more appropriate theoretical basis.

The federal personal name cyberpiracy legislation provides an example of a regulation that arguably evidences an unjust enrichment rationale.[73] The provision does not require a complainant to establish a trademark in her name in order to bring an action against a cybersquatter. The provision is limited in operation in that the cybersquatter must have a clear sale motive. Thus, the operation of a clickfarm under another person's name will not run afoul of its terms. This provision would thus be irrelevant to Scenario 3 in Box 7.1, for example. This scenario involves an unauthorized fan website including a commercial clickfarm. However, the provision would likely apply to Scenario 2. This scenario is more of a straightforward cybersquatting case.

The use of an unjust enrichment rationale to support the development of more accessible personal domain name regulations may be useful for future practice in the domain space. This approach would support the drafting of simple dispute resolution procedures like the UDRP, but more broadly based on preventing unjust commercial profits relating to the use of another person's name in the domain space.[74] A restitutionary approach still leaves ample room to protect purely expressive uses of personal names. In other words, the conduct of the registrants in Scenarios 1 and 4 in Box 7.1 would likely be protected as they relate predominantly to speech and do not implicate commerce. Scenario 3 (the unauthorized fan website that contains a clickfarm) is more problematic because it combines commercial profits with expression. Nevertheless, a restitutionary policy rationale for regulation might assist in developing the appropriate contours for dealing with these kinds of situations more effectively in practice.

---

[72] *William J. Clinton*, National Arbitration Forum, Claim No. FA0904001256123, available at http://domains.adrforum.com/domains/decisions/1256123.htm.

[73] 15 U.S.C. § 8131(1)(A).

[74] See, for example, Lipton, *Celebrity in Cyberspace*, *supra* note 55, at 1512–26 (crafting a new personal domain name dispute resolution policy along similar lines).

7.3.2.2 Culturally and geographically significant words and phrases

The regulatory matrix is even less certain in the area of culturally and geographically significant words and phrases such as ubuntu, uluru and amazon. These kinds of words only attain trademark status if they have sufficient secondary meaning in association with the offering of goods or services.[75] It is important for these terms to be available for legitimate expressive uses in the domain space.[76] For example, traders from a particular region will often want to use a geographical term to indicate the geographical source of the goods, as opposed to the manufacturing source.[77] Any regulation that inhibits the use of a geographical or cultural term in the domain space must take into account the delicate balance of uses to which such a term may be put in practice. The lack of a principled theoretical basis for domain name regulation has hindered the development of effective regulations in the context of cultural and geographic indicators.[78] Consider the hypothetical scenarios set out in Box 7.2.

As was the case with the personal name scenarios in Box 7.1, the available domain name regulations focus on trademark policy. A complainant who cannot establish a trademark in a geographic or cultural term will have little meaningful recourse against a registrant. In some cases, the registrant itself may hold a valid trademark in the name, such as the 'amazon.com' domain name in Scenario 1 in Box 7.2. Thus, the regulations would protect that registrant against challenges from those with other interests in the domain name.[79] It is an open question whether this is an appropriate result as a matter of policy. In other words, the regulatory approach has been taken by default that trademark rights currently take precedence over other legitimate interests.[80]

---

75 Lindsay, *supra* note 41, at 225.

76 *Id.* at 225–6.

77 *Id.* at 225 ('The inclusion of a geographical term in a registered trade mark always gives rise to particular difficulties. The difficulties arise because, although it may be desirable to use a geographical term to indicate the source of goods or services, registration would prevent the legitimate use of the geographical term in a descriptive sense by other traders.').

78 *Id.* at 224–5 (noting that the World Intellectual Property Organization has, to date, declined to develop specific protections for geographical terms because of the lack of clear international principles on which such protections might be based).

79 For a more detailed discussion of the issue of multiple competing interests in a domain name, see discussion in Jacqueline Lipton, *A Winning Solution for YouTube and Utube? Corresponding Trademarks and Domain Name Sharing*, 21 Harvard J. Law and Technology 509 (2008).

80 Lipton, *Beyond Cybersquatting*, *supra* note 57, at 1363 ('current dispute resolution mechanisms are focused on the protection of commercial trademark

BOX 7.2 HYPOTHETICAL SCENARIOS INVOLVING CULTURAL AND GEOGRAPHIC INDICATORS IN THE DOMAIN SPACE

Scenario 1. A popular online bookstore registers a domain name that corresponds with the name of a famous landmark. A group of manufacturers located near the landmark that uses its name in marketing their products and services wishes to use the name in the domain space.[a]

Scenario 2. The official tourist bureau for a popular skiing region utilizes the name of the region in its domain name. A trademark holder with registered trademark interests in the relevant term seeks transfer of the domain name.[b]

Scenario 3. A domain name speculator registers a group of domain names corresponding with well-known geographical terms in the hope of making money from clickfarms on associated websites. Her aim is to target Internet users who might be seeking information about the geographic locations. The click-through advertisements are not specifically associated with any of the geographic locations.

Scenario 4. The President of the United States happens to have a last name that corresponds with the name of a city in Japan. The '.com' version of the name is registered to the city offices for the Japanese city. The President wants to use the name for his new online open government initiative.

[a] LINDSAY, *supra* note 41, at 229 (describing the example of the 'amazon.com' trademark).
[b] This hypothetical is loosely based on *Kur- und Verkehrsverein St Moritz v StMoritz.com*, WIPO arbitration and mediation center, Case No. D2000–0617 (17 August, 2000), available at www.wipo.int/amc/en/domains/decisions/html/2000/d2000-0617.html, last accessed March 16, 2010.

Existing regulations generally protect purely expressive uses of a domain name as legitimate uses, even against trademark holders. Thus, the trademark holder in Scenario 2 will likely be out of luck provided that the tourist bureau is using the name for expressive, rather than com-

---

interests, often to the detriment of other socially important interests that may inhere in a given domain name.').

mercial, purposes.[81] The lines between expressive and commercial uses may become blurred if the registrant has a dual purpose in registering the name. Not all commercial purposes are in bad faith, although courts and arbitrators may be more protective of purely expressive uses than of uses that combine expressive and commercial motives. While a number of adjudicators have been sympathetic to those with expressive purposes, it is worth reiterating that free speech is not expressly identified as a legitimate use in either the ACPA or the UDRP.[82] It is not impossible that a registrant whose primary motivation is expressive could be found to be acting in bad faith.

Scenarios 3 and 4 in Box 7.2 raise complex issues that are not particularly effectively addressed under current regulations. While some of the domain names in Scenario 3 may correspond with trademarks, they are also general terms that might attract Internet users to the registrant's clickfarm irrespective of any association with a particular mark. While it is possible that the registrant had a sale motive in the back of her mind when she registered the names, it is not clear that her actions are in bad faith in the traditional cybersquatting sense. The registration of multiple domain names corresponding with other people's trademarks is an express bad faith factor under both the ACPA and the UDRP.[83] However, the registration of domain names corresponding with cultural and geographic terms that *may* correspond in some cases with trademarks is not the same as the intentional registration of trademarks in the domain space. The motivations for the conduct are different. Unlike traditional cybersquatting, the former scenario relies on happenstance. If it happens that a domain name relates to someone's trademark, the registrant might serendipitously profit from clickfarm custom by Internet users seeking the trademark holder's official website.

The trademark-focused provisions of the UDRP and other domain name regulations are confusing in application in situations like Scenario 3. As the policy underpinnings for the regulations lie in trademark protection, there is no guidance to arbitrators and judges as to the correct approach to take in disputes involving these kinds of names. Presumably, in many situations like Scenario 3, arbitrators and judges will find the registrant's use of relevant terms to be legitimate. If there was no motive

---

81 See *Kur- und Verkehrsverein St Moritz*, WIPO Case No. D2000–0617, available at www.wipo.int/amc/en/domains/decisions/html/2000/d2000-0617.html.

82 In October 2006, however, under the Trademark Dilution Revision Act, criticism and commentary were inserted into the Lanham Act as a defense for trademark dilution: 15 U.S.C. § 1125(c)(3)(A)(ii).

83 15 U.S.C. § 1125(d)(1)(B)(i)(VIII); UDRP, para. 4(b)(ii).

to profit from someone else's trademark, the application of rules based largely on trademark policy is not very helpful. This is evidenced in row 3 of Table 7.1 suggesting that most uses of cultural and geographic words that are not trademarked are legitimate.

Current trademark-focused policy has nothing to say about whether this is in fact the right result in the domain space as a matter of more general theory. It is not clear whether we need specific regulations to protect cultural and geographic indicators that are not trademarked. If so, such regulations might usefully be based on unjust enrichment. Irrespective of trademark interests, it may be worthwhile to develop rules that prevent, say, clickfarmers from making commercial profits that capitalize on words and phrases that have particular significance to one or more cultural groups, even if that significance is not manifested in a trademark right. In some cases, the words and phrases may have a proprietary connection with a particular cultural group, but more likely than not, an unjust enrichment rationale will be the best fit. Under this rationale, it would be possible to develop rules based on the notion that a registrant should not be unjustly enriched at the expense of a group of people with a legitimate interest in a particular word or phrase.

Scenario 4 in Box 7.2 is another problematic situation. It does not involve any trademarks at all, unless the Japanese city officials have trademarked the city's name or the President has established sufficient secondary meaning in his name to support a trademark.[84] In the absence of trademark rights, current regulations give little guidance as to who has a better right to the domain name. It is an open question whether any set of rules should be developed for rare scenarios like this. It may be preferable to deal with them on a case-by-case basis. In any event, the adoption

---

[84] High-level politicians have had some success in establishing trademarks in their personal names: *William J. Clinton*, National Arbitration Forum, Claim No. FA0904001256123, available at http://domains.adrforum.com/domains/decisions/1256123.htm ('Reluctantly, the Panelist concludes that President Clinton has established a common law mark in his name. A mark is a secondary identifier of the source of goods and services. President Clinton's best-selling books are probably enough to qualify his personal name as a common law mark.'); *Hillary Rodham Clinton*, National Arbitration Forum, Claim No. FA0502000414641, available at www.arb-forum.com/domains/decisions/414641.htm ('The Panel finds that complainant's uncontested allegations establish common law rights in the Hillary Clinton mark sufficient to grant standing under the UDRP. complainant alleges that the Hillary Clinton mark has become distinctive through complainant's use and exposure of the mark in the marketplace and through use of the mark in connection with complainant's political activities, including a successful Senate campaign.').

of a theoretical basis for domain name regulation based on unjust enrichment may be helpful in delineating the kinds of conduct that should *not* be regulated at all. A regulatory approach premised on unjust enrichment at the expense of another would militate against regulating situations like Scenario 4 in Box 7.2 as there is no obvious unfair benefit in this case at the expense of the President. The adoption of a clear theoretical basis for domain name regulation that is broader than mere trademark policy may better delineate which situations require some form of redress and which simply involve a balance of competing legitimate interests in the domain space.

7.3.2.3 Generic terms

Generic terms raise a distinct set of policy issues. Generic terms are broader than other classes of words and phrases in the domain space. They include words like love, joy, business and hope, not to mention sex, the subject of one of the most intriguing domain name battles fought outside the bounds of trademark law.[85] More recently, 'P2P.com' has been the subject of controversy in the domain space.[86] Generic terms are generally neither trademarked nor trademarkable, subject to some relatively rare exceptions.[87] Nevertheless, they are often valuable cyber-realty. A survey of the top 25 reported domain name sales at the end of 2007 illustrates that generic terms generally raised the largest sales revenues of any domain names in that year.[88] 'Porn.com' raised almost US$10 million dollars, while 'business.com' and 'diamond.com' tied at US$7.5 million apiece.[89] Even names like 'fish.com' raised just over US$1 million dollars, while 'if.com' and 'rock.com' tied at US$1 million.[90]

Again, current trademark-focused rules are a poor fit for conflicts that arise in relation to generic domain names. A registrant of multiple generic terms in the domain space may have a variety of commercial and

---

[85] *Kremen v Cohen*, 337 F.3d 1024 (9th Cir. 2003) (finding domain name to be property for the purposes of the Californian statutory tort of conversion).

[86] Purva Patel, *supra* note 32.

[87] LINDSAY, *supra* note 41, at 352 ('A generic term is a name of a product or service itself. Given that, by definition, a generic term cannot operate to distinguish the source of goods or services, it might be thought that anyone should be free to register a generic term as a domain name. What is generic in one part of the world may, however, be distinctive in another part of the world. Moreover, a term that is descriptive rather than generic may become distinctive and acquire trade mark rights.').

[88] KESMODEL, *supra* note 2, at 193.

[89] *Id.*

[90] *Id.*

expressive motives, none of which likely has anything to do with interfering with a trademark holder's rights. There is a healthy and active market in generic domain names that has developed outside the realm of existing trademark-focused regulations.[91] This raises a number of issues for regulators, including the foundational question as to whether there is ever a valid theoretical justification for regulating generic domain names. The answer to this question depends on how much of a free market approach one is prepared to take with respect to the domain space.

To the extent that regulations have been found wanting in the context of generic terms, the underlying theoretical quandary has related to the categorization of generic names as intangible property. In other words, a property rights rationale for domain name regulation potentially comes into play here. For example, the 'sex.com' domain name was the subject of a conversion action under Californian law.[92] This dispute arose in circumstances where the name was, in effect, converted for the purposes of the Californian statute by a fraudulent request to its registrar to transfer the name to a party who had no legal entitlement to it. A similar situation arose more recently in the case of the 'P2P.com' domain name. Registrants of generic names that are 'stolen' in this way have very little guidance as to their rights. The regulatory impulse to date has been to gravitate towards property theory and explain the conflict in terms of the misappropriation of another's property.

However, as noted above, property analogies can be problematic in the domain space because they never apply perfectly to the virtual world. The attraction of the property theory is that it fits the way people routinely think about domain names. Markets for trading in domain names have developed over the years, and people treat domain names as proprietary assets.[93] Despite the market approach, the judicial verdict has been less clear. While some judges have accepted domain names as intangible property, others have not.[94] This might be a good time in the development of domain name jurisprudence to make a clear decision one way or the other.

---

91 *Id.* at 24, 30.

92 *Kremen v Cohen*, 337 F.3d 1024 (9th Cir. 2003).

93 *Id.* at 1030 ('like other forms of property, domain names are valued, bought and sold, often for millions of dollars').

94 *Kremen v Cohen*, 337 F.3d 1024 (9th Cir. 2003) (accepting domain names as property for the purposes of Californian statutory conversion action); *Network Solutions v Umbro International*, 529 S.E. 2d 9 (Va. 2000) (court not prepared to accept domain names as property for the purposes of a garnishment action); Patel, *supra* note 32 ('domain names aren't physical property, but a right to contract . . . because owners pay for the right to use the name', citing Mr Jeff Becker, an intellectual property attorney from Dallas).

In other words, regulators could make a policy decision to accept domain names as a form of property, and thus accept a property rights rationale for their regulation. This would include allowing more ready access to trespass and conversion actions in cases involving generic domain names. Alternatively, regulators could make the opposite decision and deny domain names proprietary status. Any subsequent regulations might then have to be based on an unjust enrichment rationale.

This chapter suggests that the property model may be preferable for several reasons. It best accords with the way market participants relate to domain names. Even though a domain name is a form of contractual license from a registrar to a registrant,[95] it results in a valuable asset that is freely traded on the open market, and that is occasionally stolen by a bad faith actor. Even though a transfer of a domain name is, in reality, a deregistration from the original registrant and reregistration to the new registrant, it is now treated routinely as a seamless transfer as if the name was being handed directly from the original registrant to the new registrant. Further, the acceptance of a property rights rationale for regulating generic domain names could take advantage of existing property-based laws such as theft and conversion and simply extend them judicially to virtual property, as was the case with the 'sex.com' name under Californian conversion law.

7.3.2.4 Typosquatting

Typosquatting has been defined as 'taking advantage of common misspellings made by Internet users who are looking for a particular site of a particular provider of goods or services, in order to obtain some benefit therefrom'.[96] This definition covers typosquatting in relation to trademarks, but theoretically one could just as easily squat on other words and phrases. One might register common misspellings of generic words, personal names, and cultural or geographic indictors in the hope of attracting Internet custom. For example, a domain name speculator who could not afford to bargain for 'porn.com'[97] might just as easily register 'pron.com' in the hope of attracting customers.[98] Such conduct is unlikely to amount to bad faith or to be regulated in any way under existing domain name rules because it does not implicate any trademark interests. The most

---

[95] Patel, *supra* note 32.

[96] LINDSAY, *supra* note 41, at 259, citing *Shields v Zuccarini*, 254 F.3d 476, 483 (3d Cir., 2001).

[97] The actual 'porn.com' domain name most recently sold for US$9.50 million: KESMODEL, *supra* note 2, at 193.

[98] At the time of writing, the domain name 'pron.com' was in fact registered for this purpose.

common forms of typosquatting involve trademarks and, to some extent, personal names.[99]

Typosquatting that involves misspelling a trademark is currently regulated by the ACPA and the UDRP. Each of these rules covers situations where the domain name is identical *or confusingly similar* to a trademark.[100] However, where a domain name corresponds with a person's name, the complainant will be out of luck unless she can establish a trademark in her name. Typosquatting is also prohibited under the federal personal name cyberpiracy provisions.[101] Misspellings of generic, cultural and geographic terms that do not correspond with trademarks do not currently raise the specter of regulation. There is perhaps no reason why they should, but again it is a question that has not received any meaningful regulatory attention.

Typosquatting, particularly with respect to trademarks and some personal names, should be an easy issue in the regulatory context. The fact that someone has gone to the trouble of registering a deliberate misspelling of someone else's mark or name may suggest a bad faith motive in and of itself. It may therefore raise an initial presumption of bad faith commercial conduct that should be regulated as a matter of policy. This presumption might be rebutted by the registrant in certain circumstances. The question then arises as to the basis on which such conduct should be regulated as a policy matter. Typosquatting, at least as it relates to trademarks, can be, and currently is, regulated under the trademark policy rationale.

Under this approach, commercially profitable uses of a misspelling of another's mark in the domain space attract sanctions, while purely expressive uses might not. We might therefore expect the regulation of typosquatting on trademarks to mirror the regulation of 'sucks'-type domain names relating to trademarks. While speech should be protected, unfair commercial advantage-taking should not. A brief look back at Table 7.1 suggests that there are potentially some differences in the application of current regulations to typosquatting as compared with 'sucks'-type domain names. It appears that typosquatting more readily attracts sanctions than the registration of 'sucks'-type domain names. This is unsurprising given that the deliberate misspelling of a mark is more likely to be undertaken for a commercial purpose than the registration of a 'sucks'-type domain

---

99 See Table 7.1, rows 5 and 6.

100 15 U.S.C. § 1125(d)(1)(A)(ii)(I), (II); UDRP, para. 4(a)(i).

101 15 U.S.C. § 8131(1)(A).

name. The latter tend more often to be used for commentary and criticism while the former tend to be used more for unfair commercial advantage.

Over time, savvy domain name speculators have come to use 'sucks'-type domains for commercial purposes, hiding behind the pejorative term to clothe their conduct in the guise of speech. As observed by David Lindsay, the use of 'sucks'-type domain names in this way is termed 'sham speech'.[102] While still amenable to regulation under a trademark policy rationale, arbitrators and judges approaching sham speech websites must be careful to apply the trademark-protecting laws as robustly as they would in the case of typosquatting.

This discussion has not yet touched on typosquatting on personal names. Many personal names are commercially valuable in spite of the potential lack of trademark protection. This is one reason why Congress adopted specific anti-cybersquatting rules relating to personal names.[103] In the case of typosquatting on a nontrademarked personal name, a trademark policy rationale cannot be the basis for regulation. Presumably, a property rights rationale is likewise not a particularly good fit in the absence of clearly accepted property rights in personal names.[104] So again, the only viable theoretical justification would be unjust enrichment. Drawing on unjust enrichment theory, one could develop accessible rules for individuals aggrieved by typosquatting on their names in the domain space for unfair commercial profit motives.

7.4 ROLE OF THE REGISTRAR

One piece of the puzzle missing from the preceding discussion relates to the role of domain name registrars. A significant advantage of creating a clearer theoretical basis for domain name regulation would, in fact, be increased clarity as to the role and potential liability of domain name registrars. Existing law and policy has been unclear about the extent to which a domain name registrar should be liable for bad faith conduct by domain name registrants. There are arguments both for and against the imposition of such liability. In early trademark-focused cases, registrars were routinely added as litigants in trademark infringement and dilution actions.[105] This was an obvious strategy for plaintiffs. The registrar was

---

102 Lindsay, *supra* note 41, at 262.

103 15 U.S.C. § 8131(1)(A).

104 McKenna, *supra* note 31, at 247.

105 See, for example, *Lockheed Martin Corp v Network Solutions Inc.*, 194 F.3d 980 (9th Cir. 1999); Philip Zadeik, *Domain Name Disputes: The United*

often much easier to locate than the registrant. The registrar may also have deeper pockets than the registrant. The registrar also maintained the necessary contact information about the registrant. Moreover, in early domain name cases, the registrar was typically Network Solutions situated in Reston, Virginia.[106] This made the assertion of jurisdiction under the Lanham Act an easy matter for potential plaintiffs.

The registrar was obviously complicit in the registration in that it had taken the registrant's money and handed out a domain name that corresponded with the plaintiff's mark. Thus, it was fairly easy to argue at least contributory trademark infringement or dilution. Because Network Solutions was not particularly well financed in its early days, and was simply implementing what was initially thought to be a purely technical process, its officers were not trained to detect and prevent trademark infringement.[107] It was possible to argue that once a registrar had knowledge, in the form of a complaint by a trademark holder, that a domain name registration potentially infringed the mark, it should take action to cancel the registration.[108] While this view had some merit, it potentially put the registrar in the role of having to adjudicate between two competing claims if the registrant itself has asserted a legitimate interest in the domain name. Most domain name registrars are ill-equipped to determine the appropriate outcome of disputes involving competing claims in a domain name.

Other Internet intermediaries have faced similar situations. Many Internet service providers have been asked to remove material contributed by their users on the basis that it infringes a copyright,[109] infringes a

---

States Experience, available at http://library.findlaw.com/1999/Jan/1/129411.html#footnote9, last accessed August 10, 2009 ('NSI become concerned when companies who could not work out any resolution started suing NSI.').

[106] Early domain name registration over gTLDs was handled by Network Solutions, based in Reston, Virginia: MILTON MUELLER, RULING THE ROOT: INTERNET GOVERNANCE AND THE TAMING OF CYBERSPACE 1–2 (2004) ('Reston, Virginia, was . . . ground zero of the commercial Internet explosion of the mid-1990s. The region was home to Network Solutions, Inc. (NSI), the government contractor that had turned domain name registration into a multimillion dollar business and that was the site of the critical A root server, the central source of data for coordinating the world's Internet names.').

[107] Zadeik, *supra* note 105 (describing early attempts by Network Solutions to avoid having to take on significant costs associated with ascertaining true trademark ownership associated with domain names).

[108] This was argued unsuccessfully in *Lockheed Martin Corp. v Network Solutions Inc.*, 194 F.3d 980 (9th Cir. 1999).

[109] *A&M Recording v Napster*, 239 F.3d 1004 (9th Cir. 2001) (alleged copyright infringement by operators of popular peer-to-peer file sharing service).

trademark,[110] or is defamatory.[111] Internet intermediaries are often not in a position to ascertain the validity of these claims. Ultimately, Congress has legislated in some of these areas in an attempt to clarify the responsibility of the intermediaries. Thus, § 230 of the Communications Decency Act provides a safe harbor for Internet intermediaries against liability for the speech of others.[112] This applies often in the defamation context to prevent a chilling affect on Internet speech that might result if the gateway services enabling online speech faced legal liability for the speech of others.[113] In the copyright context, the Digital Millennium Copyright Act also provides a safe harbor from copyright infringement for Internet service providers that have acted expeditiously in removing infringing material on receipt of a notice by the copyright holder.[114]

The role of domain name registrars in terms of their liability for the conduct of their users has been variously dealt with in the context of domain name regulation. Much of the rule-making here is contractual. Since being joined as defendants in early trademark cases, domain name registrars quickly inserted into their registration policies clauses that disclaimed liability for trademark infringement. These clauses squarely placed the onus on registrants to ensure that they were not infringing other people's trademark rights or other legal interests.[115] The UDRP is a significant part of this contractual approach. It contractually binds registrants to submit to mandatory arbitrations if a trademark owner complains about the registration of a domain name.[116] Under the UDRP, the registrar represents that it will abide by decisions of arbitrators and domestic courts on

---

110 *Playboy v Netscape*, 354 F.3d 1020 (9th Cir. 2004) (alleged trademark infringement by search engine operators).

111 *Zeran v America Online*, 129 F.3d 327 (4th Cir. 1997) (action against Internet service provider for liability for defamatory comments posted by user of the service).

112 47 U.S.C.A. § 230(c)(1).

113 Examples include *Zeran v America Online*, 129 F.3d 327 (4th Cir. 1997); *Blumenthal v Drudge*, 992 F. Supp. 44 (D.D.C. 1998).

114 17 U.S.C. § 512(c).

115 UDRP, para. 2 ('By applying to register a domain name, or by asking us to maintain or renew a domain name registration, you hereby represent and warrant to us that (a) the statements that you made in your Registration Agreement are complete and accurate; (b) to your knowledge, the registration of the domain name will not infringe upon or otherwise violate the rights of any third party; (c) you are not registering the domain name for an unlawful purpose; and (d) you will not knowingly use the domain name in violation of any applicable laws or regulations. It is your responsibility to determine whether your domain name registration infringes or violates someone else's rights.').

116 UDRP, para. 4(a).

matters relating to rights in domain names.[117] These contractual measures take much of the early pressure off registrars by making it clear that they do not – and cannot be expected to – take initial responsibility for bad faith registrations in breach of trademark policy. However, they do not go much beyond trademark policy.

While UDRP arbitrators may squeeze disputes involving domain names of unclear trademark status within their jurisdiction, the expressed justification must always be finding a trademark interest in a word or phrase in the domain space. In other words, a UDRP arbitrator, seeking to be sympathetic to the holder of an interest in a personal name or geographic term, might order the transfer of a domain name corresponding to such a term. However, in these cases the arbitrator must find a trademark right in that name or term on which to base the transfer order. There is no action available under the UDRP without a trademark.[118] This fact may have caused some arbitrators to overly readily accept trademarks in words that have not unequivocally achieved this status.[119] The fact that the UDRP is the most accessible avenue of recourse for domain name complainants might motivate some arbitrators too readily to find trademarks in personal names and cultural and geographic indicators. This in itself may be a sufficient argument for identifying and developing theoretical justifications for domain name regulation outside of trademark policy.

At this point in time, the adoption of regulations that are accessible to disputants, but that encompass broader policy aims, such as the prevention of unjust enrichment more generally, may be a useful development that will lead to more coherent regulations in the future. Such an approach may be instructive not only for domain name disputes per se, but also for disputes involving Internet search engines more generally. Also, the forthcoming extension of the domain space to incorporate new gTLDs would benefit from a clearer understanding of the kinds of policies that should be reflected in the resolution of disputes involving domain names.[120]

The adoption of a more comprehensive and coherent theoretical frame-

---

[117] *Id.* para. 3(b), (c).

[118] *Id.* para. 4(a)(i).

[119] With respect to personal names, see, for example, Lipton, *Celebrity in Cyberspace*, *supra* note 55, at 1527 ('The continued development of personal domain name jurisprudence based on trademark principles threatens to warp the boundaries of trademark law and to unjustifiably extend trademark practice online into areas where the alleged trademarks are mere fictions . . . In any event, the application of the trademark-based UDRP to personal domain name disputes is clearly creating inconsistent results.').

[120] Farley, *supra* note 6 (generally criticizing the proposal for new gTLDs for its unclear policy underpinnings that are overly focused on trademark principles).

work for domain name disputes would bring with it a need to clarify the extent to which domain name registrars might be held liable for infringements of protected interests in domain names. In the trademark policy arena, a decision has been made that registrars are not generally required to take responsibility for the registration of trademarked terms, but are required to abide by remedies granted by arbitrators and courts.[121] As a cost-benefit exercise, this makes sense, particularly given the easily accessible mechanism now available for trademark holders to protect their interests under the UDRP.

The question remains as to whether there are other areas of domain name policy that may require a different balance of interests in terms of the potential liability of registrars. The obvious example is the relatively rare situation involving conversion or theft of domain names, secured by a wrongdoer fraudulently approaching a registrar for transfer of a name originally registered to someone else. These situations raise a different cost-benefit analysis to the trademark issues addressed by the UDRP. In the case of fraudulent conversions of domain names involving generic terms the domain name registrar is implicated in a different way to the way in which it is typically involved in a trademark-focused dispute. In the latter situation, the registrar is simply performing its typical functions of processing often large volumes of applications for currently unregistered domain names. In contrast, the former situation involves a request to transfer a domain name from an existing registrant into the hands of a new registrant. In these cases, it is reasonable to expect the registrar to be vigilant to ensure that the original registrant has indeed acquiesced to the transfer. In the case of any doubt, it is not difficult for the registrar to send an email to the original registrant to verify the transfer.

The Ninth Circuit Court took this view in the 'sex.com' case. Holding Network Solutions, the registrar, secondarily liable for conversion under the Californian statute, the court noted that Network Solutions had made no effort to contact the original registrant of the domain name before giving the name away on the basis of a facially suspect letter from a third party who had subsequently left the jurisdiction.[122] While accepting that the third party (Cohen) was the guilty party in the case, the court felt that there was nothing inappropriate about holding Network Solutions responsible for giving away the domain name when it could have taken

121 UDRP, para. 3(b), (c).

122 *Kremen v Cohen*, 337 F.3d 1024,1035 (2003) ('Network Solutions made no effort to contact Kremen before giving away his domain name, despite receiving a facially suspect letter from a third party. A jury would be justified in finding it was unreasonably careless.').

simple precautions to ensure that the transfer request was not fraudulent.[123]

With respect to an argument that had been accepted by the district court about the policy problems inherent in imposing liability on domain name registrars, the Ninth Circuit countered as follows:

> The district court was worried that 'the threat of litigation threatens to stifle the registration system by requiring further regulations by [Network Solutions] and potential increases in fees' . . . Given that Network Solutions' 'regulations' evidently allowed it to hand over a registrant's domain name on the basis of a facially suspect letter without even contacting him, 'further regulations' don't seem like such a bad idea. And the prospect of higher fees presents no issue here that it doesn't in any other context. A bank could lower ATM fees if it didn't have to pay security guards, but we doubt that most depositors would think that was a good idea.[124]

In fraudulent transfer situations there is a good argument for imposing liability on a domain name registrar if the registrar has not taken inexpensive and simple precautions to ensure the validity of a transfer request. The question remains as to what is the appropriate policy justification for the imposition of such liability. While the Ninth Circuit was prepared to rely on the property rights rationale underpinning the Californian conversion statute,[125] its holding is specific to its interpretation of that statute. A more widely accepted property rights rationale for these kinds of cases might lead to judicial interpretations of existing legislation in other states that would more readily accept property rights in generic domain names in support of these kinds of holdings. At the present time, a property rights approach to domain name disputes is not generally accepted and some situations involving alleged conversion of others' generic domain names have proved difficult to resolve as a matter of law.[126]

Alternatively, an unjust enrichment rationale would be a possibility for remedying fraudulent transfer situations. Where a fraudulent transferee is unjustly enriched at the expense of the original registrant, the domain name registry might be held liable for facilitating the unjust enrichment. Unlike the property rights approach, the unjust enrichment rationale probably calls for new regulations that are less focused on property than

---

123 *Id.*

124 *Id.* at 1035–6.

125 *Id.* at 1030.

126 *Network Solutions v Umbro International*, 529 S.E. 2d 9 (Va. 2000) (court not prepared to accept domain names as property for the purposes of a garnishment action); Patel, *supra* note 32.

current conversion laws. It may ultimately be possible to develop a new kind of UDRP that is more squarely based on the unjust enrichment concept and is not limited to trademark policy. This would effectively allow a cost-effective and accessible avenue of recourse for complainants and might also side-step the question of registrar liability, because registrars would presumably continue to be bound by private arbitral decisions involving domain names. Perhaps the system could work towards a general unjust enrichment model to capture unjust commercial conduct in the domain space involving any kind of word or phrase. In the meantime, registrants faced with fraudulent transfer situations may have to rely on a property rights rationale and pursue actions under existing theft and conversion laws.

7.5 CHAPTER SUMMARY

This chapter has surveyed the way in which the domain name system currently suffers from a lack of cohesive and coherent underlying theory. This is partly the result of a lack of focus on domain name issues outside trademark-oriented disputes. Importantly, there is no single entity that has global constitutional competence to create an overarching policy for domain name regulation. Nevertheless, the gaps and inconsistencies in current regulations are causing problems of application in practice. This chapter has suggested that:

(1) the domain name system requires the identification and development of a more comprehensive underlying theoretical framework;
(2) such a framework should not be purely premised on trademark policy;
(3) a new theoretical framework might usefully be modeled on a combination of trademark policy, restitution theory and property theory;
(4) developing a tripartite framework drawing on synergies between these three theoretical justifications would more effectively facilitate future developments in domain name regulation and practice, and would better address the needs of today's domain name markets.

The final chapter draws together the issues raised throughout the book on finding an appropriate balance between trademark protection, free speech, and other interests in the domain space. It further considers the most appropriate future approaches to domain name regulation.

8. Conclusions

This book has focused on aspects of domain name regulation that have not yet been addressed comprehensively in existing literature. Most prior discussion of domain names, particularly in the 1990s and early years of the new millennium, focused on the need to protect trademark holders against bad faith commercial conduct. Dennis Toeppen and his fellow cybersquatters were the initial touch points for concern in the early years of the domain name system.[1] Regulators were in an invidious position because no one had clear policy-making authority for domain name disputes at a more global or comprehensive level. Arguably, there is still no one clear body that has the authority to regulate all aspects of domain name policy, including concerns about trademarks, personal names, political speech and legitimate interests in cultural and geographic words and phrases.

While the Internet Corporation for Assigned Names and Numbers (ICANN) has assumed administrative control over the technological aspects of the system, its mandate is to make policy only to the extent required in support of its technical functions.[2] The World Intellectual Property Organization (WIPO) has assisted ICANN in developing some domain name policy,[3] but WIPO's mandate is focused on the protection of intellectual property rights. National and state legislatures can obviously make some laws relating to domain names, but these are bound to be piecemeal, as evidenced by current practices. Within federal systems, powers to regulate intellectual property rights usually vest in the central government,[4] while powers over other issues

[1] See discussion at 1.1, *supra*.

[2] ICANN's mission statement contemplates that ICANN makes policy that is 'reasonably and appropriately' related to its technical functions: ICANN Bylaws, art. 1, section 1, available at www.icann.org/en/general/bylaws.htm, last accessed July 24, 2009.

[3] See, for example, WIPO's Domain Name Dispute Resolution resources, available at www.wipo.int/amc/en/domains/, last accessed July 24, 2009.

[4] For example, the United States government is empowered to regulate copyrights and patents under the 'arts and sciences' clause of the federal Constitution

that might impact domain name practice may reside at the state or provincial levels.[5]

Thus, there is no one clear body at the global, or even at the national level, that can assume responsibility for developing clear, comprehensive and global domain name policy. This leaves open the possibility of a bottom up approach to domain name regulation that relies on a combination of ICANN, accredited domain name registrars, courts, arbitrators and domestic legislatures to develop principles for regulation that can effectively balance competing interests in domain names. Such an approach has a number of advantages over attempts to formulate a top down global policy. A bottom up approach can be pragmatically focused on problems occurring in the real world. It also has the advantage of incorporating a number of competing perspectives. The ability to include diverse perspectives on domain name regulation is extremely important because a number of interests implicated in the domain space relate to cultural values such as free speech and privacy. These cultural values often differ more significantly from jurisdiction to jurisdiction than policies underlying the protection of commercial and intellectual property rights.

The aim of this book has been to provide some guidance to private bodies, courts, legislatures and arbitrators as they approach future issues involving domain name regulation. There is likely to be increasing pressure on these entities to develop approaches to domain name policy that better accommodate competing legitimate interests in the domain space, and that more clearly delineate good faith from bad faith conduct. Hopefully, the issues identified and examined in this book will provide at least a useful starting point for developing an expanded approach to domain name policy in the future.

Domain names are unlike any other form of cyberproperty in that they are the closest analogy to real property online. Unlike digital copyright works, for example, a domain name is rivalrous. It can only exist in the hands of one entity at a time.[6] Even domain name sharing arrangements

---

(art. 1, clause 8, subpara. (viii)), and the power to regulate trademarks is derived from the 'commerce' clause (art. 1, clause 8, subpara. (iii)).

5 See, for example, Cal. Elections Code, § 18320; Cal. Business and Professions Code, §§ 17525–17526.

6 DAVID KESMODEL, THE DOMAIN GAME: HOW PEOPLE GET RICH FROM INTERNET DOMAIN NAMES 23 (2008) ('Domain names raised a host of new and perplexing questions in the field of intellectual-property law, especially when it came to trademarks. One problem was that only one company could register a domain, whereas under trademark law, multiple companies were entitled to use the same name, as long as they operated in different industries. That's why United Airlines, United Van Lines, and other companies using "United" could peacefully coexist. But only one entity

would require one single entity to be registered as the domain name holder.[7] This creates completely different challenges for regulators than those arising in other areas of intellectual property law. If only one person can hold a domain name, rules have to be developed for prioritizing competing interests in a given domain name.

The initial approach to this problem was the 'first come, first served' system employed in the early days of the domain name system. This soon caused problems when trademark holders began to complain about cybersquatters: people who realized there was much money to be made by beating trademark holders to the registration of intuitive domain names and then profiting from selling the names.[8] As domestic courts began to side with trademark holders on this issue,[9] ICANN was forced to rethink its position on policy neutrality. It thus implemented the UDRP, but shortly thereafter policy development came to a relatively abrupt halt.[10]

This history is understandable. Trademark holders are a much more powerful lobby, both domestically and globally, than people concerned about free speech, personality rights, privacy rights and cultural and geographic interests. It makes sense that those with the power to lobby achieved the protection they desired. However, unless future law and policy-makers are aware of the importance of protecting competing interests online, the current approach to domain name regulation has the potential to significantly chill speech and relegate other important social and cultural interests to the background in what has the potential to be an unparalleled global communications medium – the Internet. Even within the commercial realm, the lack of any policy for dealing with competing

---

could register united.com. Trademark law also allowed for companies in different regions to share a name, but that was not practical on the borderless Internet.').

[7] See discussion at 2.4, *supra*.

[8] Jonathan Nilsen, *Mixing Oil with Water: Resolving the Differences Between Domain Names and Trademark Law*, 1 J. HIGH TECH. L. 47, 51 (2002) ('Cybersquatting has been defined several ways. The most general definition of a cybersquatter is a person who registers a domain name that matches a well-known company for the purpose of ransoming it to that company.').

[9] See, for example, *Panavision Int'l L.P. v Toeppen*, 141 F.3d 1316 (9th Cir. 1998).

[10] Jacqueline Lipton, *Beyond Cybersquatting: Taking Domain Name Disputes Past Trademark Policy*, 40 WAKE FOREST L. REV. 1361, 1363 (2005) ('[C]urrent dispute resolution mechanisms are focused on the protection of commercial trademark interests, often to the detriment of other socially important interests that may inhere in a given domain name. If the global information society continues down the current road of protecting these interests at all costs, other important social norms relating to Internet use will not have a chance to develop, and the Internet will become permanently skewed in favor of commercial trademark interests.').

legitimate trademark interests outside of 'first come, first served' is potentially wasteful. It may be that other approaches, such as domain name sharing, could lead to more efficient commercial uses of certain domain names.[11]

While these initial balances have not been achieved under the existing domain name system, new technological advancements in the domain space are likely to tilt Internet activity even more in favor of trademark holders unless a more inclusive approach can be taken in the future. The proposed introduction by ICANN of new gTLDs, for example, implicates the balance between trademark and other interests in web addresses. Concerns about the need to balance trademarks with other interests in the domain space are not likely to go away in the future. In fact, the questions are likely to become more complex as new technological developments come online. Hopefully, this book will be the starting point for a discussion that focuses more squarely on developing an appropriate policy balance – and policy basis – for balancing competing interests in domain names.

[11] See 2.4, *supra*.

Index